Southgate House

A Derbyshire Country Mansion and Its Inhabitants through the Centuries

Christiane Müller-Hazenbos

GHP

published by Golden House Publications
London 2014

Cover front
Copyright Derbyshire Record Office, Matlock/Picture the Past (DCBR000405) and Andrea Gubisch, Berlin

Cover back
Pencil drawing of Southgate Stables by Graham Duckmanton, Worksop (1984)

Printed in the United Kingdom

ISBN 978-1-906137-36-6

In memory of two sturdy old ladies: Cecile Joan Nicholson of Bank Top Road and Joan Mary Bletcher of Jubb Close, The Brecks, Rotherham. I wish I had seized the chance while you were still around to tell you how much I owe you both.

C, February 1, 2012: I still have your pencil drawing from a house on the road to Chesterfield of which I enclose a photo. It served as a reference to me for many, many years and I still look at it whenever I pass it (...). Do you still remember this drawing?!
G, February 14, 2012: The old buildings on Chesterfield road are still there.
G, April 25, 2012: I have also included a copy of a painting of the old buildings on the Chesterfield Road. The buildings are called Southgate Stables.

Table of Contents

Acknowledgements

Every house has a story to tell. To me this is the story of Southgate House and its inhabitants and of a friendship. In autumn 2012 I embarked on a very strange journey. A journey which not only took me far back into England's distant past, complete *terra incognita* to me until then, but also almost 30 years back into my own past when as a 14-year old pupil I spent my summer holidays in Rotherham, and to one evening in August 1984 when I took part in a pencil drawing class by a Worksop artist. I never forgot this lesson and it later played a decisive role when choosing my future career path as an archaeologist and draughtswoman, which has since taken me on various excavations to the Near and Middle East. What is more this artist gave me the product of that lesson as a present: a demonstration drawing which depicts Southgate Stables, the old stable building of Southgate House near Clowne in Derbyshire. I have cherished the drawing ever since, but it took another 28 years when by a fortunate coincidence in January 2012 I traced the drawing's creator on the internet. In next to no time the artist and I established a very inspiring correspondence and struck up a remarkable friendship. In the course of our exchange of letters the building depicted in the pencil drawing excited my curiosity and I decided that I wanted to know more about it and its history. It then took another year and a half to write this book.

When I began writing seriously in early spring 2013 I had no idea what was awaiting me, and I certainly had no inkling of the overwhelming amount of source material that I would find and the wonderful things I would experience whilst researching on Southgate House and Estate. It was hard to believe that such a fascinating universe was unfolding before my eyes, and how the lives of all the various Bowdon and Butler-Bowdon family members, as well as of the inhabitants of Clowne and Barlborough, of Chapel-en-le-Frith, of Beighton Fields Priory, of Spinkhill and Pleasington Old and New Hall would captivate me. I became immersed in a world previously unknown to me and I soon felt close to persons who had long since passed away. What were first names soon took on faces and came alive to me. Actions became comprehensible the more I found out about the fate of Southgate House and Estate over the course of the past 250 years. Not only did this venture begin to open up my horizons, but also along the way I experienced such incredible generosity from both my English and German friends - and I found new friends and acquaintances, all of whom believed in me and the project without question. My gratitude for their selfless support is beyond measure. This makes clear that writing a book is never an individual achievement and I want to thank those who took the time and contributed:

Thanks to my husband Joost Hazenbos (Berlin) for his never ending patience and support. Joost, you took the load off me without complaint and endured the frequent retreats into the reclusion I needed for reading, researching and writing.

Thanks to my parents Elke and the late Hans-H. Müller (Bremerhaven) for the foresight that regular stays in England would improve my command of the English language and for teaching me that the past matters.

Thanks to Barbara and Graham Duckmanton (Worksop). This book is for you both. Graham, your countless altruistic contributions to the project in 2013 and 2014 were invaluable and I will be forever grateful, for everything. Barbara, your kind and warm-hearted hospitality was, and is, overwhelming and I cannot thank you enough.

Thanks to Sonia and Mike Levers of Dukeries Art Gallery (Worksop) for passing on an important letter.

Thanks to Edward Werner Austin (Warrington) for his immeasurably resourceful and enthusiastic research in 2012 and 2013. The preliminary compilation of material in 2012 would not have been possible without you, and without your further help in 2013 and 2014 this book would not exist today. You're a star, Eddie! Thanks also to Kathleen Armitage. Kath, your cordial welcomes during my frequent visits to Warrington mean so much.

Thanks to Tony and Teresa Bak (Worksop) for welcoming me at Barlborough Heritage and Resource Centre in April and September 2013, and for generously sharing their extensive knowledge with me. Tony, you have been so incredibly patient, answering to my numerous questions over the months so kindly. Your support for this project has been unwavering and words are not enough to express my appreciation.

Thanks to Andrea Gubisch (Berlin) for advice on graphic layout and for making scans and designs. You worked miracles on the Butler-Bowdon family tree, Andrea! But what is even more important: thank you for your unquestioning friendship. I would not have been able to accomplish this project without you (or anything else for that matter).

Thanks to Humphrey Butler-Bowdon (London). I hesitated for a long time as to whether I should get in touch, but was rewarded with such an abundance of detailed information on the more recent members of the Butler-Bowdon family, for which I am extremely grateful. Thank you, Humphrey, for pointing out the E and O problem. You saved me from a huge mistake.

Thanks to Lord Petre (John, 18th and present Baron Petre of Ingatestone Hall) for generously providing helpful information.

Thanks to June Pearce (Clowne) for sharing her childhood memories of life at Southgate Estate with me, and in doing so bringing the past back to life. June, your way of looking at the world is really special and left a deep impression on me. I am so glad we met and became friends.

Thanks to Mary Jones (Killamarsh) for writing down her recollections of her youth in Harlesthorpe and her expeditions to the "Secret Garden". Mary, your contributions to the project were so rich in detail, it was a joy including them in to the manuscript - and without you I would not be the proud owner of varifocals today. Thanks for caring.

Thanks to Mona Ives (Barlborough) who in September 2013 kindly allowed me to interview her on life as Maid Domestic at Southgate House during the early 1930s. Sharing her recollections with me of a time now long gone was a very touching experience and gave me valuable first-hand information on "how it was" behind the scenes in a country house.

Thanks to Ruby Thorpe (Clowne) for talking about old times in April 2014 and for letting me participate on her memories of Southgate House.

Thanks to Derek Bower (Branton) for sharing the memories of his youth at Toll Bar Cottage with me. Derek, I am greatly indebted to you, especially since your explanations solved one of the great riddles of Southgate Estate. Searching for POW Erich Siegel together with you turned into a remarkably emotional experience.

Thanks to Heide and Georg Barczynski (Friedelsheim), daughter and son-in-law of the late Erich Siegel, and also to Klaus Siegel (Mutterstadt), son of Erich Siegel. Despite contacting them of the blue, a stranger requesting information dear to their hearts, all three decided to help me to learn more about Erich's life. It was a wonderful experience to connect with strangers and I am so happy they decided to contribute to this book.

Thanks to Father Peter D McGuire, Parish Priest of the Church of the Immaculate Conception (Spinkhill), for meticulously gathering information on the burials of various members of the Butler-Bowdon family at Spinkhill cemetery for me, and thus filling in a number of gaps in my manuscript. Also my thanks for our inspiring correspondence, and for showing us around Spinkhill Church in April 2014.

Ein Dankeschön an Paul D Walker (Eckington) for looking through his box-files for me in search of supplementary information on the Butler-Bowdon family history. Paul, without your book on Spinkhill Church I would never have heard of Henry (5) Bowdon's diary. I enjoyed our subsequent correspondence about Hardman & Co., Catholic saints and all other Catholic matters immensely. Thanks to Father Michael Beattie S.J. of Mount St. Mary's College (Spinkhill) for additional backup.

Thanks to Canon Anthony Dolan, archivist of the Roman Catholic Diocese of Nottingham (Nottingham), for successfully searching their archives for additional information on the Butler-Bowdon family. Vielen Dank!

Thanks to Geoffrey Holdsworth (Clowne) for kindly providing me with details on the Van Dyk family and their businesses at Worksop and at Southgate House.

Thanks to Terry Richardson (Clowne) for the beautiful old black and white photographs of Clowne - important contributions to the book.

Thanks to Tom White (Clowne) for telling me more about the military history of Southgate Stables during WWII.

Thanks to Mavis and John Aston (Creswell) - a chance meeting in a supermarket in Clowne in September 2013 which proved to be very fruitful.

Both supplied me with vivid descriptions on how life was in the area during WWII.

Thanks to Allan Bailey (Clowne) and his allies of Clowne Local History Society.

Thanks to Peter Hopkins (Whitwell) of Whitwell Local History Group.

Thanks to Les Wheatcroft, the convivial proprietor of Acorn Lodge (Worksop). Your guesthouse is the best place to stay in Worksop for any researcher. Truly a home from home!

Thanks to Alan and Joyce Taylor (Chapel-en-le-Frith) for the great correspondence and the resulting friendship following our first meeting in Chapel-en-le-Frith April 2013. Thank you also for introducing me to the wonderful John Hodgkinson.

Thanks to John Hodgkinson, an intrepid and most entertaining inhabitant of Chapel-en-le-Frith, for showing me around his beautiful hometown in April 2013, for telling me about his life, for making me laugh so much and for walking down Bowden Lane with me. If there ever was a true British gentleman, a man of sterling qualities, then it is John!

Thanks to Derbyshire County Council/Record Office (Matlock) and the dedicated archivists Rebecca Sheldon, Anne Lawley, Mark Smith, Paul Beattie and their colleagues for supporting my research in 2012, 2013 and 2014. Their input was of invaluable help. Doing research in Matlock was one of the most enjoyable things I have ever done in my academic career.

Thanks to Rebecca Volk, archivist at the Archives of the British Province of the Society of Jesus (London) for finding some very revealing records on Henry (5) Bowdon.

Thanks to Vinai Solanki, History Curator at Blackburn Museum and Art Gallery (Blackburn), for his generous supply of details on the history of Blackburn, the cotton industry and for providing background information on the contents of the painting of Vladimir Osipovich Sherwood.

Thanks to Rebecca Hill, Curator of Fine Art at Blackburn Museum and Art Gallery (Blackburn), for the unbureaucratic and complaisant way of processing of my enquiries and for the lovely correspondence on our respective professions.

Thanks to Colin Pritt of www.blackburnpast.com (Blackburn) for allowing me to use images from his very recommendable website on the history of Blackburn and for letting me know how to pronounce Pleasington correctly.

Thanks to Martin Child, Parish Historian (Blackburn) for freely supplying me with everything I wanted to know about the stained glass window of Pleasington Priory.

Thanks to Nicola Crews and Michael Hunkin of Birmingham Archives/Library of Birmingham (Birmingham) for their help and support regarding my requests.

Thanks to Martin Ellis, Curator (Applied Art), Birmingham Museums Trust, Birmingham Museums and Art Gallery (Birmingham), for looking through the Hardman firm's warehouse books and the related design index for me, providing me with useful information.

Thanks to Tim Williams of Pugin Hardman & Powell Ltd. (Lichfield) for looking up information in "dusty books" for me, albeit without results.

Thanks to Sheena Charrett, Business Officer at English Heritage (Northampton) for advising me on the extent of English Heritage's involvement with the structural repairs of Southgate Stables.

Thanks to Craig Murray of the Imperial War Museum (London) for answering my questions on military titles and ranks in great detail.

Thanks to Mark Pearsall of the National Archives (London) for answering my questions on administrative ranks and titles and for giving me further information on military history.

Thanks to Alastair Massie of the National Army Museum (London) for trying to solve the riddle of a very enigmatic census entry even though it proved impossible.

Thanks to Joy Hales (Editor) and Amy Noton (Editorial Assistant) of "Derbyshire Life & Countryside" (Derby) for sending me copies of two articles published in the magazine by return of mail.

Thanks to Eva Stoewer of the "Tracing Service of the German Red Cross" (Munich) for checking their files on POW camps in England and on returning German soldiers.

Thanks to Stephan Kühmayer of "Deutsche Dienststelle (WASt) for the notification of next-of-kin of members of the former German Wehrmacht who were killed in action" (Berlin) who set the world on fire and made the impossible possible by tracing the German POW Erich Siegel for me. Unfortunately we were too late. The respective chapter in the book was possibly the most emotional one for me, and I am very grateful for the support given so abundantly to me.

Thanks to Achim Koch of the German Bundesarchiv, Abteilung Militärarchiv (Department Military Archives) (Freiburg im Breisgau). He searched their archives for me, looking for references to Southgate House and Barlborough.

Thanks to Robert Vogt of Botanischer Garten and Botanisches Museum Berlin-Dahlem (Berlin) for patiently answering my questions on *Myosotis*, *Vinca* and *Primula* in funerary contexts.

Thanks to David Hawkins (Minster Lovell/London) for explaining the layout of an English mediaeval town and the meaning of the word "gate" in this context to me.

Thanks to Anne Hartigan and Reginald Eaton (Birmingham) for the lift from Birmingham airport to the Library of Birmingham and pointing out the sights of their fascinating hometown to me in April 2014.

Thanks to Marjolijne and Marc Lauxtermann (Woodstock) for accommodation and lovely talks in April 2014.

Thanks to Magdalena Frost (Berlin) for patiently proof-reading my manuscript, always reliable and absolutely ingenious. Magdalena, if you ever despaired on my "Denglish" syntax and my notoriously wrong use of prepositions you were kind enough to not let me know.

Thanks to Tobias Krämer, Managing Director of archaeform GmbH (Berlin), for tolerantly enduring my private extra workload during working hours, allowing me to be distracted from office work every so often to do some research or send one of my many private E-mails. I know my fast and noisy typing drove you round the bend, Tobias. But thanks anyway.

Thanks to Annette Zippelius (Bad Windsheim), the best travel management assistant ever.

Thanks to Carsten Fischer (Berlin/Kuala Lumpur) for giving me a straight tip. My research took an unexpected turn because of this.

Thanks to Ingeborg Pietschmann (Bremerhaven) for explaining wood conservation to me.

And finally thanks to all my friends near and far for their countless contributions: Maria-Stella Anastasopoulou (Oradea/Stockholm), Bram Calcoen (Antwerp), Ulrike Dubiel (Berlin), Hannelore Fricke (Berlin), Anna Gorial (Delingsdorf), Wolfram Grajetzki (London), Joyce Hunter (Scarborough), Rüdiger Kelm (Friedrichstadt), Marion Krieten (Bremerhaven), Heidrun Ohk (Berlin), Ursula Rohloff (Köln) and all the many others who cannot be named here. You all listened to me, often with angelic patience, you carried me, and you made me go on when I was about to pack it all in and surrender, when I again and yet again doubted myself and lost faith in my idea.

And a special thanks to Henriette-Albertina, my beloved furry companion, who patiently kept me company during the endless evening hours of researching and typing, and who always knew when it was time for her treats, thus reminding me when to call it a day. She is the best cat a writer could wish for; in fact she is the best cat in the world. From her I learned that giving up is not an option.

Thanks to Amy MacDonald, Henry Priestman, Jez Lowe, Show of Hands and Paul McCartney. Their music is the soundtrack to this work.

All mistakes regarding the content of the book are undeniably mine. As an Egyptologist (and not a historian of modern era) I am not familiar in professionally dealing with records and sources from Georgian and Victorian England.

Christiane Müller-Hazenbos, Berlin in July 2014

Specification of Southgate House / Worksop Road (A619)

SK 47 NE PARISH OF CLOWNE WORKSOP ROAD
1/117 (South Side)
26.8.65 Southgate House
II

Description: Southgate House
Grade: II
Date Listed: 26 August 1965
English Heritage Building ID: 79287

Location: A619, Clowne, Derbyshire S43 4TD
Locality: Clowne
Local Authority: Bolsover District Council
County: Derbyshire
Country: England
Postcode: S43 4TD

Small country house, now an (*sic!*) hotel. Late C18. Painted render with painted stone dressings and chamfered quoins. Hipped Welsh slate roof. Stacks hidden in the roof valley. Three storeys. Plinth and first floor bands. East elevation of three symmetrical bays. The centre bay advanced and pedimented. Central tripartite entrance with round-arched fanlight over the doorway. Flanked by glazing bar sashes with keystones. Broad Venetian window above with ashlar surround. Flanked by glazing bar sashes with keystones. The top floor has a central tripartite window, its centre light with segmental arched head. Flanked by glazing bar sashes with keystones.

Listing National Grid Reference: SK4980577108

Sources:
http://www.britishlistedbuildings.co.uk/en-79287-southgate-house-clowne-derbyshire (viewed 17/10/2012)
http://list.english-heritage.org.uk/resultsingle.aspx?uid=1108959 (viewed 17/10/2012)

Specification of Southgate Stables / Worksop Road (A619)

SK 47 NE PARISH OF CLOWNE WORKSOP ROAD
1/118 (North Side)
Southgate Stables
21.4.80 including wall to south
enclosing stable yard
II

Description: Southgate Stables, Including Wall to South Enclosing Stable Yard
Grade: II
Date Listed: 21 April 1980
English Heritage Building ID: 79288

Location: A619, Clowne, Derbyshire S43 4TB
Locality: Clowne
Local Authority: Bolsover District Council
County: Derbyshire
Country: England
Postcode: S43 4TB

Pair of cottages, stables and coach house, and walls. Mid C19. Coursed rubble sandstone with sandstone dressings and quoins. Welsh slate roofs with stone coped gables with moulded kneelers. Brick ridge and gable stacks. One and two storeys. A long range and two cross ranges enclosing a courtyard. The cottages form the east wing. Symmetrical four bay east elevation. Each cottage has a central doorway with segmental arch, half glazed door and overlight; flanked by tripartite sashes under segmental arches. Two single bar sashes above, under segmental arches. The long south elevation has a square tower near the centre, with pyramid roof. Doorway to the ground floor with keyed dressed stone surround. Circular window above, and blind rectangular window above again. To the right are two segmental arched carriage entrances, with later brick and glazed infill, and further doorways, with a circular window above. To the left is a C20 garage entrance and a dressed stone doorway. To the left again is a two storey L-range which has to south, a C20 garage entrance and above, a dressed stone circular window flanked by square windows with keyed lintels. The return elevation has a central doorway with keyed dressed stone surround, flanked by windows with keyed lintels. The first floor has a circular window flanked by square windows with keyed lintels. The gable end to the road has two blind segmental arches and a shuttered circular opening above. The fourth side of the courtyard is enclosed by a rubblestone wall with rounded copings.

Listing National Grid Reference: SK4989677166

Sources:
http://www.britishlistedbuildings.co.uk/en-79288-southgate-stables-including-wall-to-south (viewed 17/10/2012)
http://list.english-heritage.org.uk/resultsingle.aspx?uid=1045918 (viewed 17/10/2012)

List of Figures

Figure 1 Map showing border triangle of Derbyshire, Nottinghamshire and South Yorkshire

1. Introduction

The aim of this book is to examine one of the most iconic features of English architecture: the country house. In this particular case the focus will be on Southgate House, a Derbyshire country mansion, its history and its inhabitants over the course of two and a half centuries.

Southgate House is a classical example of a modest Georgian country house, a small but sparkling gem situated in the north-eastern corner of Derbyshire in the border triangle of Derbyshire, Nottinghamshire and South Yorkshire (53.288836°N 1.254169°W, Figure 1). For the most part it belonged to the Butler-Bowdon family, members of the landed gentry originating from Lancashire. Southgate House was the family's main seat for a certain period of time and is therefore an example of a country house which was permanently inhabited, rather than merely a summer residence for affluent metropolitans or industrialists.

What follows is divided into several parts. The first two chapters form short abstracts on the history of the English country house, followed by brief overview of what characterises the Derbyshire country house. The next chapter looks at two poems of the same name, "The Stately Homes of England", but which have different standpoints, before the buildings of Southgate House, Southgate Stables, Southgate Cottages and Southgate Camp are explored in all their different manifestations over the centuries. The inhabitants of Southgate Estate shaped their surroundings and the Butler-Bowdon family in particular was instrumental in that development. Yet neither are the occupants on the other side of the "green baize door", the physical and ideological curtain that separated those above stairs from those below for centuries, forgotten. Without domestic personnel no mansion could have functioned, and yet all too often the living and working conditions of those employed as staff are either romanticised or simply ignored, their contributions and hard labour taken for granted. The numerous occupants of the farms and cottages connected to the estate, as well as their living conditions as tenants and leaseholders, have also been examined. Southgate House has been home to some beautiful treasures of art whose particular historical relevance is described. The Butler-Bowdon family's other properties, such as Bowden Hall in Chapel-en-le-Frith, Pleasington (New and Old) Hall near Blackburn, and Beighton Fields Priory and Barlborough House in Barlborough are also visited. The last chapter of the book is dedicated to the times when Southgate Estate served as a camp for prisoners of war during the Second World War.

There are many different approaches to the subject of the "country house", the most common of which is to view it in the context of its social or architectural history. Since the circumstances under which I could carry out my research on Southgate House were restricted[1], I chose to rest the focus on the social component of the house.[2] Fortunately, all sources related to Southgate House and Estate available to me could be approached in this way. A detailed examination of the architecture was not possible[3], but could also not be completely ignored in the book.

2. "A stern and silent pride"[4] - The English Country House

Different aspects of the "English Country House" have been covered extensively by specialist books. Many of which take divergent points of view and a substantial amount of research on the subject has been conducted over the years.[5] The focus of analysis varies according to the different authors' opinions, assessments and predilections (e. g. social history, architectural history), which often leads to varying definitions and interpretations. Today innovative research and interdisciplinary approaches continue to shed new light on the subject.[6] Occasionally, however, overlapping evaluations and inconsistent use of terms can lead to confusion, and sometimes even the houses themselves cause similar problems due to their changing functions or waning relevance over the centuries.[7] All countryside mansions do however fall under the three categories of "stately home", "manor house" and "country house".

The term "stately home" in particular seems generally to be avoided by most academics, as apparently not all great houses in the country were initially designed to be "stately". As expressions of power and wealth

---

[1] Most of my work was conducted from abroad as I am not a resident of the UK; also I had no additional funding at my disposal.

[2] The exponent of this approach is Girouard, *English Country House*. This is critically examined by Arnold, Dana, "The Country House: Form, Function and Meaning", in: Arnold, *Georgian Country House*, p. 16ff.

[3] I refer to a professional evaluation of the architectural situation of the buildings of Southgate Estate, i.e. the building history and a determination of construction phases. This certainly would be very revealing, but would require a more substantial financial foundation.

[4] Quote from "Land of Hope and Glory" by Arthur Christopher Benson (1862-1925).

[5] Selected standard works on the topic are Girouard, Mark, *Life in the English Country House, A Social and Architectural History*, Harmondsworth 1980; Muthesius, Hermann, *The English House* (edited by Dennis Sharp), Oxford 1987 (originally published in 1904/1905); Jenkins, Simon, *England's Thousand Best Houses*, London 2009; Cook, Olive, *The English House through Seven Centuries*, Harmondsworth 1984; Mandler, Peter, *The Fall and Rise of the Stately Home*, New Haven/London 2009; Arnold, Dana, *The Georgian Country House, Architecture, Landscape and Society*, Stroud 2013; Ferry, Kathryn, *The Victorian Home*, Oxford 2012; Robinson, John Martin, *The English Country Estate*, London 1988; Horn, Pamela, *Life in the Victorian Country House*, Oxford 2010.

[6] Arnold, *Georgian Country House*, p. xi.

[7] Arnold, Dana, "1 The Country House: Form, Function and Meaning", in: Arnold, *Georgian Country House*, p. xiii, p. 3.

executed in stone or brick they predominantly served as icons of social control and the dominance of the ruling classes; but on the other hand they also functioned, equally importantly on an economic level.[8] The term "stately" principally refers to English country houses built on a palatial scale (sometimes based on old buildings which preceded them, such as castles or secularised monasteries or abbeys). They were to serve as status symbols for the social élite and statesmen in England, and as a setting in which to entertain the royal family and other members of the aristocracy. Today's usage of the term "stately home" refers to large country mansions that are partly open to the public.

The "manor house" is - as the name implies - defined as the administrative centre of a manor's feudal estate, and was owned by the landed gentry. Such houses functioned on a local level. They were often situated in a village near the church and formed the nucleus of secular village life.[9] Such houses could also be very grand and lavishly designed; some were also converted secularised monasteries or abbeys.

The contrast to the manor house, the "country house" is defined as a smaller mansion situated in the countryside.[10] It was originally intended to be a counterpart to the town house, owned by wealthy individuals who split their time between the tranquility of rural life and the hustle and bustle of the big city[11], but it sometimes also served as a full-time residence for members of

---

[8] Arnold, Dana, "1 The Country House: Form, Function and Meaning", in: Arnold, *Georgian Country House*, p. 16. According to Mark Girouard (Girouard, *English Country House*, p. 2ff.) country houses were "power houses" designed to reflect either the owners' actual power or ambitions of power. Under favourable prerequisites country houses could generate quite a considerable yearly income and provide work for a substantial number of people; cf. Horn, *Victorian Country House*, p. 13. The term "stately home" was coined by Victorian poet Felicia Dorothea Hemans (see Chapter 5).

[9] Girouard, *English Country House*, p. 78; Bishop, *Country House Revisited*, p. 9.

[10] Outlined by Dana Arnold as "(...) the interaction of aristocratic and bourgeois ideals which together with an agrarian economy created a vision of class unity bound together in the notions of patriotism, national prosperity and happiness.", cf. Arnold, *Georgian Country House*, p. xiii.

[11] Social life followed a strict time table, especially during the Victorian era; cf. Horn, *Victorian Country House*, p. 96f., p. 102: whole families spent the Season in London, which usually began in April or May and lasted until July, and was the social focal of the year. If they did not return to their country seats the rest of the summer was spent either at the seaside or abroad, and Christmas was then spent at their main seat. All of this would be punctuated by regular visits to acquaintances at other country houses. Those who owned more than one property made sure that they visited each one at least once a year in order to assert their political and social influence in the surrounding area and to oversee the running of the estate. In most cases visits were arranged in order to combine business with pleasure, for example by coinciding with political or sporting events, or other pursuits such as hunting.

the landed gentry.[12] Aside from this, for people living in rural communities country houses were places of employment and often local country meetings were also held there. Examples of this architectural phenomenon can still be found today scattered in various shapes and sizes all across England. Like manor houses they were the fixed stars of their estates. Architecturally, the origins of the country houses are the mediaeval hall. The houses themselves have witnessed an evolution over the last 500 years. Originally larger houses were built with fortifications and were seen to reflect the position as feudal lords of their owners. The period of stability under the Tudors saw the first great houses built without fortifications. During the formal act of the English Reformation, Henry VIII (1491-1547) dissolved all monastic institutions in Britain, transferred their valuable assets to the higher secular ranks of society, and divided up the vacated land. Elizabeth H Bishop writes that "as much as a quarter of the total area of England was transferred to the country's landowning class". Those monasteries which were not converted into residential mansions were left to fall into disrepair and later became sources of building material.[13] It is not until the latter part of Elisabeth I's reign (1533-1663) and the subsequent years of the reign of James I (1566-1625) that mansions were first designed by architects, a trend which soon became very popular.[14]

During the first half of the 17th century landowners began in earnest to build large scale country houses. Many members of the ruling class took the decision to erect new, upscale houses which reflected the tastes of the time as well as the owner's social and political influence, often abandoning or even demolishing their ancestral homes in the process.[15] Over the course of the same century some house owners sought to build even more lavish and prestigious residences. No expenses were spared and more often than not left the owner in financial ruin. It was in this way that a number of houses later became stately homes.[16] Over the course of time the display of culture (such as collecting books to form a library or a collection of works of art or antiquities etc.) "became an essential part of the image of a worthy ruling class", says

---

[12] In Victorian times inhabitants of country houses often profited from living in greater informality than in the city; cf. Horn, *Victorian Country House*, p. 17 (image).

[13] Bishop, *Country House Revisited*, p. 8 (referring to Robinson, *English Country Estate*, p. 42). According to Arnold, Dana, "1 The Country House: Form, Function and Meaning", in: Arnold, *Georgian Country House*, p. 18 and Arnold, Dana. "9 Living off the Land: Innovations in Farming Practices and Farm Design", in: Arnold, *Georgian Country House*, p. 154: in 1688 15-20% of usable or workable land belonged to the large landowners (those with estates comprising of more than 10,000 acres). This figure had risen to 20-25% by 1790. The landed gentry (whether the wealthy notables or the less affluent, but influential squirearchy) held between 15 and 20% throughout the period.

[14] Jenkins, *Best Houses*, p. xl.

[15] Bishop, *Country House Revisited*, p. 9 (referring to Mandler, *Fall and Rise*, p. 7).

[16] Jenkins, *Best Houses*, p. xivf.

Mark Girouard, and the country house in particular functioned as the showcase of the refinement of manners of its owner[17]: "The polite world saw themselves as an elite, whose claim to run the country was based on having a stake in it as property owners, and was reinforced by the culture, education and *savoir-faire* of which its country houses were an advertisement."[18] Growing wealth resulting from income in the manufacturing world and commerce sector enabled Britons to purchase vast amounts of land to build on and the 18th century was a heyday for nobility and moneyed aristocracy. Country houses in Palladian and Neoclassical style multiplied; a phenomenon which did not meet its match before or since the Elizabethan era.[19]

The 18th century, however, also was the time which, due to various accumulating sociopolitical factors, saw a "growing gap between the polite world of the gentry and the impolite world of servants, farmers and smallholders. In terms of the country house this meant an increasing split between gentry upstairs and non-gentry downstairs".[20] We all remember the legendary TV series "Upstairs, Downstairs" from 1971, which depicted life in an Edwardian and Post-Edwardian England by using the microcosm of a London townhouse where the servants lived "downstairs", and their masters resided "upstairs". Recently, against the even more impressive backdrops of enormous English country mansions, the same subject was brought back into focus by the very popular TV series "Gosford Park" (2001[21]) and "Downton Abbey" (since 2010[22]), both written by Julian Fellowes. Most readers will therefore have clear picture in their minds how these houses looked, functioned and were maintained and how the concept of those "above stairs" and those of "below stairs" worked.[23] This strict division lasted until the economically difficult Post Napoleonic time (from 1815 onwards)[24] and later the agricultural depression of the 1870s[25] again threatened the system.

---

17 Girouard, *English Country House*, p. 180.

18 Girouard, *English Country House*, p. 189.

19 Hobsbawm, *Industry and Empire*, p. 58f.; Jenkins, *Best Houses*, p. xviif.

20 Girouard, *English Country House*, p. 184.

21 Predominantly shot at Wrotham Park, Hertfordshire.

22 Shot at Highclere Castle, Hampshire.

23 No-one has described the allocation of the tasks of those "below stairs" more detailed than Hermann in 1904/1905 in his book (Muthesius, *English House*, p. 70f., p. 96ff). See also Powell, *Below Stairs*.

24 For more information on the subject see Appendix 1.

25 The years between 1873 and 1896 are known as the "Great Depression" when the economy in Britain stagnated; characterise by falling prices, profits and rates of interest, and the country no longer was the "workshop of the world" (the "Great Depression" was, however, a world-wide phenomenon, not limited to Britain). The reasons for the agricultural depression were manifold: primarily, an increase in world food supplies and the incapability of the British farmers to respond to free trade, resulted in the collapse of grain prices due to competition from cheaper products and

Up until the Great Depression in the 1870s, estates with country houses at the centre generated income for their owners which often more than not proved enough to live on. But landowners were never farmers; they rarely earned their money by working the land. Money was earned from the tenants and the rent they paid to their land lord.[26] From the Middle Ages until well into the 19th century the country house was the ideal investment for "anyone who had made money by any means, and was ambitious for himself and his family".[27] Consequently, money was primarily held in the country and less so in towns, and landowners rather than merchants were the prevalent class.[28]

For those of the country gentry or landed aristocracy who managed to weather difficult economic times their houses often remained full-time residencies in the Victorian era (1837-1901). As previously mentioned, these houses figured prominently in their respective surroundings, being centres of employment for many rural communities. Conversely, estates with country houses at their core provided their owners, not only those of hereditary gentry but also those of the newly rich class with additional incomes.[29] Whilst benefiting from security and repose a rural estate offered, few had a real understanding of the fact that theses houses were no longer merely places of amusement and distraction, but were entities with duties and responsibilities. The houses and estates were attractive to those who had made their money in manufacture or commerce as they embodied a sense of continuity which could be passed on to future generations which industry could. Unlike German and American business men who reinvested their profits in their factories, English industrial tycoons invested in their real estate which they continually sought to enlarge.[30]

The failure of agriculture and the subsequent Great Depression led to radical changes in the landed society of Britain. Many relinquished their positions, and they ultimately ceased to be of national importance.[31] A great number of these landholders found themselves encumbered with debts, income generated from agricultural rents unable to cover even the interest incurred. In order to facilitate the sale of family heirlooms to try and keep

---

imports from USA; additionally, low farm worker's wages led to a drift of labour from the countryside towards towns, which resulted in increasing depopulation of rural areas. British steel production was out-competed by Germany and the United States, and Britain found itself the weakest of these three industrial powers; cf. Brown, *Economic change: Agriculture*; Hobsbawm, *Industry and Empire*, p. 105ff., p. 112.

26 Girouard, *English Country House*, p. 3; Arnold, Dana, "1 The Country House: Form, Function and Meaning", in: Arnold, *Georgian Country House*, p. 18.

27 Girouard, *English Country House*, p. 3.

28 Girouard, *English Country House*, p. 2.

29 Jenkins, *Best Houses*, p. xvii; Bishop, *Country House Revisited*, p. 9.

30 Jenkins, *Best Houses*, p. xviiif.; Hobsbawm, *Industry and Empire*, p. 160ff.

31 Hobsbawm, *Industry and Empire*, p. 105ff., p. 179.

mounting debts at bay, the Settled Land Law of 1882[32] was introduced. But the tide could not be turned: landowners were forced to annexe parts of the estate property or at least outlying parts (some invested income generated this way shares).[33] Other houses had to be demolished or were left to fall into disrepair. The extent of these measures varied depending on the individual circumstances of the affected families.[34]

Those who best weathered the storm of the agricultural slump where those who had additional sources of income (e.g. a family business, shares, rental income from town properties). Yet, the lesson was learnt by all. The landowning classes and the business world became increasingly close bedfellows. Before the mid 19th century anyone with links to trade was accepted as a true member of the upper class. Any money made in this way had to be reinvested in land. By 1900 the newly rich were both continuing to work and profit from industry and taking over country houses and assuming titles. It had become entirely acceptable to be a business man and a landowner. Along with the newly rich there were still those families who due to stubbornness, pride or lack of ingenuity continued to struggle on living off the rents of their farms, but in the face of unprofitable agriculture and rising prices, taxes and wages lived in ever-increasing shabbiness. On the other hand there were also the upper class families who had so much wealth that they could afford to live as they always had. Both groups looked down on the new arrivals, yet basically it was this new group which who saved the institution of the country house.[35]

A strong belief of the upper class rested was that in times of uncertainty land was safe.[36] It could not be burnt down or drowned at sea, nor could it be stolen or blown up. This belief in the reliability of land was one of the main reasons why people chose to invest in it. Owning land meant having an

---

32 Encyclopedia Britannica, *English Settled Land Acts*; http://www.legislation.gov.uk/ukpga/Vict/45-46/38/section/25 (viewed 21/05/2013). Such land acts gave landholders extra power. This was meant to promote development and maintenance of (mostly neglected) land and "could be financed with Capital Trust Money including transportation, infrastructure, residential, commons, and waterways", cf. Talen, *Codes Project*.

33 Harris, *No Voice from the Hall*, p. 2. Other means of survival were to send their sons to work in the City or for them to marry daughters of tycoons, whose generous dowries enabled them to maintain and extend their country seats; cf. Girouard, *English Country House*, p. 300f.

34 Harris, *No Voice from the Hall*, p. 2. More than 5% of country houses were demolished between WWII and WWII; cf. Bishop, *Country House Revisited*, p. 10 (referring to Mandler, *Fall and Rise*, p. 9).

35 Jenkins, *Best Houses*, p. xviiff.; Horn, *Victorian Country House*, p. 13, p. 62; Girouard, *English Country House*, p. 300f., p. 304. The newcomers not only bought existing old houses, but were also keen on building completely new houses.

36 Girouard, *English Country House*, p. 298.

enduring stake in the country.[37] But after 1900 arguments for buying a country property no longer held sway. Investing large amounts of money in such houses was seen both politically and socially irrelevant as well as financially unwise. It was more sensible own a house in the country (with no land attached) than a country house. It was soon possible to reach political heights without owning a country house or even having any country-house connections at all.[38] Declining numbers of servants meant life in the country house changed further still. Families forced to tighten their belts reduced the size of their households and the increase in technology also meant that there was less work for domestic staff.[39]

The third crisis suffered by the country house, its outcome identical to the previous one, took place during the Armistice in 1918. The grievous loss of male family members (be that the head of the family, the eldest son, or younger brother who perished on some foreign battlefield during the First Word War) left a mark on British society. In WWI there was not compulsory requisition, but the remaining house owners saw it as their duty to offer their houses for use as hospitals, convalescent homes or other purposes.[40] These houses of course suffered from this alienation. Finally, economic recession and increased taxation forced many owners of historic houses to give up their estates and mansions[41] which were then sold (as a whole or by dissolving the estates into single lots). When, in the wake of the war and later in the post-war boomtime, owners sold their land, there were a wealth of willing purchasers including tenant farmers looking to buy their holdings and those who had come into money and were looking for a country seat as a symbol of their social success.[42] Again other houses were simply demolished or were left to fall into disrepair. John Harris estimates the number of country houses lost at 300 to 400.[43] After the First World War domestic staff were even harder to come by. Offices and factories proved more attractive offering workers more independence as well as better pay. Large houses now had to be easier to clean and run with comfortable accommodation in order to appeal to servants.[44]

The surviving estates faced the same fate again both during and in the aftermath of WWII, but with a slightly different reason. Even before the

---

37 Girouard, *English Country House*, p. 300.

38 Girouard, *English Country House*, p. 301f.

39 Girouard, *English Country House*, p. 308.

40 Horn, *Victorian Country House*, p. 122.

41 Horn, *Victorian Country House*, p. 115, p. 120; Girouard, *English Country House*, p. 308: first imposed in 1894, death duties were then increased in 1909 and again in 1919. Both income tax and servant's wages continued to rise steadily.

42 Hobsbawm, *Industry and Empire*, p. 14, p. 179.

43 Craven, Stanley, *Derbyshire Country House*, p. 11; Harris, *No Voice from the Hall*, p. 2f.; Girouard, *English Country House*, p. 316; Horn, *Victorian Country House*, p. 121f.

44 Girouard, *English Country House*, p. 309.

beginning of the war some house owners chose to offer up their homes to accommodate schools or to house those evacuated from urban areas, this being preferable to compulsory requisition. However, it made little difference. The development John Harris calls the "Dunkirk Spirit" (for "after Dunkirk[45] nearly every country house had some role to play in the war effort, either through compulsory requisition or as a result of its owner voluntarily offering it for patriotic uses") spelt disaster for most country houses.[46] The total number of houses requisitioned by the government's compulsory order by 1945 has never been fully ascertained, but according to John Harris the number must have approached at least 2,000 houses. In direct vicinity to the great houses, Nissen huts or prefabricated camps for military use and other military installations were erected on the estate's grounds, often destroying carefully cultivated gardens and landscapes. In general, requisitioned houses were not treated with any caution; in particular "lesser houses often suffered a lack of maintenance and custodial respect".[47] These chaotic circumstances of neglect and abandonment did not end with the war, but continued to exist well into the 1960s and beyond.[48]

The advent of income and inheritance tax (new estates duty payable on the death of the owner established in 1894), increasing costs of labour and the Depression were further blows to owners of large houses and estates.[49] Those proprietors who managed to overcome difficult times had to adapt to the new circumstances in order to get by. "Even if there had been any awareness that a valuable heritage was being destroyed, there were few means of rescue: no amenity societies concerned with the problem, no National Trust, no state grants, and no developed tourism - and apart from schools, private mental homes and some local authority adaptations, there were few alternative uses".[50] The luckier owners were able to open their houses and gardens to the public or allowing their homes to be converted into museums. Smaller mansions without big estates attached had a higher rate of survival, and were often converted into comfortable private residences.[51] The romance of the country house certainly helped their owners win sympathy, interest and financial aid which helped in the constant battle against taxes and running

---

[45] The Battle of Dunkirk took place between May 26 and June 4, 1940. It was part of the Battle of France on the Western Front and was fought between the allied forces and the Germans. Its goal was to defend and rescue British and other allied soldiers in Europe, cf. Hickman, *World War II: Battle and Evacuation of Dunkirk.*

[46] Harris, *No Voice from the Hall*, p. 1f.; Horn, *Victorian Country House*, p. 122.

[47] Harris, *No Voice from the Hall*, p. 5.

[48] Harris, *No Voice from the Hall*, p. 4f.; Horn, *Victorian Country House*, p. 122.

[49] Jenkins, *Best Houses*, p. xxii.; Horn, *Victorian Country House*, p. 115.

[50] Harris, *No Voice from the Hall*, p. 3.

[51] Craven, Stanley, *Derbyshire Country House*, p. 11; Girouard, *English Country House*, p. 318; Jenkins, *Best Houses*, p. xxiii: "with a portfolio of tax reliefs, charitable trusts, maintenance allowances and grants evolved with a quid pro quo of public access."

costs, "in a curious reversal of history, instead of the houses existing as means to support the ends of their owners, the owners now tend to be seen as means to support the survival of their houses".[52] A large number of English Houses today are owned by the National Trust, in the hands of the government's English Heritage or belong to the Historic Houses Association.[53] Mark Girouard writes in 1978: "Even if a considerable number (of country houses) belong to families who have owned them for many generations, such families could no longer conceivably be described as a ruling class. A few owners of country houses are still engaged in running the country or the county, but the old automatic correlation between the ownership of an estate and the right to execute power has vanished. The most that country houses now bring their owners is an accepted constitutional position, as patrons of local and national good causes."[54] This can be augmented by Pamela Horn's statement that "many of the largest magnates have remained major owners of country estates".[55]

Southgate House and Estate is a mirror of its times, the classical paragon of an English country house which has weathered the stormy seas of history relatively unscathed. Its good fortune is no doubt largely due to the prudent conduct of its owners, the Butler-Bowdon family and the sensible owners succeeding them. The available historical sources show not only how Southgate thrived and expanded, how outbuildings, farms and arable land were added to the estate, but also how the house suffered during the great agricultural depression at the end of the 19th century[56], how it witnessed the tragic consequences of WWI[57], and how it played its part in the drastic measures that were undertaken during the Second World War[58] until it was finally granted a new life today as a splendid hotel and restaurant.[59]

---

52 Girouard, *English Country House*, p. 318.

53 Jenkins, *Best Houses*, p. xxiii; Horn, *Victorian Country House*, p. 122: "It was this loss that prompted the passage of legislation in 1937 enabling stately-home owners to donate their property to the National Trust. In return for tax concessions, and, in some cases, continued residence, they gave permission for limited public access by visitors and tourists (...)."

54 Girouard, *English Country House*, p. 318.

55 Horn, *Victorian Country House*, p. 124. According to her, in the year 1976 1,500 families were listed as owners of nearly a third of the rural land of England and Wales.

56 See Chapter 8.

57 See Chapter 8.

58 Southgate Estate was requisitioned at the beginning of WWII as a temporary accommodation for members of British army regiments. Towards the end of the war it served as a POW Camp which was transformed into a squatter camp after the war (see Chapter 25).

59 Hotel and Restaurant Van Dyk (and until recently Van Dyk's Garden Centre).

3. "Romanes eunt domus"[60] - Excursus on the Concept of the Country House

As an archaeologist I could not resist taking a look into a more distant past when researching the origins of the English country house. What I did find shows that it cannot be viewed purely as a product of its own time. The Scottish archaeologist and historian Neil Oliver summarises the background facts in his recently published book on the history of ancient Britain as follows: "The Roman villa operated exactly like a Victorian country house. It was a luxurious home at the centre of a working estate that generated a rich income for its owners. As well as providing accommodation for the family itself, there would also have been space set aside for domestic servants and for those who worked the land. If all of that sounds familiar then it is necessary to remember once more the impact of such a concept on native Britons. Even after decades, even after a couple of hundred years of Roman rule, the majority of Britons were still used to roundhouses - simple, single-roomed homes where all the business of life was performed in one open space centred around a hearth. The Roman villa by contrast was everything we visualise when we think about somewhere to live: rectangular buildings with straight walls and corners; separate rooms with doors providing privacy; corridors linking one space to another; more than one way in or out; glazed windows; tiled floors and tiled roofs; running water."[61]

When the Romans made Britannia part of their empire during the 1st century AD (43 AD invasion under Emperor Claudius), they essentially brought their whole way of life with them. Among other things, the institution of a comfortable and luxurious messuage they called *villa rustica*, which was reserved for highly decorated officers of the Roman army and other high-ranking and prosperous members of Roman society expatriated to foreign shores, as well as for the Romanised British elite.[62] The idea that proceedings and circumstances at a *villa rustica* were akin to those at a Victorian country house is debatable for many reasons, and certainly comes across a bit unorthodox at first sight, but it is not entirely inconceivable that the concept of a country house as an economic and utilitarian unit (with masters and servants together under one roof) was not an indigenous British idea of the early Middle Ages, but was in fact brought to the British Isles about 2,000 years ago from the Continent.

---

60 Brian's Latin Lesson, quote from the movie "The Life of Brian" by the comedy group Monty Python (1979).

61 Oliver, *Ancient Britain*, p. 398f.

62 To date ca. 800 Roman villas have been archaeologically identified in Britain until today. This may sound like a lot, but in fact they constitute only 1% of all rural settlements in the south of England; cf. Oliver, *Ancient Britain*, p. 402. For further reading on the subject see Perring, Dominic, *The Roman House in Britain*, London 2001; Percival, John, *The Roman Villa*, London 1976.

With the end of the Roman rule in Britain in 410 AD, the luxurious Roman villas in Britain were largely abandoned. Some were left to fall into disrepair and disappeared from sight completely[63], and others were taken over for different purposes, but evidently some sort of formative living tradition had been so successfully established in Britain that it never totally forfeited its popularity over the following centuries.[64] Historian H P R Finberg was the first scholar to suggest "a correlation which seems to have emerged between the extent of Roman villa-estates and Saxon and post-Conquest parish boundaries".[65] The archaeological remains on the Ditchley Park estate near Charlbury in Oxfordshire could hold a link between Roman and Anglo-Saxon times: "The case of Ditchley does not, of course, prove continuity of occupation at the villa from Roman to Saxon period; but it does show that the Saxon settlers encountered the estate in visible and defined form, and something occurred in their rural society which perpetuated the estate as a recognized unit. A possible correlation between Anglo-Saxon estates and Roman villas is also now being observed in the Butcombe area of north Somerset."[66]

However, these observations should not in any way be used as a rule of thumb for the whole of Britain. Whereas in the big towns and cities in the south of Britain such as *Calleva Atrebatum*/Silchester, *Camolodunum*/Colchester, *Londinium*/London, *Verulamium*/St Albans or *Eboracum*/York a Britano-Roman society enjoyed a metropolitan life with all its amenities (interconnected road networks lined with houses, shops and workshops, mass public entertainment, water supply, unlimited access to all sorts of Roman and continental commodities such as luxury goods and exotic food), life for at least 90% of the people elsewhere continued as it always had. Depending on the region, settlement patterns ranged from fortified Iron Age hill forts with specific interior developments to undefended farming settlements providing homes for extended families and small rural villages. People lived on largely unaffected by what was changing around them, and living patterns remained much the same as they always had.[67] According to Neil Oliver the secret of Roman success in Britain "was to leave people to live the way they wanted, provided they paid their dues and made no trouble".

---

[63] Oliver, *Ancient Britain*, p. 399.

[64] Cook, *English House* , p. 12f., p. 16.

[65] Craven, Stanley, *Derbyshire Country House*, p. 10.

[66] Cf. The Agrarian History of England and Wales: Volume I.II, Prehistory to AD 1042, ed. by H P R Finberg, Cambridge 2011 (paperback edition), p. 246 and footnote 1 (referring to the research of H P R Finberg, Roman and Saxon Withington, Leicester 1955, = Lucerna, London 1964, p. 21-65). Apparently Ditchley is also the nucleus for another architectural feature in Britain, - the timber-framed building. Reintroduced by the Anglo-Saxon this was "the pride of English domestic architecture in the late fourteenth and succeeding centuries"; cf. Cook, *English House*, p. 16.

[67] Oliver, *Ancient Britain*, p. 343ff. , p. 360, p. 386ff., p. 402f.

As long as they stuck to the rules, people far away from the urban centres "had much choice about just how Roman they actually wanted to be".[68]

4. "To thee belongs the rural reign"[69] - The Derbyshire Country House

The concept of an elaborate home for the landed gentry and the idea of a country home far away from the noise, the dirt and the danger of diseases of the big cities for those better-off in society has always been an integral part of architectural development and can be observed everywhere where urbanisation took place. Seen in this context Derbyshire is no exception to the rule. In a meritorious manner historian Maxwell Craven and museum curator Michael Stanley have compiled an exhaustive study of the county's history and its manor houses, whose results form the basis of this chapter.

Derbyshire is one of Britain's oldest cultural landscapes and the continuity of settlement is one of the main features of the county. Settlements in Derbyshire can be traced as far back as the Paleolithic Age, with Creswell Crags being one of the oldest known inhabited areas in the whole of Britain.[70] Bronze and Iron Age housing is attested in the Derbyshire lowlands, especially along the valley of the river Trent, the region's main artery of communication. Upland monuments such as Arbor Low also provide

---

[68] Oliver, *Ancient Britain*, p. 403.

[69] Quote from "Rule, Britannia!", song from the poem of the same name by James Thomson (1700-1748) and David Mallet (ca. 1705-1765), set to music by composer Thomas Augustine Arne (1710-1778), first performed in 1740.

[70] Habitation of the caves is attested for Neanderthal people (40,000-50,0000 years ago), by Cro Magnon (time of the last Ice Age), during Paleolithic, Mesolithic and Neolithic periods, in Bronze Age, under Roman rule, and in post-mediaeval times. Given that the tip of the ice sheet terminated only ca. 50 km north of what is today Sheffield, the Palaeolithic inhabitants of Creswell Crags lived "closer to the sharp end than any other known sites of human habitation in Britain". One outstanding archaeological find from the Paleolithic Age was made at the so-called Robin Hood's Cave at Creswell Crags: a small piece of rib bone (ca. 5-7 cm in length) engraved with the depiction of a horse head. Moreover, Creswell Crags is the only example of Ice Age/Paleolithic cave art on the British Isles and the most northerly archaeological attestation for this in Europe, depicting a bison, a stag, and a series of long-necked birds (ibis, interpreted by some as female figures), altogether displaying 90 individual engravings, made during a relatively short time, the Late Glacial Interstadial, a phase when the ice had retreated for a millennium (14,000-13,000 years ago). Soon after that the climate deteriorated again, temperatures dropped dramatically and Britain was gripped by the "Big Freeze". The land disappeared under advancing ice sheets once more, thus making human inhabitation impossible for the following ca. 2,000 years, until the climate warmed up again (beginning of the Holocene, allowing humankind to fill the empty spaces without any more interruption); cf. Oliver, *Ancient Britain*, p. 34ff.; Riden, *History of the County of Derby III*, p. 137f. For further reading on the subject see Bahn, Paul, Pettitt, Paul, *Britain's Oldest Art, The Ice Age Cave Art of Creswell Crags*, English Heritage, Swindon 2009.

evidence of human presence.[71] According to Craven and Stanley, Derbyshire is also one of the areas in Britain that shows continuous habitation from pre-Roman times until the Saxon settlements of the 6th and 7th centuries. Over the course of 500 years the style of dwelling in this mostly agricultural environment developed from simple huts to pit houses. This pattern extended into the late Anglo-Saxon, Viking and Norman eras and on to modern times. Many structures have however unfortunately often been built-over, making comprehensive archaeological research difficult.[72] There is no evidence of any kind of Roman legacy in the area, even the country estate with the *villa rustica* as its central element cannot be attested anywhere (the same applies to all other parts of highland zones of Roman Britain), in contrast to the southern and western parts of England, where the history of rural mansions can in some cases be linked with this type of living (see Chapter 3).

Due to a lack of archaeological research, little is known about post-Conquest/early mediaeval house building in Derbyshire. The earliest mansions in the county appear to have been built of wood, even in the upland zones; earliest remnants of buildings in the south however, appear to be built of stone and it later increasingly became a preferred building material in the northern parts as well.[73] In the beginning, country estates appear to have been quite large, especially those in the prosperous southern parts of Derbyshire. Following the Black Death in 1347/1348 the county was deprived of a substantial number of inhabitants, which in turn meant that free peasants were able to acquire land that had suddenly become cheaply and widely available, and marry into aristocracy.[74]

Between the mid 16th and mid 17th century many families belonged to the group of the landed gentry. They held properties whose sizes varied from smaller estates of about 400 acres in the fertile south and east, to bigger ones with 5,000 acres and more. If an owner of a small estate held the rights to exploit lead- or coal-bearing beds on his land, his chances of achieving material wealth and high renown were as good as for someone holding large amounts of moorland in the north or west.[75] Mainly because of the durability of their building materials, minor houses survived better in the upland zone, but large estates survived region-wide and additional edifices were built as great courtiers accumulated richness, agriculture developed and the mining of raw materials was intensified.[76] Derbyshire is said to be home to superb houses from almost all historical periods, rivaling the beauty of the castles of

[71] Craven, Stanley, *Derbyshire Country House*, p. 10.
[72] Craven, Stanley, *Derbyshire Country House*, p. 10.
[73] Craven, Stanley, *Derbyshire Country House*, p. 10f.
[74] Craven, Stanley, *Derbyshire Country House*, p. 11.
[75] Craven, Stanley, *Derbyshire Country House*, p. 11.
[76] Craven, Stanley, *Derbyshire Country House*, p. 11.

the Loire in France.[77] During the 18th and 19th centuries the very rich estates flourished considerably, whereas the smaller estates were absorbed. Towards the end of 19th century a new group of landowners came onto the scene: industrialists who usually bought quite modest estates. A new period of activity of house building or rebuilding in different styles commenced.[78] By marrying into families of the established gentry and thus assuming places in the social hierarchy of the county, these businessmen cast off their mercantile origins.

The majority of Derbyshire country houses were built of stone. Before the railway network connected all major cities of Britain and began entering remote rural areas (between 1830 and 1850[79]), means of transport was limited. Therefore almost every locally accessible rock type - such as sandstone, carboniferous limestone, magnesian limestone and shale - was used as building material, thus lending the architecture its pronounced local character.[80] A study of these stones has revealed that the builders utilised not only very local sources of supply, but that the material was generally obtained from within a three-mile radius of the building site. Only a few places in the country were not near any good building material and frequently a quarry was opened specifically to supply a building.[81]

Those houses which were made from brick could afford to purchase stone from further afield, e.g. for dressings or pavings, but the use of "exotic", non-local stone remained rare.[82] Stone buildings predominate the area of northern Derbyshire; brick as building material was more utilised further southwards, and yet further south again stone was the main material used.[83] Like in other parts of Britain, the earliest houses in Derbyshire were of the open-hall type with a central hearth, and owing to the availability of material were erected either from timber or stone. They were often overlain with later additions, but the main feature of all the houses is the great hall. Based on this prototype is the "typical upland Derbyshire stone built gabled manor" as well as the more elaborate type of house which features subsidiary structures, such as cross-wings set around a courtyard. During the 14th century, when many grand

---

77 Jenkins, *Best Houses*, p. 151.

78 Craven, Stanley, *Derbyshire Country House*, p. 11.

79 Hobsbawm, *Industry and Empire*, p. 88.

80 Craven, Stanley, *Derbyshire Country House*, p. 8; Muthesius, *English House*, p. 68: as a general rule houses in the north of England were traditionally made of stone, whilst those in the midlands and parts of the south were predominantly made of wood and those in and around London were made of brick. For the stones used for building in Derbyshire see also Cook, *English House*, p. 137.

81Craven, Stanley, *Derbyshire Country House*, p. 8; a possible example for Southgate Estate cf. Land Values Map (Duties on Land Values), Derbyshire Record Office, *Ref. No. D595.*

82 Craven, Stanley, *Derbyshire Country House*, p. 8.

83 Craven, Stanley, *Derbyshire Country House*, p. 8.

houses in England were erected as fortified houses, a number of buildings in Derbyshire were more residentially laid out and of a non-defensive type.[84] Historian Philip Riden states that surviving minor buildings in the region of north-east Derbyshire date from the period of the Great Rebuilding, which took place there "after 1600 rather than before. The typical farmhouse or cottage of that period was built of rubble limestone walling with a pantile roof, materials which give the area more in common with adjoining Nottinghamshire villages than the parishes of the coalfields to the west, were timber-framing and thatched roofs were replaced with sandstone walls and stone-flagged roofs."[85]

By the end of the English Civil War (1642-1651), classicism in the tradition of Inigo Jones became popular in the area, its best examples being Bretby Hall near Burton-upon-Trent, which found imitators in the centre and the north of the Derbyshire, and the first great Baroque building in the county, Chatsworth House. The latter set standards for further building activity and led to an, up until then, unheard of conjuncture in construction work in the area.[86] The work was executed to a comparatively high standard solely by local tradesmen (but nowhere reached the standards of Chatsworth House).[87] Around 1740, not quite a hundred years later, the nationwide house-building boom slowed down. Palladian architecture, already popular elsewhere in the country, had not yet reached Derbyshire or else it was considered at the time to be too conservative or too costly for local standards.[88] But gradually over time both a provincial Palladian and neo-classical style found their way into Derbyshire; the most notable architect of this provincial movement being Joseph Pickford of Derby (1734-1782).[89] The late 18th century architecture in the northern half of the county was largely influenced by men from Yorkshire (e.g. Sheffield architect Joseph Badger or architect William Lindley from Doncaster[90], see Chapter 8), and from the 19th century onwards also by architects from Manchester. But already towards the end of the 18th century the architecture and settings of the manor houses became more arbitrary, and local traditions disappeared with improved transport connections and the changes that society in Derbyshire, as elsewhere, underwent.[91] By the early

---

[84] Craven, Stanley, *Derbyshire Country House*, p. 12.

[85] Riden, *History of the County of Derby III*, p. 6.

[86] Craven, Stanley, *Derbyshire Country House*, p. 12.

[87] Craven, Stanley, *Derbyshire Country House*, p. 13.

[88] Craven, Stanley, *Derbyshire Country House*, p. 13.

[89] Craven, Stanley, *Derbyshire Country House*, p. 14; http://www.derbyshireuk.net/pickford.html (viewed 29/01/2014).

[90] Craven, Stanley, *Derbyshire Country House*, p. 14.

[91] Craven, Stanley, *Derbyshire Country House*, p. 15.

19th century an increasing number of architects of national repute were undertaking building work in Derbyshire.[92]

To sum up, it is perhaps best to let Craven and Stanley speak for themselves: ".... the richness of Derbyshire scenery is matched triumphantly by the variety of seats built thereon, the wide range of the materials which that scenery reflects, and the skill of the artists and craftsmen who built them, so many of them native to the area."[93] They emphasise that to them, the hallmark of the Derbyshire landscape and its development is that builders and architects of country houses had enough common sense over the centuries to use local materials which blended into the landscape.[94]

5. "The Stately Homes of England"

It was the British poet Felicia Dorothea Hemans (1793-1835)[95] who first coined the term "Stately Home" in her poem "The Homes of England" written in 1827.[96] In this work she aspires to give her readers an understanding of that one special feature of her cherished native country: the English House in all its glory, each set in its respective surrounding. Every stanza describes a different type of household for every level of society and emphasises how every home in England adds to the overall to the beauty and grace of the country. She wants to open her readers' eyes to the landscape of England, which she herself holds so dear. She paints a vivid picture of the nation and within it all its charming houses come alive.

The stately Homes of England,
How beautiful they stand!
Amidst their tall ancestral trees,
O'er all the pleasant land.
The deer across their greensward bound
Thro' shade and sunny gleam,
And the swan glides past them with the sound
Of some rejoicing stream.

The merry Homes of England!
Around their hearths by night,
What gladsome looks of household love

[92] Craven, Stanley, *Derbyshire Country House*, p. 14.

[93] Craven, Stanley, *Derbyshire Country House*, p. 15.

[94] Craven, Stanley, *Derbyshire Country House*, p. 10.

[95] Felicia Dorothea Hemans predominantly dealt with Romantic themes such as nature, the picturesque, childhood innocence, travels abroad, liberty, or the heroic. Hers was a female voice pitched between Victorian sentiment and chauvinism; cf. Encyclopedia Britannica, *Felicia Dorothea Hemans*; Teymur, *Felicia Dorothea Hemans*.

[96] "The Homes of England" by Hemans, *Records of Woman*, p. 169ff.

Meet in the ruddy light!
There woman's voice flows forth in song,
Or childhood's tale is told,
Or lips move tunefully along
Some glorious page of old.

The blessed Homes of England!
How softly on their bowers
Is laid the holy quietness
That breathes from Sabbath-hours!
Solemn, yet sweet, the church-bell's chime
Floats thro' their woods at morn;
All other sounds, in that still time,
Of breeze and leaf are born.

The Cottage Homes of England!
By thousands on her plains,
They are smiling o'er the silvery brooks,
And round the hamlet-fanes.
Thro' glowing orchards forth they peep,
Each from its nook of leaves,
And fearless there the lowly sleep,
As the bird beneath the eaves.

The free, fair Homes of England!
Long, long, in hut and hall,
May hearts of native proof be rear'd
To guard each hallow'd wall!
And green for ever be the groves,
And bright the flowery sod,
Where first the child's glad spirit loves
Its country and its God!

With this ode Hemans professes the value of the traditional way of things by looking to the past for an ideal English society. However, apart from this being a glorifying measure and a romantic stylistic device, it is also a misleading romantic idealisation of a phenomenon in English history which although undeniably beautiful, at the same time represents only a small segment of society which lived rather detached from the surroundings and whose experience differed considerably from that of the rest of the world. With the developing industrialisation in England (from 1780 onwards) and its ancillary effects, large swathes of the working classes found themselves living under disastrous conditions in the large cities[97] (such as Manchester and London), or were facing extreme poverty, for example as agricultural labourers while the minority of society, the landed gentry, dominated British politics and social life.[98] British historian Eric J Hobsbawm says: "The large landowners were rich and powerful, and the rich and powerful were landowners"[99], and "To belong to the upper classes meant to own an estate and a 'seat'. Landownership was the price of entry into high politics."[100] A seat in Parliament ensured control over the fate of politics, meaning one was acting in one's own interest. This system was based on votes and the more votes they had, the more seats could be gained in the House of Commons. By the early 18th century Parliament had waged and won its battle against the monarchy and influence in the House of Commons had become the new basis of power.[101] The landed gentry favoured and supported Toryism, as they believed it to be the best representation of their interests. In addition to this owning land was not just a way of generating money for its proprietors, it was also considered a way of life with all its exclusive amenities.[102] Even in times of agricultural hardship (e.g. between 1815 and the 1830s or during the Great Depression) the social predominance of the British nobility remained untouched, and their political influence outside of the towns and cities unchallenged.[103] Blake Morrison in his essay in "The Guardian" on grand houses as a national literary obsession goes even further by citing the Russian dramatist Anton Pavlovich Chekhov from his work "The Cherry Orchard". The left-wing student Trofimov has nothing good to say about the land-owning caste, condemning them as "serf-owners, possessors of living souls", "living in debit, at someone else's expense, at the expense of those who you wouldn't allow to cross your threshold".[104]

Blake Morrison writes further: "(...) there's a mythology surrounding English country houses that extols them as 'magical places' and their owners as wise custodians who tend the land, look after their tenants and servants,

---

97 Hobsbawm, *Industry and Empire*, p. 63ff.

98 Hobsbawm, *Industry and Empire*, p. 71.

99 Hobsbawm, *Industry and Empire*, p. 76; by 1760 ca. three quarters of the cultivated land was in the hands of landlords, occupying free-holders held 15-20%, and a "peasantry" had ceased to exist.

100 Hobsbawm, *Industry and Empire*, New York 1999, p. 75.

101 In large part this success was down to the estate owners' tenantry as tenants would normally vote as instructed by their landlords, cf. Girouard, *English Country House*, p. 184.

102 Hobsbawm, *Industry and Empire*, p. 76f.

103 Hobsbawm, *Industry and Empire*, p. 58: "The British aristocracy and gentry were thus little affected by industrialization, except for the better. Their rents swelled with the demand for farm produce, the expansion of cities (whose soil they owned) and of mines, forges and railways (which were situated on their estates)."

104 Morrison, "The Country House and the English Novel".

devote their lives to public service, fill their galleries with beautiful pictures and their libraries with rare books, and are unfailingly hospitable to friends and guests. Predictably, the most zealous purveyors of the myth have been aristocrats themselves, who depict their homes not as monuments to power and wealth but as embodiments of grace and gentility."[105] As seductive as it may be, it is indispensable to dispel the popular myth, the cult of the English country house, which is fuelled by not only by popular novels about country houses but also by TV documentaries, films and series that "allow us to luxuriate in places we could never own"[106] and to project our personal dreams of living a grander, altogether better life. Even today "aristo-Anglophilia" is a phenomenon which still hold considerable influence, and "forthright political condemnation" (…) is rare in British fiction"[107], but the yawning chasm of social imbalances and the self-aggrandisement of the upper classes are made unequivocally clear by a song named "The Stately Homes of England" by Noël Coward (from his musical in two acts "Operette", performed in 1938, written in 1937).[108] The cloying sentimentality of Heman's poem made him compose a satirical version laced an astute irony and a wicked sense of humour:

Lord Elderley, Lord Borrowmere,
Lord Sickert and Lord Camp,
With every virtue, every grace,
Ah what avails the sceptred race,
Here you see-the four of us,
And there are so many more of us
Eldest sons that must succeed.

---

[105] He refers to Mark Girouard's anthology *A Country House Companion*, cf. Morrison, "The Country House and the English Novel"; see also Horn, *Victorian Country House*, p. 124: "In modern Britain surviving stately-home owners see themselves as custodians of their land and heritage rather than as leaders of society and arbiters of political and economic policy, either nationally or in the rural communities where they live."

[106] Morrison, "The Country House and the English Novel".

[107] Morrison, "The Country House and the English Novel".

[108] Sir Noël Peirce Coward (16/12/1899-26/03/1973) was an English playwright, actor, and composer who is most widely known for his sharply observed comedies on social behaviour; cf. Encyclopedia Britannica, *Sir Noël Coward.* Text retrieved from Schiano, Adams, Strafford, *SongMeanings*. "Short introduction by Noël Coward: "In "Operette" at His Majesty's Theatre London in 1938, four elegant young gentlemen sauntered onto the stage in deep evening dress and top hats and capes and scarves. They represented the cynical, the cheerful aristocracy of the early 1900s. I must now ask your indulgence while I transform myself into this impeccable quartet: The Stately Homes of England."", cf. http://www.wepsite.de/Noel_Coward,The_Stately_Homes_of_England.htm (viewed 31/07/2013).

We know how Caesar conquered Gaul
And how to whack a cricket ball;
Apart from this, our education lacks co-ordination.
Though we're young and tentative
And rather rip-representative,
Scions of a noble breed,
We are the products of those homes serene and stately
Which only lately
Seem to have run to seed!

The Stately Homes of England,
How beautiful they stand,
To prove the upper classes
Have still the upper hand;
Though the fact that they have to be rebuilt
And frequently mortgaged to the hilt
Is inclined to take the gilt
Off the gingerbread,
And certainly damps the fun
Of the eldest son-
But still we won't be beaten,
We'll scrimp and scrape and save,
The playing fields of Eton
Have made us frightfully brave-
And though if the Van Dycks have to go
And we pawn the Bechstein Grand,
We'll stand
By the Stately Homes of England.

Here you see
The pick of us,
You may be heartily sick of us,
Still with sense
We're all imbued.
Our homes command extensive views
And with assistance from the Jews
We have been able to dispose of
Rows and rows and rows of
Gainsboroughs and Lawrences,
Some sporting prints of Aunt Florence's,
Some of which were rather rude.
Although we sometimes flaunt our family conventions,
Our good intentions
Mustn't be misconstrued.

The Stately Homes of England
We proudly represent,
We only keep them up for
Americans to rent,
Though the pipes that supply the bathroom burst
And the lavatory makes you fear the worst,
It was used by Charles the First
Quite informally,
And later by George the Fourth
On a journey north.
The State Apartments keep their
Historical renown,
It's wiser not to sleep there
In case they tumble down'
But still if they ever catch on fire
Which, with any luck, they might
We'll fight
For the Stately Homes of England

The Stately Homes of England,
Though rather in the lurch,
Provide a lot of chances
For Psychical Research-
There's the ghost of a crazy younger son
Who murdered, in thirteen fifty-one,
An extremely rowdy Nun
Who resented it,
And people who come to call
Meet her in the hall.
The baby in the guest wing,
Who crouches by the grate,
Was walled up in the west wing
In fourteen twenty-eight.
If anyone spots
The Queen of Scots
In a hand-embroidered shroud
We're proud
Of the Stately Homes of England.

Lord Elderley, Lord Borrowmere,
Lord Sickert and Lord Camp,
Behold us in our hours of ease,
Uncertain, coy and hard to please.

Reading in Debrett of us,
This fine Patrician quartette of us,
We can feel extremely proud,
Our ancient lineage we trace
Back to the cradle of the Race
Before those beastly Roman bowmen
Bitched our local Yeomen.
Through the new democracy
May pain the old Aristocracy
We've not winced nor cried aloud,
Under the bludgeonings of chance what will be- will be.
Our heads will still be
Bloody but quite unbowed!

The Stately Homes of England
In valley, dale and glen
Produce a race of charming,
Innocuous young men.
Though our mental equipment may be slight
And we barely distinguish left from right,
We are quite prepared to fight
For our principles,
Though none of us know so far
What they really are.
Our duty to the nation,
It's only fair to state,
Lies not in pro-creation
But what we pro-create;
And so we can cry
With kindling eye
As to married like we go,
What ho!
For the Stately Homes of England!

The Stately Homes of England,
Although a trifle bleak,
Historically speaking,
Are more or less unique.
We've a cousin who won the Golden Fleece
And a very peculiar fowling-piece
Which was sent to Cromwell's niece,
Who detested it,
And rapidly sent it back
With a dirty crack.

A note we have from Chaucer
Contains a bawdy joke.
We also have a saucer
That Bloody Mary broke.
We've two pairs of tights
King Arthur's Knights
Had completely worn away.
Sing Hey!
For the Stately Homes of England.

The Stately Homes of England,
Tho' rather on the blink
Provide a lot of reasons
For what we do and think.
Tho' we freely admit we may be wrong,
Our conviction that we are right is strong
Tho' it may not be for long,
We'll hold on to it
We might as well hold the bat
Till they knock us flat
Our dignity of race may
Retire into its shell
Our Minister of Grace may
Defend us none too well
But still if a child
Becomes too wild
And we're forced to use the rod,
Thank God
For the Stately Homes of England.

So when writing a book on an English manor house one should never let slip from view that it is not a self-evident manifestation representative of the whole of English society over the past centuries. No matter how tempting it is to let oneself be enamoured by the undeniable beauty and elegance of the architecture, style and design every grand structure from stately home to manor house, even down to the most modest country house, one must remember that they were often erected at the expense of those less fortunate. However, I cannot deny the fascination for Southgate House and Estate and its history which developed over the course of my research and I must admit that I thoroughly fell for its charms.

6. The Buildings of Southgate House, Southgate Stables, Southgate Cottages and Southgate Camp

The Georgian country house of **Southgate House** is situated on Worksop Road in Clowne, Derbyshire. An integral part of the architectural ensemble is the historic sandstone building of **Southgate Stables** on the opposite side of the lane. The present-day Hotel Van Dyk is comprised of what used to be **Southgate House**; **Southgate Stables** together with several farms and servants' and workers' **Cottages** belonged to the estate.

Southgate House was built in the middle the 18th century.[109] It is a pretty, three storey high house of moderate size, built of stone with painted cement render and a slate roof. The house underwent minor structural changes during the late 19th and early 20th century when a chapel built of brick was added to the main house. Southgate House was possibly preceded by another building.

Southgate Stables as they stand today were erected in the middle of the 19th century, but stables as part of Southgate Estate are already mentioned as early as 1787. Structural additions to the building were made during the 20th century[110] and in 1990 major renovation works were carried out.[111] According to English Heritage both buildings, the house and the stables, are Grade II listed under the Planning (Listed Buildings and Conservation Areas) Act 1990 as amended for its special architectural or historic interest.[112]

Southgate Cottages (or "Cottages at The Avenue") must have been erected before 1897 and existed until at least 1947; they were possibly demolished in 1957 when the road connecting Chesterfield and Worksop was widened. According to the Land Values Map of 1909/1910 the ensemble originally consisted of two houses; one larger rectangular one to the west, set back from the main road by a couple of metres, and a smaller, rather square building located directly on the road to the east.[113] Evidently both houses, originally erected of sandstone ashlar and brick, did not have any special architectural relevance. Another cottage belonging to Southgate Estate was the former tollhouse facility situated alongside the Chesterfield and Worksop Turnpike

---

[109] British Listed Buildings, *Southgate House, Clowne*; English Heritage, *Southgate House*.

[110] British Listed Buildings, *Southgate Stables*; English Heritage, *Southgate Stables*.

[111] Picture The Past, *Southgate Stables (103754)*; Picture The Past, *Southgate Stables (103755)*; Picture The Past, *Southgate Stables (103756)*.

[112] English Heritage, *Southgate Stables*. "The Planning (Listed Buildings and Conservation Areas) Act 1990 required all Local Planning Authorities to determine which parts of their areas were of special architectural or historic interest and to designate them as conservation areas, in order to preserve or enhance the character and appearance of the area. It is also their duty to review them from time to time, and to determine whether any further parts of their areas should also be designated as conservation areas."; cf. Stroud, *Derbyshire Extensive Urban Survey*, p. 20.

[113] Compare Land Values Map (Duties on Land Values), Derbyshire Record Office, *Ref. No. D595*.

Road during the 18th and 19th century (see Chapter 14.4). This building was also demolished in 1957 during the road construction works. There are three more cottages which belonged to Southgate Estate as attested in a record dated 1947: "Cottage at Harlesthorpe Dam", "Cottage at Rotherham Road" and "The Hermitage" (see Chapters 14.6, 14.7, 14.8). A fourth cottage mentioned in the record as "Cottage at Stableyard" is identical to "Southgate Stables" (see Chapter 14.3).

Southgate Camp is a fourth and ephemeral element of the estate. It served as a camp for Prisoner of War and later as accommodation for squatters after the prisoners had left, and continued to exist as cheap and primitive housing well in the early 1960s (see Chapter 25).

7. "The Shifts and Changes in the Patterns of Life"[114] - The Area and the Village of Clowne

The village of Clowne, part of the parish of Bolsover, is comprised of a total area of 1,922 acres. It lies on the peak of a magnesian limestone ridge, which runs along a north south alignment from Durham through Yorkshire, Derbyshire and which ends in the southern end of Nottinghamshire. Over the centuries the limestone has been mined intensively. Additionally since the Industrial Revolution, the land has been mined for coal, a rich source of which lies under the ground.[115]

Clowne is situated in the direct vicinity of the Palaeolithic site of Creswell Crags and has a similarly long history. Whaley Shelters I and II are sites of Mesolithic and Neolithic cave/rock shelters, and four Neolithic burials have been found in one of the seven caves/rock fissures (used as rock shelters) at Markland Grips.[116] A surface find of a spearhead found half a mile south-west of Markland Grips in plough-soil has been dated as Middle Bronze Age.[117] A place called Ash Tree Cave in Burnhill Grips is another relevant archaeological site. Finds made there date from Palaeolithic to Roman times.[118]

---

114 Quote from the song "Timeless Skies" written by Al Stewart, from the album "Time Passages" (1978).

115 Riden, *History of the County of Derby III*, p. 107ff.; NN, "Focus on: Clowne", p. 21 (content of article based on information by Clowne Local Historic Society, http://www.clownevillage.co.uk).

116 Riden, *History of the County of Derby III*, p. 137. "Grip" in this context comes from a word meaning "ditch" or "furrow" hinting to the course of the water rather than the limestone cliffs, cf. NN, "Focus on: Clowne", p. 21. According to Riden, the word derives from the dialect "grip" meaning "small watercourse".

117 Riden, *History of the County of Derby III*, p. 137; NN, "Focus on: Clowne", p. 24.

118 NN, "Focus on: Clowne", p. 24. More archaeological finds have been made in and around the neighbouring village of Whitwell: two Mesolithic sites at Steetley and Bondhay; stray finds of flints and other artefacts from Mesolithic, Neolithic Era and Bronze Age and Roman times from several find places within the parish, a Neolithic

The area supposedly belongs to one of the highest points in Britain and therefore has always been of strategical importance as an observation point owing to its far-reaching views. Hollinhill and Markland Grips are a series of deep glacial valleys originating from the end of the last Ice Age. The river Wollen, which forms the boundary with Whitwell, has created the deep valley of Hollinhill Grips in the magnesian limestone ridge which in the Iron Age was the territorial boundary between the Corieltauvi people[119] and the Brigantes[120]. The Wollen is joined by another river, which cuts through the valley of Markland Grips. The confluence of both rivers formed a triangular-shaped promontory[121] which has been identified as the site of a Corieltauvi fortification, an Iron Age settlement directly south of A616/Sheffield Road halfway between Clowne and Creswell.[122] This fortification certainly served to reinforce the boundary between the two tribes and belongs to a number of other, similar pre-Roman archaeological sites such as Bolsover and Scarcliffe Park.[123] The fort was protected to the west by triple ramparts and ditches and had three entrances. The whole site measures ca. 10.5 acres. So far only limited excavation has taken place. There are traces of latter secondary colonisation (2nd and 3rd century and ca. 1200).[124]

In Roman times a fort known today as Camp Hill[125] guarded at least one major ancient ridge track[126], which ran through Clowne in a north-south direction. Archaeologists were able to identify a second track heading towards

---

long cairn near Whitwell quarry, a Romano-British settlement with enclosed round huts near Scratta Wood, and a Roman coin hoard from a field east of Gapsick Lane; cf. Riden, *History of the County of Derby III*, p. 165.

119 The Corieltauvi (or Coritani) were a Celtic tribe of largely agricultural people who settled in the East Midlands (incl. Derbyshire) prior to the Roman conquest and later became *civitas* of Roman Britain, their capital was Leicester; cf. http://www.historyfiles.co.uk/KingListsBritain/BritainCoritani.htm (viewed 03/04/2014). The find place in Clowne shows an abundance of industrial waste dating from the 2nd century which led excavators to the conclusion that it was a later adopted settlement and which makes a military use unlikely; cf. Pearcy, *Forts*.

120 The Brigantes were the inhabitants of the region south of the Antonine Wall including among other areas Yorkshire and the land to the west and into the Peak District, cf. Encyclopedia Britannica, *Brigantes*; Beresford, "Scarcliffe Park", p. 10.

121 Riden, *History of the County of Derby III*, p. 137.

122 Riden, *Elmton*, p. 2, p. 5f.; Beresford, "Scarcliffe Park", p. 10, figure 6; http://www.burrows.co.uk/bolsoverguide/10TheM.htm (viewed 19/05/2013); NN, "Focus on: Clowne", p. 22. The promontory is denoted as "Camp" on the map sheet 19.11 of the Land Values Map of 1909/1910 (Derbyshire Record Office, *Ref. No. D595*).

123 Beresford, "Scarcliffe Park", p. 3-18.

124 Riden, *History of the County of Derby III*, p. 138; NN, "Focus on: Clowne", p. 23: dating by the find of several coins and Gaulish Samian Ware.

125 Riden, *History of the County of Derby III*, p. 137; NN, "Focus on: Clowne", p. 23.

126 For more information on the subject see Appendix 2.

Chesterfield in 1990.[127] The camp was situated north of The Oaks farm in Elmton Common[128] and was possibly used as a day camp by the Romans as they moved northwards heading for Brigantian-occupied territory.[129] Purportedly, several ancient spearheads have been found there, as well as a couple of old coins, including the find of one silver coin around 1895 with a bust and the word *Caesar* on its reverse. Similar finds of Romano-British origin made at Oxpasture Lane at Whaley Hall (late 1st to 3rd century) give hint to a seemingly meagre and largely agrarian economy, which did not make use of imported pottery. Coal and wood served as fuel.[130]

More detailed information on the region is available from the early Middle Ages (11th century) onwards: "Clune Manor" together with 4 other manors or estates in the vicinity (Barlborough, Whitwell, Eckington and Wales) was bequeathed by Wulfric Spot(t), an Anglo-Saxon nobleman and founder and patron of Burton Abbey who died ca. 1004[131], to thegn Morcar (chief thegn of the Seven Boroughs, killed 1015[132]) between 1002 and 1004.[133] Apparently Clowne "was not merely a manor, parts being in the manors of Barleburg (Barlborough) and part in Witewelle (Whitwell). So Clowne itself was an identifiable community apart from the manor."[134]

The settlement of Clowne appears in three entries in the Domesday Book as Clune[135] (the name perhaps deriving from Clun, a Celtic river name[136]).

---

127 Arkwright Colliery Opencast Colliery appraisal of 1990; cf. NN, "Focus on: Clowne", p. 24: "These routes are probably the reason the hillfort and the Roman fort were built, as trade and hospitality would have been an economic addition to the local residents and so defending them would have been of great importance."

128 Riden, *Elmton*, p. 5; Riden, *History of the County of Derby III*, p. 136f. and fig. 46 (Frithwood Lane just outside Creswell).

129 NN, "Focus on: Clowne", p. 23.

130 Riden, *History of the County of Derby III*, p. 138; see also Bishop, "An Archaeological Resource Assessment of Roman Nottinghamshire", p. 1-9.

131 Baxter, Stephen et al., *Prosopography of Anglo-Saxon England* (Wulfric).

132 Baxter, Stephen et al., *Prosopography of Anglo-Saxon England* (Morcar).

133 Riden, *History of the County of Derby III*, p. 2ff, p. 112; Stroud, *Derbyshire Extensive Urban Survey*, p. 3; http://www.clownevillage.co.uk/clowne-hist/noatable%20dates2.htm (viewed 19/05/2013); NN, "Focus on: Clowne", p. 24.

134 http://www.burrows.co.uk/bolsoverguide/10TheM.htm (viewed 19/05/2013). "The township itself was split between the estate of Clowne and that of Whitwell and Barlborough held by Leofnoth."; cf. NN, "Focus on: Clowne", p. 24.

135 Domesday Book, Folio 277r, 278v and 281r (for 1086); cf. The National Archives, *Domesday*; Powell-Smith, *Open Domesday*.

136 http://www.clownevillage.co.uk/history/history.html (viewed 10/07/2013); Barlborough Heritage and Research Centre, *Local Walks* interprets the word as "a place of many springs". "Several springs are mentioned in historical documents such as "Bawne Spring", "West Springs" and "Little Spring Wood"."; cf. NN, "Focus on: Clowne", p. 21. Philip Riden offers another explanation for the origin of the word: a little river that rises in Barlborough and flows towards Creswell could have been

According to research by Philip Riden, by 1066 Clowne, measured at one carucate.[137] The settlement was split into two smaller estates, two bovates[138] of sokeland being ascribed to the large manor of Barlborough, and six bovates remained separate (and only briefly until 1086 when it was merged in the manor of Bolsover) by one of the king's thegns[139] named Ernwy/Earnwig (of Stanton).[140] A separate manor of Clowne does not seem to have existed.[141]

Earnwig's share excluded, the other aforementioned seignuries were held by Leofnoth by 1066 and passed to Ralph Fitz Hubert after the Conquest (both thegns are listed in the Domesday Book for Clowne).[142] According to an article in Worksop Life Magazine based on information provided by Clowne Local Historical Society the land in question in Clowne was "called an estate rather than manor as there is no mention of one here until 1485".[143]

During the Middle Ages all the manors (or estates) in question had free tenants; Clowne parish, which was split between the manors of Barlborough and Bolsover, was held by a group of influential freeholders.[144] However, it seems that other sub settlements never extended to more than one main house, sometimes with a few cottages attached, such as Harlesthorpe[145], which, as we will later see, will become the geographical focus of this

Clowne's namesake. Its name is identical with the name of the river Clun in Shropshire and could have been transferred to Derbyshire in Anglo-Saxon times; cf. Riden, *History of the County of Derby III*, p. 107 and footnote 9. I suspect this description refers to the stream whose modern name is river Wollen (see above).

137 A carucate is a land measure (the word meaning deriving from the Latin word *caruca* = plough). It describes the amount of land which could be ploughed by one plough team; cf. http://www.domesdaybook.co.uk/glossary.html (viewed 02/02/2014).

138 A bovate (also named oxgang) is an old land measurement. One bovate is equivalent to ca. 15 English acres (= 1/8 carucate/hide). It describes the amount of land which could be ploughed using one trek ox (one carucate was the area which could be ploughed with a team of eight oxen); cf. Rowlett, *How many?*

139 A thegn (or thane) is a feudal lord or nobleman in Anglo-Saxon England; cf. Encyclopedia Britannica, *Thane*.

140 Riden, *History of the County of Derby III*, p. 2ff., p. 112; Domesday Book, Folio 278v.

141 Riden, *History of the County of Derby III*, p. 112.

142 For more details see Riden, *History of the County of Derby III*, p. 2ff; p. 15f.; Domesday Book, Folio 277r.

143 NN, "Focus on: Clowne", p. 28. The article also observes that over the course of twenty years, between the time of Norman Conquest and the Domesday Book, the value of land in Clowne plummeted to less than half that what it had been: 20 Shillings to 8. Only eight villagers are mentioned in the Domesday Book, which leads us to suspect that, as elsewhere in Derbyshire, the village experienced an economic downturn. However, whether this was due to disease or to the "harrying of the north" remains a mystery to this day.

144 Riden, *History of the County of Derby III*, p. 4.

145 Riden, *History of the County of Derby III*, p. 2.

research. A number of gentry estates of lesser size came about due to the rising elite in Barlborough and Clowne in the 17th century, which according to Philip Riden, mainly centred on Park Hall, Beighton Fields, Southgate House, and Romeley Hall.[146]

According to Magna Britannia (1817), after ca. 800 years[147] Clowne must still have been situated on the boundary between the manor of Barlborough and the manor of Bolsover[148], but the line dividing the two places cannot be defined precisely. Records only disclose more detailed information for the year 1829 when it was stated that the larger share of Clowne was situated within Bolsover manor and for the year 1874 when the land south and east of Hickingwood Lane was described to belong to Bolsover, the land north and west of it to Barlborough.[149] Further modifications of the boundary took place in 1885 and 1935 when part of Barlborough civil parish (including the mining village of New Barlborough) was incorporated into Clowne.[150] At the end of the 19th century the parish of Clowne covered 1,922 acres of land[151], located towards the northeastern corner of Scarsdale Hundred. The parish was surrounded by Bolsover to the south, Elmton and Whitwell to the east, Barlborough to the north and Staveley to the west; the boundaries to the respective settlements were not defined in a very conventional way.[152] During the mid of 20th century a boundary line between Whitwell and Clowne was situated along the A619 between Southgate House and (the now ruins of) Southgate Cottages.[153]

Not much is known about Clowne during the early Middle Ages, but the village has two puzzling features remaining from that time. The first is the church St. John the Baptist, founded in the early 12th century (1138), which was initially dedicated as "All Saints"[154]. When built it seems that it was

---

146 Riden, *History of the County of Derby III*, p. 6. *Pace* Mr Riden, but as far as it is known there is no verified attestation for Southgate House in the 17th century.

147 This invariance is perhaps at least partially owed to the fact that no major estates in the region were held by the church, so the area was not affected much by the radical changes the Dissolution of the Monasteries in the 16th century (see Chapter 13) brought with it; cf. Riden, *History of the County of Derby III*, p. 5.

148 Magna Britannia is a topographical account of 9 counties of Great Britain including Derbyshire and was published between 1806 and 1822 by Daniel and Samuel Lysons; cf. Lysons, *Magna Britannia, Clown*, p. 89ff.

149 Riden, *History of the County of Derby III*, p. 112. The writing of Hickingwood varies and can be Hickingwood, Hickin Wood or Hickinwood.

150 Riden, *History of the County of Derby III*, p. 107.

151 Kelly's *Directory*, p. 98f.

152 Riden, *History of the County of Derby III*, p. 107.

153 Information disclosed by Derek Bower in a private E-mail correspondence with the author on May 23, 2013.

154 http://www.clownevillage.co.uk/clowne-hist/noatable%20dates2.htm (viewed 19/05/2013); http://www.stjohnclowne.org/history.htm (viewed 22/05/2013).

deliberately situated just outside the settlement. There is neither any archaeological nor historical evidence for a previous habitation in the near vicinity of the church, nor any known tenurial reason why the church was originally built quasi *extra muros*. Perhaps the near-by junction of two important roads led to the development of Clowne happening there, rather than in the proximity of the Lord's house.[155] The church website reports that the building was initially a monastic foundation, located in close proximity to the Ridgeway route from Mansfield to Worksop Priory, providing comfort and shelter for passing travellers.[156] Today, the church is incorporated in the village, situated on Church Lane towards the southeastern corner of the settlement. The other peculiarity is a 14th century stone cross (modified in the 17th century) on The Green at the junction of Rectory Road and Mill Street. It is not unlikely that a small market was held here in the Middle Ages, but no market charter for Clowne is attested.[157] The church and the cross are the village's only surviving mediaeval structures.

The Black Death that wiped out large parts of the population of Derbyshire did not spare Clowne in the mid of the 14th century (1348-1350). Its victims were buried on what is today called "Barlborough Links".[158]

The oldest remaining house appears to date from the mid 17th century or possibly later. It is a former farmhouse built of limestone and sandstone, positioned on 106 High Street. It bears a date stone inscribed with "WGA 1758".[159]

During the late Middle Ages/Early Modern Age the parish of Clowne was a small settlement with a rather steady number of inhabitants: in 1563 the presence of 55 families is attested. But the growth of the village came to a dramatic halt with the outbreak of "The Great Plague of Chesterfield" which peaked in June 1587 and again in 1606. It claimed so many lives in Clowne that they could not all be buried in the local churchyard, but many had to be interred at "Monument Field" north of the settlement (also named "Plague Field").[160] In 1664 there were 42 households documented in the portion within the Bolsover constabulary (at that time the Barlborough part was not counted separately). Another count in 1676 reveals 278 conformists (members of the English state church) and nonconformists. In 1700 Clowne was comprised of ca. 400 inhabitants. In 1751 the number of families counted was 87, but only 70 in 1772. 78 houses were counted in the early 1780s and 97 in 1801, inhabited

---

155 Riden, *History of the County of Derby III*, p. 4, p. 109.

156 http://www.stjohnclowne.org/history.htm (viewed 22/05/2013).

157 Riden, *History of the County of Derby III*, p. 109.

158 http://www.clownevillage.co.uk/clowne-hist/noatable%20dates2.htm (viewed 19/05/2013).

159 Riden, *History of the County of Derby III*, p. 109; Riden, *Clowne*, p. 7 and footnote 3: initials unidentified.

160 http://www.burrows.co.uk/bolsoverguide/10TheM.htm (viewed 19/05/2013).

by 484 people. During the mid 19th century, the population slowly began to rise: 637 people were counted in 1831 (living in 134 houses) and 677 people in 1841. The number fell to 600 in 1851, and increased again to 701 in 1861.[161] It can be estimated that during these times Clowne was a predominantly farming community with 50% of Clowne's inhabitants working on the land.[162] The other half occupied supporting trades, worked in shops or ran small businesses.[163]

While farming remained an essential branch of trade for Clowne[164], the situation changed significantly when the coal mining industry took over as the main economic activity. The exposed coal measures appear to have already been exploited on a small scale in the 17th century, as well as some limestone and sandstone.[165] Extensive coal mining in Clowne began in the 1870s when a "Miss Bowdon" cut the first sod for Southgate Colliery in 1875 (under a lease from 1874 from the Butler-Bowdon estate to Shireoaks Colliery Company[166]). Work was taken up in earnest at the mine in 1877[167] which

---

161 http://www.clownevillage.co.uk/clowne-hist/noatable%20dates2.htm (viewed 19/05/2013), http://www.burrows.co.uk/bolsoverguide/10TheM.htm (viewed 19/05/2013); Riden, *History of the County of Derby III*, p. 107. According to the mentioned years (1841, 1851 etc.) these numbers are based on the decennial censuses of England and Wales. Pigot & Co.s *National Commercial Directory for 1828-29* (Pigot & Co.s *1828-29*), p. 112 numbers the parish at about 600.

162 The land (owned by the Duke of Portland and, among others, members of the Bowdon and Butler-Bowdon family) yielded fair crops of wheat, barley and turnips; cf. Kelly's *Directory*, p. 98f.

163 http://www.burrows.co.uk/bolsoverguide/10TheM.htm (viewed 19/05/2013). Pigot & Co.s *1828-29*, p. 112 attests, among others, a small manufactory of sail cloth, which in probability will have been Bowden (*sic!*), Malkin & Co." (or "Bowden (*sic!*) & Co.", see Chapter 22.1).

164 Twenty Farmers were recorded for the parish at the beginning of the 20th century, one having had his own flour mill; cf. http://www.burrows.co.uk/bolsoverguide/10TheM.htm (viewed 19/05/2013).

165 Coal mines are attested for Clowne in 1652. In the course of an Inclosure Act of 1778 the coal was reserved for the Duke of Portland; cf. Riden, *History of the County of Derby III*, p. 118ff. (also p. 107); Riden, *Clowne*, p. 2, p. 10.

166 "(…) the trustees of the will of Henry Bowden of Southgate House (…) leased the coal (…) for 40 years from 1872 to the Shireoaks Colliery Company, with the usual powers to work coal (…) and other minerals."; cf. Riden, *History of the County of Derby III*, p. 119. According to him (p. 119 and footnote 5) Shireoaks Colliery Company also purchased "the freehold of small areas of surface at Southgate in 1873-1874, 1876, and 1891." Shireoaks Colliery Company Ltd. is named as owner of the colliery in 1910/1911 on p. 7, 10 and 68 in the Book of Records of the Land Values Map (Derbyshire Record Office, *Ref. No. D595*).

167 Riden, *History of the County of Derby III*, p. 119; Bridgewater, *Southgate Colliery*; http://www.clownevillage.co.uk/clowne-hist/noatable%20dates2.htm (viewed 19/05/2013). "Miss Bowdon" was presumably one of the two daughters of Henry (5) Bowdon.

caused the economic focus to change and the population of Clowne to increase considerably (1871: 1,002 persons, 1881: 1,812 persons, 1891: 2,349 persons, and 1901: 3,896 persons counted[168]), with the development reaching its peak in 1911 at 6,037 inhabitants. The number of residents declined after that to 5,880 in 1921 and 5,917 in 1931. In the course of a boundary change of 1935 the total number of people rose to 6,106 in 1951 and remained stable for 20 years. With new land released for new housing the population grew once more to 6,846 in 1981, 7,234 in 1991, 7,447 in 2001 and 7,590 in 2011.[169]

The University of Nottingham holds an interesting record regarding the above-mentioned lease of Southgate Colliery.[170] It is a correspondence covering a time span of six years (between 16/04/1867 and 11/09/1873) between the 5th Duke of Portland[171] and the two Bowdon brothers Henry (5) and John (5) and a number of other local business men. The Bowdons expressed an interest in renting coal-bearing land from the Duke of Portland at Whitwell in order to exploit the coal under Southgate Estate, of which some of the Duke's land would have been affected as well as the local infrastructure. The Duke preferred to buy out the land and minerals in question to which John (5) was possibly open, but the proposal was turned down in favour of a compromise of to jointly explore the minerals and the promise by the Bowdon brothers to give the Duke of Portland the "first refusal on any sale of the lands or minerals of the Southgate Estate". The negotiations included the Duke's explicit wish that the landscape not be spoiled by the site of the pit, in as far as that he would not have been affected by the sight and the activities of the mine in his ancestral estate in Welbeck Abbey.[172]

At its peak Southgate Colliery employed around 400 men (300 men underground, 100 on the surface). By 1900 the mine had been sunk about a thousand feet and produced some 600 tons of hard coal every day (Figure 2). Steam winding engines, installed in 1887, helped quarrying. A large chimney, built in 1890, extracted the steam of the engines, but was blown down on May

---

168 Riden, *History of the County of Derby III*, p. 2; Kelly's *Directory*, p. 98f.; http://www.burrows.co.uk/bolsoverguide/10TheM.htm (viewed 19/05/2013).

169 Riden, *History of the County of Derby III*, p. 2.; http://www.burrows.co.uk/bolsoverguide/10TheM.htm (viewed 19/05/2013).

170 University of Nottingham, *Ref. No. Pl E12/9/6/1/31-175.*

171 William John Cavendish Cavendish-Scott-Bentinck, 5th Duke of Portland (12/09/1800-06/12/1879); cf. Lundy, *Peerage* (Person Page 961). Eric J Hobsbawm writes in the Chapter "Agriculture 1750-1850" (Hobsbawm, *Industry and Empire*) on p. 85: "The really large landlord did not necessarily depend on agricultural rents. He might enjoy the fruits of rising urban real-estate values, or the profits of mines and railways which a fortunate providence had placed under or on his land."

172 The Duke of Portland was the owner/occupier of Welbeck Abbey and the Parente and Bentinck families occupy parts of the house until today; cf. Lundy, *Peerage* (Person Page 1367).

9, 1951.[173] A tragic cage accident occurred at Southgate Colliery in 1911, and of 12 men involved three were killed.[174]

Unusually for the time, Clowne had two railway stations (neither of which exist today), one was opened in 1888 (Midland Railway), the other in 1897 (Lancashire, Derbyshire and East Coast Railway). Both lines served local transportation as well as the colliery (Figure 3), the rail connexion thus contributing to the expansion of Clowne. All lines are closed today.[175]

The colliery turned its last coal in 1929 and ceased to exist on January 17 of that year. It was flooded by a sudden ingress of water from an adjacent pit; thankfully no-one was harmed during the incident. In 1955 the colliery was opened up for a second time in order to support the construction of a link to the colliery in the neighbouring village of Creswell. This was eventually abandoned, and the shafts and colliery site were filled in and cleared by 1961.[176]

Another building from Clowne's historical past is the old half-timbered publican house on Mill Street; it was one of four Inns, which, alongside four Ale Houses and eight other businesses, sold alcoholic beverages in the village.[177] An old photograph in possession of Barlborough Heritage and Resource Centre provides evidence of the "The Bowden (*sic!*) Arms".[178] An article in the Derbyshire Courier dated November 9, 1850 mentions the said place, at that time owned by a Mr and Mrs Roberts. The text refers to a meeting of Mr George Unwin and other local dignitaries on the occasion of receiving rents arising from the estates (*sic!*) of J B Bowdon, Esq. by Mr Unwin. The participants of the occasion spent a harmonious evening with an excellent dinner, raising loyal toasts to the Lord Lieutenant of the County and the Duke of Portland, John (5) Butler-Bowdon, his wife and family, W H De Rhodes, Esq. and Mr Unwin senior. The toasts "were given and cordially responded to, in expression of good feelings towards the several parties", and "the conviviality being heightened by several excellent songs". The same newspaper makes mention of a similar occasion a couple of days earlier on

---

173 Bridgewater, *Southgate Colliery;* http://www.clownevillage.co.uk/clowne-hist/noatable%20dates2.htm (viewed 19/05/2013). For a short reference to the colliery see Linacre, *How it was*, p. 8.

174 http://www.clownevillage.co.uk/clowne-hist/noatable%20dates2.htm (viewed 19/05/2013).

175 Bridgewater, *Southgate Colliery;* Riden, *History of the County of Derby III*, p. 108f., p. 135 (for more detailed information on the railway situation). Yet Clowne became connected to the new and fast developing nationwide railway network comparatively late, the first wave of building activities took place between 1835 and 1837, a second, much bigger one between 1845 and 1847; cf. Hobsbawm, *Industry and Empire*, p. 88.

176 Bridgewater, *Southgate Colliery.*

177 http://www.burrows.co.uk/bolsoverguide/10TheM.htm (viewed 19/05/2013).

178 A contemporary picture of this building is in possession of Tony Bak of Barlborough Heritage and Resource Centre.

October 30, 1850 at an inn in Whitwell, when again the receipt of rents was celebrated with a small get-together. A toast was given, among others, to J B Bowdon, Esq. The text sheds an interesting light on the relationship between the named landowners and their tenants: "The party spent a few hours pleasantly and agreeably, as is usual on such occasions where the tenants live under kind and liberal landlords."[179]

The rapid growth of Clowne at the beginning of the 20th century (mainly between 1890 and WWI), triggered by the development of the colliery, necessitated the extensive demolition of older buildings. It did not take long before Clowne had overtaken the neighbouring villages of Barlborough and Whitwell, and soon became a local shopping centre (the first Co-op opened in 1898[180]) as well as a place to catch the train. New houses, shops and offices made of red brick were erected as well as terraced housings which spread up North Road. Rather than creating a new, separate colliery village detached from the old settlement, existing street fronts were rebuilt and new roads were developed. This building activity heralded the start of a new public infrastructure: the education sector was developed[181], the first cinema opened its doors on Rectory Road in 1911[182], there was a gasworks (on Station Road) and a police station (on Rotherham Road) and a cricket and a football ground

---

179 Thanks to Tony Bak of Barlborough Heritage and Resource Centre for kindly providing me with this information.

180 http://www.clownevillage.co.uk/clowne-hist/noatable%20dates2.htm (viewed 19/05/2013).

181 Education found its way into Clowne in the 16th century by means of Rector William Inskip (1528-1582), who founded the first school which is notable for a village the size of Clowne and for the fact that there already were schools in the vicinity (Staveley, Chesterfield). It can be assumed that this first school did not last long; cf. http://www.burrows.co.uk/bolsoverguide/10TheM.htm (viewed 19/05/2013). The next verifiable information on the matter stems from 1727, when the foundations for a longer-lasting school education in Clowne were laid. In 1734 the first school with the aim of educating the poorest children of the village was opened; cf. http://www.clownevillage.co.uk/clowne-hist/noatable%20dates2.htm (viewed 19/05/2013); according to Pigot & Co.s *1828-29*, p. 112 a free school for twenty-four boys and girls was endowed in 1730. Children of Clowne continued to attend the school throughout the century, until it came under the control of the state in the 1870s. By the beginning of the 20th century Clowne boasted two schools; cf. http://www.burrows.co.uk/bolsoverguide/10TheM.htm (viewed 19/05/2013). For a complete and detailed overview of the development in education in Clowne see Riden, *History of the County of Derby III*, p. 122ff.

182 Riden, *History of the County of Derby III*, p. 121. According to Sylvia R Linacre (Linacre, *How it was*, p. 68), it was called "The Palace" and showed three different films a week; see also http://www.clownevillage.co.uk/clowne-hist/noatable%20dates2.htm (viewed 19/05/2013). According to this source the cinema was originally named "Picture Hall" before receiving its new name, "Picture Palace", in 1935. The cinema was closed in 1961.

were opened to the public.[183] To sum up Philip Riden states that "within barely twenty years Clowne had changed from a farming village into a small mining town."[184]

With the end of WWI and the closure of Southgate Colliery the number of inhabitants decreased and the size of the town remained constant. Only after the end of the Second World War, with the erection of new estates at Hickinwood on Creswell Road (initiated by the rural district council with purpose-built shops and a variety of houses) did Clowne begin to grow again. This area was popular amongst the mine workers at Creswell and the employees of the new hosiery and knitwear factory built on the grounds of the former Southgate Colliery.[185] More land was released for housing, new schools were built and the technical college on Rectory Road (opened in 1931) was expanded. The closure of the coal mines in the region during the 1980s and 1990s lead to further deterioration of the town and its central commercial core, which was further intensified by the poor layout of the town. Apparently the whole Bolsover area deteriorated so badly in the wake of the closure of the collieries that it became one of the poorest in the whole of England. Clowne Technical College was closed in 2002. At the same time in an area closer towards Barlborough some opencast coalmines working were established, the A616 was realigned ("Barlborough Links") and land was again released for more housing and commercial buildings. This led to a further decline of Clowne's old town centre, where the only notable development was the opening of a very large Tesco supermarket in 2003, and the opening of a new college campus in 2005.[186] Today Clowne is on the up again and a pretty little country town on the edge of Derbyshire and the shires of South Yorkshire and Nottinghamshire and the bustling cities within. It is within easy reach of the Peak District and Sherwood Forest and close to many places of beauty such as the Yorkshire Dales and the North York Moors.

8. "Southgate House is a delightful residence."[187] – The History of Southgate House

Southgate House was built on land known as Harlesthorpe, part of the parish of Clowne, situated northeast of the village.[188] The place may have originated

[183] Riden, *History of the County of Derby III*, p. 110f.

[184] Riden, *History of the County of Derby III*, p. 111.

[185] Riden, *History of the County of Derby III*, p. 111, p. 118.

[186] Riden, *History of the County of Derby III*, p. 8, p. 111f., p. 117, p. 127, p. 120 and footnote 15 referring to an article in Derbyshire Times dated November 13, 2003 ("Tesco ... bringing more people into Clowne who ... would also spend money at other shops"). This is opposed by "Don't let Tesco be the death of Clowne", an article in the Worksop Guardian on August 15, 2003 where local shopkeepers express their concern that their trades may suffer as a result of the competition (cf. NN, "Don't let Tesco be the death of Clowne").

[187] Glover, *History*, p. 305.

and also received its name sometime between the end of the 9th century and the 11th century.[189] One of the earliest recorded mentions of Harlesthorpe dates back to the early reign of Henry III (1207-1272) when Adam of Cridling (with the name affix "'Lord of Whitwell") transferred ownership of the land at Harlesthorpe to his sister, Alice of Cridling.[190] Philip Riden describes Harlesthorpe as a "quasi manorial-free tenement" during the Middle Ages[191] whose name can be translated as "Thóraldr's farm".[192] Most likely it was a separate estate by 1632 when it was "described as parcel of the manor of Whitwell".[193] Referred to as "manor of Harlesthope" in the 14th century, it changed hands several times over the centuries. Records mention such names as Adam and Alice Taylor, John Leicester, Geoffrey and Joan Leicester, Sir William Bingham, Roger Folville; Joan, wife of Philip Maybank, Thomas Walton (14th century); William and Joan Walton and family members (15th century); John and Joan Ryce, John Clerk, George Pierrepont and Sir Henry Pierrepont (16th century); Henry Barker (17th century); Thomas Ashe, John Bourke, and members of the Staniforth family (18th century).[194]

In the middle of the 19th century the Duke of Portland was lord of the manor (which was partly copyhold[195]), sharing it with several owners, including Henry (5) Bowdon, Esq. and later on Major John (6) Erdeswick Butler-Bowdon (of Pleasington Hall, Lancashire). The Bowdon family can be traced back to 17th century Chapel-en-le-Frith and further back in time again to Bowdon near Altrincham, Greater Manchester.[196] Apparently not much is known from the time when they left the village of Bowdon and moved to Chapel-en-le-Frith, and also not from the time around 1650 when they quit Chapel-en-le-Frith until the 1690s when they allegedly arrived in Beighton

---

188 Riden, *History of the County of Derby III*, p. 122.

189 Riden, *History of the County of Derby III*, p. 110.

190 Riden, *History of the County of Derby III*, p. 112. According to Riden, *Clowne, Manors and other Estates*, p. 3 "this grant may represent the creation of Harlesthorpe as a separate estate".

191 Riden, *History of the County of Derby III*, p. 110.

192 Earlier known as "Tharlesthorpe"; cf. Riden, *History of the County of Derby III*, p. 110; according to Mr Riden the toponym derives from the combination of "an Old Norse personal name with a common Scandinavian final element"; the word "thorpe" in Old and Middle English stands for a hamlet, a small village or small estate (related to Old Norse); cf. http://www.dictionary.reference.com/browse/thorp (viewed 02/02/2014).

193 Riden, *History of the County of Derby III*, p. 112.

194 Riden, *History of the County of Derby III*, p. 16, p. 112f., p. 186.

195 For more information on the subject see Appendix 3.

196 For a family tree see Glover, *History*, p. 304; White's *1875*, p. 732-733; information on the origin of the family from Bowdon disclosed in a personal E-mail correspondence between Humphrey Butler-Bowdon and the author on November 25, 2013.

Fields Priory in the parish of Barlborough.[197] On November 4, 1691 (?, marriage settlement date) however, Henry (1) Bowdon married Mary Hewit(t) of Shireoaks in second marriage.[198] Mary brought the manor of Beighton Fields Priory into the Bowdon family. Her inheritance included the estate of Harlesthorpe, on whose lands the mansion of Southgate was erected a century later on.[199] According to Philip Riden, Beighton Fields Priory became the new residence of the Bowdons until Henry (3) Bowdon acquired the Harlesthorpe estate and built a new stately home on the south side of the main road to Worksop which was named Southgate House, and which became the Bowdon family's home in the 1820s.[200] Parallely, Beighton Fields Priory remained in the possession of the Bowdon family, and in the year 1829 Henry Bowdon is mentioned as the freeholder[201] of Southgate House, Clowne.[202] Maxwell Craven writes that the architect of Southgate House is not known, but he

---

197 Chris Bowden writes in 2007 on http://archiver.rootsweb.ancestry.com/th/read/CHESHIRE/2007-12/1196623064 (viewed 14/06/2013): "(...) Previous generations of Genealogists have also queried the claims of the Beighton fields family to be of the same line as those of Bowden Hall. Butler Bowden claims that papers proving connections were destroyed during the penal times when Catholics were prevented from inheriting and papers were lost during this period. (…)"

198 Chris Bowden (in Bowden, *Bowdon Marriage*) names 04/11/1691 as date of marriage settlement. The year 1691 is supported by a document held by Sheffield Archives (*Ref. No. MD5439*, original document not viewed personally), being an inventory of husbandry ware at Beighton Fields attributed to Henry Bowdon and dated 1691 (from the deeds and papers of the "Bowdens of Bowden" relating to Chapel-en-le-Frith and Beighton Fields). This information does not go together with 1665 as the year of death of Henry (1). Derbyshire County Council, *Bulmer's Derby 1895*, p. 208 gives the year 1665 as the date of marriage which seems plausible; information disclosed by Tony Bak in personal E-Mail correspondences with the author on June 11, 2013 and January 14, 2014. Teresa Staples in her personal recollections also refers to this date (information by kind courtesy of Father Peter D McGuire in a private E-Mail correspondence with the author on May 18, 2014). Another marriage date (1603) derives from a text (anonymous and undated, therefore entirely built on sand) held by Barlborough Heritage and Research Centre.

199 Craven, "Southgate House, Clowne", p. 57.

200 In the year 1829 according to http://www.clownevillage.co.uk/clowne-hist/noatable%20dates2.htm (viewed 19/05/2013).

201 For detailed information on land-tenure see Appendix 4.

202 Riden, *Clowne, Manors and other Estates*, p. 2; also Riden, *History of the County of Derby III*, p. 25, p. 112 and p. 122: "… Clowne was for centuries a parish of small freeholders and non-resident land-owners. The largest estates were the freeholds at Romeley and Harlesthorpe. Neither appears to have included much land in Clowne itself, and after Southgate House was built on the Harlesthorpe estate (…) its owners looked more to Barlborough than to Clowne."

thinks it was possibly Joseph Badger of Sheffield[203], who worked in the surrounding area (Renishaw, Oakes Park) and could have built the house at the behest of the Bowdon family.[204] The southwards facing front of the mansion house at Romeley (today a ruin)[205], originally situated between Clowne and Stanfree and therefore not far away from Southgate House, bears some vague resemblance to the latter, according to a painting by Swiss artist Samuel Hieronymus Grimm (1733-1794[206]). Romeley House has been attributed to the Doncaster architect William Lindley (ca. 1739-1818) in ca. 1790.[207]

Opposing this basically coherent conjecture are a couple of other documents which prove that Southgate House and Estate go back much further in time. First and foremost, there is the last will of a George Staniforth, Gentleman of Barlborough, Derbyshire composed on February 2 and February 7, 1757 and executed on August 23, 1757. This record makes a compelling case for the identity of the owner of Southgate House many years before the Bowdon family came into play, and it conclusively explains the naming of the manor house in Clowne, which, according to Tony Bak of Barlborough Heritage and Resource Centre, derives from the Staniforth's previous homestead on an outward road named Southgate, in the Southgate district of Eckington (see Chapter 23).[208] Unfortunately, we do not learn anything about the inhabitants of Southgate House in 1757, as they remain unnamed in the

---

[203] Joseph Badger (b. 1738 in Derbyshire - d. 1817) was a carpenter, joiner, builder and architect active in the mid 18th to early 19th centuries. He had a yard in Orchard Street, Sheffield; cf. http://www.zoominfo.com/p/Joseph-Badger/656577613 (viewed 03/07/2013); Parks & Gardens UK, *Joseph Badger*; Craven, Stanley, *Derbyshire Country House*, p. 14.

[204] Craven, "Southgate House, Clowne", p. 57.

[205] Craven, Stanley, *Derbyshire Country House*, p. 178f.; Riden, *History of the County of Derby III*, p. 116f.

[206] Manco, *Researching Historic Buildings*.

[207] Craven, Stanley, *Derbyshire Country House*, p. 178f.; http://www.clownevillage.co.uk/history/history.html (viewed 10/07/2013); Hull, *Parlington Hall*.

[208] In a personal E-mail correspondence Tony Bak informed me on June 8, 2014 that the earliest attestation he has found of the Staniforth family in Eckington is 1602. Barlborough Heritage and Research Centre, *Interesting Facts*: "Southgate House was built by a certain Mr. Staniforth, 'Southgate' was also the name given to his previous home in the Southgate District of Eckington." See also Riden, *History of the County of Derby III*, p. 113. Derbyshire Record Office in Matlock holds a document that contains an undated site plan of the building in question as well as a proposed reconstruction (architectural drawing) of a property for Capt. Francis Osbert S Sitwell dated 1937 (*Ref. No. D6573/Box 53/26-27*). For general information on the history of Eckington and Southgate Old House see Stroud, *Derbyshire Extensive Urban Survey*, especially p. 14 (Southgate Old House = listed building dated to the 17th century), also see English Heritage, *Southgate Old House*); British Listed Buildings, *Southgate Old House, Eckington.*

testament. Perhaps the house stood temporarily empty and was only used by the Staniforth family as temporary residence when their presence was required in the area. At the deposit of his will, George Staniforth apparently lived with his family (his wife Hannah, his two sons Charles and Jeremiah and his two daughters Hannah (b. 1736) and Sarah (b. 1738)) in a messuage consisting of a dwelling house with orchard and garden, meadows, closes and crofts in Duffield, Derbyshire, but he bequeaths Southgate House and Farm to his son Charles, who twenty years later was attested as its inhabitant (see below).[209] This allows us to establish an approximate *terminus ante quem* for when Southgate House was built, that is to say before 1757 - which would make this house a mid-Georgian building (ca. 1740 - ca. 1800[210]).

The text in question has been preserved and is kept at the National Archives in London.[211] It is a handwritten document composed in Secretary Hand or Court Hand (used for government or legal documents). George

---

209 The results of an on-line research (www.ancestrylibrary.com) carried out by Tony Bak were kindly placed at my disposal by Mr Bak on April 20, 2013. They yield the information that a Mr Staniforth (without a first name given) subscribed a book edition of Shakespeare's plays in 1774; he is specified with basic information (1751-1775) and an address: Southgate House. It remains unclear whether this refers to Southgate House in Eckington or to Southgate House in Clowne. The person in question cannot be Charles Staniforth who was alive in 1777, and it cannot have been his brother Jeremiah, also mentioned in the last will of George Staniforth dated 1757, as Jeremiah Staniforth (no basic information) is later attested as an inhabitant of Litfield, Derbyshire (another messuage at Litfield being owned by the Staniforth family according to George Staniforth's last will). He is described as "deceased" with two surviving sons, George (a surgeon) and John (a miller) in a document held by Rotherham Archives dated August 3 and 4, 1807 (Rotherham Metropolitan Borough, Archives and Local Studies Section, *Ref. No. 213/C/53/2*, original document not viewed personally). This record deals with a lease and the release of a messuage "with wine and liquor vaults adjoining, stable, yard, etc." in Millgate, Rotherham. The first names of various Staniforth family members pertaining to the Old Testament allow the assumption that the family could have been Quakers. Unfortunately I could not find any proof for this theory. The matter was discussed with Tony Bak of Barlborough Heritage and Resource Centre by E-mail on July 10, 2013. He said that of the Quaker records he holds none show the Staniforth surname. The Quakers in Derbyshire met at Chesterfield and many were buried at the graveyard of Handsworth Woodhouse, Sheffield. Only seven tombstones have survived there (in a private residents' back garden). For members of the Staniforth family in the year 1790 and their dealings with their part of the manor of Harlesthorpe also see Riden, *Clowne, Manors and other Estates*, p. 4.

210 For principal periods of English domestic architecture see Jenkins, *Best Houses*, p. xl.

211 By kind communication of Tony Bak in a personal E-Mail correspondence with the author on June 20, 2013; The National Archives London, *Ref. No. PROB 11/832/232*. According to a list of burials in Barlborough in 1757, a George Staniforth was buried there on April 1, 1757 (cf. Spencer, *Barlborough Burials 1757*), but since the testament is dated August 23, 1757 this cannot be the George Staniforth in question.

Staniforth informs his heirs (in extracts): "(...) Southgate House and Farm as the same were late in the possession of Emmanuel Richardson[212] lying in the several parishes of Barlbrough (*sic!*) Whitwell and Clown (*sic!*) in the County of Derby (...) and it is also my Will and Desire and I Do hereby direct and appoint that as soon as my Daughter Hannah Staniforth[213] shall arrive at the Age of one and twenty years or marry which shall first happen that the said Francis Bower and Samuel Turner my Trustees shall settle upon my Son Charles Staniforth all that my said Messuage or Tenement and Lands with the Appurtenances so called Southgate House and Farm he paying thereout to my Daughter Hannah the sum of five hundred pounds (...)". Through this source we learn not only of the Staniforth's family background, but also that Southgate Estate possibly had a prepossessor, Emmanuel Richardson. Here we encounter problems as to explaining the naming of Southgate House, though but it cannot be ruled out that at that time Southgate was still known as Harlesthorpe.[214]

With reference to Wirksworth parish records, the Wirksworth website[215] lists a very interesting incident which took place twenty years later on, in 1777, when George Woodhead, blacksmith of Clowne, stood accused of having assaulted, at a place not specified, a Charles Staniforth of Southgate House, Clowne. Charles of course was the son and heir of George Staniforth as mentioned in his testament. For reasons unknown no prosecution was brought about. Evidently Charles Staniforth pressed no charges against George Woodhead, which seems surprising. Under normal conditions the charge of a simple blacksmith making an assault on someone of the landed gentry would have been very serious. Perhaps there had been heavy drinking involved (resulting in attenuating circumstances?), or Mr Staniforth had a

212 The reading of the surname Richardson is very tentative and entirely unsupported. It is solely my personal interpretation of the handwriting in the copy of the will provided by the National Archives.

213 http://search.ancestry.com/cgi-bin/sse.dll?rank=1&new=1&MSAV=1&msT=1&gss=angs-g&gsfn=George&gsln=Staniforth&msbdy=1735&msbpn__ftp=Eckington%2C+Derbyshire%2C+England&msddy=1737&msdpn__ftp=Eckington%2C+Derbyshire%2C+England&cpxt=0&catBucket=rstp&uidh=000&cp=0&gl=42&so=2 (viewed 26/06/2013) lists a Hannah Staniforth born in 1736, Derbyshire, England, who could be the above mentioned daughter of George Staniforth. The same site lists a Sarah Staniforth born in 1738, Derbyshire, England, who could be the oldest daughter of George Staniforth who is also mentioned in his last will, here stated as the wife of Mr Thomas Clark of Chesterfield. See also Riden, *Clowne, Manors and other Estates*, p. 4.

214 This is supported by Riden, *History of the County of Derby III*, p. 113.

215 Wirksworth website on www.wirksworth.org.uk: Palmer, John, http://www.wirksworth.org.uk/CRM16.htm (2003) (viewed 14/06/2013), covering records from all Derbyshire, among others having indexed criminal records from Derbyshire Petty and Quarter Sessions.

skeleton in his closet which he did not want uncovered. This of course is mere speculation, but it is possible that something tragic happened in Clowne in 1777. In the Parish of Clowne the death of an Elizabeth Woodhead, aged 65, wife of a George Woodhead, is registered for March 2, 1777.[216] Could there be a link between the two incidents?

A brief but very enlightening newspaper advertisement from the year 1787 publicised on the website of Barlborough Heritage and Resource Centre provides us with further information on the property situation of Southgate Estate.[217] Evidently, George Staniforth's son Charles Staniforth had died (possibly shortly before) and Southgate House in Clowne was advertised to be let on February 24, 1787 in the London Evening Post: "To be lett (*sic!*), and entered upon at Lady-Day next, Southgate House near Barlbrough (*sic!*) in the county of Derby, being an exceeding (*sic!*) good new built stone messuage. Fit for the residence of a genteel family consisting of a drawing room 25 f. by 15 f., dining room 18 f. 6 j. by 16 f., breakfast parlour 16 f. by 12 f. with an exceeding good kitchen, and pantry, on the low floor three good vaulted cellars, very good chambers and garrets of the whole; with brewhouse, back kitchen, barn, stables, chaff-house and other necessary conveniences, together with a good garden, well walled, and planted with choice fruit trees in full bearing; and about 43 acres of included arable meadow, and pasture land adjoining the house. Southgate-House was the late residence of Mr. Staniforth[218], deceased, and is ready fitted up; in a pleasent (*sic!*) healthy situation, and fine sporting country; adjoins the turnpike-road from Chesterfield to Worksop, and from Mansfield to Rotherham. To view the premises, apply at the house and for further particulars to Mr. Fletcher, of Whitwell, near Worksop, Notts., who will treat for the same."[219]

Apart from the detailed and revealing description of the House and Estate, the advertisement includes one striking detail: the house is described as "an exceeding good new built stone messuage". This means that the predecessor

---

[216] Spencer, *Clowne Burials*. Peter Hopkins lists a number of people with those names for baptisms in the parish of Whitwell, but none of them fit regarding the dates in the present case; cf. Hopkins, *Woodhead*, but the list of burials from the same website (http://www.wlhg.co.uk/Graves_index.htm, viewed 08/01/2014) names a George Woodhead who died on 21/04/1777. This may however simply be a coincidence as the name Woodhead is very common in the area.

[217] Barlborough Heritage and Research Centre, *Interesting Facts*.

[218] According to the Barlborough Heritage and Resource Centre website, Mr Staniforth was a scythe and sickle manufacturer in Sheffield around 1780; cf. Barlborough Heritage and Research Centre, *Interesting Facts* and The National Archives, *Ref. No. STA*, attested in 1928: Thomas Staniforth & Co Ltd, scythe and sickle manufacturers of Severquick Works, Hackenthorpe, Sheffield; company established in 1743.

[219] Barlborough Heritage and Research Centre, *Interesting Facts*. For a comprehensive analysis on the layout of large and small country houses in England see Muthesius, *English House*, p. 79ff., p. 124ff.

building of George Staniforth's Southgate House must have been demolished and rebuilt, presumably around 1786.[220] This means that the newly erected building can also be attributed to the mid-Georgian period. I could not trace any contemporary drawings, paintings or plans from that time. Contemporary photographs from the 1900s of Southgate House (Figures 4 to 7) show at that time a striking resemblance to the Georgian mansion of Walden Place, Saffron Walden, Essex (erected ca. 1740). Albeit that that particular house was built of red brick and has a couple of more windows, it is almost a spitting image of Southgate House with its façade layout and the design of the truncated pyramid roof with the chimneys.[221] Also Romeley House near Stanfree, southwest of Clowne, seems to have shared some outer features with Southgate House (see above).

Southgate House as it presents itself today has certainly undergone exterior and interior changes over the two hundred years since it was built, so not everything of its original appearance has been preserved, but it seems as if these changes have not been major. Various black and white photographs from the past decennia show a modest-sized square and compact house almost resembling an urban villa with three storeys, a truncated pyramid of a roof with two chimneys to the left and to the right and a centred pediment; the frontage of the building bearing a strong geometrical segmentation gained by means of horizontal and vertical alignments in the strictest symmetry. The decreasing size of the windows with every floor serves to further underline the vertical façade design. Alterations to the exterior layout, apart from times when the mansion was partially or entirely covered by climbing plants, could not be detected on the basis of the available photographs, but today the two chimneys have gone (for more structural changes see below). The tripartite front is entirely unembellished, but it reverberates the spirit of the Georgian era/Neoclassic period - although in an extremely reduced and sober way. Following the needs of today's use, the interior of the house has undoubtedly seen some changes in regard to room arrangements and its floor plan, but what is clearly left from the original structural shell are its strikingly low ceilings. A professional architectonic survey would prove the constructional development of the house with more certainty, but this unfortunately count not be accomplished within the framework of this research.

Historian Philip Riden gives a detailed description of the building: "Southgate House is built of brick (later covered in cement render) dressed in stone, beneath a hipped roof on which pantiles have replaced Welsh slate. It is of three storeys with a principal front to the east of three bays, the central one breaking forward slightly beneath a pediment. Both the main doorway and the first-floor window above it are Venetian; on the second floor a lunette

---

[220] This issue was discussed with Tony Bak in a private E-Mail correspondence with the author on June 21, 2013.

[221] Cook, *English House*, p. 191 (photo of Walden Place).

window has been replaced with another tripartite window. All three have stone surrounds. The other windows have gauged brick lintels, each centred with a stone keyblock. The side elevations are of four bays. In the 1870s a private Roman Catholic chapel, designed by Charles Hansom, was erected to the north of the house, linked to it by a single-storey extension."[222]

Interestingly enough, the Land Values Map of 1909/1910 features the presence of a quarry as part of Southgate Estate.[223] The quarry is situated on the north side Worksop Road (A619), ca. 200 m to the west of the crossroads of Gapsick Lane/Gipsyhill Lane. If we accord credibility to the observations of Craven and Stanley[224], it is not impossible that this could have been the stone pit for the erection of the "new built stone messuage" of Southgate House. We do not know when the quarry became part of Southgate Estate, so this idea is only a tentative proposal. If stone material from the quarry was not used to erect the manor house itself, then it was possibly used at a later point in time for building the various outbuildings that belonged to the estate and perhaps also as a source of income for the owners. Lastly, it is remarkable that the advertisement refers to "meadow, and pasture land adjoining the house" but does not explicitly make mention of farms or anything else that lets the reader conclude that Southgate House was part of a much larger estate with farm buildings (as attested by the will of George Staniforth).

Unless there was not another unknown acquiring party who owned Southgate House and Estate for a very short period of time, we can safely conclude that Henry (3) Bowdon was the purchaser of Southgate and it was he who possibly commissioned an architect (the above mentioned Joseph Badger?) to further fit out the already existing building. Somehow the date of the advertisement (1787) seems to be a bit early for a possible purchase date if we believe Philip Riden, who refers to Stephen Glover's text of 1829: "…it was purchased and rebuilt at a great expense by the present proprietor (he refers to Henry (3) Bowdon), and is now become the chief family seat."[225] However, since Stephen Glover's other observations on the Bowdon family's genealogy

---

[222] Riden, *History of the County of Derby III*, p. 113f. *Pace* Mr Riden, but the dating of the chapel had to be reconsidered (see below) as well as the use of brick as building material. *Pace* also Mr Craven, "Southgate House, Clowne", p. 57 who also states that Southgate House is a "two and a half storey brick house". Southgate House is built of stone, only the private chapel was erected in brick; see above article in the London Evening Post of 1787 ("an exceeding good new built stone messuage") and cf. Sale Particulars of 1938, document held by Derbyshire Record Office, *Ref. No. D1300/11/1*, p. 5. According to the same document, the single-storey extension link was a glass passage-way. Tony Bak adds in a personal E-mail correspondence dated January 26, 2014 that is was common practice in England to cover brickwork with rendering as it became unfashionable.

[223] Derbyshire Record Office, *Ref. No. D595.*

[224] Craven, Stanley, *Derbyshire Country House*, p. 8.

[225] Riden, *Clowne, Manors and other Estates*, p. 4, footnote 6 (= Glover, *History*, p. 305).

are not precise in a couple of points[226] I am inclined not to rely too heavily on his observations. The facts deriving from the original sources speak for themselves. Philip Riden has comprehensively solved the riddle in his recently published book: Charles Staniforth, according to his research, a surgeon died at Southgate in 1787, and was "'universally lamented for his humanity and skill', which he was always ready to apply for the benefit of the poor of the neighbourhood."[227] According to Riden "the house was then let to Henry Bowden of Beightonfields in Barlborough, who bought the estate from Staniforth's widow and daughters in 1790."[228]

Philip Riden's comprehensive description of Southgate House (see above) is followed by mentioning a three-sided range of stables, a coach house and cottages which "may also date from Henry Bowden's time".[229] Following the break-up of the estate these structures have been since converted into private residences. According to Mr Riden's research, "the main house and the stables stand on the site of older buildings, which Henry (3) Bowdon was said to have rebuilt "at a great expense"."[230] He also laid out a small park, plantations and gardens around Southgate House. By 1920 the park had ceased to exist, and to this day only some of the woodland remains.[231]

John (4) Peter Bruno Bowdon inherited Southgate Estate upon the death of his father Henry (3) Bowdon in 1833. Until that date he and his wife had lived

---

[226] For example he omits a whole generation of the Bowdon family; observed by Riden, *Barlborough*, p. 36, footnote 2.

[227] Riden, *History of the County of Derby III*, p. 113 and footnote 10 (Riden refers to a newspaper article published in the Derby Mercury dated January 11, 1787).

[228] Riden, *History of the County of Derby III*, p. 113 and footnotes 11, 12 and 13. Regarding letting the house to the Bowdons Riden refers to a newspaper article in The Derby Mercury dated February 6, 1787; regarding the later purchase he refers to various sources such as a document held by the National Archives, London, *Ref. No. CP 43/828, rot. 286* (Court of Common Pleas: Recovery Rolls between October 1789 and October 1790, subjects: conveyancing; original document not viewed personally), a newspaper article in The Derby Mercury dated October 21, 1790 (and later years), and other sources. See also Turner, "A More Unobserved and Convenient Location", endnote 59: "The steady rise of the Bowden (*sic!*) family is of interest. The 1705-6 Papist Returns refer to 'Mr Bowden (*sic!*) of Barlborough, yeoman' as a widower of small estate worth about £16 pa; in 1717 Henry Boden (*sic!*) registered his estate at something over £36 pa (the author here cites R. Clark, The Derbyshire Papist Returns of 1705-6, 1983). A few generations later, the family having acquired also Southgate House some four miles to the east, made successive marriages into the Erdeswick and Ferrers families (…)." (I owe this information to Paul D Walker, quoted in a personal E-mail communication dated June 17, 2014).

[229] Riden, *History of the County of Derby III*, p. 114.

[230] Riden, *Clowne, Manors and other Estates*, p. 7, source cf. footnotes 3 and 4 (footnote 4 = Glover, *History*, p. 304-305).

[231] Riden, *History of the County of Derby III*, p. 114f.

at Beighton Fields Priory.[232] He is attested as a resident of "Southgate house" in Pigot & Co.s National Commercial Directory of Derbyshire for 1835.[233] It can be presumed that he lived at Southgate House until his demise in 1850, when the house passed into the hands of his son Henry (5) Bowdon.

Although Henry (5) Bowdon, his wife Harriet and their two daughters were the members of the Bowdon family who lived the longest at Southgate House, little is known about them apart from the entries in the decennial censuses of England and Wales (verified for 1851, 1861, 1871), Henry's commemorable 21st birthday party in 1835, the births of his two daughters in 1854 and 1857 and his funeral in 1875 (see Chapter 11). After his death Harriet and her two daughters moved to Beighton Fields Priory (as attested by the census of 1881). Henry (5) Bowdon must have been a very respected member of the local community because when his funeral took place the local people honoured him as his remains were transferred to their final resting place in Beighton Fields Priory (article in The Derbyshire Times and Chesterfield Herald report on May 12, 1875), and he must have been quite a character. A document containing correspondence concerning land and minerals at Southgate between the Duke of Portland, John (5) and Henry (5) Bowdon and some other local business men between the years 1867 and 1873 (see Chapter 24) attest his "restiveness".[234] The Duke of Portland was evidently a person of distinction and would like to think he could just put any number of obstacles in people's way and get away with it; however, it looks like Henry (5) Bowdon was not willing to let him get everything his own way.

In 1857 the Bowdon family still belonged to the group of main owners of Southgate House.[235] But four years after the death of Henry (5) Bowdon in 1875, on January 25, 1879, The Derbyshire Times and Chesterfield Herald announces an extensive auction sale at Southgate House, instructed by Colonel John (6) Erdeswick Butler-Bowdon for February 4, 1879 (Figure 16)[236]: "Southgate House, near Cl(owne) Sale of live and dead farm(ing sto)ck and agricultural prod(uc)e. Messrs. Mayor and Son are instructed by Colonel Erdeswick Butler-Bodon (*sic!*), to sell by auction, upon the farm premises, as above on Tuesday, February 4th, 1879, the live and dead farming stock. And agricultural produce, viz.: - Live stock. – Brown mare, "Diamond", aged, in-foal to Mr. Hudson's horse; grey mare, aged; powerful brown mare, 4 years old, supposed in-foal, perfectly quiet and a good worker; a promising brown colt, 2 years old, by Hudson's horse, "Matchless;" brown yearling filly foal. 1 fat cow, fit for the butcher: well fleshed red and white heifer; 16 in-lamb ewes,

232 Riden, *Barlborough*, p. 37.

233 Pigot & Co.s *1835*.

234 University of Nottingham, *Ref. No. Pl E12/9/6/1/31-175* (original document not viewed personally).

235 Riden, *Clowne, Manors and other Estates*, p. 2.

236 http://www.britishnewspaperarchive.co.uk (viewed 27/10/2012).

4 fat ewes, 4 hogs, two-shear tub, 4 couples fowls, 5 dozen pigeons, 4 porket pigs. Agricultural produce. – Wheat stack with straw, the produce of 1½ acres; oat stack and straw, the produce of over 4 acres; wheat stack and straw, the produce of 5 acres; stack of oat straw, stack of wheat straw, part stack of seeds, (///tons), cob of old seeds, about 2 acres of swede turnips. Dead stock, &c. – Cart saddles and breachings, collars and blufts, plough pads, long gears, chop bin, sack barrow, yard barrow, tumbrel, corn bin, turnip chopper for beasts, ditto for sheep, weighing machine and 16½ stone weights, winnowing machine, chisel harrows, wood plough (Cook's), 3 score fleaks, 4 sheep troughs, set of 3 harrows, one pair ditto, broad wheel cart with sideboards and shelvings, 1 other cart with iron arms, water barrel with fixed iron pump and suction pipe, horse rake, iron horse hoe, drag, stone water trough, wood roller, scrawler, stack cloth, (7 by 8 yards,) turnip drill, several ladders, pig cratch, pairing knives, forks, rakes, small tools, buckets, and about 30 sacks, cart rope, and sundries. The produce to be removed or consumed before the 25th March next. Refreshment by ticket at 12 o'clock. Business to commence at 12.30." This meticulous list leaves the impression of grave problems. Was it the general economic climate (the effects of the agricultural depression) which forced the Butler-Bowdon's to take up such drastic action[237], or was it caused by the aftermath of Henry (5) Bowdon's death and the possible inability of Harriet Bowdon, the widow, and her daughters to keep Southgate Estate running? Southgate Estate must have been a quite large agricultural enterprise in the 1870s which presumably was to a certain extend self-sustaining.

The convergence of the tragic circumstances of Henry Bowdon's death and the great agricultural depression of the 1870s clearly left its mark on Southgate Estate, just like on most estate property elsewhere in England.[238] This is not only attested by the advertisement in The Derbyshire Times and Chesterfield Herald from January 25, 1879, but also by the fact that Southgate House stood apparently empty and the lands left uncultivated for an unknown period of time around/before 1881, and was not very much later temporarily let to tenants (see Chapter 11). Evidently, the Butler-Bowdons belonged to those

---

[237] An undated letter from a bundle of documents held by the British Jesuit Archives in London (*Ref. No. MQ/1*) by Henry (5) Bowdon to George Tickell, Rector of Mount St. Mary's College in 1859, sheds a light the on possible economic difficulties at Southgate Estate. Henry (5) Bowdon writes: "(...) I received your letter expecting the Bench rents I will pay you some money a little later I have many tenants in arreer (*sic!*) which makes money scarce. Yours truly H Bowdon." (for bench rents see Chapter 24).

[238] Eric J Hobsbawm (Hobsbawm, *Industry and Empire*) critically remarks on p. 85: "Moreover, by the 1840s farming was distinctly a minority interest. It occupied no more than a quarter of the population and less than this share of the national income. When the nobility abandoned agriculture – as happened in 1846, and even more obviously in 1879 – all that was left was a minority pressure group stiffened by a bloc of fox-hunting back bench MPs."

families of the landed gentry who when faced with the new difficult economic situation did not have many alternative resources to fall back on other than their lands and their share of Southgate Colliery, and since there possibly were not too many valuable assets that could be liquidated (or they wanted to part from), and domestic staff had already been substantially reduced (see Chapter 14), so moving out of the main house, leaving it to stand empty or letting it to better-off people appeared to be the best solution for the time being.[239] And indeed, the newly renovated building of Southgate House is advertised to be let on December 27, 1882 in The Derbyshire Times and Chesterfield Herald.[240] This notification, revealing in more ways than one, gives another detailed description of the building: "This desirable residence, containing two entrance halls, drawing and dining rooms, kitchens, servant's offices, thirteen bed and dressing rooms, two w.c.'s, also coach house, and three stall stables, saddle room, &c., with good kitchen garden and extensive pleasure grounds. It is situated on the turnpike road[241] from Barlborough to Worksop, it is within a mile of two churches, 2½ miles from a Catholic church, and about three miles from Eckington and Whitwell Stations on the Midland and M. S. and L. Railways[242]. It has just been painted and decorated inside and out. Should a farm be desired any quantity of land may be had, also the shooting over about 650 acres, it is also within easy reach of the meets of the Grove and Rufford Hounds[243]. (...)"[244]

In 1891 and 1895 Major John (6) Erdeswick Butler-Bowdon is named as freeholder of one of three large estates in Clowne[245], but in the 1890s the house

---

239 Horn, *Victorian Country House*, p. 115, p. 118.

240 http://www.britishnewspaperarchive.co.uk (viewed 27/10/2012).

241 The establishing of a network of turnpike roads and fast coaches contributed enormously to connecting town and county people, and it meant country gentlemen could enjoy the spoils of city life; cf. Girouard, *English Country House*, p. 218.

242 Midland Railway ran a branch from the North Midland main line at Staveley to the Mansfield-Worksop Line near Creswell and opened a station in Clowne in 1888; M. S. and L. Railways = Manchester, Sheffield and Lincolnshire Railway at Beighton. For this line Clowne acquired a second railway station in 1897; cf. Riden, *Clowne*, p. 5f. (see Chapter 7).

243 A hunting lodge, at that particular time situated in Grove County, today it is located in Barnby Moor; cf. Grove & Rufford Hunt, *Hunt History*.

244 The land agent in charge for this case was Mr George Unwin, Esq., of Whitwell, Chesterfield who was responsible for many of the Butler-Bowdon's real estate transactions (see Chapters 11 and 14.2.2). Pigot & Co.s *1828-29*, p. 112 lists a George Unwin as "land surveyor" in 1828/1829 (father?). A second company, "Garlick, Park and Sykes", operating from Winckley Square, Preston, Lancashire, could also be contacted for the auction proceedings. Garlick, Park and Sykes were surveyors and architects, cf. British Listed Buildings, *20, 21 Winckley Square, Preston*.

245 Major John (6) Erdeswick Butler-Bowdon of Pleasington Hall, Lancashire is named in Kelly's *Directory*, p. 98f. as one of three principal owners of the land of Clowne in 1891.

was let to a tenant, Harry Aldam Fowler. In the **1891** census of England and Wales the occupation of Harry Aldam Fowler is stated as "MA Oxon", he was therefore an academic who had studied at Oxford. He later became a renowned businessman in the Chesterfield area. The Hotel Van Dyk website names him as the "most notable tenant" of Southgate House.[246] The Fowlers are the classic example of country house inhabitants of the time as they apparently belonged to the group of newly rich businessmen who could afford to hire a country house when the landed gentry and higher ranks of society faced serious economic problems.

In the year 1900 the Butler-Bowdons are back.[247] Until 1929 John (6) Erdeswick Butler-Bowdon, his second wife Monica Mary and their children lived at Southgate House (later also his third wife Mary Monica). This period is marked by two notions: religion and tragic loss. Religious life played a major role at Southgate Estate. Roman Catholic worshippers from Clowne and neighbouring parishes such as Whitwell and Elmton met in the above mentioned little chapel at Southgate House which was originally built only as the private chapel for the Catholic Butler-Bowdon family.[248] As in the above quotation, the chapel is repeatedly mentioned in the current literature as having been commissioned in the 1870s by Lady Monica Mary Petre (daughter of William Bernard, 12th Lord Petre), second wife of Colonel John (6) Erdeswick Butler-Bowdon, and designed by the Roman Catholic Victorian architect Charles Francis Hansom (1817-1888).[249] When comparing the assumed date of commission with the lifetime of Monica Mary Petre this statement needs some consideration. In the first instance Monica Mary was

---

[246] http://www.vandykhotel.co.uk/assets/vision-mag-spring-2012_web.pdf, p. 2 (viewed 25/10/2012) referring to Craven, "Southgate House, Clowne", p. 58.

[247] Staples, *My Parish*, p. 1. Martin Child gives the year 1902 for their relocation (Child, *Pleasington Priory*, p. 54).

[248] Hopkins, *Churches and Religion*; Picture The Past, *Southgate House (000405)*. See also Derbyshire Record Office, *Ref. No. D1300/11/1*, p. 5, emphasising the word "private".

[249] According to Craven, "Southgate House, Clowne", p. 57 the chapel was a reduced version of a chapel which Hansom added to another manor house, Derwent Hall, which fell victim to the industrial growth of Sheffield, Derby, Nottingham and Leicester and their increased need for water in 1944; cf. Beckett, *Lost Heritage*. Charles Francis Hansom was an architect from York who primarily designed in the Gothic Revival style for a solid and illustrious Catholic clientele. He was the brother of Joseph Aloysius Hansom (1803-1882, architect, creator of the Hansom safety cab, and for a short time partner of Edward Welby Pugin, see Chapter 20) with whom he temporarily practised in partnership; cf. Dictionary of Scottish Architects, *Charles Francis Hansom* and Dictionary of Scottish Architects, *Joseph Aloysius Hansom*; Riden, *Clowne, Manors and other Estates*, p. 6. Joseph Aloysius Hansom was the architect of Mount St. Mary's College in Spinkhill. He built the first College buildings there in 1840; cf. http://www.derbyshireheritage.co.uk/Menu/Townsandvillages/Spinkhill.php (viewed 31/08/2013).

born in 1861 and married John (6) Butler-Bowdon in 1879, so perhaps the 1880s or even the 1890s as a time for commissioning the chapel are much more plausible (possibly shortly after the last of their ten children, Basil, was born in 1898).[250] A small detail, however, may solve the riddle: attached to the outer wall of the chapel, facing towards the east, is a washed-out square plaque made of render (ca. 1 m x 50 cm), today painted in white with a raised frame, bearing the Latin inscription *ad maiorem dei gloriam* ("For the greater glory of God") impressed into the render in capital letters.[251] Below the words is a date which is possibly 1901, but it is almost illegible.[252] This plaque is very likely a foundation plaque, but carved or painted pious inscriptions in appropriate places were popular among country house owners who wanted to publicly display their religiousness (Figures 6 and 8, below the chapel window the plaque is clearly visible edged in black).[253] By 1901 the architect Charles Hansom[254] was long dead but it certainly cannot be ruled out that the plans

---

250 See Chapter 10 and Chapter 20 in particular.

251 Inscription examined on-site by Graham and Barbara Duckmanton and the author on April 22, 2013. *ad maiorem dei gloriam* is also known as the abbreviation AMDG (also *omnia ad maiorem dei gloriam*, "all for the greater glory of God"). It is the Latin motto of the Jesuits, standing for service to belief and commitment to justice. The Jesuits are a male religious congregation within the auspices of the Roman Catholic Church (also named the Society of Jesus, *Societas Iesu*, SI, S.J., SJ); cf. http://sjweb.info (viewed 14/11/13); http://www.jesuit.org.uk (viewed 14/11/2013); http://www.jesuiten.org/home.html (viewed 12/05/2014). Their main objectives are reflecting upon what Christ would have done if he were living in our times and expressing that Christ is their only master and that there is no one superior to him. The Jesuits played a great role in the European educational system since the Middle Ages (Ignatius of Loyola). The order aims at preparing young people to live according to the principles of the Christian conception of the human being, thus making them "men (and women) for the others". According to Father Peter McGuire of the Church of the Immaculate Conception at Spinkhill, the Pole family of Park Hall, Spinkhill introduced the Jesuits to the area (result of a personal communication on April 28, 2014). See Kelly, *Historical Notes*, p, 126f., Walker, *Church of the Immaculate Conception*, p. 7ff. (also on the general history of the Society of Jesus in the area).

252 The date 1901 is supported by the personal recollections of Teresa Staples; cf. Staples, *My Parish*, p. 1 and by Peter Hopkins (Hopkins, *Churches and Religion*). But since the contours of the letters and numbers on the plaque are quite blurred, it cannot be excluded that the year in question could also be 1904 or 1907 (the latter suggested by Paul D Walker in a personal E-mail to the author on June 3, 2014, see also Chapter 20).

253 For chapels and pious inscriptions see Girouard, *English Country House*, p. 273.

254 The Hansoms were quite active in the area: Charles's brother Joseph Aloysius Hansom not only built Mount St. Mary's College, he also was the architect of the Church of the Immaculate Conception in Spinkhill (completed in 1846). The event of the opening of Spinkhill church found echo in the newspapers: under "Opening of a New Roman Catholic Church" in the Chesterfield Reporter & Derbyshire Chronicle dated September 25, 1846 those attending include "J. B. Bowden (*sic!*), Esq, Southgate

for the lay-out and design of the chapel do indeed go back to an earlier date (viz his lifetime) and were originally initiated by John (6) Erdeswick Butler-Bowdon and his wife.[255] The actual builder remains unknown but sources reveal that the chapel was laid out as a temporary brick structure.[256] Father A I Whittet S.J. in the Nottingham Diocesan Yearbook of 1953 describes the chapel as "a splendid record of apostolic zeal on the part of the Butler-Bowden (*sic!*) family, and the villagers (the author: of Clowne[257]) must be ever grateful to this ancient and devoted Catholic family."[258]

Philip Riden found out that public mission services were taken up at Southgate Chapel, dedicated to the Sacred Heart and Our Lady of Victories in 1902 or 1903[259], they were then temporarily moved to premises in Mill Street, Clowne[260], but later returned to Southgate House again until ca. 1945 or later.[261] The domestic chapel seemed to have had a priest of its own who was

---

House & family (...) H. Bowden (*sic!*), Esq (...) J Butler Bowden (*sic!*), Esq" (thanks to Paul D Walker for this annotation, disclosed in a personal E-mail correspondence with the author on July 4, 2014; the listed persons are John (4) Peter Bruno Bowdon, Henry (5) Bowdon and John (5) Butler-Bowdon). Many Old Catholic families were associated with the adjacent Mount St. Mary's College as well, among them the Butler-Bowdons, the Constable Maxwells and the Ferrers (see Chapter 10); cf. Walker, *Church of the Immaculate Conception*, p. 24ff. and 35f.

255 Catholic families, among them the Petres, were patrons of many ecclesiastical building projects; cf. Walker, *Church of the Immaculate Conception*, p. 29.

256 Cf. Sale Particulars of 1938, document held by Derbyshire Record Office, *Ref. No. D1300/11/1*, p. 5. Former Clowne inhabitant Derek Bower suspects that the chapel was possibly a "chapel of ease" for the church at Spinkhill, which is the nearest Roman Catholic Church; information disclosed in a private E-mail correspondence between him and the author on October 10, 2013. In literature it is referred to as a mass centre; cf. Staples, *My Parish*, p. 1 and Walker, *Church of the Immaculate Conception*, p. 56.

257 According to Bishop Robert Brindle's *Quinquennial* ("*Ad Limina*") report to Rome, there were 156 Catholics living in Clowne in 1908; information by kind courtesy of Canon Anthony Dolan by E-mail on May 19, 2014.

258 "New Church-Hall at Clowne" by Father A J Whittet, in: Nottingham Diocesan Yearbook 1953, p. 160f.; information by kind courtesy of Canon Anthony Dolan by E-mail on May 19, 2014.

259 Riden, *History of the County of Derby III*, p. 133. In Riden, *Clowne, Religious Life* the author quotes on p. 13/footnote 3 Kelly's Derbyshire Directories from 1909 and 1925 and adds that the chapel is not mentioned in earlier directories. For the name-giving of Southgate Chapel see below Chapter 20.

260 Presumably the place in question was the "Bowden (*sic!*) Arms", cf. the additional recollections of Mrs Staples (information by kind courtesy of Father Peter D McGuire in a private E-Mail correspondence with the author on May 18, 2014).

261 Riden, *History of the County of Derby III*, p. 133. From the recollections of former Clowne inhabitant Teresa Staples (1916-2001): "The Catholics of Clowne were allowed to worship in this private chapel, previously they had gone to Barlborough House, another mass centre at the home of Colonel Butler Bowdon's (*sic!*) brother. I understand that a mass centre was opened in Mill Street, Clowne about 1903 but closed

withdrawn in 1908 and since 1917 has been in the care of the Spinkhill Jesuits.[262] The **1911** census of England and Wales[263] attests the presence of a Roman Catholic priest named Wilfried Tonge at Southgate House. Former Clowne inhabitant Teresa Staples writes in her personal recollections that she remembers priests of Mount St. Mary's preaching at Southgate Chapel when she was a child (in the 1920s). One of them, Father Joseph Kendall, used to call at Southgate House on Saturday afternoons, heard confessions in the chapel and dined with the Butler-Bowdons and also stayed overnight.[264] According to her, mass was said at Southgate at 10.30 am every Sunday, except the first Sunday of the month when mass began at 9.00 am. On these Sundays there was a short communion service at 7.30 am which Mrs Staples attended with her brothers, her sister and the maids "from the big house". Southgate Chapel was in use until 1950.[265] Over the years members of the parishes of Spinkhill,

---

after two years, the Catholics then resumed their worship at Southgate."; cf. Staples, *My Parish*, p. 1.

262 From a typescript account (ca. 1955) of the Parishes of the Roman Catholic Diocese of Nottingham by Canon G D Sweeney, archivist of the diocese; information by kind courtesy of Canon Anthony Dolan by E-mail on May 19, 2014.

263 "The 1911 census for England and Wales was taken on the night of Sunday 2 April, 1911. The count included all individual households, plus institutions such as prisons, workhouses, naval vessels and merchant vessels, and it also attempted to make an approximate count of the homeless.", "In common with the censuses that preceded it, it recorded the following information: Where an individual lived Their age at the time of the census, Who (what relatives) they were living with, Their place of birth, Occupation.", "Also, depending on an individual's circumstances, additional information could include: Who their guests were on the night of the census, The number of servants they had (if any), Whether they were an employee or employer, Details of nationality, Duration of current marriage, Details of any illnesses or conditions each family member had, and the date these began.", cf. http://www.1911census.co.uk/Content/default.aspx?r=24 (viewed 29/10/2012). In 1911 Clowne was part of the town of Worksop and therefore located in Nottinghamshire (http://www.findmypast.co.uk, viewed 16/09/2013). It is interesting to follow the course taken by the enumerator that day: he began his survey with Southgate House, then followed the course of the road on its southern side eastwards to Southgate Cottages/The Avenue, crossed the road to its northern side, went in westerly direction to Southgate Stables, went north to Walls Farm and then straight down south to Hickingwood Farm before proceeding towards Whitwell Common.

264 Staples, *My Parish*, p. 2f., p. 5. Father Kendall, who left Clowne in 1938 after 22 years of service, drove around on his motor bike that refused to start on its own volition and needed to be pushed before it churned to life.

265 Cf. a correspondence between Hardman Studios, Birmingham (see Chapter 20) and Rev. A I Whittet of Mount St. Mary's College, Spinkhill from the years 1952 and 1953 on elements of furnishing of Southgate Chapel and the newly built church on Creswell Road, Clowne (Church of Sacred Heart and Our Lady of Victories, see Chapter 20) (Birmingham City Archives at the Birmingham City Library, *Ref. No. MS*

Barlborough and Whitwell joined together in trying to establish a centre for Catholic mass in Whitwell.[266] The building of such a chapel as an addition to a country house was a hallmark of the time. Over the course of the Victorian era, both families of old money and those of the newly-rich middle classes rediscovered moral values, with domesticity and religion playing the main part, and found that the display of their personal piety could be adequately expressed by a private place of worship.[267] Southgate Chapel was deconsecrated at an unascertainable date in the 1950s and is now one of the dining rooms at the Van Dyk Hotel.[268]

Little else is recorded for Southgate House and Estate during these years into which the proceedings of the First World War fall, a time with grave consequences for families throughout Britain and especially for those of landed estate and inheritable property whose families looked back on generations of military tradition.[269] The Butler-Bowdons were not spared this fate. An undeniably inconceivable loss for the family, but on a scale that did not affect the continuance of the estate[270], was the death of Basil Joseph Bernard Butler-Bowdon, youngest son of John (6) Erdeswick Butler-Bowdon and his second wife Monica Mary[271], Second Lieutenant of the 2nd Battalion, Lancashire Fusiliers, who was killed in action on March 28, 1918 aged 19 on one of the battlefields in northern France.[272] He was commissioned on January 16, 1918 and was posted to his battalion in the first week of March 1918. Three weeks later he lost his life in "Operation Michael", the big and final German

---

175/A/4/5/3/67, File 67 (C)). The record refers to the "disused Chapel of Southgate House".

266 Hopkins, *Churches and Religion*.

267 Girouard, *English Country House*, p. 270f.

268 Craven, "Southgate House, Clowne", p. 58 ("function room").

269 The death toll was devastating: "(...) one in five of the peers and their sons under the age of fifty who served in the War were killed."; cf. Horn, *Victorian Country House*, p. 120.

270 Married women of the landed gentry in the Victorian era were under pressure to bear sons who could inherit the estate and ensure that it remained within the family; cf. Horn, *Victorian Country House*, p. 49.

271 Two more sons of John (6) Erdeswick and Monica Mary Butler-Bowdon also died prematurely, one as an infant, the other one in 1904 in the aftermath of the Boer War in South Africa (1899-1902) (see Chapter 10).

272 A short notice in the category "Et Caetera" (*sic!*) in the Catholic weekly newspaper The Tablet dated October 16, 1918 informs the readers about the following: "Second-Lieut. Basil Joseph Bernard Butler-Bowdon, Lancashire Fusiliers, reported missing near Fampoux since March 28, is now officially presumed to have been killed in action on that date. He was nineteen years of age, and the youngest son of Colonel and the late Hon. Mrs. Butler-Bowdon, of Pleasington Hall, Lancashire, and Southgate House, Derbyshire. He was educated at Downside."; cf. The Tablet, *Cietera, 26th October 1918*. Downside School is a Catholic co-educational boarding and day school in Stratton-on-the-Fosse near Bath, Somerset.

spring offensive which started on March 21, 1918, also known as "Kaiserschlacht".[273] The Clowne War Memorial on "The Green", North Road, Clowne, honours his memory together with the names of 97 male Clowne inhabitants who gave their lives during the Great War and WWII.[274] His name is also listed on Arras Memorial, Pas de Calais, France.[275] And there is more information on that tragic event: upon auction sale of Southgate House and Estate in 1938 potential purchasers were informed of the following in the Sale Particulars: "(...) (The Chapel is a temporary Brick Structure and can remain or not, as the purchaser desires, but if pulled down or converted to other uses, the Vendor reserves the stained-glass window and the memorial brass).".[276] Through an auction which took place on October 1, 2013 this particular brass plaque came into the possession of Barlborough Heritage and Research Centre. Its commemorative text is flanked on the top left by the Butler-Bowdon family coat of arms and on the top right by the badge of the Lancashire Fusiliers[277] and reads: "Of your Charity / Pray for / the repose of the Soul of / Basil Butler-Bowdon / Lieutenant 2nd Batt. the Lancashire Fusiliers / who was killed in action on March 28th 1918 at / Fampoux near Arras, where, by the gallantry of / the Third British Army the German onrush / was stemmed and broken. / *Requiescat in Pace*." (Figure 9).[278] According to Tony Bak of Barlborough Heritage and Research Centre, the plaque was manufactured by John Hardman & Co. of Birmingham, a company which operated in partnership with Augustus Welby Northmore Pugin (1812-1852), a well-known Arts and Crafts architect, designer and exponent of Gothic Revival style, and his descendants (see Chapter 20).[279] The Pugins and the

---

273 Baker, *The First Battles of the Somme*; details on Basil Butler-Bowdon cf. Derbyshire Courier Report October 26th, 1918 & The Royal Fusiliers Report 21st February, 2007; article retrieved from Ancestry.co.uk's Military Records by Tony Bak and kindly provided to me, information disclosed in a private E-mail correspondence on July 14, 2013.

274 Freer, *Descendants of William the Conqueror*: the names of the fallen of the Great War are engraved in black letters on the front panel of the plinth of Clowne War Memorial under the caption "In grateful remembrance of the men of Clowne who fell for their country in the war 1914-1919"; cf. English, *Clowne War Memorial*: "Butler Bowden / no initial / Lt."

275 Commonwealth War Graves Commission, *Casualty Details* (Basil Butler-Bowdon).

276 Cf. Sale Particulars of 1938, p. 5 (Derbyshire Record Office, *Ref. No. D1300/11/1*). For more information on memorial brasses see Meara, David, *Victorian Memorial Brasses*, London 1983.

277 The Lancashire Fusiliers badge depicts an Egyptian sphinx and the word Egypt because the company was engaged in the Egyptian Campaign (1793-1802); see also Baker, *Lancashire Fusiliers*.

278 For further information Basil Butler-Bowdon and the Battle of Fampoux see Appendix 5.

279 Information disclosed in a private E-mail correspondence between Tony Bak and the author of October 1 and 2, 2013. A Biography on A W N Pugin: Hill, Rosemary,

Hardmans were staunch Roman Catholics; which is possibly why the John Hardman & Co. made the plaque by order of the Butler-Bowdons - and it is also possible that they were even personally acquainted with the family.[280] The auction took place in Banbury, Oxfordshire, and since this is not very far from Birmingham it is not entirely unlikely that the plaque somehow came from the former inventory of John Hardman & Co. by a circuitous route. Birmingham City Archives at the Birmingham City Library hold a file referring to "Butler-Bowden (*sic!*) Brass"[281], assumingly containing a correspondence or memo of John Hardman & Co. Upon a personal inspection on April 22, 2014 at the Birmingham City Archives the folder surprisingly turned out to be empty. The plaque arrived in Barlborough, however, with an accompanying memorandum ("note to be added to parcel in the safe") of John Hardman Studios (43 Newhall Hill, Birmingham 1) dated May 27, 1953. It reads: "A Butler-Bowdon brass, originally carried out for Southgate House, Clowne, in 1920. Removed when the house passed out of the hands of the family in 1952.[282] It was intended to re-fix the brass at Pleasington Priory, but

---

God's Architect: Pugin and the Building of Romantic Britain, London 2007; Pugin himself has written a couple of treatises, among others Pugin, Augustus Welby, *The True Principles of Pointed of Christian Architecture and An Apology for the Revival of Christian Architecture*, London 1841, see also http://www.birminghamheritage.org.uk/pugin.html (viewed 02/11/2013); http://www.thepuginsociety.co.uk (viewed 02/11/2013).

280 Banerjee, *John Hardman & Co.*; Victoria & Albert Museum, *Style Guide: Gothic Revival*; Ferry, *Victorian Home*, p. 67f. Gothic Revival is described as imitation Mediaeval style in 19th century art, which in the course of a general resurgence of the church and growth of Roman Catholicism was applied mostly in sacred architecture (between 1830 and 1900), but also in a civic and domestic context. The forms and patters of designs were derived from those found in the craftsmanship of the Middle Ages. Rigorous study was often interwoven with a more imaginative vision of Mediaeval chivalry and romance. A W N Pugin in particular strived to reinstate pre-Reformation faith together with its architecture, combining a flair for publicity with the religious zeal of a convert to Catholicism. For more about John Hardman & Co. see Chapter 20.

281 Birmingham City Archives at the Birmingham City Library, *Ref. No. MS 175/A/4/5/3/41, File 41 (B).*

282 The mention of the year 1952 is peculiar. Only a few sources refer to the first half or mid 1950s as the time when the Butler-Bowdons gave up ownership of Southgate House, but the majority of sources (original documents, eye witnesses) suggest a much earlier date (auction in 1938). Humphrey Butler-Bowdon suggested that perhaps the family retained some land or interest, but this is only an assumption (personal E-mail correspondence with the author on November 25, 2013). Another explanation may be that according to Peter Hopkins from Whitwell Local History Group, Southgate Chapel continued to be in use until 1950 (see above); cf. Hopkins, *Churches and Religion*. According to June Pearce, Southgate Chapel remained in use even longer than that (until the mid/late 1950s or even early 1960s; information disclosed in a personal E-mail correspondence with the author on January 10, 2014). Meanwhile Southgate

the Bishop's permission to do this could not be obtained.[283] Lieut. Col. Butler-Bowdon advised us 24th. May, 1953, we were to scrap the brass, but we informed him that it will be stored pending any future possible use." A very wise decision!

The tragedy of losing one of their sons in the Great War notwithstanding, Southgate Estate was further developed by the Butler-Bowdons: the Land Values Map of 1909/1910[284] shows nineteen different units of Southgate Estate: Forrest's Plantation, Harlesthorpe Cottages, Square Plantation (with Southgate House and Stables), Wall's Plantation, Wall's Holt, an old quarry, Southgate Cottages, Hickin Wood, Harlesthorpe Lane Cottages ("Lake View"), a house at "Rodgwood", Harlesthorpe and a bungalow on Station Road, Clowne and eight different stretches and patches of woodland along road and land boundaries (among others at Whitebrick Moor). The related Book of Reference records John (6) Erdeswick Butler-Bowdon for ownership of Southgate Estate and lists all his properties along with their respective tenants.

When John (6) Erdeswick Butler-Bowdon passed away in 1929, the ownership of Southgate House and Estate passed into the hands of his son William Erdeswick Ignatius (also apparent from the Electoral Rolls of Derbyshire). The presence of William Erdeswick Ignatius Butler-Bowdon and his family on Southgate Estate is additionally attested for the years 1932[285] and 1934[286]. According to a document of the Sale Particulars (sale by auction on Tuesday, March 15, 1938, "at 3.30 p.m., precisely") held by Derbyshire County Council/Derbyshire Record Office in Matlock[287], "Southgate house remained in the family till sold as part of 23 lots, including farms and cottages, by Lt Col W Butler-Bowdon."[288] That the auction catalogue survives to this day is a piece of good fortune as it gives a detailed description of Southgate House and its estate in 1938 (Figure 10). It is advertised as a "delightfully-situated

---

House was apparently unoccupied and stood empty. The plaque possibly remained in the chapel until it was desecrated/went out of use and was returned to John Hardman Studios by order of William Erdeswick Butler-Bowdon around 1952.

[283] For the significance of Pleasington Priory see Chapter 21. The role of the above mentioned bishop could not be determined.

[284] Document held by Derbyshire Record Office, *Ref. No. D595.*

[285] Riden, *Clowne, Manor and other Estates*, p. 5.

[286] Kelliher, "Rediscovery of Margery Kempe", p. 260f.

[287] Derbyshire Record Office, Ref. No. D1300/11/1: the auctioneers were Eadon, Lockwood & Riddle F.A.I, the auction took place at The Saleroom, St. James's Street in Sheffield; the solicitors were Arnold, Folks, Chadwick & Co., 15, Bolton Street, Piccadilly, London, W. I., the land agent was W Burman, F.S.I., F.L.A.S., Estate Office, Kiveton Park, Nr. Sheffield.

[288] This is William Erdeswick Ignatius Butler-Bowdon (1880-1956); Picture The Past, *Southgate House (000405).*

Georgian medium-sized Residence (Modernised[289] and in Excellent Order) (...) with delightful Views and Garden, Parkland, and Avenue of fine Beech Trees." The quantity in decimal acreage for residence and grounds was estimated at 8,516. Together with this "6 First Class Farms (let to excellent tenants)" were offered, as well as "Several Small Holdings, 16 Cottages, Fishing Lake, Woodlands etc. Also valuable building land (...)". This description is followed by an account of the outbuildings of Southgate House, which were the Stables (see Chapter 14.3), and a description of the surrounding gardens: "The Gardens are well laid out, also there is a very productive walled-in Kitchen Garden with Greenhouse, Potting Shed, Frames etc., also there is a Servants' Tennis Court in the Paddock across the Road. (...) Also well-cultivated Parkland with good Levels. Paddocks of Grassland and well-grown Woodlands[290], Plantations, etc." Page 2 of the Particulars uses the typical real estate language we recognise today. The location of the estate is over-embellished: "(...) the House backs the Main Chesterfield to Worksop Road (which is not a busy thoroughfare and little night traffic), (...)". Although to that time the road was much narrower and bendier than it is today, everyone who uses the A619 regularly nowadays will know very well that this statement must have been a shameless and undisguised lie, even in 1938.

The most valuable part of the Sale Particulars of 1938 is the detailed description of Southgate House itself: "The Charmingly-Situated and Well-Timbered Freehold Residential and Sporting Estate known as Southgate House, Near Clown, Derbyshire." It is said to be "well proportioned without being too large, and it was modernized about 8 years ago at considerable expense." The ground floor of the house contains an entrance hall, a dining room, a library, a smoke room, a cloak room with WC." The glass passage-way to the annexed chapel must have been a special feature as well as it is mentioned also in the list. Two staircases connected the ground floor to the two storeys above. The first floor provided space for four principal bedrooms with two dressing rooms, two tiled bathrooms, two WCs, three secondary bedrooms for the servants, another bathroom and WC, a housemaid's closet, a heated linen room, a heated cupboard, a china cupboard and other not specified rooms. On the second floor a large landing led to a play room, three more bedrooms, two box rooms and a housemaid's pantry. A well-equipped kitchen is mentioned, along with a scullery, a servant's hall, a butler's pantry, a strong room, a larder, a store room, a boot room and "excellent arched

---

289 Page 5 of the auction catalogue conveys it was modernised "about 8 years ago at considerable expense" = ca. 1930 (Derbyshire Record Office, *Ref. No. D1300/11/1*).

290 Timber, larch wood in particular, from Southgate Estate must have belonged to the perpetual sources of income for the Butler-Bowdon family as is revealed by a correspondence between Henry (5) Bowdon and clergymen of Mount St. Mary's College in the 1860s, cf. British Jesuit Archives, ***Ref. No. MQ/1***.

cellaring". Central heating was provided as was electricity, water and drainage.

The Sale Particulars also list the above mentioned six "First Class Farms"[291] in detail. Whereas according to the 1909/1910 document (Land Values Map) Southgate Estate comprised of mostly agricultural land and cottages/houses with their respective tenants, in 1938 the farm houses of Springfield Farm (directly on the main road connecting Barlborough and Whitwell/A619), South Walls Farm and North Walls Farm (situated opposite each other in Walls Lane near Whitwell), Manor Farm (at the end of Harlesthorpe Lane, Clowne)[292], Little Walls Farm (located at Walls Lane between Barlborough and Whitwell) and Eastwood Cottage Farm (at White Brick Moor, off Walls Lane) and Hickinwood Farm (north of Hickingwood Lane) were part of Southgate Estate. The document gives a total of acreage including the residence and grounds, parkland, arable land, grassland, paddocks, spinney, woods, the various plantations and a piece of the lane of 800 acres! The expansion of Southgate Estate during the first third of the 20th century shows how the estate thrived in spite of the difficult economic situation in England after WWI and how fortunate the Butler-Bowdons had been in their decisions up until then.

The reason however, why the Butler-Bowdons gave up ownership of Southgate House and Estate has to remain speculative. Humphrey Butler-Bowdon informs us that Southgate House sat on a coal seem, which was mined (= Southgate Colliery) and helped to cover the running costs of Southgate Estate. Butler-Bowdon family history has it that Mr Butler-Bowdon's grandparents sold the house when they heard that the coal was to be nationalised.[293] This information somehow contradicts the fact that Southgate Colliery had already ceased mining coal in 1929, so maybe other reasons could have played a role, too. The situation must have been grave - like anywhere else in England (see Chapter 2). William John Arthur Charles James Cavendish-Bentinck, the 6th Duke of Portland[294], wrote in 1937: "When I first lived at Welbeck, the great neighbouring houses (...) were all inhabited by their owners, who (...) employed large staffs. Now, not one of them is so occupied, except for a very few days in the year, and the shooting attached to

---

[291] Indeed there are seven farms listed in the catalogue, see Chapter 16.

[292] Mary Jones reports in a private E-Mail correspondence with the author dated May 31, 2013 that the last family to farm Manor Farm were Mr and Mrs Widdowson with their son Victor. She thinks the land has since been absorbed into other farms and that a family and a vet now live in the farmhouse. Mr Widdowson could be one of the sons of John and Hannah Widdowson of Beighton Fields House, Barlborough (see Chapter 18); cf. census returns of 1841 and 1851 for Beighton Fields.

[293] According to a personal E-mail correspondence between Humphrey Butler-Bowdon and the author dated November 25, 2013.

[294] William John Arthur Charles James Cavendish-Bentinck, 6th Duke of Portland (28/12/1857-26/04/1943); cf. Lundy, *The Peerage* (Person Page 962).

them is either let or abandoned."[295] His remarks certainly include the Butler-Bowdons who had seemingly made plans to leave the area by that time. The Electoral Rolls prove that some members of the family did stay there until 1939 and that the Butler-Bowdons retained ownership of the manor of Southgate until just before WWII.[296] This is supported by Humphrey Butler-Bowdon who says that his grandparents William Erdeswick Ignatius and Gertrude Butler-Bowdon relocated to a house in Dapsland, Mayfield, Sussex in 1936.[297]

Unfortunately it proved impossible to determine how many persons were tempted by the sales offer of 1938 and who bought which share or which lot of the estate, but it appears as if the domain was bought as a whole by Sir Osbert Sitwell 5th Baronet of Renishaw (near Eckington)[298], an English writer.[299] The personal recollections of former Clowne inhabitant Derek Bower shed some light on that particular period of time. He does not remember the precise date when the Sitwells bought Southgate Estate, but he can confirm that it was around 1938 when the estate was auctioned.[300] He remembers Sir Osbert making visits to Springfield Farm and the cottage of his family (see Chapter 14.4) around that time, arriving in a horse-drawn "buggy" on more than one occasion. Springfield Farm at that time was part of Southgate Estate and Mr Bower recollects the Sitwells arranging for water supplies to be brought to the

---

295 Quote taken from Horn, *Victorian Country House*, p. 124.

296 Cf. Sale Particulars dated 1938 (Derbyshire Record Office, *Ref. No. D1300/11/1*). Craven, "Southgate House, Clowne", p. 57 who has probably not viewed the Sale Particulars of 1938 states that the sale of the house probably goes back to the period following the death of John (6) Butler Bowdon's son, Col. William Erdeswick Ignatius Butler-Bowdon (which was in 1956). William Erdeswick Ignatius' son Maurice Butler-Bowdon is attested as inhabitant of Southgate House in 1938 and 1939 by the Electoral Rolls. William Erdeswick Ignatius and Gertrude Butler-Bowdon are listed for Southgate for a last time in 1937. There is a peculiar typo for the 1938 Electoral Rolls where Maurice is stated as living at Little Walls Farm, the address prior to Southgate House in the list.

297 Their presence there is attested also for 1955; cf. Catholic Herald Archive, "£33,000 Cope to stay in England", referring to William Erdeswick Ignatius Butler-Bowdon; Kelliher, "Rediscovery of Margery Kempe", p. 261, and personal information by Humphrey Butler-Bowdon in an E-mail correspondence with the author dated November 25, 2013. When in 1955 Humphrey Butler-Bowdon's father Maurice took over the house in Sussex, his grandfather William Erdeswick Ignatius Butler-Bowdon moved to Chideock, Dorset.

298 Innes-Smith, "Plantagenet or Tudor", p. 124f.; Riden, *Clowne, Manor and other Estates*, p. 5.

299 Osbert Sitwell was a writer of WWI prose and poetry (1892-1969): Encyclopedia Britannica, *Sir Osbert Sitwell*.

300 Information disclosed to the author in a private E-mail correspondence on May 20, 2013. Tony Bak contributes in a private E-mail correspondence dated July 14, 2013 that Osbert Sitwell also bought lands at Barlborough in 1945.

farm via pipelines in 1943.[301] Sir Osbert agreed that the Bower's home, Toll Bar Cottage, could also have piped water provided the trench for the pipes was dug. This was done by William Bower, Derek Bower's father, and his uncle.

During the early months of WWII, for a period of about six months, soldiers of the 424th Battery Royal Horse Artillery[302] were billeted for military training in Barlborough (in the Church Institute, the Chapel Schoolroom, Barlborough Hall and in the village school).[303] Sylvia Linacre's account of that time points out that Southgate House was requisitioned as housing for military personnel as well[304], therefore I assumed that this more precisely meant Southgate Stables, as the horses of the RHA certainly needed adequate accommodation in the vicinity. But there were more military personnel in the area: a local gentleman called Tom White often visited the soldiers of the Cheshire Yeomanry (Figure 11)[305] as a young boy when they occupied the stables of Southgate House. He remembers them as being friendly towards him and that they allowed him to care for the horses; they spent many happy hours cleaning the horse's equipment and telling him tales of adventures which he found interesting.[306] Soldiers of Cheshire Yeomanry also occupied

---

[301] It was the duty of the landowner to maintain the outlying buildings of their estates; cf. Arnold, Dana, "9 Living off the Land: Innovations in Farming Practices and Farm Design", in: Arnold, *Georgian Country House*, p. 153.

[302] This was the 424th Battery of the Royal Horse Artillery, information disclosed by Craig Murray of the Imperial War Museum (London) by e-mail on February 26, 2013; Royal Artillery unit, the 424 Searchlight Battery, Anti-Aircraft Command; information disclosed by Mark Pearsall of the National Archives (London) by e-mail on March 4, 2013. This unit was also called the Lancashire Hussars (Yeomanry), since 1938 the 423rd and 424th Batteries were part of the 106th Lancashire Yeomanry Field Regiment based in Liverpool (75 Shaw Street); cf. http://www.desertrats.org.uk/orgartillery.htm#RHA106 (viewed 04/03/2013); Baker, *The Lancashire Hussars Yeomanry*; http://web.archive.org/web/20070814061819/http://www.ian.a.paterson.btinternet.co.uk/orgartillery.htm#RHA106 (viewed 04/03/2014); Fagan, Hogan, *Liverpool and Merseyside Remembered.*

[303] Linacre, *How it was*, p. 71, p. 73.

[304] A banner donated by the soldiers to the school children of Barlborough commemorated their stay in Barlborough; cf. Linacre, *How it was*, p. 73, p. 79.

[305] The Cheshire Yeomanry was a Cavalry Regiment active between 1797 and 2007. Their role during WWII was seeing action mainly in the Middle East (Palestine, Syria, Lebanon). They were one of the last regiments of the British Army to fight on horseback, and remained mounted until 1942 after which they lost their horses. After that they were given a new role as a Signals Regiment (Middle East, England and North-West Europe), and after May Day 1947 the regiment was reformed and equipped with tanks. For further information see Cheshire Military Museum, *The Cheshire Yeomanry*; Staples, *My Parish*, p. 6.

[306] Information contributed by June Pearce in a private E-mail correspondence with the author on December 31, 2013.

the schoolhouse of the neighbouring village of Whitwell; their officers were billeted in the Middle Club on Welbeck Street, Whitwell.[307] Teresa Staples remembers that apart from the officers of the Cheshire Yeomanry, the Middlesex Tank Corps[308] and the South Lancs[309] occupied Southgate House. According to her, the soldiers were billeted in huts in the vicinity.

A today derelict stable building on the corner of the lane at Manor Farm, Harlesthorpe was used by the War Office to stable warhorses of the Cheshire Yeomanry during WWII, too. They were very friendly with the locals and helped them when they could.[310]

After the troops had left, Southgate was converted into a POW camp for German and Italian prisoners, this camp was in use until 1946/1947 (see Chapter 25).[311] Although fraternisation between local people and detainees was strictly forbidden by the British government until Christmas 1946, the soldiers could move around freely and were a familiar sight in the village of Barlborough in their brown uniforms and were not unpopular.[312] Friendships between the German prisoners and their English neighbours were also formed in Southgate as Derek Bower remembers (see Chapter 25).

A rental/tax account book of Renishaw Hall Estate stored at Derbyshire Record Office[313] dated 1946-1961 reveals that in 1947 and 1948 the Ministry of

---

307 This is recollected by Denis and Nora Jones (Jones, *Life in the Village during World War II*).

308 The Tank Corps of Middlesex Regiment was the armoured division of the Middlesex Regiment (Duke of Cambridge's Own, 1881-1966); cf. Forces War Records, *Middlesex Regiment.*

309 The South Lancashire Regiment (Prince of Wales's Volunteers) was a regiment of the British Army between 1881 and 1958; cf. Forces War Records, *South Lancashire Regiment.*

310 Information contributed by June Pearce in a private E-mail correspondence with the author on September 25, 2013 and January 31, 2014.

311 Linacre, *How it was*, p. 79; Riden, *Clowne, Manor and other Estates*, p. 5, footnote 4; http://www.clownevillage.co.uk/feedback/feedback.htm (viewed 19/05/2013).

312 Richards, *Life in Britain for German Prisoners of War*; Linacre, *How it was*, p. 79. Friendships were counterproductive in the view of British wartime propaganda, because the danger was that the stereotypical picture of the fanatic, dangerous Nazi German could be caused to falter if British citizens were to come into direct contact with German POWs. The War Office saw a problem with keeping the prisoners under guard, and the Foreign Office feared acts of reprisals against British prisoners in German detention; cf. Held, *Kriegsgefangenschaft in Großbritannien*, p. 149.

313 Derbyshire Record Office, *Ref. No. D6573/Box 120/5* Derbyshire County Council/Derbyshire Record Office and Derby Diocesan Record Office, *Sitwell of Renishaw: Estate Records*, p. 1f. These papers chiefly relate to the time of Sir George (2) Reresby Sitwell (1860-1943, see Chapter 23) and his son, Sir Osbert Sitwell (1892-1969); furthermore the compendium comprises of a couple of earlier documents dating into the times of Francis Sitwell (1728-1793). The papers consist of estate rentals and accounts from late 19th to 20th century, of plans (mostly of collieries), and of other

Works paid rents to the Renishaw Hall Estate on a semi-annual base for renting Southgate House together with the gardens and woodland of the estate. This information is only an isolated segment in a greater whole. The complete time-span of this rental contract could unfortunately not be fully determined. However, the tenancy is significant: the Ministry of Works, a department of the British government, was at that time responsible for requisitioning property for wartime use.[314] It is therefore very likely that they were responsible for establishing the POW camp on the grounds of Southgate Estate.

For the years between 1948 and 1961 the Electoral Rolls of Derbyshire, kept at Derbyshire Record Office in Matlock, a place called "Southgate Camp" with 40 inhabitants is recorded, all occupants bear English names. Nissen huts, originally erected at Southgate Estate for the prisoners of war (see Chapter 25), were let to squatters and miners after the war. It is interesting to note that for the years 1948 to 1962 no inhabitants are registered for Southgate House in the Electoral Rolls. Mary Jones, an inhabitant of Clowne, disclosed in a private correspondence that she thinks that the house was not occupied during the 1940s and 1950s because as children, when playing in the woods and the fields close to Southgate House, they would climb over the wall into the grounds which they called the "Secret Garden". A family she went to school with swore that the house was haunted, that there was a private chapel and her friends said that they had often seen ghostly goings on at night (which would have to be proved).[315]

Ruby Thorpe, aged 85 in 2014 and a former inhabitant of 10, Harlesthorpe Cottages (granddaughter of Mrs and Mr Woolley, see Chapter 14.6), also remembers that Southgate House had a large, walled garden where the greenhouses of former Van Dyk's nurseries used to stand. The wall was about 8 feet/2.5m high to keep people out, and peaches grew against the wall. It seemed like a food paradise full of fruits and vegetables for some of the farm workers who lived nearby. The wall of course served to keep them out.[316] Colonel William Erdeswick Ignatius Butler-Bowdon was friends with Ruby Thorpe's grandparents and like everybody else they were allowed to walk through the woods of Southgate. Mrs Thorpe recalls the woods, the "Secret

---

properties in North Derbyshire and South Yorkshire. According to Derbyshire Record Office personal and family papers have been retained at Renishaw Hall, Eckington.

314 The National Archives, *Ministry of Works.*

315 Information disclosed in a private E-mail correspondence with the author on May 29, 2013.

316 Information disclosed in a personal E-mail by June Pearce after a personal meeting with Ruby Thorpe on March 25, 2014. There were also blackcurrant bushes, gooseberry bushes, and raspberry bushes, and Ruby's grandmother used to go to get blackcurrants from there to make jam (information disclosed by Ruby Thorpe during a personal meeting in Clowne on April 27, 2014.).

Garden" of Mary Jones, as a big park with many beautiful and massive trees.[317] She used to go there very often. There were bluebells to be found there as well as cowslips, violets, celandines, and "you pick them, but were told not to pick more than a dozen".

A remarkable detail is that the London Gazette from January 22, 1963 lists a Cornelis Josef van Dijk known as Cornelis Josef Van Dyk, as Market Gardener; Southgate House for November 12, 1962.[318] This is intriguing as judging by the name, the Van Dyk family who decided to settle in Clowne around that time must have originally come from the Netherlands. Unfortunately Van Dyk is an extremely common Dutch name, so it proves impossible to find out more about the background of this undoubtedly interesting sideshow. The same applies to later owners and inhabitants of Southgate House also bearing Dutch surnames: Plug and Plug-Kroon (see Chapter 14).

According to Maxwell Craven, the Van Dyk brothers bought Southgate House after the death of Col. William Erdeswick Ignatius Butler-Bowdon (in 1965) and converted it into a garden shop and plant nursery.[319] This information could be revised by the recollections of Geoffrey Holdsworth, a former employee of the Van Dyks and to this day inhabitant of one of the bungalows on the grounds of Southgate House.[320] He remembers that the Van Dyk brothers originally had a business in Clumber Park near Worksop where they grew and sold fruit and vegetables from 1949 to 1956. The land they cultivated was leased from the National Trust. They also had a retail shop at Bridge Street in Worksop between 1950 and 1957, incidentally it was the first self-service shop in England (the building today is a branch of Lloyds TSB Bank). The Van Dyks had a large regular order to supply the Royal Oak pub in Barlborough with flowers and vegetables for the restaurant. It was whilst they were delivering the orders that they noticed that Southgate House was vacant and decided they would like to buy it and develop their business. The house was then purchased from the Sitwell family in 1955 through Hollingsworth estate agency.[321] The shop business at Worksop was closed

317 According to Mrs Thorpe's grandfather, one of these trees was called "Old Woman's Hat". It had dark red leaves and was shaped like a hat with one branch shooting up like a feather.

318 The London Gazette from January 22, 1963, p. 717; cf. http://www.london-gazette.co.uk/issues/42901/pages/ (viewed 29/10/2012).

319 Craven, "Southgate House, Clowne", p. 58.

320 Information disclosed in a personal communication between June Pearce and Geoffrey Holdsworth and transmitted to the author by E-mail by June Pearce on November 8, 2013. Geoffrey Holdsworth worked for the Van Dyks from the age of 14 until he retired, taking time out for National Service between 1957 and 1959.

321 In a personal E-mail to the author dated November 16, 2013 June Pearce quotes a local source who remembers a family owning Southgate House before the Van Dyks,

when the Van Dyks moved to Southgate House in 1957. Southgate House was at that time in a state of disrepair and needed a lot of renovation. The Van Dyks built greenhouses and opened for business in the same year (1957). Geoffrey Holdsworth says at this time the Van Dyk Garden Centre was one of only three in England.[322] He recalls the Van Dyks as astute businessmen with great foresight. However, according to June Pearce, an inhabitant of Clowne, tradition has it that the local people thought the Van Dyks were daft to take on such a large property, but against all prophecies of doom the nurseries became a thriving business.[323] The brothers bought land on the opposite side of the road from Sitwell Estate (to the west of Southgate Stables). Their plan was to develop it as an agricultural or horticultural showground. The local council however refused planning permission and the grounds were used only as an extension of the greenhouses, even though it can be assumed that a showground would have been a great asset to the area. The nurseries apparently enjoyed a good reputation in the surrounding area and were a popular destination as Chesterfield-born screenwriter and author Deric Longden recalls in his book "I'm a Stranger Here Myself": "My mother's favourite place for a day out was Chatsworth Park and then Van Dyke's (*sic!*) nursery, with MFI running it close in third place."[324]

According to the Electoral Rolls, the Van Dyks are attested as inhabitants of Southgate House since the year 1963 when they built two bungalows at the rear of the premises for their personal use.[325] However, the Van Dyks were very active business people and not only had the retail shop in Worksop but for a short time one in the village of Clowne as well (1957-1959).[326] June Pearce relates in addition to this that the Van Dyk brothers were good friends of her

---

the Fellowes-Long. Unfortunately I could not fit this information into the chronology verified by the available sources.

322 The others are Bernard's Nurseries of Rugby, Warwickshire (which still exists today) and Geoff Smith's of Otley (Wharfedale), West Yorkshire (according to the recollections of Geoffrey Holdsworth (November 8, 2013)).

323 Information disclosed in a private E-mail correspondence between June Pearce and the author on May 24, 2013.

324 Longden, *I'm a Stranger Here Myself*, p. 33 (MFI was a furniture warehouse in Chesterfield selling low-priced self-assembly furniture). Deric Longden also refers to "Van Dyke's nursery" in another novel: "She (his mother) smiled. It seemed she would like that. There were so many places, Van Dyke's nursery, Calver, Bakewell market - lots of them."; cf. Longden, *Lost for Words*, p. 226. On p. 229ff. Mr Longden describes the nurseries a little more detailed (aisles, a separate shop) and the sorts of gardening goods which were sold there. He also makes mention of a café with a goldfish pond on the premises.

325 Remembered by Geoffrey Holdsworth (November 8, 2013).

326 Information disclosed in a private E-mail correspondence between June Pearce and the author on October 6, 2013, and remembered by Geoffrey Holdsworth (November 8, 2013).

father's who had a transport business and delivered all the building materials the Van Dyk's used to build the greenhouses.[327] Her cousin Mary Jones remembers that the Van Dyk brothers started with one greenhouse growing tomatoes and eventually grew into a prosperous garden centre. It was not big by today's standards, but Mary Jones recalls that they had wonderful plants for sale. She loved the place and would often walk by to see what was new. If one of the brothers were in they would always stop and talk to the customers and give advice to everyone. According to Mrs Jones, they must have been good people to work for because a boy she knew from her class at school, Michael Gregory who lived in Barlborough, went straight from school to work there and was still employed there when the nurseries closed (similar to Geoffrey Holdsworth who spent all his working life at Van Dyk's Garden Centre).[328]

Not only did the Van Dyk brothers and their families build bungalows behind the hotel, they also gave some of the loyal workers a plot of land to build their own bungalows (for example in 1966 to the families of Geoffrey Holdsworth and Michael Hannon, both men still live there today, see Chapter 14); according to Mary Jones Mr Gregory also owned of these bungalows.[329]

In 1966 the Van Dyk brothers opened the mansion as a hotel. Three years later, in 1969, they sold both businesses again. According to the recollections of Geoffrey Holdsworth, Dirk and Jacob Plug-Kroon purchased the business from the Van Dyks and continued the nursery business.[330] Van Dyk's Garden Centre and Nurseries ceased to exist in August 2011.[331] The former Mansfield Brewery was the owner of Southgate House/Van Dyk Hotel for a couple of years (see Chapter 14) until CPS Leisure (today Hotel Van Dyk Ltd., Eyre

---

[327] Information disclosed in a private E-mail correspondence between June Pearce and the author on May 24, 2013.

[328] Information disclosed in a private E-mail correspondence between Mary Jones and the author on October 1, 2013; further details during a personal meeting in Clowne on September 22, 2013. Mrs Jones says that she used to see him often going about his duties and always asked for advice on any plants she had bought.

[329] Information disclosed in private E-mail correspondences between Mary Jones and the author on May 29, 2013 and on October 1, 2013.

[330] Remembered by Geoffrey Holdsworth; information disclosed in a private E-mail correspondence between June Pearce and the author on November 8, 2013. The exact date of the purchase is unknown.

[331] Riden, *Clowne, Manors and other Estates*, p. 5; http://www.vandykhotel.co.uk/ (viewed 25/10/2012). The Worksop Guardian (NN, "Sewing seeds of friendship", dated September 20, 2011) reports: "A Garden Centre that has ceased trading after 54 years last month has donated a tree (...) provide a permanent reminder of Van Dyk Garden Centre". Information also disclosed by Mary Jones in a private E-mail correspondence with the author on June 15, 2013. Upon a personal visit in April 2014 I saw that the nurseries/greenhouses had been demolished.

family) bought the place in 2002.[332] The Van Dyk Hotel continues to be a successful business. Geoffrey Holdsworth adds that currently development is underway to extend the house premises to accommodate 70 additional bedrooms, and a seafood restaurant is to be created inside the old tea rooms.

9. The Land Values Maps and associated Books of Reference ("Domesday Books")

The possibly most substantial graphic representation of the extent of Southgate Estate are the so-called "Land Values Maps" whose working copies are stored at the Derbyshire Record Office in Matlock.[333] Their final copies, as well as the related Field Books are preserved at the National Archives in London. These associated "Domesday Books" (Reference Books) are also stored at Matlock Archives. The maps and books were produced in the course of the Finance Act 1910 which required a comprehensive survey of landownership in the United Kingdom.[334] There was no need to register ownership of land in England, so the Land Values Maps and their related reference books can be viewed as "the first available documentary evidence linking property ownership to a map".[335] This forms a solitary document as neither before nor after have any other endeavours been made to compile this kind of information until the modern times Land Registry began its work. The Books of Reference form the basis for the later Tax Rate Books.

The maps were executed on a scale of 1:2500. Coloured borders or colour washes indicate the boundaries of individual properties. Since in reality country estates did not necessarily consist of one large piece of land, s-shaped hooks connected their disjointed elements on the maps. Every single unit of an estate received an assessment number which was listed in the Reference Books. Derbyshire was subdivided into four council areas, Clowne Rural District with Southgate Estate belonging to the area of Chesterfield. All units

---

332 http://www.vandykhotel.co.uk/assets/vision-mag-spring-2012_web.pdf, p. 2 (viewed 25/10/2012) says that the ownership lasted for over 30 years which is slightly overestimated. The time span covers ca. 20 years from the late 1970s/early 1980s until 2002. Mansfield Brewery (founded in 1855) ceased to exist in 1999 when it was taken over by another brewing business; cf. http://www.marstons.co.uk/about/Heritage.aspx (viewed 07/03/2014); Richmond, Turton, *Brewing Industry*, p. 226.

333 Derbyshire Record Office, *Ref. No. D595* (D595/R1/1/16, sheets 19/7 and 19/11); Booth, *Belper Derbyshire*.

334 "Record of Valuations made by the Commissioners of Inland Revenues, in accordance with the provisions of Part I. of the Finance (1909/10) Act, 1910.", Lloyd George's Domesday Survey, part of his "People's Budget" dated 1909; cf. Booth, *Belper Derbyshire*.

335 Booth, *Belper Derbyshire*. Apparently the maps are older than the Books of Reference, the margin on the foot of Sheet 19/11 for example says: "Zincographed and Published at the Ordnance Survey, Southampton 1898".

of Southgate Estate received markings in violet on Sheet 19/7 and in light brown on Sheet 19/11. Altogether Sheet 19/7 shows sixteen different units of Southgate Estate in 1910[336]: Forrest's Plantation, Harlesthorpe Cottages, Square Plantation (with Southgate House and Stables, Figure 12), Wall's Plantation, Wall's Holt, an old quarry, Southgate Cottages, Hickin Wood and eight different stretches and patches of woodland along road and land boundaries: two patches along Rotherham Road, a large area of wood south of Southgate House, two patches of woodland east of Hickin Wood, another patch north of Hickin Wood, woodland north of the quarry and woodland near Whitebrick Moor. Supplementing this Sheet 19/11 shows ten different units comprising of the cottages of Harlesthorpe Lane ("Lake View"), "Rodgwood", Harlesthorpe, agricultural land at Harlesthorpe and Hollin Hill and a built-up plot on Station Road, Clowne as also being parts of Southgate Estate. The related Reference Book names Col. John (6) E Butler-Bowdon as owner of Southgate Estate and lists all his properties with their respective tenants.[337]

10. "Vanus est honor" - The Bowdon and Butler-Bowdon Men

When starting my research on Southgate House and Estate it was not my intention to examine the family history of the Bowdons and Butler-Bowdons. However, the longer I dealt with matters, the clearer it became that it was absolutely necessary to give my attention to this widely ramified family, and I discovered an intriguing entity with a compelling history.

The front of a small, open-hearth fireplace in a corner of a room in Barlborough House is adorned with the Bowdon and Butler family's motto (the overmantel is decorated with a large Butler-Bowdon family coat of arms, Figure 13).[338] This maxim, executed in golden capital letters and flanked by elements from the Butler (right) and Bowdon (left) crests, is striking as it does not seem to make much sense on first sight: *vanus est honor*, honour is vain. In a normal context, honour is considered to be one of the most worthy human traits. So why should it be vain (conceited) or vain (futile)? The explanation must be found somewhere else: possibly the Butler-Bowdons believed that honour could only exist between human beings, but for themselves being a Catholic family and therefore tuned towards belief and religious life more than worldly matters, honour between humans did not have a great significance and was therefore to be considered "vain". So "vain" in this case is not used in the sense of vanity but rather as something futile, insubstantial, hollow or illusory in an earthly way.[339] This assumption is supported by the

336 Sheet 19/7.

337 Pages 1, 6, 38 and 50 of the book.

338 Referring to photo by courtesy of Tony Bak of Barlborough Heritage and Research Centre.

339 Result of a personal conversation with Joost Hazenbos on May 2, 2013.

Latin motto of the Society of Jesus on the plaque on wall of the chapel of Southgate House: *ad maiorem dei gloriam* – "For the greater glory of God" (see Chapter 8).

Apparently, the name "Bowdon" (and its variations such as Bowden and Bodon) is not overly common in England but there seem to be a couple of sources which give us hints to its origin.[340] I do not feel secure about the reliability of the information available to me and fear to tread on shaky ground, but I presume it makes sense to mention at least some suggestions. One explanation for the name of Bowdon/Bowden could be the derivation from an Old Frisian personal name "Botha/o" which means "messenger, harbinger" and a Germanic patronymic form, "Bode(n)". Another explanation possibly lies in locational surnames, e.g. from places of that name in Scotland or England. In the counties Devon, Derbyshire and Cheshire, "Bowdon" means "hill shaped like a bow", deriving from the Old English pre-7th century/Anglo-Saxon word "boga-dun(n)", bow (-shaped) or bow weapon hill, or curved hill, or a bend. Also, it could derive from topographical surnames, referring to someone who lived at the top of a hill ("dun"), from "bufan dune", "above the hill".[341] A name Bowden attested in Leicestershire is recorded as "Bugedone" in the Domesday Book of 1086, and is said to come from the Old English female personal name "Burcge" (masculine "Buga"/"Beoga"), and "dun"; hence "Burcge's hill".[342] The initial part of "boga-dun(n)" may have its origin in "berg" which could imply the use of a hill as a meeting place with "don"/"dun" meaning (fortified) stronghold, thus it can be interpreted as "hill fort".[343] In accordance with this assumption, another source says that the Bowdon/Bowden family took their surname from a place name (Gaelic "both an duin", house on the hill) whose roots lie with Viking settlers in ancient times, or come from someone having lived on the lands of Bowden in Roxburghshire, Scotland where the family had purportedly held lands since the early Middle Ages.[344] The same source offers another explanation for the origin of the name: Cheshire, where the Bowdons

340 McNeal Dodgson, *Place-Names of Cheshire*, p. 204; http://www.communigate.co.uk/chesh/altrincham/page3.html(viewed 30/11/2013); http://www.surnamedb.com/Surname/Boden (viewed 10/04/2013); http://www.surnamedb.com/Surname/bowden#ixzz2gI0QxBJo (viewed 29/09/2013).

341 http://www.surnamedb.com/Surname/Boden (viewed 10/04/2013).

342 http://www.surnamedb.com/Surname/bowden#ixzz2gI0QxBJo (viewed 29/09/2013).

343 http://www.communigate.co.uk/chesh/altrincham/page3.html (viewed 30/11/2013).

344 http://www.surnamedb.com/Surname/bowden#ixzz2gI0QxBJo (viewed 29/09/2013); http://www.houseofnames.com/bowden-family-crest (viewed 10/04/2013). This source does not give any verifiable background information and is therefore to be treated with the utmost caution.

allegedly held a family seat and were granted lands by Duke William of Normandy (William the Conqueror, ca. 1028-1087), their liege Lord, for their presence at the Battle of Hastings (1066). In this context these Bowdons are said to originally stem from a place called Bodin in Normandy, France.[345] This assumption is supported by the explanations in Burke's book on the Landed Gentry: the family came to Britain at the time of the Conquest carrying the name of Bodin or Bowdon.[346]

The earliest recorded spellings of the family name are said to be that of a Richard de Boulden, dated ca. 1200, in *Liber S. Marie de Calchou Registrum Kelso* (1113-1567), Scotland, during the reign of King William "The Lion" of Scotland (1165-1214); that of a Walter Bodin, dated 1273 in the Oxfordshire Hundred Rolls, a census of England and Wales during the 13th century (during the reign of Edward I, 1273-1307)[347]; that of a Richard de Bouldone, Parson of the Parish of Edistone, Devon (?), who rendered homage in 1296; a John de Boghedon, who appeared in the Place Names of Devonshire in 1333; and a William de Bolden, who was Abbot of Kelso in 1370 (as recorded in the Monastic Annals of Teviotdale near Hawick, Roxburghshire). According to the sources available to me, there was also a Thomas Boden who appeared in the Register of the University of Oxford in 1583, and a Sarah, daughter of an Edward Bowden, mentioned along with the date of February 2, 1624. Unfortunately it is not possible to connect the above mentioned Thomas Boden to one of "our" Bowdon men, but it is striking that he bears one of the favoured first names at that time, which again might just have been a coincidence.

All the sources which have been consulted over the course of this research, indeed give diverse spellings for the family name Bowdon. It is either spelt Bowdon, Bowden, or sometimes Bodon. At the time when governments introduced tax collections and population censuses (e.g. in England the Poll Tax and the compilation of the Domesday Book, both in the 11th century) surnames became necessary in order to be able to tell people and families apart. Over the course of time, surnames tended to change, often leading to a large number of variants[348]; the difference in spelling in some cases is accounted for by poor or indifferent spelling by enumerators, transcribers and later on newspaper editors etc. However, all Bowdon/Bowden/Bodon names in the sources I consulted are the same. Also birth and death dates of the respective family members are not always concurrent in the consulted

---

345 http://www.houseofnames.com/bowden-family-crest (viewed 10/04/2013). This source does not give any verifiable background information and is therefore to be treated with caution especially as there is apparently is no place of that name in France today.

346 Burke, Burke, *Genealogical and Heraldic History*, p. 125: name appearing in the Battle Abbey Roll.

347 The National Archives, *Hundred Rolls*.

348 http://www.surnamedb.com/Surname/Boden (viewed 10/04/2013).

interpretations of the source material, thus stemming from confusion of the various Thomas, George, John and Henry Bowdons and other Bowdon men in the Bowdon family.

The name Butler is of Norman-French origin. It is widely recognised as originating before 1066, and recordings of the name are even scarcer in France itself. In a sense the name derives from a job description from the Old French word "bouteillier" (the "one who supplies the (wine) bottles", responsible for looking after and serving the alcoholic beverages[349]). However, to have "bouteillier" in the surname must somehow represent status within a royal or at least noble, household, similar to names such as Marshall (Master of the Horse), the Steward (Head of the Estate), the (dis)Spencer (Head of Provisions) and other occupations. However, the fact that when in 1171 Theodore Fitzwalter accompanied King Henry II on his conquest of Ireland he assigned the title "Chief Butler of Ireland" and later took the name "Butler" as his family name, shows us that the original Butlers must have been considered more than mere servants. In 1055 the first ever recording of the surname was recorded as Hugo Buteiller (calendar of preserved ancient documents of France, reign of King Henry I of France, 1031-1060).[350]

Both the Bowdon as well as the Butler family had their own coat of arms which requires a short description in this context. The main element of the Bowdon coat of arms is a striding lion on a black background turning left in the first quarter. All other three quarters remain undecorated (the fourth is coloured in black). No less than 94 coats of arms have been granted in England and Ireland to people bearing the name Butler and its derivates. The original and ancient crest showed the blazon of a red field, a chevron between three goblets, all executed in gold.[351] The Butler-Bowdon family coat of arms shows the combination of both crests; the first and third quarter is dedicated to the Bowdon crest, the second and forth quarter bear the Butler elements (Figure 14 and Chapter 10).[352]

I attempted to draw an abbreviated and very tentative genealogical tree of the Bowdon and Butler-Bowdon family which is surely amendable (Figure 30).[353] In possession of Barlborough Heritage and Resource Centre is a copy of

---

349 Girouard, *English Country House*, p. 22.

350 Burke, Burke, *Genealogical and Heraldic History*, p. 125; http://www.surnamedb.com/Surname/butler#ixzz2gI0gFEKf (viewed 29/09/2013).

351 http://www.surnamedb.com/Surname/butler#ixzz2gI0gFEKf (viewed 29/09/2013).

352 For a more detailed description of the Butler-Bowdon family coat of arms see Appendix 6.

353 I am mostly relying on the 10-yearly censuses of England and Wales, on Burke, Burke, *Genealogical and Heraldic History*, p. 125f.; Glover, *History*, p. 304-305; White's *1875*, p. 732-733; Bowden, *Bowdon Marriage*; Abram, *Parish of Blackburn*, p. 80; http://www.uk.mundia.com/gb/Search/Results?surname=BUTLER%20BOWDON&birthPlace=United%20Kingdom (viewed 25/05/2013); Riden, *Barlborough*, p. 36ff.;

an imposing Bowdon family tree on parchment, captioned "Pedigree Bowdon of Southgate and Beightonfields formerly of Bowdon Hall Co. Derby" and originally designed and illustrated by Lancelot George B Butler-Bowdon who managed to trace the family history back to 1450 (Figure 15). The parchment measures 6 feet and 6 inches x 2 feet. The last entry is from 1841, the year when the Bowdon family was united with the Butler family in marriage (see Chapter 21). This information was also used in compiling the following list.[354]

Thomas (1) Bowdon, b. xxxx - d. xxxx, of **Bowden Hall of Chapel-en-le-Frith and Wheston-in-Peak**[355], living 1450

Nicholas (1) Bowdon, b. xxxx - d. xxxx, of **Bowden Hall**, allegedly attested in ca. 1477[356]

George (1) Bowdon, b. xxxx - d. xxxx, of **Bowden Hall**, Esq., son of Thomas (1) Bowdon, living in 1495, married to Barbara Bagshaw(e), daughter of Nicholas Bagshaw of Abney, Esq.; two sons: Edward and George (2)

Edward (1) Bowdon, b. xxxx - d. xxxx, Esq., first son of George (1) Bowdon and Barbara Bagshaw, living 1611, unmarried and *d.s.p.*

George (2) Bowdon, b. 1537 - d. xxxx, of **Bowden Hall**, Esq., second son of George (1) Bowdon and Barbara Bagshaw, living 1550, still living 1611, married to Ellen Pole, daughter of Austin Pole of Langley, Co. Derby, Esq.; three sons: Thomas (2), George (3), German (1), one daughter: Ann (married to Roland Smith, Esq., of Waterford, Ireland)

Thomas (2) Bowdon, b. 1629 - d. xxxx (died in his father's lifetime) of **Bowden Hall**, first son of George (2) Bowdon and Ellen Pole, married to Anne Bagshaw(e), second daughter of Henry Bagshawe of Ridge, Co. Derby, Esq., in first marriage and Ellen Shrigley in second marriage[357]; four sons with Anne Bagshaw(e): Nicholas (2), George (4), Edward (3), Thomas (3)

Lundy, *Peerage;* Estcourt, Payne, *Catholic nonjurors;* http://www.angelfire.com/realm/gotha/Part15.htm (viewed 15/08/2013); Craven, "Southgate House, Clowne", p. 57.

[354] Information disclosed in private E-mail correspondence between Tony Bak and the author on July 16 and September 1, 2013. I was able to examine the family tree during a personal visit to Barlborough Heritage and Research Centre on September 21, 2013. Apparently, there must be more information on that matter as Sheffield Archives hold a record (*Ref. No. MD5444*, original document not viewed personally) labelled "Pedigree of Bowden" covering the years 1547 to 1803 from the deeds and papers of the "Bowdens of Bowden" relating to Chapel-en-le-Frith and Beighton Fields.

[355] Craven, "Southgate House, Clowne", p. 57. According to a newspaper article titled "Heroes Every One" in the Worksop Guardian dated January 11, 1918, Thomas Bowdon commanded the garrison at Bolsover Castle (information disclosed in a private E-mail correspondence between Tony Bak and the author on June 25, 2013).

[356] Craven, Stanley, *Derbyshire Country House*, p. 38.

[357] The family tree facsimile in possession of Barlborough Heritage and Research Centre withholds information on details of this second marriage.

(attested in 1661), and three daughters: Elizabeth (attested in 1661), Anne (attested in 1661), Dorothy; Edward (3), Thomas (3), Elizabeth, Anne and Dorothy all died without issue

George (3) Bowdon, b. xxxx - d. xxxx, of Bowdon, Esq., second son of George (2) Bowdon and Ellen (1) Pole, married to Ellen Bowdon, daughter of George Bowdon of Bowdon, Esq., Cheshire, two sons: William, Edward (2) (living in 1611)

German (1) Bowdon, b. xxxx - d. xxxx, Esq., third son of George (2) Bowdon and Ellen Pole, married to Florence Bradburn, daughter of Nicholas Bradburn of Bradburn, Esq., no issue

Nicholas (2) Bowdon, b. xxxx - d. xxxx, first son of Thomas (2) Bowdon and Anne Bagshawe, unmarried, living in 1611

Nicholas (X) Bowdon, b. xxxx - d. 1637, of **Bowden Hall**, married to Alice Creswell on 18/01/1633, one son: Thomas (X)[358]

George (4) Bowdon, b. ca. 1599 - d. 1658 ("living 1636, died 1658 aged 57, was a benefactor to the County of Derby"[359]), heir of **Bowdon Hall**, second son of Thomas (2) Bowdon and Anne Bagshawe, married to

Dorothy Browne (d. 24/01/1637), daughter of Nicholas Browne of Marsh Hall (near Chapel-en-le-Frith) on 24/04/1621 in Chapel-en-le-Frith, thirteen children: Nicholas (3) (b. 1622, baptised 23/02/1622 - d. 1667/ 20/03/1668 /1670/1680), George (5) (b. 1627, baptised 04/06/1627 – d. 1633), Thomas (4) (b. 1629, baptised 20/09/1629), Edmund (b. 1632, baptised 05/01/1632), Valentine (b. 1633, baptised 27/02/1633), Jermyne/German (2) (b. 1633?, baptised 03/06/1633?), Benjamin (b. 1635, baptised 01/04/1635[360]), Dorothy (b. 1625, baptised 27/02/1625, living in 1634, wife of John Haye of Lime/Lyme, Co. Chester[361]), Elizabeth (b. 1623, baptised 27/03/1623 - d. 1641, unmarried), Ann (buried 06/12/1641[362], unmarried), Barbara (b. 1626, baptised 01/05/1626 - d. 1633), Ellen (b. 1637 – d. 1637, buried

---

358 This Nicholas does not appear on the Bowdon family tree of Barlborough Heritage and Research Centre and could not be related to any Bowdon family member; cf. Bowden, *Bowdon Marriage*. The same source mentions a Charles Bowdon, b. xxxx – d. 1649, son of a George Bowdon, "buried in ye quire of North Isle" of the Bowdon quire of the church in Chapel-en-le-Frith on 06/07/1649, and a George Bowdon, b. xxxx - d. 1680. Neither person could be connected to any known members of the Bowden family for that period.

359 Cf. Bowdon family tree, Barlborough Heritage and Research Centre.

360 There is a last will of Benjamin Bowden of Stapleford which is listed in the Canterbury Wills; cf. The National Archives, *Wills 1384-1858* and *Ref. No. PROB 11* (series, specific document not viewed personally) made between 1384 and 12 January 1858, these records are of the Prerogative Court of Canterbury (PCC) wills. Source for this information: Bowden, *Bowdon Marriage*.

361 Bowden, *Bowdon Marriage*.

362 Bowden, *Bowdon Marriage*.

24/01/1637), Mary (b. 1628, baptised 03/09/1628 - d. 1633); one of the surviving daughters carried the estate out of the family

Nicholas (3) Bowdon of Bowdon, Esq., b. 02/1622 - d. 1667/ 20/03/1668[363]/1670/1680, of **Bowden Hall**, first son of George (4) Bowdon and Dorothy Browne, married in first marriage to a female with the surname Woodruffe, daughter of a Mr Woodruffe of Hope, Derbyshire (barrister at law), no issue[364]; married to Mary Barnby in second marriage on 30/09/1652, three sons: Barnby, Thomas (5) and Robert, one daughter NN (died young)

William Bowdon, b. xxxx - d. xxxx, first son of George (3) Bowdon and Ellen Pole, married to an unknown female, one daughter: Cecily Bowdon (married to Austin Pole)

Edward (2) Bowdon, b. xxxx - d. xxxx, second son of George (3) Bowdon and Ellen (1) Pole, living in 1611, married to an unknown female, one son: George (6)

Barnby Bowdon, b. xxxx - d. ca. 1674, first son of Nicholas (3) Bowdon and Mary Barnby, unmarried/*d.s.p.*

Thomas (5) Bowdon, b. xxxx - d. xxxx, of Barnby, Co. York and Bowdon, Co. Derby, second son of Nicholas (3) Bowdon and Mary Barnby, unmarried/*d.s.p.*

Robert Bowdon, b. xx/05/1656[365] - d. xx/03/1681, third son of Nicholas (3) Bowdon and Mary Barnby, unmarried/*d.s.p.*

George (5) Bowdon, b. 1627 - d. xxxx, of Coventry (?), Gentleman, Esq., of Bowdon (aged 55 in 1681), second son of George (4) Bowdon and Dorothy Browne, unmarried/*d.s.p.*[366]

Thomas (4) Edward/Edmund Valentine Bowdon, b. 1629 - d. xxxx, third son of George (4) Bowdon and Dorothy Browne, attested in 1677 or 1680 for Bowden Hall, died unmarried

German (2) Bowdon (b. 1633 - d. xxxx) of Melton Mowbray, Esq., Co. Leicester, fourth son of George (4) Bowdon and Dorothy Browne, aged 48 in 1681, married to Elizabeth Thorpe, daughter of John Thorpe of Melton Mowbray, two sons: George (7) aged 11 in 1681, Thomas (6) aged 8 in 1681, four daughters: Elizabeth aged 6 in 1618, Anne aged 3 in 1681, Mary died young, Dorothy aged 1 in 1681

---

363 A Nicholas Bowden of Bowden Esq. is buried in the north isle of the Bowden quire of the church in Chapel-en-le-Frith on 10/03/1668 according to register extracts; cf. Bowden, *Bowdon Marriage*.

364 Cf. Bowdon family tree, Barlborough Heritage and Research Centre.

365 Robert was baptised on 28/05/1656, cf. Bowden, *Bowdon Marriage*.

366 According to Chris Bowden (Bowden, *Bowdon Marriage*), George (5) Bowdon had two daughters; one of them took Bowden Hall Estate out of the possession of the family.

Benjamin Bowdon (b. 03/04/1635 /1637 - d. xxxx) of Stapleford, Co. Leicester, fifth son of George (4) Bowdon and Dorothy Browne, aged 44 in 1681, married to Elizabeth Goodhand, daughter of a Mr Goodhand, Co. Leicester

William Bowdon, b. xxxx - d. xxxx, first son of George (3) and Ellen Bowdon, one daughter: Cecily Bowdon (married to Austin Pole, Esq., of Langley)

Edward Bowdon, b. xxxx - d. xxxx, Esq., second son of George (3) and Ellen Bowdon, married to NN, one son: George (7)

George (6) Bowdon, b. xxxx - d. xxxx, Esq., son of Edward (2) Bowdon, married to Ellen (2) Pole of Langley, daughter of Austin Pole and Cecily Bowdon, two sons: Henry (1), John (1)

Henry (1) Bowdon, b. xxxx - d. 1665 (plague?), of **Beighton Fields**, Co. Derby, Esq., first son of George (6) Bowdon and Ellen (2) Pole, married to Mary Hewit(t)/Hewett 04/11/1691 (?), heiress of **Beighton Fields** ("of the ancient family of Hewit of Shireoaks, Co. Notts."), no offspring, Henry "left Beightonfields and all his other estates his nephew Henry Bowdon"[367] (= Henry (2) Bowdon)

John (1) Bowdon, b. xxxx - d. 1665 (plague), second son of George (7) Bowdon and Ellen (2) Pole, Captain in the Army, married to Alice Beard, daughter of Beard of Beard Hall, Co. Derby[368], one son: Henry (2)

Henry (2) Bowdon: b: xxxx - d. xxxx, of **Beighton Fields**, Yeoman, son of John (1) Bowdon and Alice Beard, nephew of Henry (1) Bowdon, married to a female with the surname Alleyne (Allen), sister of John Alleyne of Wheston/Whetstone Hall, Esq., "who left Whetstone to his nephew John Bowdon, Esq., in 1700"[369] (= John (2) Bowdon), marriage year ca. 1690, one son: John (2)

John (2) Bowdon: b. 31/08/1695 - d. 01/03/1764 or 01/07/1764, of **Beighton Fields**, Yeoman, son of Henry (2) Bowdon and a female with the surname Alleyne (Allen)[370]; married to Mary Barker (b. 1700 - d. 1728), daughter of Barker of Barlborough, Esq., in first marriage (1719), children: Elizabeth/Mary (married to a male "Johnson of Sheffield, Esq., Co. Warwick, brother to her father's third wife", one son: Cesar Johnson, *d.s.p.*)[371] and John (3), second marriage with Margaret, daughter of Nelson

---

367 Cf. Bowdon family tree, Barlborough Heritage and Research Centre.

368 Cf. Bowdon family tree, Barlborough Heritage and Research Centre.

369 Cf. Bowdon family tree, Barlborough Heritage and Research Centre; Craven, Stanley, *Derbyshire Country House*, p. 221.

370 The last will of John Alleyne dated September 27, 1726 names "John Bowden (*sic!*) the younger, eldest son and heir of my nephew John Bowden (*sic!*) of Beighton Fields co. Derby, gent". The source further quotes "condition of John Bowden (*sic!*) the elder during the minority of John Bowden (*sic!*), dated Sept 1726, signed by John Bowden (*sic!*) and Henry Bowden (*sic!*)", cf. Lockie, *Wills of Derbyshire*; Estcourt, Payne, *Catholic nonjurors*, p. 30f. (giving another date of the will: December 22, 1724).

371 Cf. Bowdon family tree, Barlborough Heritage and Research Centre: the name Elizabeth is crossed out and is overwritten by the word Mary.

of T/F(?)ayrehxxx[372], Esq., Co. Lancashire and widow of R Sherborn Esq. of Stoneyhurst[373] 1739, one son: Thomas (7); third marriage with Mary, daughter of Johnson of Shelfield, Esq., Co. Warwick (d. 1785[374]), four sons: George (8), James (1), Joseph Cesar (attested in 1737), Martin (attested in 1746); five daughters: Charlotte (b. 1748 - d. 20/08/1807, married to Richard Butler of Pleasington Hall), Ann(e) (1) (attested in 1736, married to a John Bowdon of Beighton Fields = John (3) Bowdon?), Frances (attested in 1740), Alice, Mary[375]

John (3) Bowdon: b. 14/05/1722 - d. xxxx, of **Beighton Fields**, son of John (2) and his first wife Mary Barker, married to Alice, daughter of George Johnson of Shelfield, Esq., Co. Warwick, one son: Henry (3), secondly married possibly to his younger half sister Ann Bowdon, daughter of John (2) and his third wife Mary Bowdon, no issue

Thomas (7) Bowdon, b. 20/08/1731 / 06/08/1741 - d. 30/05/1779, of **Barlborough**, Esq., son of John (2) Bowdon and Margaret Nelson, died unmarried and without issue

George (8) Bowdon, b. 09/10/1743 - d. 1791, of **Radford/Oxfordshire**, Esq., first son of John (2) Bowdon and Mary Johnson, married to Elizabeth, daughter of Clements/Tufton of Oxfordshire, Esq. (d. 1804), three sons: George (9), John (no number given, died 16/01/1825 unmarried in Oxfordshire), Joseph (of **Sedgeley Park**, Reverend, priest in the Catholic church, d. 1844), two daughters: Mary, Ann (2)

George (9) Bowdon, b. xxxx - d. 18/02/1822, Esq., first son of George (8) Bowdon and Elizabeth Clements, married to Eleanor (d. 26.03.1836), daughter of Harison (*sic!*), Esq., Co. Lancashire, four children: Mary (d. 23/08/1842), Eliza (married to Phillip Hickin of Wolverhampton, Esq., no issue), Ann(e) (3) (married to James Vinn of Brussels, Esq., d. 10/06/1843 in Belgium), George (10) (died young)

James (1) Bowdon, b. 14 or 15/11/1744 - d. xxxx, of **Staveley**, Co. Derby, Esq., second son of John (2) Bowdon and Mary Johnson, married to Elizabeth, daughter of Reverend Yates, Rector of Clown, Co. Derby (she d. 09/09/1796), no offspring

---

372 Place name illegible on Bowdon family tree, Barlborough Heritage and Research Centre.

373 Stonyhurst was the place of residence of the Sherbourn family in Lancashire, Cf. Bowdon family tree, Barlborough Heritage and Research Centre.

374 "Sister to Alice who married John Bowdon Esq.", cf. Bowdon family tree, Barlborough Heritage and Research Centre. Mary left a substantial last will; cf. The National Archives, London, *Ref. No. PROB 11/1127/218*; cf. http://www.nationalarchives.gov.uk/SearchUI/details/D414056?descriptiontype=Full&ref=PROB11/1127/218 (viewed 08/06/2013), see Chapter 22.1.

375 Ann(e), Joseph Cesar, Martin, Frances, Alice and Mary are denoted as "all dead" in the Bowdon family tree.

Richard (1) Butler, b. 17/11/1747 - d. 1779, of **Pleasington Hall**, Co. Lancashire, Esq., married to Charlotte Bowdon on 02/10/1771 in Barlborough[376], daughter of John (2) Bowdon and Mary Johnson, three children: (Richard) John Francis (b. 19/01/1774 - d. 1821 / 13/09/1824[377]), Mary-Anne (b. 01/06/1777 - d. 09/03/1840), Ann (4) (b. 21/02/1778 - d. 1835) [378]

Henry (3) Bowdon, b. 02/02/1754[379] - d. 26/02/1833, living in 1831, son of John (3) Bowdon and Alice Johnson, of **Southgate House**, married to Mary Erdeswick ("only daughter of Joseph son of Sampson Erdeswick of Sandon Hall Esq., Co. Stafford"[380]) (date of marriage 30/11/1775[381]), Mary died at Southgate 06/04/1791[382], three children: John (4) Peter Bruno, Henry (4) (died young), Barbara (died as infant)

John (4) Peter Bruno Bowdon, b. 1787 - d. 17/12/1850, son of Henry (3) Bowdon and Mary Erdeswick, of **Southgate House and Beighton Fields**, married to Mary Martha Ferrers on 26/02/1812[383], living 1831, High Sheriff for Derbyshire in 1841[384], three sons: Henry (5), John (5), James (2) (died as infant[385]), five daughters: Helena-Mary (married Peter Constable Maxwell in 1834, d. 16/06/1851; six children)[386], Barbara Magdalen (b. 1819, married

---

376 FamilySearch, *England Marriages*.

377 Above the sacristy door of Pleasington Priory there is a memorial plaque in the memory of (Richard) John Francis Butler. It bears a Latin inscription: "*Orate Pro Anima Johannis Francisci Butleri de Pleasington / Armiceri / Qui Aedem Hanc / Deo in Honorem Piis Catholicis in Solatium / Suis Sumptibus Extruxit Ornavit Dotavit / Vixit Annos L / Obiit die XIII Septembris Anno Domini / MDCCCXXIV*", which translated into English reads: "Pray for the soul of John Francis Butler of Pleasington, Gentleman, who built this edifice in the honour of God and for the pious Catholics as solace, adorned it and furnished it. He lived 50 years. He died on the day of 13th September in the year of Our Lord 1824"; cf. Child, *Pleasington Priory*, p. 54. A metal plaque on the stone floor outside the sacristy reads: "I. F. Butler Esquire 1824" (information disclosed in personal E-mail correspondences between Martin Child and the author on May 31 and June 1, 2014).

378 The Bowdon family tree at Barlborough Heritage and Research Centre states "no issue" for this marriage.

379 NN, "Diary of Henry Bowdon", p. 138 (see also Chapter 14.3).

380 Cf. Bowdon family tree, Barlborough Heritage and Research Centre.

381 Information "copied from an old vellum roll in the possession of Colonel Butler-Bowdon of Pleasington"; cf. Genealogical Society of Utah, *Erdeswick pedigree*.

382 Genealogical Society of Utah, *Erdeswick pedigree*.

383 Date of marriage settlement was 20/02/1812 according to a grant of Mary Martha Bowdon (née Ferrers) to her son Henry (5) Bowdon; cf. Shakespeare Centre Library and Archive, *Ref. No. DR 422/77* (dated 02/05/1839).

384 http://www.london-gazette.co.uk/issues/19948/pages/303 (issue dated 05/02/1841) (viewed 22/07/2013).

385 James (2) Bowdon is not mentioned in the Bowdon family tree.

386 Lundy, *Peerage* (Person Page 6036).

Edward Wright, Esq., of Kelvedon Hall, Essex in 1849 in Clowne)[387], Fanny Willoughby (later became a nun)[388], Eliza Jemima (b. 1826 - d. 20/01/1872), Caroline Erdeswick (d. 06/11/1842)

Henry (5) Bowdon, b. 07/08/1814 (Barlborough) - d. 03/05/1875 (Southgate House, Clowne), first son of John (4) Peter Bruno and Mary Martha Bowdon (née Ferrers), Magistrate and Deputy Lieutenant for the County of Derby, married to Harriet (Henrietta Mathilda) Blount(-Petre) on 08/11/1853[389] or 11/05/1853[390]; census 1851: aged 36, census 1861: aged 46, census 1871: aged 55, still married to Harriet (30/09/1832 - 31/03/1885), two daughters: Alice Elizabeth Mary (b. xx/07 or 08/1854 - d. 04/10/1933, married to (Count[391]) Ireneo Paolo Del Monaco on 15/02/1890, five children) and Constance M (b. 17/07/1857 - d. 30/03/1901, married to William Francis Lee on 19/07/1892[392], no issue)

John (5) Peter Bruno Butler-Bowdon, b. 14/09/1815 - d. 03/03/1878[393], heir of **Pleasington Hall**[394] by the bequest his cousin Mary Anne Butler (daughter of Richard and Charlotte Butler) in 1840, second son of John (4) Peter Bruno and Mary Martha Bowdon (née Ferrers), Magistrate and Deputy Lieutenant of Lancashire, Chairman of the County Magistrates in the Lower Division of the Hundred in Blackburn, Chairman of the NE Lancashire Liberal Association, married to Amelia Catherine Frances

---

387 http://www.findmypast.co.uk (Marriage Parish Records) (viewed 16/09/2013); White's *1875*, p. 733.

388 White's *1875*, p. 733.

389 Doubtful: De La Caille Ruvigny and Raineval, *Plantagenet roll*, p. 41.

390 Clarke, "From Riches to Rags", p. 14; http://www.angelfire.com/realm/gotha/Part15.htm (viewed 15/08/2013).

391 Ireneo Paolo Del Monaco was a member of the Italian aristocracy. He is quoted as "Count" (= Conte) on the website www.emedals.com (eMedals, *A 1916 Canadian Memorial Cross*), subsequently making his wife Alice "Countess" Del Monaco. See also Clarke, "From Riches to Rags", p. 14.

392 http://www.angelfire.com/realm/gotha/Part15.htm (viewed 15/08/2013).

393 Gravestone in Pleasington Priory. This gravestone is situated on the floor outside the sacristy. Information by kind courtesy of Martin Child in a personal E-mail correspondence with the author on May 31, 2014. The full text reads: "Of your charity pray for the souls of Amelia Catherine Frances Butler Bowdon of Pleasington Hall, born May 16th 1815, died November 24th 1874, Mary Frances Amelia Butler Bowdon, daughter of the above born August 21st 1852, died February 16th 1859. Madeleine Mary Butler Bowdon died October 12th 1877, aged 24 years. John Butler Bowdon born 14th September 1815, died 3rd March 1878, aged 62. Jermyne T. Butler Bowdon born 18th September 1853, died 19th November 1899. On whose souls sweet Jesus have mercy."

394 John (5) is the second son of John (4) Peter Bruno Bowdon, he inherited Pleasington Hall in Lancashire in 1840 from a cousin, Mary Anne Butler, cf. Craven, "Southgate House, Clowne", p. 57; Abram, *Parish of Blackburn*, p. 80; Farrer, Brownbill, *History of the County of Lancaster*, p. 266-269.

Whitgreave (b. 16/05/1815[395] - d. 24/11/1874) on 01/05/1849[396], children: John (6) Erdeswick, Lancelot George, Jermyn Thomas (b. 18/09/1853 - d. 10/11/1879[397]), Bruno Aloysius (b. 1858 - d. 1940 in Weymouth, Dorset[398]), Mary Frances Amelia (b. 21/08/1852 - d. 16/02/1859[399])

John (6) Erdeswick Butler-Bowdon, b. 16/02/1850 (Rugeley, Staffordshire) - d. 02/01/1929 (Pleasington, Lancashire, of **Pleasington Hall** and heir of Southgate House and Beighton Fields Priory[400], Major/Lt.-Col./Gentleman J P Late Col Militia/Late Colonel Commander 3rd Batt. East Lancashire Regiment[401], census 1901: aged 51, census 1911: aged 61, son of John (5) Butler-Bowdon and Amelia Whitgreave, brother of Lancelot George B Butler-Bowdon; married to his cousin Madel(e)ine Mary Wright[402] (b. 1853 - d. 12/10/1877[403]) in 1876 in first marriage (no issue), second marriage to Hon. Monica Mary Petre on 05/02/1879[404] (b. xx/02/1861, Portland Place, London - d. 15/05/1907, Pleasington, Lancashire), ten children: William Erdeswick Ignatius, Leonard Joseph Bruno, Bernard Joseph, Basil Joseph Bernard, Theresa Mary Sophia (b. 1882 - d. 28/03/1963, Worthing, Sussex), Monica Mary Rose (b. 1884 - d. 1907, Riding Mills, Northumberland?), Angela Mary Josephine (b. 21/05/1885, Pleasington Hall - d. 1973, London), Gladys Mary Ella (b. 1886 - d. 1959, London), Ursula Mary Cora (b. 1889/1890 - d. 1955, Cuckfield, Sussex), Isabel-Mary Helena (b. xx/09/1893 - d. 12/01/1921, Yorkshire)[405]; married to Mary Monica

---

[395] Gravestone in Pleasington Priory. Information by kind courtesy of Martin Child in a personal E-mail correspondence with the author on May 31, 2014.

[396] Parker, *Wolverhampton History and Heritage Website*.

[397] Gravestone in Pleasington Priory. Information by kind courtesy of Martin Child in a personal E-mail correspondence with the author on May 31, 2014.

[398] Bruno Aloysius married a Constance Mary Andrew on August 22, 1881 in Guarlford, Worcestershire and had two daughters with her; cf. http://www.guarlford.org.uk/remember_charles_andrew.htm (viewed 02/04/2013); he is buried in Melcombe Regis, Dorset; cf. http://www.findmypast.co.uk (Burials Parish Records) (viewed 16/09/2013).

[399] A metal plaque on a pillar of Pleasington Priory bears the following inscription: "Sacred to the memory of Frances Amelia, only daughter of John and Amelia Butler Bowdon of Pleasington. Born Aug. 21st 1852. Died Feb 16th 1859. R.I.P." Information by kind courtesy of Martin Child in a personal E-mail correspondence with the author on May 31, 2014.

[400] Riden, *Barlborough*, p. 37.

[401] Farrer, Brownbill, *History of the County of Lancaster*, p. 266-269.

[402] Daughter of Barbara Wright (née Bowdon), granddaughter of John (4) Peter Bruno Bowdon.

[403] Gravestone in Pleasington Priory. Information by kind courtesy of Martin Child in a personal E-mail correspondence with the author on May 31, 2014.

[404] De La Caille Ruvigny and Raineval, *Plantagenet roll*, p. 41.

[405] Freer, *Descendants of William the Conqueror*; five of the six daughters became nuns, cf. Riden, *Barlborough*, p. 38.

Walm(e)sley (b. 1852 - d. 09/09/1937, London) in third marriage in 1909 or 1910, no issue

William Erdeswick Ignatius Butler-Bowdon, b. 16/01/1880 (Manchester Square, London, Middlesex) - d. 30/03/1956 (Bridport, Dorset), Lieutenant Colonel and Deputy Lieutenant[406], D.S.O., married to Gertrude Mary de Trafford (b. 23/09/1888 - d. 15/03/1983, Dorchester) on 28/09/1909 in Haunton, Staffordshire, two sons: Maurice Erdeswick and Anthony William

Leonard Joseph Bruno Butler-Bowdon, b. 02/02/1881 (Pleasington, Lancashire) - d. 24/12/1904 (South Africa)

Bernard Joseph Butler-Bowdon, b. 30/10/1896 - d. 11/05/1897 (Hampshire)

Basil Joseph Bernard Butler-Bowdon, b. 05/11/1898 (Bournemouth) - d. 28/03/1918 (Fampoux near Arras, France), Lieutenant

Maurice Erdeswick Butler-Bowdon, b. 04/07/1910 (Cornwall) - d. 14/06/1984 (Chichester, Sussex)[407], 1927/1929 Midshipman Royal Navy[408], later Lieutenant (1941)[409] and Captain, son of William Erdeswick Ignatius Butler-Bowdon and Gertrude Mary de Trafford, married to Anne Darlington on 15/04/1939 in London, three children

---

406 Deputy Lieutenant (DL) in the UK is a military commission. A DL is subject to the Lord Lieutenant of a lieutenancy county or area and normally renders either civil or military service in the local community; cf. http://www.legislation.gov.uk/ukpga/1997/23/section/2 (viewed 04/03/2014). Furthermore William Erdeswick Ignatius Butler-Bowdon was also decorated with the King's and Queen's Medals (with six clasps) and with the award of the Companion, Distinguished Service Order (D.S.O.), a military decoration conferred on officers of the armed forces for "highly successful command and leadership during active operations"; cf. https://www.gov.uk/medals-campaigns-descriptions-and-eligibility (viewed 03/04/2014). A newspaper article titled "Heroes Every One" in Worksop Guardian dated January 11, 1918 lists his military career in detail (information disclosed in a private E-mail correspondence between Tony Bak and the author on June 25, 2013). During the Anglo-Boer War (1899-1902) war he served in the Duke of Cornwall's Light Infantry; cf. http://www.findmypast.co.uk (Anglo-Boer War records) (viewed 04/09/2013).

407 Freer, *Descendants of William the Conqueror*; Lundy, *Peerage* (Person Page 7594); http://www.angelfire.com/realm/gotha/Part15.htm (viewed 15/08/2013).

408 Kelliher, "Rediscovery of Margery Kempe", p. 260.

409 Cherrett, *World War II Today*; account of Lord Louis Mountbatten on the battle for Crete (bombardment of Maleme airfield) where their destroyer, the HMS Kelly, sunk on May 23, 1941: "(…) I saw the navigator, Lieutenant Maurice Butler-Bowdon, with his back to the ship. I yelled to him 'Swim like hell' because I was afraid that the propellers would hit him. We both managed to get clear, but only by a matter of six or seven yards. (…)"

Anthony William Butler-Bowdon, b. 30/07/1913 (Eynsford, Kent) - d. 09/02/2001[410], son of William Erdeswick Ignatius Butler-Bowdon and Gertrude Mary de Trafford, married to Marion Pollock, seven children

Lancelot George B Butler-Bowdon, b. 28/03/1851 (Pleasington, Lancashire) - d. 12/09/1909 (Riding Mill, Northumberland?), of **Barlborough House**, Captain and Major, son of John (5) Butler-Bowdon and Amelia Whitgreave, brother of John (6) Erdeswick Butler-Bowdon, census 1891: aged 40, married to Ella Cicely Mary Clifton-Wykeham Lelgarde Rawdon-Hastings (b. 22/11/1856 – d. 02/07/1912) on 30/07/1879[411], son of John (5) Butler-Bowdon and Amelia Whitgreave, brother of John (6) Erdeswick Butler-Bowdon

John (7) W Lancelot Wykeham Butler-Bowdon, 25th and last Lord Grey de Ruthyn[412], b. 25/10/1883 (Pleasington Hall, Lancashire) - d. 25/10/1963, of **Barlborough House**, Justice of Peace, son of Lancelot George B Butler-Bowdon and Ella Cicely Mary Bowdon (née Clifton-Wykeham (?) Lelgarde Rawdon Hastings, b. 1858 - d. 1912), grandson of John (5) Butler-Bowdon[413]

Out of respect for the privacy of family members of the Butler-Bowdon family alive today, I let the family tree end at this point. The family line continues to this day through Maurice and Anthony Butler-Bowdon.[414] One member may be mentioned however: the contemporary British artist and painter Humphrey Ocean, born Humphrey Anthony Erdeswick Butler-Bowdon on June 22, 1951, first son of Maurice Butler-Bowdon.[415] He kindly pointed out to me that the Bowdon family originated from a place called Bowdon outside Manchester (today Greater Manchester, near Altrincham, Cheshire), consequently "Bowdon" is to be considered as the correct spelling of the family name, and will therefore be used throughout this book.[416]

---

410 Freer, *Descendants of William the Conqueror*; Lundy, *Peerage* (Person Page 7594); http://www.angelfire.com/realm/gotha/Part15.htm (viewed 15/08/2013).

411 Lundy, *Peerage* (Person Page 3446); Lancelot George Butler-Bowdon was extremely popular among the people of Barlborough, cf. Linacre, *How it was*, p. 64, see also Chapter 22.

412 Lundy, *Peerage* (Person Page 3446); "Lancelot Butler Bowden (*sic!*), Lord Grey de Ruthyn of Barlborough House was the twenty-fifth baron of Britain's seventh oldest barony and was bearer of the Royal Golden Spurs."; cf. Linacre, *How it was,* p. 64, see also Chapter 22.

413 Craven, "Southgate House, Clowne", p. 57; Abram, *Parish of Blackburn*, p. 80.

414 Freer, *Descendants of William the Conqueror.*

415 http://www.humphreyocean.com (viewed 09/09/2013).

416 Information disclosed in personal E-mail correspondence between Humphrey Butler-Bowdon and the author on November 25, 2013. According to him his father Maurice spent his life correcting people on the misspelling of Bowdon (disclosed in personal E-mail correspondence between Humphrey Butler-Bowdon and the author on November 26, 2013). See also Victoria & Albert Museum, *Cope* on the Butler-Bowdon

Further research yielded a substantial number of members of a Bowden family from Bowden Middlecale (today Hayfield and New Mills, two villages ca. 6 km north of Chapel-en-le-Frith), attested for example by 17th century court papers.[417] They partly bear the familiar Bowdon first names such as Nicholas, Thomas and John, and are also described as recusants[418] just as the members of the (Butler-) Bowdon family of Chapel-en-le-Frith, Beighton Fields, Barlborough and Clowne, but none of them seem to fit to the dates of "our" Bowdons. Available sources do not reveal any common roots. It is not possible to find reliable references to any other Bowdons than the ones linked to Bowden Hall/Chapel-en-le-Frith on the copy of a family tree on parchment which Tony Bak holds for Barlborough Heritage and Resource Centre. However, Hayfield and New Mills are situated in close proximity to Chapel-en-le-Frith; hence it is difficult not to envision that the Hayfield Bowdens may have been a distant sideline, perhaps the "poor relatives" (court papers for example list a Thomas Bowden of Hayfield as yeoman for September 1634, and a Ralph Bowden as overseer for ca. 1689). The old place name "Bowden Middlecale", though obsolete today, contains the word "Bowden" which is intriguing as is the fact that there are more "Bowden" places in the vicinity such as the famous "Bowden Bridge"[419] and a "Bowden Lane" in Chapel-en-le-Frith. On the other hand, "Bowden" seems to be a quite common surname in Derbyshire, Cheshire and Lancashire to this day, so the occurrence of identical names may again just be a coincidence.

---

cope (see Chapter 19): "(...) the spelling of the original owner's is Butler-Bowdon when he (text refers to William Erdeswick Ignatius) signs letters; his name is mispellt (*sic!*) as Bowden in certain letters addressed to or about him in 1955." According to Philip Riden, it was John (6) Erdeswick Butler-Bowdon, Humphrey Butler-Bowdon's great-grandfather, who changed the spelling of the surname from Bowden to Bowdon; cf. Riden, *History of the County of Derby III*, p. 113; the spelling "Bowdon" however can be seen on various gravestones of family members of preceding generations at Beighton Fields Priory and Spinkhill cemetery (see Chapters 12 and 18).

417 Spencer, *Yesterday's Journeys, Law and Order*; http://www.tribalpages.com/tribe/familytree?uid=akfraser&surname=Bowden (viewed 12/07/2013) (the latter sources refer to the 19th and 20th centuries). The author of http://archiver.rootsweb.ancestry.com/th/read/CHESHIRE/2007-12/1196623064 (viewed 14/06/2013), Chris Bowden, says that he descends from a Bowden family from Hayfield and New Mills, which probably were Quakers.

418 Recusants were mainly members of the Roman Catholic Church who refused to conform to the Anglican doctrine and to attend services of the Church of England. They faced fines and punishments and were entered in the so-called "Recusant Rolls"; cf. Walker, *Church of the Immaculate Conception*, p. 7.

419 Bowden Bridge is the site near where the mass trespass of Kinder Scout started on April 24, 1932, a demonstration to make the public aware of the fact that walkers in England and Wales until then were denied access to areas of open country; its final result was the Countryside and Rights of Way Act 2000; cf. Glasby, *Mass Trespass on Kinder Scout*.

11. "I read the news today"[420] - Southgate in the Press

Between the years 1835 and 1899 Southgate Estate is mentioned in announcements in various newspapers.[421]

Henry (5) Bowdon's 21st birthday was celebrated with a jamboree, a party so impressive that it was mentioned in the Derbyshire Mercury on August 12, **1835**. A large party of relatives and friends were invited to Southgate House on the day in question, the festivities not being restricted to members of the family, but also including the tenants of Southgate Estate. 200 guests partook an excellent dinner under a canopy on the lawn with "the desirable accompaniment of ale, of very superior quality". Toasts were raised and speeches were made. The evening was spent with a "sumptuous dinner at the mansion", followed by a ball where "an excellent quadrille band was in attendance". The party lasted until the small hours of the next day. "The cannon planted in front of the house, was fired repeatedly during the day" and wives and family members of the tenants also did not miss out, they were treated to tea and refreshments at Beighton Fields and at Clowne.[422]

Pleasing news was announced in the London Morning Post on August 2, **1854**: the birth of a daughter to the Lady of Henry (5) Bowdon of Southgate House (= Alice E M Bowdon)[423], and the Nottingham Guardian on July 23, **1857** and The Derbyshire Times and Chesterfield Herald on July 25, 1857 report the birth of another daughter to Henry (5) and Harriet Bowdon on July 17, 1857 (= Constance M Bowdon).[424]

People knew how to celebrate in Clowne. The Derbyshire Times and Chesterfield Herald reports on April 22, **1871** on the occasion of the sick-club

---

420 Quote from the song "A Day in Life" written by John Lennon and Paul McCartney, from the Beatles' album "Sgt. Peppers Lonely Hearts Club Band" (1967).

421 These are only selected articles. The on-line database of http://www.britishnewspaperarchive.co.uk/ holds much more textual information.

422 Information courtesy of Tony Bak of Barlborough Heritage and Resource Centre. The cannon evidently had figured prominently. It belonged to a set of two cannons originally deriving from the residence of a certain Captain Eyre from the neighbouring village of Mosborough. They were removed to Southgate House under a Mr Bowdon, one of the Captain's executors, presumably Henry's father John (4) Butler-Bowdon; cf. Foster, *Description of Mosborough, Chapter I*. Ruby Thorpe also remembers the cannon in the front garden of Southgate House (information disclosed by E-mail by June Pearce after a personal meeting with Ruby Thorpe on March 25, 2014 and also during a personal meeting with the author in Clowne on April 27, 2014).

423 http://www.britishnewspaperarchive.co.uk/ (viewed 02/05/2014). I owe this hint to Alan Taylor (personal E-mail correspondence on May 2, 2014).

424 http://www.britishnewspaperarchive.co.uk/ (viewed 25/06/2013); baptised in 1857 in Carburton & Clowne; cf. http://www.findmypast.co.uk (Baptism Parish Records) (viewed 16/09/2013), Constance's elder sister Alice was baptised in 1854 in Carburton & Clowne, too.

meeting[425] in April 10, 1871 whose members first gathered at the Angel Inn in Clowne, and then proceeded to walk, accompanied by a brass band, in procession to the parish church where a small religious service took place, and were later regaled with beer by Henry (5) Bowdon at Southgate House and finished the day off with an opulent dinner. Toasts were raised, songs were sung and among others Henry Bowdon gave £1 as a subscription to the club.[426]

The marriage of John (6) Erdeswick Butler-Bowdon to Madeline Mary Wright receives a long and exhaustive article in The Derbyshire Times of February 10, **1877**.[427] Although the text of the article uses the occasion to describe at great lengths the history of the Butler-Bowdon family, the article's main intention is to report on an invitation to a dinner extended to the tenantry of the Butler-Bowdon family, hosted by the steward Mr G Unwin, Esq., of Whitwell. Many names of the participating male tenants such as Froggatt, Warriner, Ellis, Richardson, Garfitt et al. can be traced in the available resource material. Toasts were raised and good wishes were expressed on the occasion. The bride was described in a speech as someone who possessed "beauty of mind as well as dress". The feast was also used for political transactions including plans to developing Clowne into a thriving community when Shireoaks Colliery Company would soon reach the main coal and be able to introduce gas. The following day the tenants and their female family members received a special treatment when tea was provided, presided over by Mrs Unwin. A ball was hosted in the evening and a quadrille band from Worksop enlisted to provide enjoyable entertainment. At that time no one could anticipate that this marriage would not last long; Mary died in the same year.

On January 25, **1879** The Derbyshire Times and Chesterfield Herald announces an extensive auction sale of farming stock and agricultural produce of Southgate House, instructed by Colonel John (6) Erdeswick Butler-Bodon (*sic!*) for February 4, 1879 (see Chapter 8 and Figure 16).[428]

The newly renovated "Desirable Residence" of Southgate House is to let on December 27, **1882**. The advertisement in The Derbyshire Times and Chesterfield Herald gives a full description of the state of the layout of the building and the estate and, among other features, mentions a "three stall stable" which without doubt is Southgate Stables. It also says "saddle room" which would have been part of the same building (Figure 17).[429]

425 Sick-clubs were part of English Poor-law medicine with the aim to alleviate sickness amongst the labouring classes, cf. Toler T Maunsell, "Provident Dispensaries or Independent Sick Clubs".

426 http://www.britishnewspaperarchive.co.uk/ (viewed 25/06/2013).

427 http://www.britishnewspaperarchive.co.uk/ (viewed 25/06/2013).

428 http://www.britishnewspaperarchive.co.uk/ (viewed 29/10/2012).

429 http://www.britishnewspaperarchive.co.uk/ (viewed 29/10/2012).

The Manchester Courier and Lancashire General Advertiser reports on January 21, **1885** on a serious accident on ice on the pond of Southgate House on Sunday, January 18, 1885. Three people of Clowne, Samuel Hibbert, a collier, Albert Draper, a blacksmith, and Catherine Rounds, a domestic servant, lost their lives when the ice gave way (Figure 18).[430]

In **1897** the household furniture and effects of a Mrs C Smith of Southgate Cottages, who is retiring from her work as housekeeper, are announced to be sold by auction. This information was revealed by The Derbyshire Times and Chesterfield Herald on August 28, 1897 (Figure 19).[431]

The Fowler family, temporary inhabitants of Southgate House during the last decade of the 19th century, receive little attention throughout the whole research on Southgate Estate and in the number of records and sources consulted, but are at least referenced in the newspapers - mainly for peculiar incidents: on May 10, **1899** The Derbyshire Times and Chesterfield Herald reports the following: "Spare the Rod, Spoil[432] -" - Clowne Boys steal Ducklings and suffer accordingly. One good hiding is worth a dozen fines, where boys are offenders, although Samuel and Frank Smith, two Clowne lads may not be of the same opinion after their interview with a burly member of the County police force, who is a wonderful adept at wielding the birch-rod. These youngsters were summoned for stealing five ducklings, the property of Mr H. A. Fowler, of Southgate, at Eckington on Monday. Wm. Kennedy (11) told Major Butler-Bowdon and Mr. R. Eyre that about half-past five on the 2nd inst., he went and fed the poultry and missed five ducklings. He saw the two Smiths sitting on a fence, and they ran away when they saw him. He followed them and found the ducklings in their pockets. He took possession of the poultry and placed them in a coop with guard before it. Next morning the guard was moved, and three of the ducklings were missing. Sergt. Miles said he charged the lads with stealing the ducklings, and they said they had put them through the fence. He searched and found the three produced. Defendants were each ordered to receive six strokes with the birch rod, and the Magistrates advised them to be careful in the future."[433] Draconian measures!

---

430 http://www.britishnewspaperarchive.co.uk/ (viewed 29/10/2012). According to http://www.clownevillage.co.uk/history/history.html (viewed 10/07/2013), the pond in question was Bumpmill Pond at Harlesthorpe.

431 http://www.britishnewspaperarchive.co.uk/ (viewed 29/10/2012).

432 The complete saying would be "Spare the rod (and) spoil the child", but the newspaper article only gives an abbreviated quotation. The meaning of the saying is that children will only flourish by corporal punishment for their wrongdoings, the original notion deriving from the Bible, Proverbs 13:24: "He that spareth his rod hateth his son: but he that loveth him chasteneth him betimes".

433 http://www.britishnewspaperarchive.co.uk/ (viewed 25/06/2013); note the presence of Major (Lancelot G B) Butler-Bowdon, at that time residing at Barlborough House in Barlborough.

"Adding Injury to Insult - An Aggressive Barge Boy" titles The Derbyshire Times and Chesterfield Herald on November 8, **1899**.[434] "It was adding injury to insult the way Harry Piggott, a canal boat lad, of Worksop, treated Mr Wm. Ed. Nesfield Fowler, on Sunday. In the afternoon of that day Mr Fowler was told by his father's lad, Wm. Kennedy, that some lads were throwing stones at some tame pheasants on the lawn of Southgate House, Clowne. Mr Fowler went out and saw Piggott. He asked him his name, and he gave that of Fred Johnson. He said he came from Staveley, but not giving satisfactory answers to questions. Mr Fowler said he would telephone Staveley and see if this was correct. On hearing this the lad made off, and Mr Fowler went after him. When they had gone about five yards, Piggott turned and struck at his pursuer with his stick. Mr Fowler closed with him and Piggott struck him twice with his fists. He was ecured (*sic!*), but would not give any name and address and was taken to the police station. At Eckington on Monday he was charged with assaulting Mr Fowler, and on pleading guilty was fined 5s and the costs."

In order to give an impression of what a Justice of the Peace, in this case Lancelot George B Butler-Bowdon, had to deal with at a local Petty Session[435] during the 19th century, I collected some additional example newspaper articles from the years 1885, 1886 and 1888.[436] The Derby Daily Telegraph of July 6, **1885** reports on a bar fight between two patrons (both colliers) of the Duke of York public house in Eckington, who argued outside in front of the establishment and which ended up in a brutal physical assault of one of the men involved against the other. The prisoner was sentenced by Mr Butler-Bowdon and his colleagues to "£30 15s., including costs". Another article illustrates the boundless stupidity of reckless men. With noticeable relish The Derbyshire Times and Chesterfield Herald gives an account on September 18, **1886** of a "mad freak", in fact an employee of the Postal Telegraph Department, walking on telegraph wires at Dronfield. The man walked along the telegraph wires from one post to the next, "there being two rows of wires, he had got in between, with one foot on each of the bottom wires. Then holding on by the higher wires, he walked along from one post to another". His high-wire act attracted quite a crowd of spectators, but the stunt was brought to a sudden end by the appearance of a local Dronfield police constable passing by on his duty round. Mr Butler-Bowdon and his colleague

---

[434] http://www.britishnewspaperarchive.co.uk/ (viewed 25/06/2013).

[435] Petty Sessions were courts of summary jurisdiction where minor crimes and routine businesses were dealt with by two or more local Justices (of the Peace). Petty Sessions were replaced by Magistrate Courts in 1974, cf. http://cambridgeshire.gov.uk/leisure/archives/catalogue/holdings/m_p/pettysessions.htm (viewed 09/09/2013).

[436] All four articles retrieved from http://www.findmypast.co.uk (British Newspapers 1710-1965) (viewed 04/09/2013).

fined the man *in absentia* 40s. and costs. The Derbyshire Times and Chesterfield Herald report on November 11, **1888** on a case of bigamy and the accused person, a collier of Eckington, who preferred to not be present at his court hearing, absconded without marrying the prosecutrix whom he had promised to marry unlawfully. The same newspaper informs its readers three days later, on November 27, **1888** about a case of poaching in Barlborough. A farm labourer and a collier stood convicted of trespassing in pursuit of game. They behaved extremely stupidly when caught in the act by the landowner's game keeper, giving themselves away. A financial penalty of 5s. each and costs were inflicted on both culprits.

11.1. "Stop all the Clocks"[437] - Obituary Notices

A few selected obituaries published in various local newspapers from 1875, 1850, 1907, 1909, 1912, 1929 and 1937 shed a light not only on death but also on life at Southgate Estate, Clowne, Barlborough and other surrounding villages.

The demise of Henry (5) Bowdon is announced in the Derbyshire Courier of May 5, **1875** (and by an identical text in The Derbyshire Times and Chesterfield Herald on May 8, 1875): "We regret to announce the death of Henry Bowdon, Esq., J. P., which took place about ten o'clock on Monday evening, at his residence, Southgate House, near Chesterfield. Mr. Bowdon had been rather unwell for some weeks, but nothing serious was anticipated by any of his family. He attended the Petty Sessions at Eckington, a week last Monday, and on Friday he was somewhat suddenly seized with an attack of bronchitis, confining him to his room. Dr. Fleming, of Harthill, the medical attendant to the family, was sent for, but the unfortunate gentleman rapidly grew worse, and expired on Monday evening as above stated. Mr. Bowdon was of a very ancient Catholic family, and was a magistrate, and Deputy Lieutenant for Derbyshire, having been placed on the Commission of the Peace in 1842, during which year his father served as High Sheriff of the County. He was the senior magistrate of this division, and had for a great number of years attended the Eckington Petty Sessions as chairman. He was a Liberal in politics, but did not take an active part in political affairs. The deceased gentleman was much respected by all classes of the community, more especially by his tenancy and the poor, by whom he will be long and affectionately remembered. Mr. Bowdon was in his 61st year, and leaves a widow and two daughters."[438]

The Derbyshire Times and Chesterfield Herald reports on May 12, **1875** on the funeral of Henry (5) Bowdon. This was probably one of the most elaborate

---

437 From the poem "Funeral Blues" by Wystan Hugh Auden (1936); cf. Fuller, *W. H. Auden*, p. 21.

438 Information courtesy of Tony Bak of Barlborough Heritage and Resource Centre on the occasion of a personal visit in Barlborough on April 20, 2013.

funeral ceremonies Clowne ever witnessed (Figure 20): "Funeral of H. Bowden (*sic!*), Esq., J. P. The remains of the late Henry Bowdon, Esq., were interred on Friday in the private burial ground of the family, at Beighton Fields Preory (*sic!*), near Barlborough. The funeral cortege left Southgate House at half-past ten and reached Spinkhill Church an hour later, when solemn high mass was celebrated. The procession then reformed, and proceeded slowly to Beighton Fields, which was reached about one o'clock. The Body of the deceased gentleman was enclosed in three coffins, the second being a lead one. The outer one bore the following inscription: - "Pray for the soul of Henry Bowden (*sic!*), of Southgate House, born in 1814, died 1875." The Requiem having been sung by the choiristers (*sic!*) the body was lowered to the grave. The procession was a very large one, and was proceded (*sic!*) by twenty constables of the Eckington division, under the command of Superintendent Cruitt. The chief mourners were Colonel and Captain Bowden (*sic!*) of Pleasington Hall, Lancashire, Captain Blunt, Reading; and J. Carrington Wright, Esq., of Kelvedon Hall, Essex. There was (*sic!*) five mourning coaches and many private carriages. Amongst those in the procession we noticed the Rev. E. B. Estcourt, Eckington; the Rev. M. Stapylton, Barlborough; Dr. Fleming, Harthill, &c. A vast concourse of people has assembled to pay their last tribute of respect to the deceased gentleman - Beighton Fields Priory as its name implies, was at one time a monastery, and has been in the Bowdon family for many generations. The burial ground is in the garden, and tablets are erected to those buried there. The following inscription is to be seen: - "Through all adversity they ever remained steadfast to the faith of the forefathers." The undertaker was Mr. Ald. Grundy, of Sheffield, and the carriages supplied by the Sheffield Carriage Company."[439]

The report on Henry (5) Bowdon's funeral immediately brings Wystan Hugh Auden's beautiful and sad poem "Funeral Blues" (written in 1936) to mind, whose first stanza echoes Victorian mourning traditions: "Stop all the clocks, cut off the telephone / Prevent the dog from barking with a juicy bone / Silence the pianos and with muffled drum / Bring out the coffin, let the mourners come." Many details in the press announcement mirror a typical Victorian era funeral and mourning process. Funeral processions were a daily occurrence at that time and grandiose funeral rituals characterised British society during the Victorian era, although admittedly funerals of the British aristocracy have always been occasions for displaying pomp and ceremony. Death, today a rather private matter, was a public one in the Victorian era. Rituals of mourning, obsolete in our day, were of highest importance of in the late 19th century; there was a great social pressure to pay respect to the deceased and to grief publicly. During the reign of Queen Victoria people usually died in their homes, surrounded by family and friends, and the corpse stayed in the home until burial, and it was here that the traditional vigil was

---

439 http://www.britishnewspaperarchive.co.uk/ (viewed 29/10/2012).

held. After a person had passed away, a ritualised process of mourning commenced whereupon all rituals connected to burying people, immortalising them and remembering the dead, had to be observed closely.[440] This included, among many other things, preparing the interior of the house according to the customs of the time (e.g. covering mirrors and furnishing portraits of the deceased with black crepe, tightly closing curtains and blinds). Females in particular, considered to be the "true vessels of grief" as ones able to express their inner feelings, had to adhere to certain dress codes, such as wearing a "mourning dress" made of crepe and in dark or muted colours.

Encasing the deceased in as many as three coffins, the middle coffin being of lead, sounds very impressive. However, encasing the corpse in three coffins was standard procedure among the better-off in society in Victorian times. The inner coffin was usually made of elm, and was lined with choice textiles. The middle one was made of lead, was soldered and carried an inscription plaque. Finally, the outer case was made of oak, and carried another richly engraved inscription plate made of brass. It was panelled with brass nails, adorned with brass handles and grips and other corresponding lid ornaments, and covered in velvet.[441] Therefore, every particular of Henry (5) Bowdon's funeral complied with a proper upper class Victorian funeral. However, 47 years later the discovery Tutankhamen's tomb in 1922 resulted in an obsession throughout British society with everything Egyptian, and so the description in the newspaper may inspire today's reader to think of the several magnificent coffins that encased the pharaoh's mummy. The labelling inscription on the outer coffin adds to that impression. In Victorian society death was celebrated, so it is not for nothing that Victorian burial customs are often compared to those of the ancient Egyptians and that grave monuments were frequently adorned with Egyptianesque elements.[442]

On December 21, **1850** the Derbyshire Courier announces the death of John (4) Peter Bruno Bowdon: "Deaths. On Tuesday, the 17th inst., at Southgate House, in the county of Derby, John Bruno Bowdon, Esq., in the sixty-fourth year of his age. Mr Bowdon filled the office of High Sheriff of this county in 1841, and was universally respected and esteemed."[443]

The second wife of John (6) Butler-Bowdon, Monica Mary Petre Butler-Bowdon, passed away on May 15, 1907 as reported by the Worksop Guardian on May 17, **1907**: "Death of Mrs. Butler Bowdon, of Clowne. After a prolonged illness, the death took place early on Wednesday morning of Mrs Butler

---

440 http://www.nps.gov/jofl/historyculture/stories.htm, containing MourningArticle2011.rtf (viewed 04/06/2013); http://www.avictorian.com/mourning.html (viewed 11/06/2014).

441 Alirangues, *Funerary Practices in the Victorian Era.*

442 Alirangues, *Funerary Practices in the Victorian Era.*

443 Information courtesy of Tony Bak of Barlborough Heritage and Resource Centre on the occasion of a personal visit in Barlborough on April 20, 2013.

Bowdon, wife of Colonel Butler Bowdon, of Southgate House, Clowne. It is a little over five years ago since her son arrived from South Africa[444], the war then being in progress, the young lieutenant bearing the marks of keen suffering. This is known to have - and, of course, naturally been a source of considerable anxiety to Mrs Butler Bowdon, but a greater trouble came about two years ago, when news arrived of the death of a younger son, who was out in South Africa[445], and there is no doubt that these distresses have hastened Mrs Bowdon's end. The deceased lady seldom participated in any public functions, but nevertheless, she was ever ready to assist in anything which was for the betterment of the place, and the lot of many has been brightened as the result of her thoughtful and kindly acts - acts which were always characterised by unostentation. She will be much missed. Col. Butler Bowdon and the members of his family have the sympathy of Clowne people in their bereavement."[446]

A short account of Monica Mary Petre Butler-Bowdon's funeral was published a few days later in Worksop Guardian on May 24, **1907**: "The Late Hon. Mrs. Butler-Bowdon. The remains of the late Hon. Mrs Butler-Bowdon, of Southgate House, Clowne, whose death was our melancholy duty to announce last week, were interred at Mount St. Mary's Churchyard, Spinkhill, on Whit-Monday morning. The beautiful church was very full, the large number present testifying to the great regard entertained for the deceased lady. Requiem Mass was sung, after which the burial took place. The following were present: - Colonel Butler-Bowdon, Captain Butler-Bowdon, Mr Basil Butler-Bowdon, Miss Angela Butler-Bowdon, Miss Gladys Butler-Bowdon, Miss Wisula (*sic!*)[447] Butler-Bowdon, Miss Isabel Butler-Bowdon, Mr and Hon. Mrs Stapleton-Bretherton, the Hon. Katherine Petre, Mr Cecil Trafford, Mr Bruno Butler-Bowdon, Mr John Butler-Bowdon, the Hon. Mrs L Butler-Bowdon, and servants. Many other members of the family were unavoidably prevented from attending. A large number of tenants and others were present. Wreaths were sent by Colonel Butler-Bowdon and family, Mr B. Butler-Bowdon, the Earl and Countess of Granard, Mr. and Hon. Mrs. E. S.

---

[444] The source is referring to William Erdeswick Butler-Bowdon; cf. a newspaper article titled "Heroes Every One" in Worksop Guardian dated January 11, 1918 (information disclosed in a private E-mail correspondence between Tony Bak and the author on June 25, 2013). W E I Butler-Bowdon went to South Africa in November 1899 and served there for two and a half years. His return to Clowne and Barlborough was celebrated with a great reception at Southgate.

[445] The source is referring to Leonard Joseph Bruno Butler-Bowdon who "succumbed to enteric while engaged at the Government Farm in South Africa"; cf. Derbyshire Courier Report October 26th, 1918 & The Royal Fusiliers Report 21st February, 2007.

[446] Information courtesy of Tony Bak of Barlborough Heritage and Resource Centre on the occasion of a personal visit in Barlborough on April 20, 2013.

[447] Misspelling for Ursula.

Trafford, the Hon. Katherine Petre, Signor[448] and Madame Del Monaco[449], Mr and Mrs Radcliffe, Mr and Mrs Verelst[450], Mr and Mrs Gainsford, Mr and Hon. Mrs. Harding, Mr. Warrener and family, and the servants at Southgate. Messrs John Walsh & Co., Ltd., Sheffield, conducted the funeral arrangements."[451]

A great loss for the parish of Barlborough was the death of Lancelot George B Butler-Bowdon two years later, on Sunday, September 12, **1909**. The Worksop Guardian of September 17, 1909 dedicates a long obituary to him (together with a portrait photograph): "Death of Major L. G. Butler Bowdon. Barlborough's loss. It is with very sincere regret that we announce this week the death of Major Lancelot George Butler Bowdon, of Barlborough House, Barlborough, which occurred on Sunday afternoon. The news of his death caused quite a shock in the neighbourhood of Barlborough and Eckington, where no man was more respected and esteemed. For about five years the Major has been ailing, suffering from Bright's disease[452], but with the exception of a period about last Christmas, when he was obliged to take to his bed for a considerable time, he has pluckily gone about attending to his

---

448 Ireneo Del Monaco originally came from Roccaraso near L'Aquila, Abruzzi, born ca. 1852 according to the 1911 census of England and Wales, listed as resident of Barlborough, Nottinghamshire on April 2, 1911; cf. http://search.ancestry.co.uk/cgi-bin/sse.dll?gl=ukicen&rank=1&new=1&so=3&MSAV=0&msT=1&gss=ms_f-80&gsln=De%20monaco&uidh=000 (viewed 05/08/2013).

449 Ireneo Paolo and Alice Elizabeth Del Monaco; Alice is the elder daughter of Henry (5) Bowdon.

450 This refers to the Verelst family of Aston Hall in Aston. The Flemish name is conspicuous and indeed the family originates from Antwerp, Belgium. Simon (John) Verelst, a painter in the court of Charles II, and his brother Harman, also an artist, settled in England in the 17th century. The latter was the great-grandfather of Harry Verelst Esq. (1834-1875) who was colonial administrator of the East Indian Company and governor of Fort William in Bengal between 1749 and 1769 and made a fortune there. He purchased a part of Aston Hall Estate and built his residence, Aston Hall, there around 1772. A portrait painting of Harry Verelst's wife Anne (daughter of Josiah Wordsworth of Wadworth Hall) by George Romney is kept at Clifton Museum, Rotherham. Harry Verelst and Lancelot George Butler-Bowdon both were County Magistrates for Eckington Petty Sessional Division, so here the connection to the Butler-Bowdon family can be found. The census returns of 1881 list a Harry William Verelst (b. 1847, unmarried at that time) as inhabitant of Aston Hall. The Verelsts gave up Aston Hall in 1928 (10 years before the Butler-Bowdons sold Southgate Estate) and the estate was broken up into several lots. The house today is a luxury hotel. The family grave can be found in the churchyard of All Saints Church in Aston; cf. http://www.rotherhamweb.co.uk/genealogy/verelst.htm (viewed 21/11/2013); Kelly's *Directory*, p. 277ff.; Newbold, *Aston Hall*.

451 Information courtesy of Tony Bak of Barlborough Heritage and Resource Centre on the occasion of a personal visit in Barlborough on April 20, 2013.

452 Kidney disease, acute or chronic nephritis.

manifold duties as a Parish and District Councillor, and a Justice of the Peace. Only a month ago he presided over the Eckington Bench, and observations were made that day as to the welcome improvement of his appearance. Shortly after that, however, his illness re-asserted itself, and last Wednesday he was obliged to take to his bed, and died, as stated on Sunday, about three o'clock in the afternoon. The deceased gentleman, who was in his 58th year, came of an old Derbyshire family, whose pedigree dates back to the Norman era. He was, however, born at Pleasington Hall, Lancashire, where his father had an estate, and where the family had lived for many years. Upon the death of his father, together with his brother, Col. Butler Bowdon, he returned to the county of his forbears, the former to reside at Southgate, Clowne, while he purchased Barlborough House. In 1879 he married the Hon. Ella, daughter of Mr. Clifton and Baroness Grey de Ruthyn, a cousin of the late Duchess of Norfolk, and they have one son, Mr. J. B. Butler-Bowdon. For many years he was connected with the North Staffordshire Militia, holding the commission of Captain, and he retired with the honorary rank of Major. At the coronation of King Edward he was one of the Gold Staffs. Major Bowdon took a considerable interest in municipal and parochial matters. He had been a Justice of the Peace for about 30 years, and, excepting Mr. J. F. Swallow, was the senior magistrate on the Eckington Bench, where his geniality and general bonhomie, together with the fact that he always tempered justice with mercy, made him a popular magistrate. He was one of the first County Councillors for Derbyshire, retiring at the last election; a member of the Worksop Board of Guardians and the Clowne Rural District Council; a member of the Eckington and District School Board, manager of the Spinkhill Roman Catholic School, and Chairman of the Barlborough Parish Council since its inception. He signalised this position each year by inviting his colleagues to dinner, a hospitality which was much appreciated by them and at which the utmost good feeling prevailed. Of late years his illness had prevented him giving the attention to these duties which he desired, but he was very faithful in his attendance at the Parish and District Council meetings where his observations had always the merit of good sense and common respect. His sympathies with the poor and suppressed were strong, and no deserving case failed to find assistance at his hands. To those in his own neighbourhood who, for petty offences, found themselves in the hands of the law, he was practically the common legal adviser. No sooner was the summons served for some small offence, than a call was made on the "Major", whose advise, - consistent with his duty as magistrate, was always at the disposal of the culprit. In politics he was a Conservative of a strong type, with a smattering of the old Tory, and a hearty dislike for Socialist theories.[453] He was a devout and earnest Roman

[453] Hobsbawm, *Industry and Empire*, p. 110: "In 1870 Britain had been Liberal. The bulk of the British bourgeoisie, the bulk of the political conscious working class, and even the old Whig section of the landed aristocracy found their political and ideological

Catholic, constant in his worshipping at Mount St. Mary's at Spinkhill. In the village of Barlborough he was held in the highest respect; by the children he was beloved, and the tiniest "nipper" got a smile and an encouraging word from him. To the poor his memory will long be dear; he was truly a man who never let his left hand know what his right did[454], and many a humble cottage will regret his loss. The Funeral. With elaborate ceremonial of the Roman Catholic Church, the interment took place yesterday morning at Spinkhill Church, near Eckington, when both at that village and at Barlborough there were evidences on every hand of the high respect and esteem in which the deceased gentleman was held. In Barlborough almost every blind was drawn, the shops had put up their shutters, and the village showed to the full its realization of the loss it has sustained. Practically the same obtained at Spinkhill, and long before the body arrived at the Church, the edifice and its environments were crowded with residents desirous of paying their last tribute of respect. The coffin was conveyed on a hearse, which was followed by a number of coaches, and the cortege arrived at the Church gates shortly after eleven o'clock, where it was met by the Rector of St. Mary's, Spinkhill, Father Lucas, Fathers Hague and Colchester, and others of the College staff, together with the choir of the college. The coffin was borne on a bier into the chancel of the Church, where it rested between a row of lighted candles. The service, which was a lengthy one, was conducted by Father Lucas, with Father Hague as Deacon and Father Colchester as Sub-deacon. Father Smith acted as Master of the Ceremonies. A Requiem Mass was sung by the College choir to a plain chant setting, and the offertory was Mendellsohn's (*sic!*) "*Beati Mortui*" As the body was taken from the Church, "*In Paradisum*" was sung to plain song; and it was repeated at the grave-side, where the "*Benedictus*" was also sung. Much of the music was unaccompanied, but Mr. Roger Fisher presided at the organ in the accompanied numbers, and played the "Dead March" (*Saul*)[455] at the conclusion of the service. The Church was appropriately draped in black for the occasion, and the chancel was beautifully decorated with palms and flowers. At the conclusion of the Mass, English prayers were said by Father Lucas, and a procession was then formed to the grave-side, consisting of the crucifier, the clergy, choir, the students of St. Mary's College,

---

expression in the party of William Ewart Gladstone. (…) By the middle of the 1890s the great Liberal Party was split, virtually of all its aristocrats and a large section of its capitalists having seceded to the Conservatives or the 'Liberal Unionists' who were to fuse with the Conservatives.", but "An independent Labour Party backed by the trade unions and inspired by socialists was about to appear."

454 This is a passage in the New Testament: Matthew 6:1-4: "(…) 3. But when you do a charitable deed, do not let your left hand know what your right hand is doing 4. that your charitable deed may be in secret; and your Father who sees in secret will Himself reward you openly."

455 "Dead March" from the oratorio "Saul" by Georg Friedrich Händel from 1738 (HWV 53), a typical funeral march.

including the members of the Society of Sodalists[456], with which the deceased was associated, the chief mourners, and friends. A circuitous route was taken to the grave, and this was lined by the children of the Spinkhill schools, and there was a huge gathering in the Churchyard. The committal portion of the service was read by Father Lucas, and the obsequies were terminated by the nearer relatives casting soil on the coffin, as is customary in the faith. The mourners were as follows:- In the first carriage, the widow, Col. Butler Bowdon (brother), Mr. Bruno Butler Bowdon (brother), and Mr. J. B. Butler Bowdon (son); the second carriage, the Duke of Norfolk, Lord Loudoun, and Lady Maud Hastings; third carriage, Miss Stapleton, Miss Figurelli, and Nurse Fenton. Also following were the servants at Barlborough House, Father Winder, Dr. Clark, Major Tudor, Mr. H. Fowler, Miss Fowler, and Mr. Cecil Fowler, Mrs. Crow and family. The Eckington Magistrates were represented by Mr. J. H. Wells and Mr. J. J. Hounsfield; the Barlborough Parish Council by Messrs. J. H. Clarkson, T. Ball, J. Rushworth, W. F. Gilbert, J. G. Hopkinson, W. Hutchins, and Jos. Robinson (clerk). Mr. John Eaton and Mr. C. Robinson represented the Clowne Rural District Council, and Mrs. Charles Robinson the managers of the Barlborough Council schools. Representing the Bowdon Pride Lodge of the Rotherham Equalised Druids[457], in their regalia, were

---

[456] Sodality (also known as a "union of prayer" or a confraternity) is a designation for a voluntary lay ecclesial movement within the Roman Catholic Church aiming for Christian charity or piety; cf. Knight, *Confraternity (Sodality)*; Knight, *Sodality*.

[457] According to Tony Bak, a former order of Druid religion in Barlborough, the secretary having been a Ben Crooks and having had some 180 members in the early 1900s (information disclosed in a private E-mail correspondence with the author on July 9, 2013); http://www.treetonweb.co.uk/features/org.htm (viewed 03/06/2013): Order of Druids (Rotherham Equalised District), founded June 30, 1888 by a Dr. Kenny. Ben Crooks is depicted as gardener in front of Southgate House on one of the old black and white photographs that exist of Southgate House (Figure 5). For the origins of druids and their rule in ancient society see Oliver, *Ancient Britain*, p. 331f. (referring to the research of Miranda Green, Cardiff University). In olden times (Iron Age) druids were advisors to the kings, acting like Old Testament prophets with their accredited abilities to see or to divine the future. They were more important than tribal leaders or kings as they overarched society, being connected on a supra-regional level all across Europe. They were respected and feared for their abilities. In their hands lay the conduction of religious ceremonies. However, what made them most arcane was that their secret knowledge was never written down, but was learned by heart and was passed on orally. Neo-Druidism has its roots in the Romanticist movement of 18th century Britain which highly revered ancient Celtic traditions of the Iron Age. The early 20th century saw modern druids developing fraternal organisations which were modelled on Freemason's lodges and which drew on ideas of romantic figures of British Druids and Bards as symbols of British spirituality. Apart from being organised fraternally a number of these groups were solely cultural, reimagining traditions from the collective consciousness of Britain; others merged together with other movements

Messrs. R. Kirk, G. Wells, G. Grundy, G. Crookes (sec.), Hy. Bagshaw, and Hy. Moore, and the general mourners included the Rev B. Darley (Harthill), Dr. Cummings, Canon Molineaux (Staveley), Dr. Clark (Anston), Mr. R. Davies (Clowne), Dr. Spencer, Mr. E. C. Tinker, Mr. Fred Barber, Supt. Andrews, Sergt. Hewitt, Mr. Harold Thompson, Mr. G. Johnson, Mr. E. Short, Mr. A. E. Hall (Eckington), Miss H. Stapleton, Messrs. H. Aves, W. Purser, G. H. Buxton, R. Buxton, J. Swift, B. Gosling, A. Warrener[458], G. Johnson, J. Hawkins, W. Clark and the Barlborough Cricket Club, of which the late Major was a patron, was represented by Messrs. A. W. Morris, W. Hazelby, and J. Turner. As the funeral procession passed through Barlborough the school children lined the streets, being under the charge of Mr. D. J. Barnfather, and at Barlborough House the flag of the Bowdon family flew at half-mast. The whole of the funeral arrangements were in the hands of Messrs. Walsh of Sheffield. Floral tributes were sent by the following: - The widow, Mrs. Locker-Lampson, Mr. and Mrs. J. F. Swallow, Mrs. Walker (Derby), Mr. and Mrs. Brailsford, Dr. Clark, Mr. and Mrs. Collins, Mr. and Mrs. Crow, the teachers and scholar of Spinkhill schools, teachers and scholars of Barlborough Council and Infant Schools, members of the Barlborough Parish Council, the Bowdon Pride Lodge, Rotherham Equalised Druids, Nurse Fenton, Mr. and Mrs. Hy. Thompson, Mr. and Mrs. T. Ball, Mr. and Mrs. J. H. Clarkson, the managers of the Barlborough schools, Mr. and Mrs. Faulkner, Mrs. J. Buxton and family, Mr. Sampson (Sheffield), the maids at Barlborough House, Mr. and Mrs. Richard Buxton, Mr. and Mrs. Aves, members of the Barlborough Hospital Committee, Supt. Andrews and police officers at Clowne, and a few friends. Public references to the late Major Butler Bowdon appear elsewhere in the issue."[459]

A eulogy for Lancelot George B Butler-Bowdon is also published in the Worksop Guardian on September 17, **1909** in the context of a monthly Clowne Council meeting: "The Late Major Bowden (*sic!*). Before the ordinary business of the meeting was proceeded with, the Chairman moved that a resolution of sympathy with the relatives of the late Major Butler Bowden (*sic!*). As long as Major Bowden (*sic!*) has been a member of the Council, he said, he had taken an interest in the work, and had done his best to get to the meetings. Mr. Robinson said they were all aware Major Bowden (*sic!*) had been a great sufferer for many years, and, though he had not attended all the meetings of the Council, he had taken a great interest in the work. All the parishioners of

happening at that time; cf. http://en.wikipedia.org/wiki/Neo-Druidism (viewed 14/06/2014).

458 Mr A Warrener held some agricultural land of Southgate Estate as a leaseholder in 1909/1910 and later on; cf. Book of References of Land Values Map, Derbyshire Record Office, *Ref. No. D595* and Electoral Rolls (see Chapters 8 and 16).

459 Information courtesy of Tony Bak of Barlborough Heritage and Resource Centre on the occasion of a personal visit in Barlborough on April 20, 2013.

Barlborough held him in highest esteem, and anyone who had approached him, either for advice or help, had not been sent empty away. He had been a real friend to the parish, and would be missed very much indeed. No gentleman in the whole county of Derby would be missed in his district so much as the late Major Bowden (*sic!*) would be in theirs'. As the colleague of the deceased gentleman, he begged to second the resolution. Mr. Eaton said he had probably had more experience of Major Bowden (*sic!*) in public life than any other member of the Council. He had met him for the last 22 years on one public body or another, and during the whole of that time he had worked most harmoniously with his colleagues, and he (Mr. Eaton) had always found him a most courteous, kind-hearted, and gentlemanly man. He re-echoed Mr. Robinson's word, so far as his own village was concerned, that Major Bowden (*sic!*) would be a much-missed man. He had attended that Council many times when he had no business to leave his own home, because he was anxious to show his interest in their work. So far as his health would allow, Major Bowden hat attended to his duties well, and he was extremely sorry for the necessity for such a resolution. (...)" The congregation expressed its sympathy and respect towards the deceased by standing up.[460] In all probability this burial ceremony was one of the biggest funeral events Barlborough and Spinkhill ever witnessed. The loss of the village's most notable inhabitant of that time led to a ceremony which again brought to life the manifold Victorian traditions of funeral ceremonies and mourning.

1912 was another fateful year for the Butler-Bowden family when Ella Cicely Mary Butler-Bowdon passed away on July 2, **1912**. The Worksop Guardian published an obituary on Ella Cicely Mary Butler-Bowdon on July 5, 1912: "Death of Hon. Mrs. Butler-Bowdon. A Loss to Barlborough. It is with great regret that we have to report the death, which took place at her residence, Barlborough House, on Tuesday morning, in her 55th year, of a popular and highly respected lady, in the person of the Hon. Mrs. E. C. Butler-Bowdon, widow of the late Major Butler-Bowdon. The deceased lady, who came to the village about 30 years ago, and who lived all her married life in Barlborough, was elder daughter of Mr. Clifton and the late Baroness Grey de Ruthyn, of Warton Hall, Lytham. She was cousin to Lady Flora Hastings, the present Duke of Norfolk's first wife. Of a most kindly disposition, Mrs. Butler-Bowdon was noted for her many acts of charity, and her generosity will be much missed in the village. She leaves one son Mr. J. W. L. Butler-Bowdon, who has the deepest sympathy of his many friends in the district. The funeral takes place to-day (Friday) at Spinkhill, at 11 a.m."[461] The announcement is

---

460 Information courtesy of Tony Bak of Barlborough Heritage and Resource Centre on the occasion of a personal visit in Barlborough on April 20, 2013.

461 Information courtesy of Tony Bak of Barlborough Heritage and Resource Centre on the occasion of a personal visit in Barlborough on April 20, 2013.

concluded with a post-mortem portrait (photograph) of the deceased dressed in black and with a black head covering.[462]

The Worksop Guardian from July 12, **1912**[463] reports on the funeral of the "Hon. Mrs Butler-Bowdon. Funeral ceremony at Spinkhill. Amidst general manifestations of regret, the funeral of the late Hon. Mrs. Butler-Bowdon took place at Spinkhill on Friday. The chief mourners were: - Mr. J. W. L. Butler-Bowdon (son), Col. and Mrs. Butler-Bowdon, and Miss Butler-Bowdon, the Duke of Norfolk, Lady Bellingham, Lord Louden, Lady Maud Hastings, Miss Kirwan, Mr. H. A. Fowler[464], Miss Fowler, Dr. Clarke, Nurse Sharp, Nurse Plumb, Mrs. Griffiths, Miss Knight, Mr. and Mrs. Arkwright, Mrs. Jackson etc. The service was taken by the Rev. Father Lucas, and was choral. The floral tributes[465] were from the deceased lady's son, Col. and Mrs. Butler-Bowdon, Lady Bellingham, Marquis and Marchioness of Bute, Duke of Norfolk, Lord Louden, Lady Maud Hastings, Mr. and Mrs. Bruno Butler-Bowdon, Mrs. Swallow, Miss Kirwan, Rev. J. D. and Mrs. Griffiths, the children and teachers at Spinkhill Schools, Mrs. Thompson and family, Mr. Reynolds, Mr. and Mrs. Moorhouse, Mr. and Mrs. Baker, Mr. and Mrs. W. Arkwright, Mrs. Jackson, "All at Marton Hall", Mr. R. Buxton and family, Nurses Sharp and Plumb, Miss Knight, Mr. and Mrs. Pepper, Mr. and Mrs. Crowe and family, "All at Barlborough Post Office", "Talbot and Violet", "Fanny and Edith"." Considering the illustrious mourners at the funeral along with family members and local people and the volume of the expressions of sympathy, Ella Cicely Butler-Bowden must have been a valued member of the parish, and well-liked throughout all social classes.

The "Death of Colonel Butler-Bowden (*sic!*) - Chairman of Eckington Justices" was announced on the front page of the Derby Daily Telegraph on January 3, **1929**.[466] "Colonel J. E. Butler-Bowden (*sic!*) died yesterday at his residence, Southgate House, Clowne, in his 79th year. For many years he represented the district o(f) th(e) Derbyshire County Council. He was also chairman of the Eckington bench of magistrates, his other public engagements including membership of the Worksop Board of Guardians, the Clowne Rural

---

462 Mourning or deathbed portraits were originally a popular Victorian tradition; cf. http://www.nps.gov/jofl/historyculture/stories.htm, containing MourningArticle2011.rtf, p. 2 (viewed 04/06/2013).

463 Information courtesy of Tony Bak of Barlborough Heritage and Resource Centre on the occasion of a personal visit in Barlborough on April 20, 2013.

464 Harry Aldam Fowler, tenant of Southgate House in 1891 with his family (see Chapter 8).

465 Laying flowers in and around the coffin and sending flowers to honour the dead were also originally a popular Victorian practice; cf. http://www.nps.gov/jofl/historyculture/stories.htm, containing MourningArticle2011.rtf, p. 2 (viewed 04/06/2013).

466 http://www.findmypast.co.uk (British Newspapers 1710-1965) (viewed 04/09/2013).

District Council, and the local Pensions and Education Committees. His eldest son was killed in the South African War, and his youngest son in the Great War. He leaves a widow, who was his third wife, and a family of one son and five daughters."

The passing of "Mrs. M. Butler-Bowdon, Former Clowne resident" and third wife and widow of John (6) Erdeswick Butler-Bowdon is made public in The Derbyshire Times of September 17, **1937**[467]: "The older generation of Clowne and Spinkhill will regret to hear of the death which took place in London on Thursday last, of Mrs. Monica Butler-Bowdon, widow of Col. J. E. Butler-Bowdon, J. P., D. L., Southgate House, Clowne. Mrs. Butler-Bowdon, who was in her 86th year, was a daughter of Mr. Herman Walmsley, Gidlow Hall, Lancashire, and was married to Col. Butler-Bowdon in 1909. She was his third wife. During her 20 years' residence at Southgate House, she endeared herself to all who had the pleasure of her acquaintance. The body was removed to Spinkhill Church in Friday, and was buried in the local churchyard on Saturday.[468] Mass was said by Father Gregson, S. J., who also officiated at the graveside. The mourners were Col. W. E. I. Butler-Bowdon (step-son) and Mrs. Butler-Bowdon, Miss de Trafford and Miss Mostyn (nieces), the Rev. Robt. de Trafford, Mr. Herman de Trafford, Mr. Francis Weld (nephews), Mr. J. L. W. Butler-Bowdon, J. P., Mr. W. Burman (estate agent), Mr. and Mrs. Liddy and Mr. Ives[469]. Flowers were sent by all the mourners."

12. "Knockin' on Heaven's Door"[470] - Spinkhill Cemetery

The churchyard of the Church of the Immaculate Conception at Spinkhill Lane, Spinkhill is not only the final resting place of Monica Mary Petre Butler-Bowdon (d. 1907 aged 47), but also of Lancelot George B Butler-Bowdon (d. 1909 aged 58) and his wife Ella Cicely Mary Butler-Bowdon (d. 1912 aged 54) and Mary Monica Butler-Bowdon (d. 1937) as reported by the contemporary local newspapers. An on-site visit by Graham Duckmanton on August 23, 2013 revealed the presence of yet more gravesites: firstly that of Eliza Jemima Bowdon (d. 1872). The text on the gravestone reads (Figure 21): "Pray for the Repose of the / Soul of/ Eliza Jemima Bowdon, / Who Died at Beightonfields

---

[467] Information courtesy of Tony Bak of Barlborough Heritage and Resource Centre on the occasion of a personal visit to Barlborough on April 20, 2013.

[468] This took place on September 11, 1937 and was the last burial of the Butler-Bowdon family at Spinkhill cemetery; information disclosed in a private E-mail correspondence between Father Peter D McGuire and the author on November 14, 2013. Details provided by Father McGuire are based on parish registers.

[469] Tenants of the Butler-Bowdons (see Chapter 14.2): John and Teresa Liddy and Henry Ives.

[470] "Knockin' on Heaven's Door" was written by Bob Dylan, from the album "Pat Garrett & Billy the Kid" (1973).

Priory / 20th January 1872. / R. I. P. / Sweet Jesus have Mercy on her Soul, / Because of Her Charity to The Poor".[471] The kerbstones surrounding Eliza Jemima's gravestone are engraved with the names of Alice, Ireneo, Enrico and Corona Del Monaco (Figures 22 to 25). The inscription for Enrico is at the front of the grave, Alice's to the right, Ireneo's to the left and Corona's is at the back. They read are as follows: "Ireneo Del Monaco died Jan. 25. 1912. Also his Wife / Alice née Bowdon (of Beightonfields Priory) died Oct. 4. 1933 / Enrico Del Monaco died 16th July 1983 aged 90 years / Corona Del Monaco died Dec. 9th 1960 (at Horsham) aged 64 years". I cannot say with certainty how many members of the Del Monaco family are buried in the same grave as Eliza Jemima or whether some of the engravings only serve as a sort of commemoration. Ireneo Del Monaco, who passed away in Worksop on January 25, 1912, is likely to have found his last resting place there, and Father Peter D McGuire of Spinkhill Church of the Immaculate Conception remembers that he buried Henry Del Monaco at Spinkhill.[472] According to him, there is a brick vault underneath the gravesite which contains a number of burials.[473]

The text on the front of the gravestone of Lancelot George B Butler-Bowdon and his wife Ella Cicely Mary Butler-Bowdon (Figure 26) reads: "Of your Charity Pray for / the Soul of / Lancelot George Butler-Bowdon / who died September 12th 1909 / aged 58 years. / And Ella his wife / who died July 2. 1912 / aged 54 years.".[474] The plinth bears an additional inscription: "Jesus Mercy. Mary Help". There is an inscription dedicated to a Margaret Helen Hughes engraved on the left hand side of the stone (for her role within the Butler-Bowdon family see Chapter 22). The inscription reads: "Of your Charity Pray for / the Soul of / Margaret Helen Hughes / who died September 19th 1908 / aged 48 years." I don't think we would be at fault if we were to deduce from the engraving that Ms Hughes is interred in the same grave as Lancelot George B Butler-Bowdon and his wife Ella.

Another tripartite gravestone consisting of stacked ashlars indicates the burials of further members of the Butler-Bowdon family (Figure 27). The top block is severely weathered and worn away which leaves us with almost no clue, but the inscription relates to Monica Mary Petre Butler-Bowdon (d. 1907): "(Pray for the Soul of) / Monica Mary / (Bowdon?) / (Born) Febr(uary)

---

471 Credit is due to Andrea Gubisch (Berlin) for assisting with deciphering the inscription (on August 30, 2013 in a private E-mail correspondence with the author).

472 Information disclosed in a personal telephone conversation with the author on November 14, 2013.

473 Information disclosed during a meeting on-site on April 28, 2014.

474 Lancelot Butler-Bowdon was buried at Spinkhill on September 16, 1909; Ella Cicely Butler-Bowdon was buried at Spinkhill on July 5, 1912; information disclosed in a private E-mail correspondence between Father Peter D McGuire and the author on November 14, 2013.

/// (1861) / (Di)ed May (15th 1907) / (Wife of John Erdeswick Butler-Bowdon?) / (of South)g(ate) Hou(se?) ///".[475] The middle block refers to her daughter Isabel-Mary Helena Butler-Bowdon (d. 1921 aged 29) and Monica Mary's husband John (6) Erdeswick Butler-Bowdon (d. 1929 aged 79): "Also / Isabel-Mary Helena / Daughter of the Above / Born September ///th 1893 / Died January 12th 1921 / Also of / John Erdeswick Butler-Bowdon / Born Feb 16th 1850 - Died Jan 2nd 1929".[476] The bottom block names John (6) Erdeswick Butler-Bowdon's third wife Mary Monica (née Walm(e)slesy, d. 1937 aged 86): "Also of Mary Monica / Daughter of Herman Walmesley and Widow of the Above / Who died on Sept. 9th 1937. / My Jesus M(ercy?)".[477] This sepulchral stone and the one belonging to Lancelot Butler-Bowdon are positioned side by side which in all likelihood was no coincidence, due to the fact that Lancelot and John (6) were brothers.

Both the burial site of Lancelot George B Butler-Bowdon and his family members and the family grave of John (6) Erdeswick-Butler-Bowdon are positioned directly alongside the main pathway leading from the churchyard gates to the church door (on the left). Eliza Jemima Bowdon's grave can be found to the left of the church door at the outer wall of the church. Behind her gravestone a white commemoration plaque for Constance Bowdon (d. 1901, see Chapter 18 and Figure 28) is attached to the church wall, under a stained glass window. The plaque reads "Of your Charity / Pray for the Soul of / Constance Mary Lee / of Beightonfields Priory / Wife of William Francis Lee / who died at Mill Hill 30th March 1901 / aged 43 years. / *"Innocens manib(u)s*

[475] This is a very tentative reading of the top stone by torchlight in the course of a nightly visit to the cemetery by Graham Duckmanton and the author on September 22, 2013. Words in brackets are uncertain and supplemented only by comparisons with the inscriptions of the other Butler-Bowdon gravestones and from other sources. Monica Mary Butler-Bowdon was buried at Spinkhill on May 19, 1907; information disclosed in a private E-mail correspondence between Father Peter D McGuire and the author on November 14, 2013. Father McGuire said he made a rubbing of the stone, but his efforts were also not crowned by success. The surface is beyond salvation.

[476] Thanks to Andrea Gubisch (Berlin) and Elke Müller (Bremerhaven) for helping with decipherment of the badly eroded writing on this part of the gravestone (on August 30, 2013 and September 1, 2013 respectively in private E-mail correspondences with the author). The burial of Isabel Maria Helen Butler-Bowdon took place on January 15, 1921, and the burial of John Erdeswick Butler-Bowdon on January 5, 1929; information disclosed in a private E-mail correspondence between Father Peter D McGuire and the author on November 14, 2013.

[477] At the end of the last row the stone is completely destroyed, the breakage leaves space for only a very short word; reading suggested by Graham Duckmanton in a private E-mail correspondence with the author on August 30, 2013.

et mundo corde" / R. I. P."[478] There is no further hint as to whether she was buried at Spinkhill cemetery.

The gravestones of Lancelot George B Butler-Bowdon (and of his wife Ella and of Margaret Hughes) and that of Eliza Jemima Bowdon, even though they passed away almost four decades apart, bear a striking resemblance. They were probably manufactured at related stonemason's workshops.[479] All final resting places of the Butler-Bowdon family at Spinkhill cemetery make a neat and well-kempt impression.

The inscription on Spinkhill First World War Memorial reads "Pray for the souls of the following who laid down their lives for their king & country in the Great War 1914-1919" and lists a number of young men of the area who were killed during that war, one of them being the son of Alice and Ireneo Del Monaco, R(omolo/Ronald) Del Monaco, Private of the 43rd Canadian Camer(o)n Highlan(de)rs (151547).[480]

The Bowdon family tree on parchment in possession of Barlborough Heritage and Research Centre names two more Bowdon family members who found their final resting place at Spinkhill: James (1) Bowdon, (b. 14 or 15/11/1744), second son of John (2) Bowdon and Mary Johnson, and George (9) Bowdon (d. 18/02/1822), first son of George (8) Bowdon and Elizabeth Clements. No gravestones relating to these two men could be identified whilst paying Spinkhill cemetery a personal visit on September 21, 2013.

I did however, make an interesting observation on that day which makes for a nice extra piece of information: directly adjacent to the left of the gravestone of Lancelot Butler-Bowdon and his family members is the grave of a certain John Joseph Baldwin Young who was the Privy Chamberlain to Pope Pius XII., "who died Friday, February 10th 1950, aged 81 years. Fortified by the Rites of the Holy Church. May he rest in Peace. Amen". Buried alongside him is his wife Margarita who was 25 years younger than her husband and who survived him by four years (Figure 29). There is no proof of a connection between the Baldwin Young family and the Butler-Bowdons, but the proximity of the gravesites is striking. Father Peter D McGuire, Parish Priest of Spinkhill (Church of the Immaculate Conception), suggested that the closeness of the gravestones could demonstrate some sort of status, and may imply that the families knew each other. About the Baldwin Young family he

---

478 *Innocens manibus et mundo corde* = Innocent in hands and clean of heart (Psalm 23.4). Mill Hill is located in Hendon, Middlesex, London.

479 The gravestone of Lancelot Butler-Bowdon reveals the name of the stone carver who manufactured the monument: T Martin from Staveley (observed on a private visit to Spinkhill cemetery on September 21, 2013); the one of Eliza-Jemima though was made by J D Waterhouse from Staveley (observed on a private visit to the cemetery on April 28, 2014).

480 For more information on Ronald Del Monaco and his brother Bernard during the Great War see Appendix 7.

could report that they were a notable Catholic family in the area and lived at The Grange, Southgate, Eckington. According to his recollections they were part of the Sheffield Young family who owned Tempered Springs, a well-respected specialist steel company (spring manufacturer).[481]

Tony Bak of Heritage and Research Centre in Barlborough pointed out to me that John (7) Lancelot Wykeham Butler-Bowdon, 25th and last Lord Grey de Ruthyn, found his last resting place - unlike all other members of the Butler-Bowdon family - at Barlborough's St James the Greater Church (buried without a headstone).[482]

13. "Read all about it"[483] - The Book of Margery Kempe

Perhaps the most fascinating tale relating to Southgate House is the tale of the incidental discovery of a unique late mediaeval manuscript entitled "The Book of Margery Kempe" in Southgate House in September 1934 (identified by Hope Emily Allen[484]). The book is the dictated spiritual autobiography of a Norfolk mystic and pilgrim named Margery Kempe of Bishop's Lynn (ca. 1373 - after 1439, today King's Lynn).[485] The manuscript is an early copy and not the original dictated by Margery Kempe herself.[486] It was drawn up some time between 1436 and 1438. The surviving manuscript was presumably written by

---

481 One famous member of the Young family is former journalist and political writer Hugo Young (1938-2003) of "The Guardian". Information disclosed in a private E-Mail correspondence and a private telephone conversation between Father Peter D McGuire and the author on November 14, 2013.

482 Information disclosed in a private E-Mail correspondence with the author on August 27 and October 20, 2013. Tony Bak adds that this is striking insofar as John (7) Lancelot Wykeham Butler-Bowdon was educated at Spinkhill. Moreover, St James Church in Barlborough belongs to the Church of England and Lord Grey of course was of Catholic origin. The last will of John (7) Lancelot Butler-Bowdon (stored in Leeds District Probate Registry?) could reveal the reasons for the burial of a member of such a staunch Catholic family in an Anglican church, but this document could not be obtained until printing of this book.

483 "Read all about it, Part III" is a song written by singer-songwriter Emili Sandé, released on her album "Our Version of Events" (2012).

484 Hope Emily Allen (1883–1960) a mediaeval scholar known for her research on the 14th-century English mystic Richard Rolle; cf. Bryn Mawr College Library Special Collections, *Hope Emily Allen Papers*; Kelliher, "Rediscovery of Margery Kempe", p. 261. A complete digital facsimile is available on-line now after "A number of teaching editions have been published in recent years - all based on a critical edition in the EETS Original series (v. 212) from 1940 by Sanford Meech and Hope Emily Allen."; cf. Fredell, Borchers et al., *The Book of Margery Kempe/Online Documentary Edition*. For a comprehensive list of essays and articles published on-line see Jokinen, *Middle English Literature: Essays and Articles/Margery Kempe*.

485 "The Book of Margery Kempe", British Library MS Additional 61823; cf. Kelliher, "Rediscovery of Margery Kempe", p. 259, footnote 3.

486 Windeatt, Kempe, *Book of Margery Kempe*, p. 9 and footnote 1.

the person whose signature can be found at the bottom of the final page.[487] It is said to be the earliest surviving text with autobiographical characteristics in the English language.[488]

Margery disengaged herself from the conventions and rules of her times and of female duties and committed herself to her spiritual vocation. In doing so she faced not only social exclusion, but also by attempting to gain personal, financial and spiritual autonomy, conflict with her fellow townspersons.[489] This in turn led to further conflicts with all possible secular and non-secular authorities within her hometown. She allegedly went on pilgrimages that took her to Europe and even as far as the Holy Land. Her mystical conversations with God, Christ, Mary and other religious persons, even "visitations" of a saint whom only she could see, are also recorded in the manuscript. She is honoured in the Church of England/the Anglican Communion.

Today the manuscript that contains annotations from four separate hands is stored in the British Library (B.L. Additional MS 61823).[490] Although the leather and paper on the front cover had been chewed by a rodent a document in the form of a letter from the year 1440 which was able to be saved from the original binding can tell us a little about the provenance and dating.[491] The first page contains the rubric "Liber Montis Gracie. This boke is of Mountegrace", written in a late 15th century hand at the top of the verso of the binding leaf. It can be assumed that some of the annotations are the work of monks of the Carthusian priory of Mount Grace in East Harlsey, N. Yorkshire (near Northallerton), home to some famous mystics and a library containing several works belonging to the same tradition.[492]

It remains unclear as to what happened to the manuscript between its origin, its removal from Mount Grace possibly during the Dissolution of the Monasteries[493], and the late 18th/early 19th century when the book reappeared

---

487 "ihesu mercy quod Salthows"; cf. Kelliher, "Rediscovery of Margery Kempe", p. 259, footnote 4.

488 Windeatt, Kempe, *Book of Margery Kempe*, p. 9.

489 Staley, *Book of Margery Kempe*, p. 1.

490 It was acquired in 1980; cf. Windeatt, Kempe, *Book of Margery Kempe*, p. 9, footnote 1.

491 Kelliher, "Rediscovery of Margery Kempe", p. 259, p. 261. William Erdeswick Ignatius Butler-Bowdon had the cover "expertly repaired".

492 Kelliher, "Rediscovery of Margery Kempe", p. 259, footnote 7.

493 Supposedly not later than the Suppression Act of 1539, the Second Act of Dissolution, an Act of the Parliament of England providing for the dissolution of 552 monasteries; cf. Jokinen, *Dissolution of the Monasteries*). During this formal act of the English Reformation, Henry VIII (1491-1547) broke up monastic institutions in Britain, dispersed their valuable assets to the higher secular ranks of society, and divided the vacant land. Elizabeth H Bishop writes that "as much as a quarter of the total area of England was transferred to the country's landowning class". Those monasteries which were not converted into residential mansions were left to fall to ruins and became quarries for building material; cf. Bishop, *Country House Revisited*, p. 8 (referring to

in the belongings of the Butler-Bowdon family. The manuscript contains two bookplates, both of Henry (3) Bowdon (1754-1833). Its last possessor was Lt.-Col. William Erdeswick Ignatius Butler-Bowdon (1880-1956). He gives an account published in "The Times" of September 30, 1934, explaining that, even though there is no actual proof of this in the case of the book of Margery Kempe, it was not uncommon at the time of the destruction and dissolution of the monasteries that valuable goods, such as books, were entrusted into the care of trustworthy Catholic families "in the hope of preserving them", the Bowdon family being one of those families.[494] What underlines this assumption is the fact that alongside the properties belonging to Mount Grace at the tome of its suppression was the advowson of the neighbouring rectory of Beighton, thus offering us an idea of how the manuscript came into the hands of the Bowdon family. It is also possible that possession of the manuscript fell to the new secular owners of Mount Grace, who handed valuables down to their various successors during the following centuries, and so finally ending up in the possession of the Bowdons.[495] It is said to have "lain in a bookshelf in the library of Pleasington Old Hall, Lancashire, next to a missal of 1340 in the rite of York".[496] From there it must have been transferred to Southgate House at an unknown time. Hilton Kelliher gives a very graphic description of the final discovery of the manuscript there in 1934, a first hand account from a letter that the eldest son of Lt.-Col. William Erdeswick Ignatius Butler-Bowdon, Capt. Maurice Butler-Bowdon, wrote to a certain Mrs D Winifred Tuck of King's Lynn on January 20, 1970.[497] He describes Southgate House as a "largish Georgian House with a big front hall" in which the members of the family had ample space for playing table tennis. When searching for a new ping pong ball a wall cupboard on one side of the fireplace had to be opened and an unruly collection of small leather-bound

---

Robinson, *English Country Estate*, p. 42). According to Arnold, Dana, "1 The Country House: Form, Function and Meaning", in: Arnold, *Georgian Country House*, p. 18 and Arnold, Dana, "9 Living off the Land: Innovations in Farming Practices and Farm Design", in: Arnold, *Georgian Country House*, p. 154 in 1688 15-20% of usable/workable land was in the hands of the great landowners (with estates comprising of more than 10,000 acres). This figure rose to 20-25% by 1790. The landed gentry (be that the wealthy notables or the less affluent, but influential squirearchy) held between 15 and 20% throughout the period.

[494] Kelliher, "Rediscovery of Margery Kempe", p. 260.

[495] Kelliher, "Rediscovery of Margery Kempe", p. 261f.

[496] According to Lt.-Col. Butler-Bowdon's statement in "The Times" of 30/09/1934; cf. Kelliher, "Rediscovery of Margery Kempe", p. 260. John (5) Erdeswick Butler-Bowdon, Maurice's grandfather, owned Pleasington New (and not Old) Hall along with Southgate House, cf. Kelliher, "Rediscovery of Margery Kempe", p. 261 and footnote 9. The Butler-Bowdons also never lived at Pleasington Old Hall; see Chapter 21.

[497] Kelliher, "Rediscovery of Margery Kempe", p. 260f.

books came to light.[498] A visitor, Charles Harvard Gibbs-Smith[499], present that very day immediately realised the value of the books and persuaded Lt.-Col. William Erdeswick Ignatius Butler-Bowdon to have them identified and their value assessed by Albert van de Put. One of the books turned out to be the above mentioned manuscript. Van de Put and Gibbs-Smith belonged to the staff of the Victoria and Albert Museum in London, but the actual identification of the book was made by Hope Emily Allen.

Somehow this whole account of events contradicts Stephen Glover's observations on the loss and destruction of papers during the persecution carried out against Catholic families[500]. He writes that many papers relating to the Bowdon family were lost or "destroyed by the persecutions frequently carried out against Catholic families"[501], but maybe this specific manuscript was a lucky exception to the rule. The same applies to a richly embroidered cope from the 14th century, owned by the Butler-Bowdon family (see Chapter 18).[502]

The "Catholic Herald" of September 9, 1954 makes mention of William Erdeswick Ignatius Butler-Bowdon's 1936 publication, a book entitled "The Book of Margery Kempe 1436".[503]

13.1. Excursus on Margery Kempe

Margery was born as Margery Brunham in Bishop's Lynn, Norfolk around 1373. She came from a respected family. She was the daughter of a burgess who held a number of honourable positions in the town (mayor and Member of Parliament, alderman of the influential Trinity Guild, coroner, Justice of Peace, chamberlain)[504]. Margery Kempe's life span covered the reigns of the

---

498 Kelliher, "Rediscovery of Margery Kempe", p. 260 quoting Maurice Butler-Bowdon citing his father William Erdeswick Ignatius with the following words: "Look (…) I am going to put this whole "-----" lot on the bonfire tomorrow (…).".

499 Charles Harvard Gibbs-Smith (22/03/1909-03/12/1981) was a British polymath who specialised in the history of aeronautics and aviation. From 1932 on he was employed as Keeper at the Victoria and Albert Museum in London. His family includes John Harvard, the founder of Harvard College; cf. http://www.information-britain.co.uk/famousbrits.php?id=1882 (viewed 05/03/2014).

500 Glover, *History*, p. 305; Burke, Burke, *Genealogical and Heraldic History*, p. 125.

501 Glover, *History*, p. 305.

502 Catholic Herald Archive, "£33,000 Cope to stay in England".

503 Catholic Herald Archive, "Acquittal of a Mystic". Selected standard works on the topic are Meech, Sanford Brown, Allen, Hope Emily, *The Book of Margery Kempe (ca 1400s), MS of Col. W. Butler-Bowdon*, Oxford 1961 (reprint); Staley, Lynn, *The Book of Margery Kempe* (translated and edited by Lynn Staley), New York 2001; Staley, Lynn, *Margery Kempe's Dissenting Fictions*, State College/University Park Pennsylvania 1994; Chappell, Julie A, *Perilous Passages: The Book of Margery Kempe, 1534-1934*, Basingstoke 2013; Butler-Bowdon, William, *The Book of Margery Kempe 1436*, London 1936.

504 Windeatt, Kempe, *Book of Margery Kempe*, p. 10.

English kings Edward III (1312-1377), Richard II (1367-1400), Henry IV (1366-1413), Henry V (1387-1422) and Henry VI (1421-1472). In the personal account of her life Margery tells the reader that she was married to John Kempe when she was 20 years old, who was also a person of standing but not equal to her father and who had some financial difficulties. Together they had 14 children; none of them are mentioned in her book except her first-born son but all of them are briefly mentioned in prayers.[505] The last attested reference to Margery Kempe is 22/05/1439. Shortly before that date she received admission to the Trinity Guild at Lynn.[506]

"The Book of Margery Kempe" actually consists of two books. Book I has 88 chapters, and Book II has 10 chapters and can be considered as a kind of addendum to Book I. Both books are preceded by a proem and a preface. The whole work is written in retrospective. At the age of 63 Margery is looking back on her life between the years 1436 and 1438. The original book has disappeared. The reason why we are familiar with the name of Margery Kempe is because of the printing of a seven page quarto pamphlet by Wynkyn de Worde[507] (date of printing ca. 1501), containing extracts from Margery's book. A single copy of this pamphlet has survived and is today stored in Cambridge University Library.[508] Additionally there exists a reprint by Henry Pepwell[509] from 1521.[510]

Margery was illiterate. She dictated the story of her life to two priests which surely led to a certain amount of "editing" and shaping from their side, but according to Barry Windeatt the links between her vigorous character and the vigour of the book's style is unmistakable. She speaks with an authentic, courageous voice (sometimes even witty, unintimidated and sharp-

---

505 Windeatt, Kempe, *Book of Margery Kempe*, p. 11.

506 Staley, *Book of Margery Kempe*, p. 1.

507 Wynkyn de Worde, originally Jan van Wynkyn (d. 1534/1535), printer and publisher in London, allegedly the first person to popularise the products of the printing press in England; cf. Encyclopedia Britannica, *Wynkyn de Worde*; http://search.lib.cam.ac.uk/?itemid=|cambrdgedb|3584483 (viewed 05/03/2014).

508 *Ref. No. STC 14924*, Cambridge University Library, Sel. 5, 27 (BMK App. II, pp. 353–357) (original document not viewed personally); cf. Scott Stokes, *Margery Kempe*.

509 Henry Pepwell (d. 1539/1540) was an English printer. He was in business from 1518 in London and involved in printing early English humanist works; cf. http://en.wikipedia.org/wiki/Henry_Pepwell (viewed 16/03/2013).

510 Windeatt, Kempe, *Book of Margery Kempe*, p. 9. It is a subchapter of a larger tract, the subchapter is titled "Here beginneth a Short Treatise of Contemplation taught by our Lord Jesu Christ, or taken out of the book of Margery Kempe, Ancress of Lynn" (*Ref. No. STC 20972*, Cambridge University Library, BL CA. 37 (variants given in BMK App. II, pp. 353–357) (original document not viewed personally); cf. Scott Stokes, *Margery Kempe*; http://www.ccel.org/g/gardner/cell/cell16.htm (viewed 16/03/2013); http://search.lib.cam.ac.uk/?itemid=|collpwdb|501567 (viewed 05/03/2014).

tongued[511]) and with unparalleled experience.[512] Margery was able to marry together the poetic language of conventional spiritual literature with an "earthly awkwardness".[513] She was an individual, an open and vivid narrator, uttering her opinions unselfconsciously. Windeatt thinks that there are indications that reveal we are dealing with an incompletely edited transcript because of the lack of shaping in the material presented and the limitations of the portrayed spiritual life.[514]

Fully aware of her deficits in literacy, Margery sought the company of people who were able to read and write and who were accustomed to contemporary spiritual literature. She learned from their conversations and subsequently became very well acquainted with the religious literature of her times[515]. She must have had a very retentive memory.

There is no focus on chronology in Margery's accounts. The passing of time and changes in life were seemingly of no great relevance to her, her writing was steered by the continuity of the purpose she saw in her own life. According to Windeatt, her recounting of her visionary and religious experiences are, strangely enough, the least individual and lively parts of her work, both style and content-wise. Other parts of her text seem to concentrate too much on the individual at the expense of an authentic spiritual awareness, as she was too overwhelmed by the trials of daily life.[516]

Margery does not provide us with any information as to her childhood. Her reflections begin with the birth of her first child in ca. 1394 and the related spiritual crisis and madness she experienced in the aftermath, possibly a singular psychotic episode (post-natal depression?)[517], from which she was rescued by a vision of Christ which she does not take seriously until later when more upsetting things had happened in her life. Her business (a grain mill and a brewery[518]) collapsed and the relationship to her husband suffered as a result. Fairly late on in life she experienced another psychotic period, and this time she chose to publicly assume a direct and special link to God as she wanted to be recognised as a person of particular religious capacity.[519]

In addition to these two episodes Margery suffered from issues such as feelings of guilt, an over active imagination, a spiritual crisis and being treated unkindly by a confessor.[520] Windeatt describes her as a "hysterical personality

---

511 Windeatt, Kempe, *Book of Margery Kempe*, p. 27.
512 Windeatt, Kempe, *Book of Margery Kempe*, p. 10.
513 Windeatt, Kempe, *Book of Margery Kempe*, p. 23f.
514 Windeatt, Kempe, *Book of Margery Kempe*, p. 24.
515 Windeatt, Kempe, *Book of Margery Kempe*, p. 15f.
516 Windeatt, Kempe, *Book of Margery Kempe*, p. 23.
517 Windeatt, Kempe, *Book of Margery Kempe*, p. 300.
518 Johnson Lewis, *Margery Kempe.*
519 Windeatt, Kempe, *Book of Margery Kempe* 2004, p. 301.
520 Alchin, *Middle Ages.*

organization".[521] She sustained a severe nervous breakdown, an again experienced a vision which calmed her and brought her back to her senses. These developments left her at odds as to how to continue her life of conflicting roles, that of a wife and mother and her desire to become a "spiritual women", for which she was criticised by her contemporaries for attempting to lead a life devoted to Christ as a married woman.[522] She decided for a life of chastity which was formalised by a vow (together with her husband, in 1403 before the Bishop of Lynn). This vow included devotion to the sacrament, frequent confessions, fasting, the use of holy images, and wearing a white dress which attracted even more criticism, as a woman of her age and standing was expected to wear black.[523]

Margery went as far as to interrupt religious services to argue with the clergy. Church authorities had her arrested and imprisoned for heresy, but they later found her innocent and released her (1417, Leicester).[524]

A further example of her abnormal behaviour was her uncontrollable sobbing and weeping at holy sites and during mass. It was at this time that she began thinking aloud and talking directly to heaven. God entered into conversation with her and she experienced very vivid visions with religious content.[525] Margery became attached to the tradition of meditation on the events of Christ's life[526], and because of her remarkably heightened and formative imagination she was able to enter into the life of Christ again and again throughout her book.[527]

At approximately the age of 40, Margery embarked on a life of pilgrimages which brought her into contact with not only the important church leaders in England (to Lincoln (1413), Canterbury (1413), Norwich (1415) and York (1417)), but also lead her across the European continent (to Assisi and Rome (1414) in Italy, to Santiago de Compostela in Spain (1417), to Aachen and Wilsnack in Germany and Danzig/Gdansk (1433), today Poland, to Norway (1433)), and as far as the Holy Land (1414). She did not deem it important to give an account of the actual travelling, choosing instead to exclude the worldly things in life, and concentrate exclusively on the spiritual matters.[528] She was often regarded as eccentric in her behaviour and was again criticised for her weeping and inappropriate white attire. Her behaviour was irritating for her fellow human beings, but since Margery saw it as persecution in the

---

521 Windeatt, Kempe, *Book of Margery Kempe*, p. 301.

522 Alchin, *Middle Ages.*

523 Windeatt, Kempe, *Book of Margery Kempe*, p. 11; Alchin, *Middle Ages.*

524 Johnson Lewis, *Margery Kempe.*

525 Windeatt, Kempe, *Book of Margery Kempe*, p. 19.

526 Windeatt, Kempe, *Book of Margery Kempe*, p. 16f.

527 Windeatt, Kempe, *Book of Margery Kempe*, p. 27.

528 Windeatt, Kempe, *Book of Margery Kempe*, p. 13.

name of Christ she regarded this as a confirmation of her actions.[529] When she finally returned from her voyages to her hometown of Lynn she was met with the same public mood (hostility on the one side, but also support on the other).[530] She suffered from the cruel words of others[531], but their failure to acknowledge her claim was for her again vindication of her path. She perceived this rejection as a persecution, which she bore for Christ's sake.[532]

Margery evidently had role models in other female mystics of her times: she strongly identified herself with St. Bridget of Sweden (1303-1373, a married mystic who made the transition from wife to bride of Christ and had a visionary experience) and Mary de Oignies of Brabant (d. 1213, with a similar life career to Margery, who later in life became a hermit and experienced visions and ecstasies)[533] and other female mystics, their experiences and narratives seem paralleled and echoed in Margery's book. It is historically documented that she met Dame Julian of Norwich[534] in Norwich and had lengthy conversations with her.[535] Unlike her contemporary who withdrew from the world and lived in peace as a recluse, Margery Kempe led a turbulent life.[536]

Throughout the book Margery refers to herself in third person as "this said creature" or "this creature". One explanation for this can be that by making herself the subject we the reader can identify the different voices of Margery Kempe, as well as emphasising the rhetorical devices employed within the book.[537]

The book is annotated by four different hands, presumably for readers interested in mystical experience.[538] Lynn Staley pays a lot of attention to two of the annotators[539]. The first set of comments, written by a neat hand in brown ink, dates to the 15th century and could possibly be related to the above mentioned priest, named Salthows. The commentator keenly stresses that a monastic reader should understand the work as a record of devotion. The second set of remarks, written in red ink, can be dated to the 16th century and is possibly the most recent of all four hands. These comments form a response

529 Windeatt, Kempe, *Book of Margery Kempe*, p. 13.

530 Windeatt, Kempe, *Book of Margery Kempe*, p. 14.

531 Windeatt, Kempe, *Book of Margery Kempe*, p. 25.

532 Windeatt, Kempe, *Book of Margery Kempe*, p. 301.

533 Windeatt, Kempe, *Book of Margery Kempe*, p. 17ff.

534 Dame Julian of Norwich was an English mystic and anchoress (a recluse nun, 1342-1416), contemporary of Margery Kempe who in contrast to her chose a life in reclusion, cf. Encyclopedia Britannica, *Julian of Norwich*.

535 Windeatt, Kempe, *Book of Margery Kempe*, p. 16 and p. 26.

536 Windeatt, Kempe, *Book of Margery Kempe*, p. 9.

537 Torn, "Margery Kempe: Madwoman or Mystic", p. 79, footnote 1; Staley, *Book of Margery Kempe*, p. 5.

538 Windeatt, Kempe, *Book of Margery Kempe*, p. 9 and footnote 2.

539 Staley, *Book of Margery Kempe*, p. 2ff.

to Kempe's text as well as being a reaction to previous comments. The writer takes up position in relation to the annotations of the writer in brown ink, concurring with the previous writer's opinions on details of the book and the coherence of the text in general. Furthermore the writer underlines in a gloss that he believes that the book belongs to the key works of contemporary piety and reveals his own fervent preoccupation with those parts of the book relating to Margery's spiritual devoutness and charity.[540] Interestingly he omits to comment on sections of the book that do not seem to fit into the pattern of accepted female devotion, instead he attempts to devalue her by only emphasising Margery's characteristics which tie in with traditional spiritual ecstasy.[541] His aim is clear: he wishes to draw the readers' attention away from Margery's inherent social radicalism. All comments have in common that they suggest ways in which mediaeval texts were considered as communal goods and therefore required commentary which related to the values of the communities in which texts were read.[542]

The academic reception of "The Book of Margery Kempe" seems to have developed in various directions over the years. From the large amount of secondary literature available, I have chosen to look at three authors with three different approaches to the subject.

Barry A Windeatt presents a translation of the text into modern English, complemented by a very concise and traditionally scholarly account of the book (introduction and extensive footnotes). To him, "The Book of Margery Kempe" is not a work which we today would understand as an autobiography. In his opinion, the aim of Margery's book was not to provide answers to the questions of subsequent readers, and was therefore not intentionally laid out as an autobiography, "as Margery herself would probably not have believed that human experience was worth recording for its own sake"[543], moreover, the focal point of the text, and Margery's main concern, was to narrate how God interacted with her and to give proof of His glory. Windeatt's synopsis is the following: "As a woman both entangled in the world and beckoned out of it (...) the extraordinary strains and variousness of Margery's life as she remembers it give her text the unevenness of living, and mean that her Book's very weakness proves its strengths, as a work of human memory and the life of the self."[544]

An entirely different view is taken by Lynn Staley[545]. She makes a very clear distinction between the person named "Kempe" and the fictional person

540 Staley assumes that the Margery's usage of affective words link her to the school of Richard Rolle; cf. Staley, *Book of Margery Kempe*, p. 3.
541 Staley, *Book of Margery Kempe*, p. 4.
542 Staley, *Book of Margery Kempe*, p. 4.
543 Windeatt, Kempe, *Book of Margery Kempe*, p. 22.
544 Windeatt, Kempe, *Book of Margery Kempe*, p. 27.
545 Staley, *Book of Margery Kempe*, p. 5.

named "Margery", believing that using this means of narration not only underlines the fictionality of the whole story, which she considers to be a mediaeval female sacred biography[546], but also enables the author to safely point out shortcomings within her milieu regarding the predominant social and religious morals and values of her times, indeed the foundations of mediaeval urban life in all its facets. Her work reveals "the disparity between social myths and social realities" (albeit maybe not contemporary realities).[547] Staley goes even further, establishing the thesis that Kempe "produces a vision of a new ecclesia, one shaped by women and women's relations, in the face of a fragmented but habitually violent and persecutory set of ruling institutions and practices."[548]

Staley dares to widen the focus from the single woman in the nucleus of an urban surrounding and to put Margery Kempe before a more general historical and geographical background.[549] Margery finds herself thrice associated with the so-called "Wycliffite Heresy"[550] (whilst staying in Leicester, York and Bristol), at a time of national unease regarding those who seemed to be at odds with the religious *status quo*. Especially during the reign of Henry V there was an increasing desire to define what nationhood meant in terms of conformity. By making Margery an example of someone living out a vernacular gospel, and challenging the secular and non-secular authorities around her, Kempe depicts a nation in which uniformity had become an end in itself and where those women in particular, who sought a life in accordance with the life of Christ had difficulty in finding acceptance and approval. Kempe lets Margery look at the religious institutions and obliterates the distinction between religious and secular arenas, and holds a mirror up to members of the church who all too often parallel their non-religious counterparts in their hunger for conformity, earthly status, riches, and influence.[551]

Staley warns however, that even though Kempe vividly describes town life, ideas of nationhood and religious institutions in her book, it could still be true that she in fact wrote a fictional account, rather than an account of the realities of her time. The most revolutionary thing about the book is the choice

---

546 Staley, *Book of Margery Kempe*, p. 1.
547 Staley, *Book of Margery Kempe*, p. 5
548 David Aers in a review on another book by Lynn Staley: "Margery Kempe's Dissenting Fictions" (1994) on amazon.de: http://www.amazon.de/Margery-Kempes-Dissenting-Fictions-Staley/dp/0271025794/ref=sr_1_5?s=books-intl-de&ie=UTF8&qid=1364477697&sr=1-5 (viewed 27/03/2013).
549 Staley, *Book of Margery Kempe*, p. 5.
550 John Wycliffe (1330-1384), reformer and dissident of the Roman Catholic church in England, his followers were known as "Lollards", members of a religious movement who flourished in England in the late 14th and early 15th century; cf. Encyclopedia Britannica, *John Wycliffe*. For further reading see Ghosh, *Wycliffite Heresy*.
551 Staley, *Book of Margery Kempe*, p. 5.

of a female voice as narrator. Yet in doing so the author chose a relatively safe position, as women did not constitute a real revolutionary threat due to their lack of legal status. Additionally Margery's strong religious faith also meant that she did not pose a serious menace to society. To Staley, Kempe is a genuine master of prose fiction, presenting all its riches and its complexities, and the difficult struggle between the needs of the individual and the draws of the community, the first-person narrator being the fantasy of a holy woman: "Such guise allowed her to inhabit a space within the status-conscious town of Lynn even as she made a story about her inability to extricate herself from codes of behaviour that have nothing to do with the freedom of the spirit lived out by Christ and the disciples."[552]

Another approach to the subject is the question of Margery's sanity. Her frequent public bouts of crying and wailing and her visions and visitations confuse and polarise the people around her. Whereas religious authorities tended to see Margery as a holy mystic, the common people rejected her and called her a devil worshipper. Astonishingly, however, she was rarely perceived as a madwoman who needed "treatment". Alison Torn, a psychologist who in her reflections subscribes to Staley's theory on Kempe as the author of Margery, examines the various phenomenons of Margery Kempe's cases of "madness".[553] She comes to the conclusion that in England at a time before the Age of Enlightenment the boundaries between madness and mysticism or religious experience and spiritual passion were drawn differently than in our secularised modern life today. Therefore, we cannot judge Margery's experiences according to our criterions, but must instead see the narrative set against its contemporary background. Margery describes her mental absences very graphically with rich detail[554], easily allowing modern scholars to deduce comprehensible psychological disorders such as psychotic spells or symptoms and affective and schizophrenic features from them.[555]

Kempe must have been aware of the similarities between spiritual ecstasy or religious fervour and madness and uses metaphors in the narrative to underline this. The author lets the reader know that the narrator is not insane, being able to recognise the differences as she herself has experienced "madness" (in which case referring to her spiritual ecstasies), and in doing so rebukes any charges of insanity by others.[556] Torn believes that all classical symptoms of psychiatric diseases which are portrayed are "truly embodied spiritual" experiences. To her, Kempe leaves us in no doubt about this, and this unshakeable belief is still perceptible today.[557] What makes this

[552] Staley, *Book of Margery Kempe*, p. 6.

[553] Torn, "Margery Kempe: Madwoman or Mystic", p. 79-89.

[554] Torn, "Margery Kempe: Madwoman or Mystic", p. 83.

[555] Torn, "Margery Kempe: Madwoman or Mystic", p. 85.

[556] Torn, "Margery Kempe: Madwoman or Mystic", p. 84.

[557] Torn, "Margery Kempe: Madwoman or Mystic", p. 86.

assumption even more plausible is that such extreme emotional eruptions as experienced by Margery, which in modern times are considered to be a sign of mental instability, were a fundamental feature of spirituality in the Middle Ages, imparting not only the gravity but also the truth of religious experience. [558] To bring it to a point: at that time "religiosity was sanity, madness amounted to a refusal to accept the truth that was God." [559], moreover, behaviour such as Margery's can be considered as a culturally bound phenomenon.[560]

Kempe also distinguishes between the times when Margery perceived her world and her visions with a "bodily eye" and when she perceived it with a "ghostly" (spiritual) eye. The vision of the bodily eye responds to external impressions, whereas the spiritual eye is connected to her inner spirituality. Consequently, God, truth and reason take place in Margery's inner world (in Augustinian tradition). Torn's best example for this is Margery's vision of being present at the crucifixion of Jesus Christ.[561]

According to Torn, Kempe the author makes a very clear distinction between reason, God and order on the one hand and madness, evil and disorder on the other (a concept evidently known to Kempe), so that true mystical experience cannot happen without exercising reason.[562] During her spells of madness Margery is described as the "victim", but after her restoration she becomes the "passive victor" in the tradition of Christian culture which transforms Margery as Kempe's voice to that of a spiritual force. The reader becomes the subject of this, reading the narrative as a spiritual lesson which along with other assumptions allows the author to conclude that "The Book of Margery Kempe" might have not only an (auto)biographic narrative, but also an attempted hagiography (narrative of a saint's life).[563] If madness is perceived in such a way, a cure can only be administered by a spiritual physician (Christ), and as there is no medical cure this makes Margery a spiritual martyr.

In the words of Torn, another strong indicator of Kempe's knowledge is the connection to the works of Richard Rolle, the 14th-century Yorkshire hermit and mystic with whose works Kempe must have been well acquainted. Many of the descriptions of Margery's experiences seem to echo Richard Rolle's experiences, one feature of English mediaeval literature which is exclusively found in the works of them both.[564]

---

558 Torn, "Margery Kempe: Madwoman or Mystic", p. 86.
559 Torn, "Margery Kempe: Madwoman or Mystic", p. 87.
560 Torn, "Margery Kempe: Madwoman or Mystic", p. 87.
561 Torn, "Margery Kempe: Madwoman or Mystic", p. 83.
562 Torn, "Margery Kempe: Madwoman or Mystic", p. 82.
563 Torn, "Margery Kempe: Madwoman or Mystic", p. 79.
564 Torn, "Margery Kempe: Madwoman or Mystic", p. 86.

From the construction of Margery as a "visionary subject and martyred object" we can, according to Torn, draw four conclusions[565]: the book legitimates and validates Margery as a holy person, the text is a guideline for married women to follow on how to make a transition to holiness, it preserves her mystical experiences for futures readers, and it corroborates her claim of sainthood. The book is aimed at two groups of potential readers: high-ranking authorities who are able to confer religious status to Margery's life and experiences, and a broader audience. By seeing Kempe within literary, social and historical context, as a reader today we should be able to recognise that Margery's religious experiences do not originate from madness.

What I, as a woman of the same age as Margery (whether real or fictional) when she set off to see the world, find personally intriguing and where I could not find references or comments in secondary literature available to me, are the missing answers to the following questions: how could a woman, who spent twenty of her fertile years pregnant and raising children, who surely had a huge household to keep going, and who allegedly ran two businesses (which went bust, so money was evidently not abundant within the family), find the time to see priests and other religious authorities, to debate religious issues with them, learn common church literature by heart and continue learning when she herself could not read and write and finally, shaken by ongoing phases of "madness" with all its consequences, leave everything behind in order to go on pilgrimages across Europe and get as far as to the Holy Land? She must have been physically and mentally exhausted; bearing in mind that travelling in the 1400s (as described by Margery herself in the book[566]) was in no way comparable to our modern standards.

14. "Upstairs, Downstairs" - The Occupants of Southgate House

By consulting the ten-yearly censuses of England and Wales it was possible to find out the names and professions of the occupants of Southgate House between 1841 and 1911.[567] The censuses for the preceding years (1801, 1811,

---

565 Torn, "Margery Kempe: Madwoman or Mystic", p. 87f.

566 Margery "is not concerned with being a travel writer" though. "We only hear of her immediate difficulties (especially the antipathy her fellow pilgrims have towards her) and of the visions and mediations experienced during her visits to holy places. To read in some of the surviving memoirs of late mediaeval travellers to the Holy Land (...) and then to remember that Margery Kempe describes almost nothing of what struck contemporary travellers as so memorably difficult and so nervously absorbing, is to register how utterly Margery's memory excludes almost everything but what she sees as the spiritual significant side of life."; cf. Windeatt, Kempe, *Book of Margery Kempe*, p. 12f.

567 It is interesting to see that in the box "Administrative County" in the entries of the censuses of 1891 and 1901 the village of Clowne to which Southgate Estate belonged was initially located in Nottinghamshire. Later on this was changed to Derbyshire by another person's handwriting.

1821 and 1831) are difficult, if not impossible, to gain access to, and they certainly do not contain as much information as their later follow-ups, so in this case I had to rely on other, rather scattered sources such as parish registers which can be found on-line.

A register of 18th century Settlement Examinations papers of Clowne parish[568] name a James Smith of Clowne, sawyer, aged 34, born in Whitwell for the year **1810,** "hired to (...) Henry Bowden (*sic!*) South Gate House. Wife and two children", and a Thomas Bell of Clowne, labourer, aged 35, born in Whitwell, "hired to (...) Mr Bowden of South Gate House".[569] The Clowne Parish Register lists two entries for **1813**. On October 7, 1813 Henry Harlow, aged 57 of Southgate, Whitwell was buried in Clowne. Not much later, on October 24, 1813 Martha Harlow, aged 76 of Southgate, Whitwell was interred. A third entry from **1816** records the burial of infant Martha Harlow, 13 weeks old of Southgate, Whitwell on April 10, 1816.[570] Unfortunately it is impossible to say in which way these people were connected to each other and what position the two adults might have held at Southgate House.

At first sight the **1841** census of England and Wales[571] sheds some interesting light on Southgate House as it only lists servants. This does not necessarily mean that the house was not occupied by the Bowdons on June 6, 1841. When the census taker visited Southgate House he met Christopher Stringfellow, aged 25, born in Derbyshire; Ann Brunt, aged 25, born in Derbyshire; Elizabeth Wells, aged 20, born in Derbyshire; Joseph Beresford, aged 15, born in Derbyshire and George Ellis, aged 15, born in Derbyshire. All members of the staff are denominated as either female or male servants without further specification (fast forward ten years to the 1851 census and we

---

568 List provided on-line by Spencer, *Yesterday's Journeys, Settlement Examinations*. Settlement Examinations are papers of quarter sessions. In the "olden days", if persons came into town from outside the parish and were trying to claim poor relief from the parish, they would have to appear before a JP who would decide if they had grounds to claim (e.g. by means of settlement certificates); if not they were removed from the parish back to where they came from, or their place of birth. People with enough money to purchase property were excluded from this rule; cf. Hitchcock, Shoemaker, Howard, McLaughlin et al., *London Lives, 1690-1800*.

569 Henry Bowden is Henry (3) Bowdon (1754-1833).

570 Spencer, *Clowne Burials*.

571 „The 1841 Census for England was taken on the night of 6 June 1841. All responses were to reflect the individual's status as of 6 June 1841 for all individuals who had spent the night in the house. People who were traveling (*sic!*) or living abroad were enumerated at the location where they spent the night on census night.", "Name of street, avenue, road, etca., House name or number, Surname of head of household, Name of persons who had spent the night in the household, Age, Sex, Person's occupation, Where born", cf. http://search.ancestry.co.uk/search/db.aspx?dbid=8978 (viewed 31/10/2012).

see that George Ellis is still in service with the household[572]). The Bowdon family meanwhile were evidently enjoying their summer vacation in Scarborough. The same census reveals at the address St. Nicholas Cliff the presence of John (4) Bruno Bowdon, aged 50, and his wife Mary Martha, also aged 50, and some of their children along with a few servants. The accompanying children were Henry (5) Bowdon, aged 26, listed as "Ind." (independent[573]), Barbara Bowdon, aged 20, Fanny Bowdon, aged 18, Jemima Bowdon, aged 16, also listed as "Ind.", and Caroline Bowdon, aged 14. The servants who accompanied the Bowdons on their holidays were Martha Bartlam, aged 35, Maria Millar, aged 22, and Joseph Wood, aged 25.

The **1851** census of England and Wales[574] lists the following members of a very large household at Southgate House: Henry (5) Bowdon, aged 36, born in Barlbro (= Barlborough), Derby is the Head of the family; his profession is

---

572 The ages seem not to add up very well, 15 in 1841 and 17 ten years later in 1851, complicated by the rounding down process used in 1841. This might be the explanation: "In the 1841 census, the age of persons over 15 was supposed to be rounded down to the nearest multiple of 5. For example, a person aged 19 would be listed as 15, a person aged 22 would be listed as age 20, and a person age 59 would be listed as 55. In practice, many census officials either did not round down at all or only rounded down for higher ages, such as over 20, or (less frequently) rounded down ages below 15. In general, the age of a person under 15 is probably accurate to within a year or two. For persons over 15, any age that is not a multiple of 5 is likely also to be accurate - for example, if a person is listed as 27, he or she probably really is 27 or thereabouts, rather than 25. The area you have to be careful of is persons over age 15 whose age is a multiple of 5 - they may be up to 4 years younger than their census listing shows – so if your ancestor is listed as 50, remember that he or she is likely actually between the ages of 50 and 54. This, of course, does not even take into account the errors made by census officials and family members reporting the ages of others! Finally, if the age of a person was unknown, children were supposed to be recorded as "under 20" and adults as "over 20"."; cf. Cochran, Whitehead, *Durham Records Online*.

573 An example: two years earlier Mary Martha Bowdon gave a grant of a legacy of £1,000 to her son Henry, "bequeathed to her by her father (...) and settled on her by marriage settlement of 20 February 1812; to hold the same, but without prejudice to the life interest of the said Mary Martha Bowdon", from a bundle of records relating to the Ferrers of Baddesley Clinton held by Shakespeare Centre Library and Archive, *Ref. No. DR 422/77* (dated 02/05/1839). There is a "similar receipt from John Bruno Bowdon, Mary Martha his wife (a daughter of the late Edward Ferrers) and Henry Bowdon their son, for £1000" (Ref. No. *DR 422/79*, dated 03/05/1839).

574 "The 1851 Census for England was taken on the night of 30 March 1851. The following information was requested: Name of street, place, road, etca., House number or name, Name of each person that had spent the night in that household, Relationship of person enumerated to the head of the family, Person's marital status, Age at last birthday (sex is indicated by which column the age is recorded in), Person's rank, profession, or occupation, Person's place of birth (if outside of England or Wales, only the country may be given), Whether blind, deaf, or idiot"; cf. http://search.ancestry.co.uk/search/db.aspx?dbid=8860 (viewed 31/10/2012).

cited as "County Magistrate".[575] He is apparently unmarried and the son of Mary M Bowdon, widow, aged 60, born in Herefordshire, who is described as a Gentlewoman Annuitant. In their household resides as visitor Caroline Ferrers, aged 54, unmarried, born in Baddesley Clinton, Warwickshire, her rank is that of Annuitant. Agatha Constable Maxwell, aged 10, born in York, is described as a niece and a Scholar at Home. Alfred Petre Constable Maxwell, aged 9, born in Richmond, is a nephew and a Scholar at Home as well as his brothers Robert de Lacy Constable Maxwell, aged 7, Wilfred Constable Maxwell, aged 7, Edward Constable Maxwell, aged 4, all born in Richmond, and a second niece named Alice Constable Maxwell, aged 3 months and also born in Richmond.[576] Nine servants were responsible for creature comforts at Southgate House - the presence of so many under-aged children surely required a lot of live-in staff: Agnes White, aged 33, unmarried, born in Middlesex, London worked as a Governess. Abraham Hibbert, aged 30, unmarried, born in Clown, Derby was the Butler[577]; George Ellis, aged 17, unmarried, born in Barlbro (*sic!*), Derby was the Footman; Elizabeth Mason, aged 34, unmarried, born in Leyburn, York was the Nurse as well as was Theresa Rose, aged 21, unmarried, born in Tinham, Lincoln. Maria Mellings, aged 31, unmarried, born in Stav(e)ley, Derby was the Lady Maid; Mary Adlington, aged 29, unmarried, born in Calow, Derby was the Cook; Mary Ellis, aged 25, unmarried, born in Whitwell, Derby was the Kitchen Maid and so was Hannah Maria Revill, aged 25, unmarried, born in Clowne, Derby. It is open to speculation as to what had befallen the Bowdon family that six under-aged children together with their governess were accommodated at Southgate House at that time, seemingly without their parents. Or were they just visitors?

The same census lists two "General Serv." from the village of Whitwell: one is Charlotte Starr, aged 17, born in Worksop, Nottinghamshire, who lived

[575] A County Magistrate is a Justice of the Peace who presides over a magistrate's court; and deals with less serious criminal cases, such as minor theft, criminal damage, assaults, public disorder and motoring offences, information disclosed by Craig Murray of the Imperial War Museum (London) by E-mail on February 26, 2013.

[576] The Bowdon family tree on parchment in possession of Barlborough Heritage and Research Centre does not list Wilfred, Edward and Alice, but gives three more names: Helena, Eustace and Frederick. When taking into consideration that the records on the family tree only go as far back as 1841 this could mean the latter three children where either grown up or did not survive until 1851.

[577] Kelly's *Directory*, p. 98f. states another Abraham Hibbard as the butcher in Clowne in the year 1891. This could be a son or grandson of A Hibbert, the butler. Sylvia R Linacre mentions the presence of a butcher in Clowne in the first third of the 20th century whereas there was none in Barlborough where her family used to live, cf. Linacre, *How it was*, p. 42.

at "Southgate Farm, Chesterfield and Worksop Road".[578] The second person was named Sarah Rich, aged 42, born in Creswell, Derbyshire. She was the daughter of the Head of Household, Robert West, and his wife Elizabeth, and had two sons, Frank and George. Both women could have been employees of the households they lived in, but since there was no other manor house in the vicinity, I find it not unreasonable to assume that both women could have belonged to the staff (daily servants) of Southgate House. Two other young ladies who also possibly worked there are listed under the address of "Highwood Lane": Sarah Newton, aged 22, born in Huntingdon, Derbyshire, and niece of the Head of Household John Tompkin is stated as "House Keeper" and Ann Wells, aged 18, born in Whitwell, Derbyshire is stated as "House Servant". This is, however, highly speculative and it cannot be ruled out that these females were the employees of the household of the dwelling on Highwood Lane.[579]

The **1861** census of England and Wales[580] allows us to conclude that there as still a large household at Southgate House in that year: Henry (5) Bowdon, aged 46, stated as born in Clowne, Derbyshire (see above) and by profession "Gentleman D L Magistrate" was Head of Household.[581] By now he was married to Harriet Bowdon, aged 29, born in Mapledurham, Oxfordshire. Together they had two daughters: Alice Bowdon, aged 6, and Constance Bowdon, aged 2, both born in Clowne, Derbyshire. Seven servants belonged to the manor: Winifred Doughty, aged 23, unmarried, born in Shenfield, Essex

---

578 Head of Household of this location was John Warriner, aged 63, born in Stanfree, Derbyshire and "Farmer of 90 Acres, employing 1 Labourer outdoor & 3 indoor". He was most likely related to all the other Warreners mentioned in this research. I am inclined to identify "Southgate Farm" with Hickingwood Farm.

579 John Tompkin, aged 62, born in Clowne, Derbyshire is cited as "Farmer of 200 Acres, employing 3 outdoor & 6 indoor labs".

580 "The 1861 Census for England was taken on the night of 7 April 1861. All responses were to reflect the individual's status as of 7 April 1861 for all individuals who had spent the night in the house. People who were traveling (*sic!*) or living abroad were enumerated at the location where they spent the night on census night." "Name of street, avenue, road, etca., House name or number, Whether property vacant or inhabited, Surname of head of household, Name of persons who had spent the night in the household, Relationship of enumerated person to head of house, Person's marital status, Age at last birthday (gender indicated by column in which age is recorded), Person's occupation, Person's place of birth, Whether blind, deaf, or idiot.", cf. http://search.ancestry.co.uk/search/db.aspx?dbid=8767 (viewed 31/10/2012).

581 A legal and administrative position: DL is deputy lieutenant for the county of Derbyshire that is a deputy for the Lord Lieutenant of Derbyshire. Several magistrates would be appointed deputy lieutenants at any one time. Magistrate means that the person in question was a justice of the peace, presumably for the county of Derbyshire. This person would therefore sit on the Derbyshire Quarter Sessions and at Petty Sessions with other magistrates, information disclosed by Mark Pearsall of the National Archives (London) by E-mail on March 4, 2013.

was the Nurse; Mary Maginnis, aged 29, unmarried, born in Ireland, was the House Maid[582]; Ellen Nichol, aged 19, unmarried, born in Newton Hall, Durham, was the Nurse Maid; Ann Ellis, aged 24, unmarried, born in Whitwell, Derbyshire was the Kitchen Maid (a relative to Mary Ellis of Whitwell/1851?); Elizabeth Barlow, aged 16, unmarried, born in Whitwell, Derbyshire was the Dairy Maid. The family had a Butler: John Bonney, aged 40, unmarried, born in Inskip, Lancashire. John Houson, aged 23, unmarried, born in Huntingdon, Yorkshire was working as a Groom.

The **1871** census of England and Wales[583] gives some indication of an even lager household at Southgate House. Henry (5) Bowdon was still Head and aged 55 at that time, born in Barlbro (*sic!*), Derbyshire. His wife Harriet Bowdon was by now aged 39, born in Mapledurham, Oxfordshire. Their two daughters, Alice E Bowdon, aged 16, born in Clown, Derbyshire, and Constance M Bowdon, aged 13, born in Clown, Derbyshire, still lived in their household. The family must have been quite well-off at that time since they could afford by then eight servants: Elizabeth Drury, aged 28, unmarried, born in Rochdale, Lancashire was the Governess; Thomas Fryer, aged 30, unmarried, born in Markington, Yorkshire was the Butler; Frank Stringfellow[584], aged 29, unmarried, born in Radford, Nottinghamshire worked as Coachman (a relative of Christopher Stringfellow/1841?); Lydia Oates, aged 28, unmarried, born in Bradfield, Yorkshire was the Cook and

---

582 The presence of Irish people in England at this period is not surprising as it coincided with the Great Potato Famine in Ireland (between 1845 and 1852) which led to emigration as a consequence of starvation and disease in Ireland; cf. Encyclopedia Britannica, *Irish Potato Famine*. For further evidence of Irish maids in the area see Linacre, *How it was*, p. 32.

583 "The 1871 census for England was taken on the night of 2 April 1871. Enumeration forms were distributed to all households a few days before the census night and the household members were required to complete the forms themselves. The next day, the enumerators collected the completed forms. All of the details from the individual forms were later sorted and copied into enumerators' books. The information requested on the census included: Address (name of the street, avenue, or road; house number) Occupant (name of each person who spent the night in the house; their birthplace and relationship to head of family) Residence (whether home was inhabited; number of rooms occupied, Personal (sex, age, marital status), Occupation (whether employer, employee, or neither), Health (whether blind, deaf, dumb, imbecile, idiot, or lunatic)"; cf. http://search.ancestry.co.uk/search/db.aspx?dbid=7619 (viewed 31/10/2012).

584 According to the Clowne parish registers we may have a very tragic case of a child's early death a year later: the registers in 1872 note the demise of twin girls with Stringfellow as their surname. It is speculative but not impossible that Frank Stringfellow, who was 30 years old at that time, had married in the meantime and was the father of little Ann and Fanny. Ann Stringfellow died one day after her birth (September 26, 1872), her sister followed her three weeks later (October 18, 1872); cf. Spencer, *Clowne Burials*.

presumably her sister Elizabeth Oates, aged 21, unmarried, born in Bradfield, Yorkshire worked as Kitchen Maid; Rachel Wilson, aged 26, unmarried, born in Overbury, Worcestershire was a House Maid as was Sarah Lomas, aged 16, unmarried, born in Whitwell, Derbyshire and Frances Wilkinson, aged 22, unmarried, born in County Durham served as Lady's Maid.

The **1881** census of England and Wales[585] provides us with no information on occupants of Southgate House, only for a "detached house" of Southgate House Estate, which surely refers to one of the outbuildings (see Chapter 14.2). Any other occupants of the Estate of Southgate are notable by their absence in the census. This could be connected to the sale of all farming stock in 1879, then trying to rent out the house in 1882 (see Chapter 11). On the other hand the census of **1881** shows that Harriet Bowdon, now 49 years old, lived in Beighton Fields Priory, was widowed and the head of the family (her rank declares her as Lady, her birthplace is given as Mapledurham, Oxfordshire). She resided there with her two unmarried daughters Alice and Constance (aged 26 and 23 now, both born in Clowne, Derbyshire). They still had four servants with them: Lydia Rowe, aged 20, unmarried, born in Swanage, Dorsetshire, Ladies Maid; Elizabeth Leyman, aged 29, unmarried, born in Lancaster, Parlour Maid; Eliza Rodgers, aged 25, unmarried, born in Clowne, Derbyshire, Cook; Sarah Mullis, aged 25, unmarried, born in Wawkshire (= Warwickshire), House Maid. These new circumstances allow us to presume that following some grave changes Southgate House stood empty and was therefore not recorded in the census.

The article that advertises Southgate House to be let in The Derbyshire Times and Chesterfield Herald of December 27, **1882** (see Chapter 11) mentions of the number of rooms at Southgate House at that time: thirteen bed and dressing rooms, two entrance halls, drawing and dining rooms, kitchens and servant's offices, and two bathrooms.

---

585 "The 1881 British Isles Census was taken on the night of 3 April 1881. The following information was requested: Name of street, avenue road, etca., House number or name, Whether or not the house was inhabited, Number of rooms occupied if less than five, Name of each person that had spent the night in that household, Relationship of person enumerated to the head of the family, Each person's marital status, Age at last birthday (sex is indicated by which column the age is recorded in), Each person's occupation, Person's place of birth, Whether deaf and dumb, blind, imbecile or idiot, or lunatica (*sic!*).", cf. http://search.ancestry.co.uk/search/db.aspx?dbid=7572 (viewed 31/10/2012).

As occupants of Southgate House the **1891** census of England and Wales[586] records an entirely new family (according to Philip Riden they were tenants[587])[588]: Head of Household was Harry Aldam Fowler, aged 40, born in York, North Yorkshire (d. 1927).[589] His wife Isabel Fowler, aged 43, was born in Scarbro (= Scarborough). They had seven children: William E Nesfield Fowler, aged 14, born in Ross-Shire, Scotland; Muriel Fowler, aged 13, born in Whittingdon, Derbyshire as was Isabel N Fowler, aged 11, Emily G Fowler, aged 9, Cecil Fowler, aged 8. Ronald Fowler, aged 5, was born in Falsgrave, Yorkshire and Geoffrey Nesfield Fowler, aged 1, was born in Clown (*sic!*), Derbyshire. All children apart from toddler Geoffrey are denoted as scholars. The Fowler household was quite large and comprised of six servants: Emily M Hayes, aged 25, single, born in Brimington, Derbyshire was Cook Domestic; Bertha Swift, aged 21, single, born in Whittington, Derbyshire was Parlourmaid Domestic; Mary Hannah Nilse, aged 16, single, born in Pilsley, Derbyshire was Kitchen Maid Domestic; Mary Ann Abel, aged 16, single, born in Staveley, Derbyshire, worked as Housemaid Domestic; Thomas W Wragg, aged 12, born in Brackenfield, Derbyshire was the Groom of the estate and James Cowley, aged 72, born in Elk(e)sley, widower, Nottinghamshire was the Gamekeeper.[590] The **1881** census lists the Fowlers as still resident at

---

[586] "The 1891 Census for England was taken on the night of 5 April 1891. All responses were to reflect the individual's status as of 5 April 1891 for all individuals who had spent the night in the house. People who were traveling (*sic!*) or living abroad were enumerated at the location where they spent the night on census night. The 1891 census has several more questions than are found on earlier census returns including questions employment status and the number of rooms occupied in the house if less than five.", "Name of street, avenue, road, etca., House name or number, Whether property vacant or inhabited, Surname of head of household, Name of persons who had spent the night in the household, Relationship of enumerated person to head of house, Person's marital status, Age at last birthday (gender indicated by column in which age is recorded) , Person's occupation, Person's place of birth. Whether blind, deaf, or idiot"; cf. http://search.ancestry.co.uk/search/db.aspx?dbid=6598 (viewed 31/10/2012).

[587] At that time they must have been tenants of John (6) Erdeswick Butler-Bowdon; compare Riden, *Clowne Manors and Estates*, p. 2 and p. 5, footnote 1 who records him as one of the principal owners of freehold estates in the parish of Clowne in 1895; cf. also Craven, "Southgate House, Clowne", p. 58.

[588] Riden, *Clowne Manors and Estates*, p. 5.

[589] Harry Aldam Fowler was the son of William Fowler of Whittington Hall which he inherited and sold in 1893, when he moved to Southgate House; cf. Craven, "Southgate House, Clowne", p. 58, but according to the census returns the family is attested at Southgate as early as 1891.

[590] A list which can be retrieved from the website of Whitwell Local History Group lists all burials of Whitwell through the centuries and relates to several elements of Southgate Estate. For "Southgate House" it reveals that the Fowler's had another daughter who died very young: Ethel Margaret Fowler (b. 1891, d. 28/08/1895); cf.

Whittington (Hall), Chesterfield, a house they inherited and the birthplace of four of their children. They lived there until 1893, when they sold Whittington Hall and moved to Southgate House.[591] They could afford to keep eight servants at that time, one of them could have been James Cowley (widower), then aged 62, who is listed in the same census but separately, his occupation described as Game Keeper and as living in Whittington, probably close to his employer whom he followed to Southgate House during the next decade. All other servants have changed. According to the censuses in **1891** the Bowdon family themselves lived in Barlborough House (Lancelot Butler-Bowdon) and Beighton Fields Priory (Harriet Bowdon) (see Chapters 18 and 22).

According to coverage in a newspaper article in The Derbyshire Times and Chesterfield Herald dated November 8, **1899**, William Nesfield Fowler, by now aged 22, still lived at Southgate House (see Chapter 8), but the **1901** census of England and Wales[592] shows that the Bowdon family is back. The Butler-Bowdons from Pleasington Hall, Lancashire (see Chapter 21 and **1891** census for Lancashire) moved to Southgate House in 1900.[593] However, after leaving Pleasington Hall the family must have made a temporary detour to the south of England[594] as John (6) Erdeswick Butler-Bowdon is attested as "formerly of Pleasington Hall but now of Bournemouth, co. Hants. esq.".[595]

Hopkins, *Graves Index*. The list further names a William Robinson (b. 1789, d. 29/04/1834), an Elizabeth Sayer (b. 1778, d. 14/11/1814), two infant girls named Alice Womble (d. 03/01/1899) and Martha Womble (d. 10/01/1900), a Mathew Wood (b. 1829, d. 04/11/1890), and a little boy named Arthur Leonard Leary (b. 1890, d. 07/09/1893, buried on Coroner's order) as residents of "Southgate". Apart for Arthur Leonard Leary, who was the son of the coal miner family Leary from Southgate Cottages (see Chapter 14.2.3), and the two little Womble girls who in all probability belonged to the Womble family of Whitwell Common Southgate (unspecified) as recorded in the 1901 census returns (Coal Miner George Womble and wife Alice with daughter Mabel Womble and stepson James Sidebottom), it proved impossible from this information to relate any listed person to a position at Southgate House or Estate.

591 http://www.vandykhotel.co.uk/assets/vision-mag-spring-2012_web.pdf, p. 2 (viewed 15/10/2012).

592 "A nationwide census was conducted in England and Wales on 31 March 1901. It contains records for 32 million people and 6 million houses. It covers the whole of England and Wales, with the exception of parts of Deal in Kent. Separate censuses were held in Scotland and Ireland. Certain parts of the records have suffered damage and therefore some information is missing, but it is largely complete."; cf. http://en.wikipedia.org/wiki/United_Kingdom_Census_1901 (viewed 31/10/2012); http://www.1901censusonline.com/ (viewed 31/10/2012).

593 Staples, *My Parish*, p. 1.

594 Child, *Pleasington Priory*, p. 54.

595 Ancient deeds relating to the manor of Clayton-le-Moors (Trappes-Lomax family of Clayton Hall), Lancashire (near Great Harwood, ca. 2 km east of Blackburn) kept in Lancashire Record Office (Lancashire Record Office, *Ref. No. DDLX 3/16* (dated 02/02/1894) and *DDLX 8/32* (dated 28/03/1894, original documents not viewed

The 1901 census lists a large number of household members of Southgate House for that year: head of the family in 1901 was John (6) Erdeswick Butler-Bowdon, aged 51, born in Rugely, Staffordshire. His occupation is given as "Gentleman J P Late Col Militia".[596] His profession has been written over with the notation "Army Off" in a different handwriting at a later point in time. His second wife, Monica E Butler-Bowdon, aged 40, born in Portland Pl, London and four of their remaining nine children were present on the day of the day of the census[597]: Theresa, aged 18, Ursula, aged 11, Isabel, aged 8, and Basil, aged 1. All children were born in Pleasington Hall, Lancashire except Basil who was born in Bournemouth, Hants. (*sic!*)[598]. Belonging to the household were eight servants: Sarah A Bentley, aged 46, widow, born in Padbury, Buckinghamshire, Maid Domestic; Edith Harrison, aged 20, single, born in Burton, Staffordshire, Housemaid Domestic; Annie Cupit, aged 20, single born in N Wingfield, Derbyshire, Scullery Maid Domestic; Harold Pearson, aged 14, from Malpas, Cheshire, Pageboy Domestic; Caroline Taylor, aged 20, single, born in Derby, Derbyshire, Nursery Maid Domestic; Katherine Moran, aged 24, single, born in Cheltenham, Gloucestershire, Nurse Domestic; Harriet L Gossor, aged 29, widow, born in Weybridge, Surrey, Cook Domestic and Mary Jones, aged 24, single, born in Candroom, N Wales, Housemaid Domestic. The parents of Teresa Staples were among the staff of the following years as she recalls that her parents came to Southgate in **1907** (see Chapter 14.1).[599]

In the Land Values Map and its related Books of Reference dated 1909/1910[600], John (6) Butler-Bowdon is recorded as the owner of Southgate Estate comprising of houses, cottages and gardens, agricultural lands and

personally) reveal that, at least in February and March 1894, John (6) Erdeswick Butler-Bowdon had his residence in Bournemouth, Hants. Bournemouth was in Hampshire until 1974 when the boundary was changed and it became part of Dorset. The writing "Hants." for Hampshire is curious. The abbreviated form is derived from the Old English "Hantum plus Scir" (meaning a district governed from the settlement today known as Southampton). The Anglo-Saxons called it "Hantumschire". At the time of the Domesday Book (1086) it was compressed into "Hantescire". Information disclosed in a private E-mail correspondence between Edward W Austin and the author on August 8, 2013.

596 This refers to a Justice of the Peace, who also appears to have been a colonel of a body of militia; a local volunteer force, whose origins extend back to Anglo-Saxon times, which could be called up in times of war. In the UK the militia ceased to exist in 1908 and became part of the Territorial Force. Information disclosed by Craig Murray of the Imperial War Museum (London) by E-mail on February 26, 2013.

597 Freer, *Descendants of William the Conqueror*. One of their originally ten children, Bernard Joseph, died as an infant in 1897.

598 For the abbreviation of "Hants." for Hampshire see above.

599 Staples, *My Parish*, p. 1.

600 Derbyshire Record Office, *Ref. No. D595*.

woodlands. He himself is listed as the occupier of Southgate House and its garden, the agricultural land as well as the woodlands (see Chapter 9).

The **1911** census of England and Wales shows a slightly reduced household: John (6) Erdeswick Butler-Bowdon and his family are still the inhabitants of Southgate House. Head of the household is, as ten years before, John (6) Erdeswick Butler-Bowdon, now aged 61, born in Rudgely, Staffordshire. His career in the army is stated here as "Col Retired Lanc Regt".[601] John Erdeswick is now married to Mary Monica Butler-Bowdon in third marriage, aged 50, born in Wigan, Lancashire, his second wife Monica Mary having passed away in 1907 (for the first wife see Chapters 8 and 10 and the family tree of the Butler-Bowdon family on Figure 30). At the day of the census their daughter-in-law was staying at Southgate House (Gertrude Mary Butler-Bowdon, née de Trafford, aged 22, born in Haselow Tormouth, Staffordshire, and married to William Erdeswick Ignatius Butler-Bowdon, the son of John (6) Erdeswick and his wife from his second marriage). Also residing at Southgate was a niece of the family, Agnes Mary de Trafford, aged 21, single, born in Haselow Tormouth, Staffordshire. A Roman Catholic priest was also present on that day: Wilfried Tonge, aged 25, born in Derby, Derbyshire. The household had four servants: Elizabeth Mottram, aged 42, single, born in Porthandwich, Cheshire, General Servant Domestic; Catherine Leese, aged 28, single, born in Bloxwich, Staffordshire, General Servant Domestic; Henrietta Loringe, aged 21, single, born in Plymouth, Devonshire, General servant Domestic and Mary McKnight, aged 16, single, born in Liverpool, Lancashire, General Servant Domestic. The **1911** census is the first census that allows an extra entry for the number of rooms in the property concerned, counting the kitchen as a room, but excluding the scullery, landing, lobby, closet or bathroom, warehouse, office, and shop. John (6) Erdeswick Butler-Bowdon, who also filled in most parts of the form and countersigned it, recorded twenty-two rooms in total for Southgate House. The sheet is countersigned by the enumerator (initials).

For the time being the censuses end with the survey of 1911. For further research on the occupants of Southgate House, Stables and Cottages in the years following 1911, I consulted various on-line sources and the Electoral Rolls of Derbyshire, available from the Derbyshire Record Office in Matlock. Several years which made strategic sense for the research were selected. John (6) Erdeswick Butler-Bowdon is named in **1912** as occupant and freeholder of houses and land at Southgate. As there was no universal suffrage for women in England before 1918 (when it was still restricted; full voting rights were not granted to women before July 2, 1928), no other members of the Butler-

[601] This stands for a retired colonel of the Lancashire Regiment. This may either refer to the honorary title of Colonel of the Regiment, which a civilian can hold; or the man may actually have held the military rank of colonel. Information disclosed by Craig Murray of the Imperial War Museum (London) by E-mail on February 26, 2013.

Bowdon family or female members of their household are listed in the Electoral Rolls. The picture for **1913** is almost identical. John (6) Erdeswick Butler-Bowdon is inhabitant and freeholder of houses and land at Southgate. Female members of family and staff remain unnoted. For May **1914** John (6) Butler-Bowdon is attested "of Southgate House, near Chesterfield, co. Derby, esq." in a document related to the manor of Clayton-le-Moors, Lancashire held by Lancashire Archives.[602] According to the Electoral Rolls in **1914** and **1915** the situation remains mostly unchanged: John (6) Erdeswick Butler-Bowdon is occupant and freeholder of house/land at Southgate and females and minors go unnoted. In the years 1916 and 1917 no Electoral Rolls were produced. In **1918** things have changed. Women have a restricted suffrage now and alongside John (6) Erdeswick Butler-Bowdon Mary Monica Butler-Bowdon, the third wife of John (6), appears again in the documents. The total number of inhabitants including personnel can still not be established however, as females under the age of 28 and minors were not recorded. Between **1920** and **1928**, John (6) Erdeswick Butler-Bowdon and Mary Monica Butler-Bowdon are the occupants of Southgate House. After John (6) Erdeswick Butler-Bowdon's death in January 1929, Southgate Estate passed into the ownership of his eldest son, William Erdeswick Ignatius Butler-Bowdon and his family. So subsequently in **1930** and **1931** it is William Erdeswick Ignatius Butler-Bowdon and his wife, Gertrude Mary Butler-Bowdon, née de Trafford, who inhabited Southgate House, and they employed two domestic servants (under-age persons who were not eligible to vote were not recorded): Annie Maria Wills and Eileen Mary Liddy. The Electoral Rolls list William Erdeswick Ignatius Butler-Bowdon and his wife, Gertrude Mary Butler-Bowdon for **1932** and also mention their first-born son Maurice Erdeswick, born in 1910.[603] Their second son Anthony William, born in 1913, is curiously enough absent from the electoral lists and remains untraceable through official sources.[604] Eileen Mary Liddy is still an employee of the Butler-Bowdons. In **1934** the household has slightly expanded: alongside William Erdeswick Ignatius, Gertrude Butler-Bowdon and Maurice

---

[602] Lancashire Record Office, *Ref. No. DDLX 3/38* dated May 21, 1914 (original document not viewed personally).

[603] Maurice Butler-Bowdon seemingly did not live at home. In the Electoral Rolls he is continuously listed as "absent" and as Naval Voter between the years 1932 and 1939, he was Midshipman and later Lieutenant and Captain of the Royal Navy (see Chapter 10).

[604] Humphrey Butler-Bowdon provided me with additional information, disclosed in a personal E-mail correspondence with the author dated November 26, 2013: "My uncle Anthony was Maurice's younger brother. In those days younger sons still figured less in records because the eldest took over the estates, in England at least." Anthony Butler-Bowdon became an architect. He lived in Italy, then in South Africa. In the 1960s he and his wife emigrated to Australia, where he set up his own architectural practise and stayed there.

Butler-Bowdon there are Eileen Mary Liddy, Ethel Reeves and Henrietta Hussey. Miss Reeves did not stay long however: in **1935** the occupants of Southgate House consist of William Erdeswick Ignatius, Gertrude and Maurice Butler-Bowdon as well as Eileen Mary Liddy and Henrietta Hussey. In addition to the Butler-Bowdon family the Electoral Rolls in **1936** list apart from Eileen Mary Liddy and Rachael Bradley as employees. Eileen Mary Liddy quit her job at that time as she got married to Arthur Maxfield (see Chapter 14.2), so in **1937** William Erdeswick Ignatius, Gertrude and Maurice Butler-Bowdon shared their house with Rachael Bradley and Annie Zilla Pendleton. The year **1938** marks another watershed when Southgate Estate apparently passed into the hands of Maurice Erdeswick Butler-Bowdon. No further family members are mentioned, the Electoral Rolls of **1938** and **1939** name him as the sole occupant.[605] In all probability his parents had by then moved to the south of England (William Erdeswick Ignatius Butler-Bowdon is attested for Dapsland, Mayfield, Sussex in 1955, see Chapter 8). British Army immediately took possession of Southgate House when WWII broke out in 1939.[606]

During the years of the Second World War no Electoral Rolls were produced, so I had to find information on occupants of Southgate House for those years through other sources. One is from a Mr Terry Boden, who in an on-line database from the year 2010 mentions that his father, Stanley Boden, was stationed at Southgate House in about **1943**, but he does not give any further details as to his father's occupation there and whether he actually lived on the premises.[607]

The picture for **1945**, when the Electoral Rolls were produced again, is somewhat diffuse. Two names are listed for Southgate House: Frances A Ashley and Margaret Jackson. It is impossible to determine the function of these two ladies in regard to Southgate House. For the following years the Electoral Rolls reveal no information on the occupants of Southgate House, the owner of the estate at that time must have been Sir Osbert Sitwell (see Chapter 8), but it seems that he did not do much in the interests of the house, nor the estate. When she was a small girl June Pearce remembers Southgate House being a little bit dilapidated and overgrown. As a child she evidently perceived it as a haunted place and writes: "We thought the 'witches' lived there."[608] From this it can be concluded that in those years Southgate House

---

605 The Electoral Rolls of 1938 show an interesting typo: Maurice Erdeswick Butler-Bowdon is accidentally recorded for the previous address in the list which is Little Walls Farm, but that must be a mistake as all other members of the Southgate household of that particular year are listed correctly in the line beneath.

606 Staples, *My Parish*, p. 5.

607 http://www.clownevillage.co.uk/feedback/feedback.htm (viewed 19/05/2013).

608 Information disclosed in a private E-Mail correspondence between June Pearce and the author on May 24, 2013.

stood empty, but from 1955 on it must have been managed remotely by the Van Dyk brothers who bought the place from the Sitwells in that year and moved into Southgate House in 1957 after having carried out extensive renovation work on the house. The London Gazette from January 22, 1963 lists a Dutchman named Cornelis Josef van Dijk known as Cornelis Josef Van Dyk working as a Market Gardener at Southgate House for November 12, **1962**.[609] Neither he nor his brother is listed in the Electoral Rolls of that year for Southgate. Even though I cannot say where Corneli/us Josef lived at that time, the new occupants of Southgate House in **1963** are his brother Petru/os Johannes Van Dyk and his wife Antonia Maria, accompanied by Stanley Shipstone, probably an employee. 1963 therefore marks the dawning of a new era and a new life for Southgate House.

In **1965** Cornelis Van Dyk and his wife Evelyn too moved into Southgate House, and Stanley Shipstone had evidently also found a wife: Ilse. According to Maxwell Craven, the Van Dyk brothers opened a nursery in Southgate in the same year.[610] They expanded their business by opening "Southgate House Hotel" in 1966, but sold both establishments again only three years later, in 1969.

The year **1968** marks the presence of an unexpected lodger at Southgate: in that very year Clowne became a parish with its own first diocesan priest, Father Calnan, who stayed for a couple of months. According to Teresa Staples, the question of his living quarters was solved by the help of the Van Dyk family. They offered the new priest accommodation at their hotel.[611]

The Electoral Rolls of **1969** reveal that Petros and Antonia Van Dyk still live at Southgate House; and Cornelis and Evelyn Van Dyk have moved to "Meadow View", newly built lodgings on the premises.[612] The new proprietors of Southgate House Hotel are Reginald and Shelagh Ferguson. And another person is listed at the same address: Joseph Calman (who will be the above mentioned Father Calnan). There is now also more accommodation on the grounds of Southgate: a place called "Southgate Nurseries" became home of the Hannon family (David, Monica J, Monica J (jnr), Michael and Christine) and to Michael Early.

A so far unrecorded property related to Southgate named "No 3 Bungalow" became the living quarters of another family in that very year: the

---

609 The London Gazette from January 22, 1963, p. 717; cf. http://www.london-gazette.co.uk/issues/42901/pages/ (viewed 29/10/2012).

610 Craven, "Southgate House, Clowne", p. 58.

611 Staples, *My Parish*, p. 10.

612 The aerial view on Google Maps (viewed 06/05/2013) shows a few freestanding houses behind the nurseries/greenhouses of the Van Dyk's Garden Centre. One of the buildings is marked as „Rose Bank"; cf. Electoral Rolls of 1995, the other houses will be „Meadow View", „Woodlands", and the bungalows.

Holdsworths (Frederick, Nellie and Geoffrey).[613] According to the recollections of Mary Jones (see Chapter 8) the Van Dyk's provided plots of land for their loyal employees to build their own bungalows directly on the premises of Southgate House[614], also possibly in order to keep short their trip to work. I believe that the adults listed in the Electoral Rolls of 1969 for Southgate were workers of Southgate Nurseries or Southgate House Hotel.

In **1970** the situation remains pretty much unchanged, only with a slightly reduced occupation: Petros and Antonia van Dyk are registered as inhabitants of Southgate House, Reginald and Shelagh Ferguson are the proprietors of "Southgate House Hotel", Cornelus and Evelyn Van Dyk live at "Meadow View", David, Monica J and Michael Hannon occupy "Woodland, Southgate Nursery", Frederick, Nellie and Geoffrey G Holdsworth are the inhabitants of "No 3 Bungalow Southgate".

My next sample from the Electoral Rolls is **1975**. In this year Petros and Antonia Van Dyk still live at Southgate House. But changes have occurred: "Southgate House Hotel" is now "Van Dyk Hotel" and its new owners and operators are Jose and Marie Romay. Two employees seem to be living with them on the premises: Christopher Oldhams and Carol F Ford. At "Meadow View" we still find Cornelus and Evelyn Van Dyk, at "Woodland Southgate Nursery" David, Monica J and Michael Hannon, and at "No 3 Bungalows Southgate Nurseries" Frederick G, Nellie, Geoffrey G and June Holdsworth.

The hotel changed hands again in the late 1970s/early 1980s when Mansfield Brewery became the new owner and with it Frank M Smith and his wife Dorothy A Smith the persons who ran the business.[615] Their presence is attested by the Electoral Rolls of **1980**. Together with them Henry Rybicki, Joel Le-Roy and Beverley Whitworth (certainly employees) are listed for "Van Dyk Hotel". In the meantime a new Dutch family has arrived: Jacob Plug and Adreana (*sic!*) D Plug-Philippo live with them under the same roof at Southgate House. The annexes are inhabited by Dirk C Plug[616] and

---

613 Another recent map available on-line (www.footpathmaps.com, viewed 15/05/2013) attests the presence of a row of five semidetached houses in Whitwell Commons today called "Southgate Bungalows". They are located directly on the southern side of the A619, ca. 150 m to the west of the crossroads of Gapsick Lane/Gipsyhill Lane, quite a bit away from Southgate House. According to Mary Jones, these bungalows have been there as long as she can remember and have nothing to do with Southgate House. The naming is just coincidental, the houses were probably named after the avenue; information disclosed in a personal E-mail correspondence between Mary Jones and the author on June 1, 2013.

614 Information disclosed in a personal E-mail correspondence between Mary Jones and the author on May 29, 2013.

615 Mr Smith was the manager of Hotel Van Dyk when it was owned by Mansfield Brewery (see Chapter 8). Information disclosed in a personal E-mail correspondence between Tony Bak and the author on February 12, 2014.

616 Jacob Plug and Dirk C Plug were presumably close relatives (brothers?).

Willenyntje[617] Plug-Kroon ("Meadow View"), David and Monica J Hannon ("Woodland, Southgate Nurseries"), and Frederick G and Nellie Holdsworth with Geoffrey and June Holdsworth ("No 3 Bungalow, Southgate Nurseries"). The **1985** Electoral Rolls record the following inhabitants for "Van Dyk Hotel": Frank M and Dorothy A Smith. A third person listed at the house is Bruce P C Holden. David and Monica J Hannon share "Woodland, Southgate Nurseries" with Christine Coddington, and Fredrick G Holdsworth lives at "No 3 Bungalows, Southgate Nurseries" together with Nellie, Geoffrey G and June Holdsworth. In **1995** Dorothy and Frank M Smith are listed at the Van Dyk Hotel together with Michael P Smith. Dirk Plug (jnr), Dirk Plug (snr), and Wilhelmina Plug-Kroon are the inhabitants of "2 Bungalow, Southgate House Nurseries"; Geoffrey and June Holdsworth occupy "Rosebank Southgate House Nurseries"; Frederick and Nellie Holdsworth are still living at "3 Southgate House Nurseries" and "Woodlands" has new occupants: Colin, Jack and Richard Goulder. Dorothy and M Frank Smith, together with James Smith and Michael Smith are registered in the Electoral Rolls of **1999** at the "Van Dyk Hotel". Cornelis G B Plug, Jacob G Plug and Adriana Plug-Philippo are the inhabitants of "Bungalow No 1, Southgate House", Wilhelma Plug is listed at "Southgate House", Dirk C G Plug, Dirk C G Plug (jnr) and Wilhelmina Plug-Kroon live at "2 Bungalow Southgate House Nurseries, Nellie Holdsworth at "3 Southgate House Nurseries", June Holdsworth at "Rosebank, Southgate House Nurseries", and Colin and Jack Goulder share "Woodlands". Since **2002** Hotel Van Dyk has been owned by the Eyre family.[618]

14.1. "A Room of One's Own"[619] - An Interview with Mona Ives

At the end of the 19th and beginning of the 20th century the choice of work in the area of Barlborough and Clowne was very limited. Men predominantly worked in the coal mines, colliery offices, shops or on farms. Jobs for women were even more few and far between, so one of the main sources of income for female workers in the region, apart from working in a jam factory in Bolsover, was to go into domestic service.[620]

Aged 92 in 2013 Esmé Mona Ives (née Godfrey) is one of the eldest inhabitants of Barlborough today. As a young girl she used to work as Maid Domestic at Southgate House. I got to know her through Tony Bak of Barlborough Heritage and Resource Centre and Mrs Ives very kindly agreed

617 Misspelling for Willemijntje, a pet name for Wilhelmina.

618 http://www.vandykhotel.co.uk/assets/vision-mag-spring-2012_web.pdf, p. 2 (viewed 25/10/2012).

619 "A Room of One's Own", essay written by Virginia Woolf (1929).

620 Riden, History of the County of Derby III, p. 7.

to an interview on her life in Gentlemen's Service.[621] She was born, christened[622] and confirmed in Clowne, but moved to Barlborough with her family when she was eleven years old. Her mother came from Nottingham and, according to Mrs Ives, was homesick all her life in Clowne; her father was a local man from New Barlborough. Even though she lived at Raines Avenue in Worksop at that time, Mrs Ives was married in Barlborough (in 1939 in St. James Church[623]) to her husband Cyril Ives (b. 21/11/1914 - d. 1973), who was a drummer in a band. Today she is widowed.

Mrs Ives was always in Gentlemen's Service. Aside from Southgate House she also worked at Worksop Manor and Barlborough House. She recalls working at Southgate House for four years in the mid 1930s.[624] She is not listed in the Electoral Rolls of those years as she was under age. Young girls often went into service when they left school at the age of fourteen, and Mrs Ives was no exception to the rule: she took up work at Southgate House when she was around fourteen or fifteen years and left at the age of nineteen when the Butler-Bowdons moved to Sussex (ca. 1939).[625] The family asked Mona to go with them, but she declined their offer and decided instead to stay in the local area.

Mrs Ives' position at Southgate house was that of the Upstairs Maid. Her tasks included taking care of the bedrooms, bathrooms, cleaning the stairs, making the fires and carrying the required coal up from the coalhouse in metal baskets. The house had certain places where servants were not allowed, and the family supervised the cleaning. The heavily brass-plated fittings around the fireplaces, the so-called "fireside companions" (accessories needed to keep the fires going such as pokers and irons), needed regular polishing. The fireside fenders were made of mesh. Another task of Mrs Ives' was the cleaning of the chapel.[626] Sunday therefore always was a busy day for her. The

---

621 The interview took place on September 21, 2013 in the presence of Tony Bak of Barlborough Heritage and Resource Centre at the home of Mrs Ives in Barlborough.

622 www.findmypast.co.uk (Parish Record Collection/Baptism Records for Carburton and Clowne) (viewed 23/10/2013).

623 www.findmypast.co.uk (Parish Record Collection/Marriage Records for Barlborough) (viewed 23/10/2013).

624 This is the time when the number of domestic servants in British household were already on the decline: by 1931 only 5% of British households still had resident servants, and this number reduced to 1% by 1951 when, except for part-time cleaners, domestic service ceased to exist; Hobsbawm, *Industry and Empire*, p. 262. For a synopsis on the chores of the household members living "below stairs" see Ferry, *Victorian Home*, p. 45ff.; Horn, *Victorian Country House*, p. 25ff.

625 Mrs Ives remained undocumented in the Electoral Rolls because she was too young to be entitled to vote when she lived and worked at Southgate House.

626 In her memoirs Teresa Staples writes that her mother, her sister and she cleaned the chapel, washed the linen, saw to the flowers and laid out the vestments every Saturday night until 1948; cf. Staples, *My Parish*, p. 5.

chapel was not very big and she describes the interior as "plain" and recalls a few pews for the worshippers. Locals attended Sunday mass, but since Mrs Ives was not a Catholic but Church of England, she never partook in the services and could therefore not say whether the Butler-Bowdons were also present.[627]

The working day at Southgate House began for the servants at 7 o'clock in the morning and lasted until 7 o'clock in the evening. Bedtime was usually around 9 o'clock at night. There was a mid-morning and a luncheon break (and most likely a dinner, but Mrs Ives did not mention this).[628] Mrs Ives received a salary of 2 pounds and 4 shillings for her work from the first week on, the salary itself was dependent on the position in the household.[629] She had half a day off per week, and each maid had a different day off in order to maintain a stabile staffing level. There was no spare time during the day when working at Southgate House, but relaxing and leisure could be found with a sandwich and a cup of tea during the breaks. Mrs Ives belonged to Southgate House's live-in staff.[630] Her room was "in the roof" and she describes it as "very bare".

Like any other maid in service Mrs Ives had to wear a uniform when on duty. This consisted of a white cap, a print dress, and a pinafore. Dresses were changed in the afternoon for the evening shift and a little apron replaced the pinny.

The servant's quarters were simple. The servant's hall had huge windows and a bare wooden floor with peg rugs, and the large wooden table had no cloth on. During rest time elevenses were taken in the servant's hall. While Mrs Ives worked at Southgate House the personnel consisted of four members

---

627 Ruby Thorpe recalls that she was also not admitted to the chapel as she was not a Catholic (information disclosed by Ruby Thorpe during a personal meeting with the author in Clowne on April 27, 2014). Teresa Staples recalls attending early Sunday service together with her siblings and the maids of Southgate house; cf. Staples, *My Parish*, p. 2.

628 For the daily routines of domestic servants and the allocation of their tasks see also Ferry, *Victorian Home*, p. 55f.

629 For comparison: in those years the average income of an employed male worker was about £3 per week; cf. Hobsbawm, *Industry and Empire*, p. 199. In her memoirs Margaret Powell reports that as a kitchen maid in the early 1920s in a household in Hove near Brighton she earned £24 a year, paid on a monthly base (= £2 per month); cf. Powell, *Below Stairs*, p. 40. When she transferred to a London household a little later she earned four pounds a year more (p. 79), and when she advanced to work as cook she received a yearly salary of £40 (p. 125). On p. 193f. she confirms the weekly wage of a male worker: her husband, a milkman, earned "three pounds five a week".

630 The presence of Mrs Ives as an inhabitant of Southgate House could not be confirmed by the Electoral Rolls, she was too young to be entitled to vote during the years she worked there.

of staff; along with herself there were a superior "head housemaid", a gardener, and a cook by herself (viz no kitchen maid). There was no footman.

Jobs for domestic personnel were normally advertised in local newspapers and servant girls often came from all over the country. Mrs Ives recalls the day when while she was working at Southgate a young girl was brought in by her father in order to work there as a maid. The girl, however, had other plans for her life and did not want to work. She escaped over the roof during her very first night at Southgate House, but was subsequently brought back by her father against her will. Mrs Ives herself could not remember how she got her position at Southgate House, but she thinks it was connected to the fact that she had made friends with one of the girls living at one of the cottages of Southgate Estate while she was still working at Worksop Manor.

As employers the Butler-Bowdons kept a distance from their staff, there was not much personal contact. But Mrs Ives had contact with the Butler-Bowdon children insofar as that some children had nannies and the housemaids often answered to the nannies as well as the family members.[631]

The servants knew the rules at Southgate House and abided by them by and large. Only when it came to taking small personal liberties in their meagre spare time did Mrs Ives develop creative strategies. The outer doors were locked in the evenings, and at that time the compound was walled and the house and gardens were closed up at nights. Mrs Ives enjoyed evenings out and often escaped through the gates to go to dances at Welbeck Tunnels. On such occasions other servants left the gate off the latch, allowing her to return safely. Dances usually finished at 10 o'clock in the evening and Mrs Ives would then walk back from Welbeck Tunnels. It once so happened that someone found the gate unlatched while Mrs Ives was still out, but her fellow worker undid the lock again for her.

The lane in front of the house at that time was not tarred, but was a dirt road. The Butler-Bowdons travelled with ponies and traps, and sometimes on horseback. There was no direct transport links to Southgate House, but a bus ran from Worksop to Clowne and passed through Southgate. There seemed not to have been any transport connection to Chesterfield in those days.

Mrs Ives remembers four cottages along the road and, according to her, one of the buildings was divided into units. She did not mention that her

---

[631] Mrs Ives corrected that statement on October 23, 2013 (conveyed in a private E-mail correspondence with Toy Bak) and said that there were teenagers at the house. This is possibly not fully precise as Maurice Butler-Bowdon was born in 1910 and his brother Anthony Butler-Bowdon in 1913, so they were hardly in their teens anymore, but the family possibly had visitors with adolescent children who stayed for longer periods of time with them.

husband to-be Cyril and his parents, Annie and Henry Ives[632], used to live in one of the cottages of Southgate Estate, namely at the "Southgate Avenue" cottages (see Chapter 14.2.3).[633] She did recall that the Butler-Bowdons kept big hunts which sometimes disturbed the washing on the line in the gardens of the cottages.

Mrs Ives has fragments of memories as to the interior of Southgate House. For example, she remembers that there were paintings on the walls[634], and that newspapers had to be laid out neatly on the tables. Another interesting detail which Mrs Ives mentioned was an inclined footpath (a so-called "foot rill") which lead down to the bottom of a pit on the grounds of Southgate Estate near Southgate House, opposite the lane heading towards the crossroads with Gapsick Lane. Near there was some open cast mining.

14.2. "A Cottage for Sale"[635] - The Occupants of Southgate Cottages

The third element of Southgate Estate is a collection of cottages, homes to people who lived and possibly worked on the grounds of Southgate over a time span of roughly a hundred years. Along with the ten-yearly censuses of the 19th and 20th century, the Land Values Map of 1909/1910 and a rental/tax account book from 1946-1961 held by Derbyshire Records Office disclose further information on this matter.

According to the Land Values Map and its related Reference Book[636], John (6) E Butler-Bowdon, himself listed as owner of Southgate House[637] (house and garden) and woods at Southgate, at that time let five separate cottages of Southgate Estate, some of some of which with gardens, to tenants in **1909/1910**: "101, Rotherham Road/103, Rotherham Road" (on the map denoted as "Harlesthorpe Cottages"), "Lake View, Harlesthorpe" (with house numbers from 1 to 10) and "The Hermitage" (according to the lists

---

632 At some stage the Ives family ran the "Dusty Miller" public house in Barlborough (according to a personal correspondence between Tony Bak and the author on October 13, 2013).

633 Annie and Henry attested as occupants between ca. 1930 and 1937, Cyril Ives in 1936 and 1937.

634 Nothing is known about the genres of these paintings. An interesting observation by Mark Girouard is that up until the late 17th century most country houses were mainly furnished with portraits, and that any other pictures were largely bought arbitrarily, often based on their subject matter. It was not until Charles I, the Earl of Arundel, and other members of the court circle began building up their collections in the 1620s and 1630s and informed buying became fashionable; cf. Girouard, *English Country House*, p. 170.

635 "A Cottage for Sale" was composed by Willard Robinson and written by Larry Conley (1929); recordings by Frank Sinatra, The Revelers and others.

636 Derbyshire Record Office, *Ref. No. D595.*

637 A ligature added by another hand at a later date in the Reference Book in front of "Southgate" could be read as "Hse" for house or "Res" for residence.

imprecisely located at Southgate whereas the proper location is in fact 400 m to the north at White Brick Moor).

In addition to this the Butler-Bowdons owned more properties at that time as the related Reference Book mentions another five buildings let to tenants, but these housings must have been of a more temporary nature, as they do not appear again in later sources. There is a cottage with garden which is described as being located at White Brick Moor whose inhabitant John Liddy is attested as an occupant of "Southgate Cottages/Cottage at The Avenue" in the census a year later, and later on as an occupant of Southgate Stables with his family (sees below Chapter 14.2). A house denoted "Rodgwood" in Harlesthorpe is let to Walter Rose, who at the same time is tenant of some agricultural land on Rotherham Road. This house, its occupant and the connected land are only mentioned in this particular record. The same applies to a bungalow at "45, Station Road, Harlesthorpe" (on the corner of Creswell Road) let to Joseph Dalwin and agricultural land and a house (?) at "262 Creswell Road, Hollin Hill" let to Benjamin James Davies (near the crossroads of Gapsick Lane).[638] George Warrener is listed as a tenant of a house and agricultural land at "Hickingwood (Farm)".[639]

A rental/tax account book held by Derbyshire Records Office lists five rented-out cottages, scattered all over the grounds of Southgate Estate in

638 Ligatures in the Reference Book in front of "262 Creswell Road, Hollin Hill", "Rotherham Rd" and "Harlesthorpe, Rodgwood" could be read as "Hse" for house or "Res" for residence, added by another hand at a later date. The same hand added "Damsbrook" as supplementary specification for the part of Clowne where "Rotherham Rd" and "Harlesthorpe, Rodgwood" were located. This toponym does not seem to be applied for an area of modern day Clowne anymore, but there is a Damsbrook Lane in the southern part of the village where B6417 intersects the village. Tony Bak informed me in a private E-mail communication on July 10, 2013 that, although there is no reference of the area being named Damsbrook, there is a Damsbrook House, a Damsbrook Farm, and a Damsbrook Drive on the outskirts of Clowne along the road to the village of Stanfree (B6418), also there is another Damsbrook Lane (diverting from B6417). Kelly's Directory of 1891 describes Damsbrook as a "hamlet" one mile south of Clowne, cf. Kelly's *Directory* p. 98f.

639 This is confirmed by the 1901 and 1911 censuses of England and Wales. Mr Warrener, unmarried in 1901 and aged 30, is listed at that address as Farmer, born in Whitwell, Derbyshire. With him in his household lived Elizabeth Winslow (?), aged 55, born in Eckington, Derbyshire. She acted as his Housekeeper Domestic. The 1911 census returns lists George Warrener, married and aged 40, Farmer, born in Whitwell, Derbyshire. He is now married to Elizabeth Warrener, aged 39 and from Scarcliffe, Derbyshire. They had two sons: George, aged 4, and William Warrener, aged 2, both born in Clown, Derbyshire. Hickinwood Farm must have been quite prosperous. Mr Warrener could afford to employ three servants: Edwin Pacey, aged 21 and unmarried, from Woolsthorpe, Lincolnshire, worked as Farm Servant, as did Alfred Kirkham, aged 25 and unmarried, from Tealby, Lincolnshire. Beatrice Froggatt, aged 16 and unmarried, born in Whitwell, Derbyshire was the household's Domestic Servant.

December **1947**: "Cottage at Harlesthorpe Dam", "Cottage at Rotherham Road", "Cottage at The Avenue", "Cottage at Stableyard"[640] and "The Hermitage"; all rents were due to Renishaw Hall Estate owned by the Sitwell family.[641] It is not verifiable from which precise point in time on all above mentioned cottages became habitable housings (or were maybe partially also farm outbuildings).

14.2.1. "Drive my Car"[642] - The Occupants of Southgate Stables

From the Sale Particulars of Southgate House of **1938** (see Chapter 8) we get a thorough description of Southgate Stables ("Lot 1") which helps us to imagine the size of the building and to understand its function: "The Outbuildings, which are situated across the Road, comprise: - 2 Men-servants' Cottages, 2 Garages (for 3 Cars), Stabling for 3, excellent Dog Kennels, Pigeon Cote, etc., etc.". The quantity in decimal acreage for residence and grounds was estimated at 0.828.[643]

Stables played a major role in the conglomerate of buildings and dependencies of a functioning estate. Some English architects went as far as to regard stable buildings as a specialised field. Mews were situated at varying distances from the main house and were invariably equipped with appurtenant elements such as coach houses and accommodation for grooms and coachmen. These could have been separate buildings, for example next to the entrance to the stables, or - like in the case of Southgate Stables - on an upper floor above the stabling and the coach-house. The general lay-out of Southgate Stables does not slavishly follow all contemporary architectural principles as listed by Hermann Muthesius in his book "The English House"[644], and all in all it is a rather small, yet in its peculiar partial symmetry, a very beautiful building. One element however, the striking square tower of Southgate Stables with its pyramid roof was apparently something no stable building could go without. Muthesius says: "A properly appointed stable-yard always has a clock that is visible from the distance. It is placed above the entrance, which is usually surmounted by a tower-like structure."[645] This feature has probably been interpreted a bit aberrantly by

---

640 "Cottage at Stableyard", the last cottage in the list in the rental/tax book of 1946-1961, denotes the east wing of Southgate Stables which today is confusingly enough called "Southgate Cottages".

641 Derbyshire Record Office, *Ref. No. D6573/Box 120/5*, page in book dated December 9, 1947; information confirmed by Mary Jones in a private E-mail correspondence with the author on June 1, 2013.

642 "Drive my Car" was written by Paul McCartney (with lyrical contributions by John Lennon) and was released on the Beatles album "Rubber Soul" (1965).

643 Derbyshire Record Office, *Ref. No. D1300/11/1*, p. 6.

644 Muthesius, *English House* , p. 102ff.; also Girouard, *English Country House*, p. 208.

645 Muthesius, *English House*. p. 104.

the architect of Southgate Stables, but if there had ever been a clock it would certainly have been attached to the tower structure.

English Heritage dates the origin of the building as mid 19th century[646] and since there is no proof of inhabitants in the censuses before 1861 I would assume that it was Henry (5) Butler-Bowdon who initiated the erection of stables as a structural addition to Southgate House. The Land Values Map of **1909/1910** clearly shows the presence of a stable yard on the northern side of Worksop Road.[647]

The above mentioned censuses and the Electoral Rolls of Derbyshire allow us to deduce information on the occupants of Southgate Stables and their professions. According to the **1861** census, a certain John Houson was working as a groom for the Bowdon household. There is case to believe that were horses on the estate at that time and that they were surely kept at Southgate Stables, a place with direct access onto the lane. It is almost certain that as a groom John Houson was professionally tied to Southgate Stables. He probably had accommodation in or next to the stables so that he was always close at hand to take care of the animals. Southgate House surely also had stable boys and other people attending to the horses but there are none listed; maybe they used people from the surrounding farms and villages that came to work on a daily basis rather than living on the premises; that is the only reason I can think of why they are not listed.

A Coachman named Frank Stringfellow is listed in the **1871** census. Like John Houson he would probably have had accommodation in or next to the coach house in order to fulfill his duties.

The **1881** census of England and Wales lists the presence of a small family living in "Southgate House (Detached House), Clown (Derby)". Thomas Ellis, aged 55, born in Whitwell, Derbyshire was the Game Keeper of Southgate House (by the term "detached house" I would assume that we are rather talking about the Stables here than Southgate Cottages in regard of Mr Ellis' profession). He was married to Mary Ann Ellis, aged 28, born in Oldcotes, Nottinghamshire. Together they had a baby daughter, Sarah J Ellis, aged 0, born in Clown, Derbyshire. From a previous marriage Fanny Mallender (Ellis), the step daughter, lived with them, aged 11, born in Clown, Derbyshire. She is listed as scholar. All family members are local people. It was at that time vital that the person who served as gamekeeper had to be well acquainted with the local countryside and wildlife (e.g. in regard of hunting). It is possible that Thomas Ellis is a descendant of George Ellis of the 1841 and 1851 censuses.

The **1891** census confirms the presence of two persons who, due to their occupations, can be connected to the outbuildings of Southgate House: Thomas W Wragg worked as a groom for the Southgate House household. To

---

646 English Heritage, *Southgate Stables.*

647 Derbyshire Record Office, *Ref. No. D595*, Sheet 19.7.

me it seems that at 12 years of age he was awfully young to be charged with the task of looking after the horses. But of course it was not uncommon during these times to start a working life at that age. James Cowley, the gamekeeper, on the other hand is one of the eldest attested persons connected to Southgate House (62 and 72 years old respectively, see above for the censuses of 1881 and 1891), again being a local man from Elkesley, six miles south of Retford.

The Land Values Map and its related Reference Book provides us with information about all dwelling houses and their inhabitants of Southgate Estate let by John (6) E Butler-Bowdon for **1909/1910**[648], naming also Southgate House and Stables, but unfortunately no particular inhabitants are mentioned for the Stables. However there is small family listed in the **1911** census for a place named simply "Southgate Clown": Ernest Dyer, aged 31, born in Stapleton, Yorkshire lived there. He was married to Isabella Dyer, aged 34, born in Lamesley, Durham. Living in the same household in 1911 was their six-year-old daughter Mary Gertrude Dyer, born in Ruddington, Nottingham. Mr Ernest Dyer's profession is stated as Chauffeur Domestic.[649] It can be assumed that Mr Dyer was the Butler-Bowdon family chauffeur and lived over in the tied houses where the Butler-Bowdon's cars were kept in the old stables. Stable staff were of course responsible for the horses and carriages, but with the changes in time and technology horse-drawn carriages became unpopular and were eventually replaced by motored vehicles, indeed by those who could afford the new luxuries. Stables staff were subsequently reduced and the remaining personnel were trained to become chauffeurs.[650] As for Southgate House in 1911 this census allows an extra entry for the number of rooms in the dwelling concerned. Mr Dyer, who completed and signed the form, noted five rooms for the place in question. The sheet is countersigned by the enumerator (initials).

The censuses of England and Wales do not give any additional evidence of individuals living at Southgate Stables. If anyone had occupied any of the outbuildings they probably have been counted as the staff of Southgate House (such as John Houson or Frank Stringfellow). We have to assume that over the years the outbuildings were continuously used as barns, storage and stables. Being a country estate the Butler-Bowdons most likely carried on keeping horses at Southgate alongside their motor cars for pleasure and country pursuits which became available in the early 1900s.[651] However, according to

---

648 Derbyshire Record Office, *Ref. No. D595.*

649 Muthesius, *English House*, p. 104: "Coachmen are assumed to be married and to run households of their own." *Quod erat demonstradum.*

650 Horn, *Victorian Country House*, p. 73: "Often they (= the former coachmen) received instruction at the factories where the cars were built, since they would be expected to carry out repairs as well as drive the vehicles."

651 Ruby Thorpe recalls three large stone steps beside the road outside Southgate House. They were used by the ladies when getting on and off their horses (information

the Electoral Rolls of Derbyshire in **1912** Ernest Dyer is listed as an occupant of what is denoted in the document as a "dwelling-house" at Southgate. His presence (and most likely that of his family whose members were not eligible to vote) is attested for Southgate Stables until **1914**. The Dyers possibly shared the stable yard with a Samuel Tidmarsh in that year; he and Ernest Dyer are both listed as occupants of "Southgate, Clowne". For **1915** only Mr Tidmarsh is listed for a "dwelling-house" at Southgate, Mr Dyer has gone. In the years 1916 and 1917 no Electoral Rolls were produced. The next information we can find on possible occupants of Southgate Stables, which provided two cottages for inhabitants, is from **1918**: Alexander Mackenzie and George Robert Taylor.

According to the Electoral Rolls of **1920** to at least **1926**, John and Roger Garfitt as well as William Hardwick and his wife Mary Hardwick could have been inhabitants of the dwelling in question, but this is only speculative as the Electoral Rolls of that year do not give any specific information other than "Southgate" in general. We also do not learn anything about the occupations of the listed persons either, as the Electoral Rolls do not give information about their age and provenance. In **1928** William Hardwick is not listed anymore, Mary Hardwick was possibly widowed and shared Southgate Stables with John and Roger Garfitt.

If we take the records of the Electoral Rolls at face value we have a stark change of occupancy at Southgate Stables for almost the next ten years: for reasons that are no longer apparent, John and Teresa Liddy are listed in the Electoral Rolls of **1930** for "Southgate House" which must be the stable building (for the Liddy family ands their quarters at "Southgate Avenue" see Chapter 14.2.3) and they remain listed at that address until **1939**. The year **1934** shows another change in the Liddy family: daughter Eileen (minor before then and therefore not present in the electoral registers) has left the family nest and is listed in the Electoral Rolls of that year as an inhabitant of Southgate House, very likely in domestic service (together with another young women, see Chapter 14). In **1934** and **1935** the two Liddy sons, Cyril John and Francis, appear in the lists, but in **1936** it is only Francis Liddy who appears to be living with his parents. In **1939** the Liddys seem to be home alone.

After the year 1939 the Electoral Rolls no longer feature inhabitants of Southgate Stables anymore, and during the years of the Second World War no Electoral Rolls were produced. But in this particular case we can gain information from other sources, such as the memoirs of Sylvia R Linacre and Tom White. Through their accounts we can find evidence for inhabitants of Southgate Stables for the early months of WWII when the 424th Battery Royal Horses Artillery was based at Barlborough (see Chapter 8).[652] It is probable

---

communicated per E-mail by June Pearce following a personal meeting with Ruby Thorpe on March 25, 2014).

[652] Riden, *Clowne, Manors and other Estates*, p. 5; Linacre, *How it was*, p. 71, p. 73, p. 79.

that the military personnel billeted there used the barracks of Southgate Stables for their cavalry (horses and staff), and they were most likely the soldiers and horses of Cheshire Yeomanry. But the four-legged inhabitants and their caretakers were apparently the last traceable occupants of Southgate Stables for some time. It almost looks like Southgate Stables ceased to exist as a dwelling house and outbuilding as Southgate House seemingly did not have need for the Stables and related domestic staff anymore after the estate was auctioned in 1938.

The new owners, Renishaw Hall Estate (Sitwell family), evidently did not allow the building to go to waste, however. The Electoral Rolls show that in **1945** "Southgate Cottages" became home to Vincent and Nora Fullwood for the next forty years.

An interesting detail is revealed in the rental/tax account book of 1946-1961 stored in the archives of Derbyshire Record Office under the headline "Southgate Estate": for a joiner's shop[653] a half years rent of 10 Shillings was paid as easement to Renishaw Hall Estate in **1947** and **1948**.[654] Unfortunately the document does not reveal the precise location of the workshop on Southgate Estate at that time, but according to the memories of June Pearce it was located at Southgate Stables.[655] The tenant was June Pearce's maternal great-uncle; his name was Arthur Maxfield. Mrs Pearce recalls that she and her mother used to visit the workshop regularly during the 1950s and 1960s. He was a carpenter and his main business was making coffins. Mrs Pearce confirms that Arthur and Eileen Maxfield lived in one of the houses attached to the old stables[656], and Arthur worked and stored his coffins in the stables. While Mrs Pearce's mother chatted with her aunt when paying the Maxfield's a visit, the children - Margaret, John and June - often had a great time playing amongst the (empty!) coffins if Mr Maxfield was not around to stop them.

A page in the above mentioned rental/tax account book lists two inhabitants (representing whole families) for "Cottage Stableyard" for December **1947**: Southgate Stables must have become a private residence which was rented out to tenants. One tenant family paid a half years rent to Renishaw Hall Estate of 9 pounds, 18 shillings and 3 halfpence; the other one

---

653 There were four joiners working in Clowne at beginning of the 20th century, cf. http://www.burrows.co.uk/bolsoverguide/10TheM.htm (viewed 19/05/2013).

654 Derbyshire Record Office, *Ref. No. D6573/Box 120/5*. Out of respect to particular individuals likely to be still alive today (assuming a lifespan of a hundred years) I am obliged to anonymise or efface the names of the persons listed in this document according to the Data Protection Act 1998 Section 33 for Research, History and Statistics whenever I quote from this source in this text.

655 Information disclosed in a private E-Mail correspondence between June Pearce and the author on June 16, 2013.

656 This information is not backed up by the Electoral Rolls of the years in question. Arthur and Eileen Maxfield are attested for 1948 in the cottages at Southgate Avenue, after that date they are not recorded for Southgate anymore.

paid 13 pounds, 16 shillings and 10 halfpence for their living quarters. This information is contradicted by the Electoral Rolls of **1947** which lists one family only for "Southgate Cottages", the Fulwoods. According to the Electoral Rolls the Maxfield family[657] had left Southgate Stables by **1948** (to live in Clowne), and the Fullwoods - evidently having been quite content with their home - stayed there until at least 1985 as attested by the electoral registers for "Southgate Cottages".

Soon after his first wife's death in the very early 1950s Arthur Maxfield's business failed and he became bankrupt, as June Pearce remembers.[658] He closed his workshop at Southgate and moved to 19 Church Street in Clowne (the presence of Arthur and Alma Maxfield is attested for that address in the Electoral Rolls of **1966**). Arthur Maxfield must have carried on his business as joiner and undertaker, because for the years 1960, 1965 and 1969 a respective shop of Mr Maxfield's is attested situated on Rectory Road in Clowne.[659]

The Fullwoods had new neighbours in the 1960s: in the years **1960**, **1961**, **1962** and **1963** Elfrida and Trevor C A(d)dlington share the cottages at Southgate Stables with them. In **1965** Trevor C A(d)dlington is alone, but there is new (but only temporary) neighbour: Frederick John Nicholson. In **1969** Trevor C A(d)dlington evidently has a new wife: Edith, and together with the Fullwoods they continue sharing Southgate Stables. One year later, in **1970**, the Fullwoods and the Ad(d)lingtons still lived together. At some stage in the following years the Ad(d)lingtons must have left.

---

[657] Derbyshire Record Office, *Ref. No. D6573/Box 120/5*, page in book dated December 9, 1947. W (= Wilfred) Maxfield was another uncle of June's mother, but quite a lot older than her. Her great-grandmother Elizabeth Maxfield had twelve surviving children (and a few more who died early in life as was typical of those times), and was a "fascinating woman, typical of the Victorian era in which she was born" as June Pearce informs in a private E-Mail correspondence with the author on June 16, 2013. It remains unclear why Wilfred Maxfield is listed as a tenant as the inhabitants at the time were Arthur and Eileen Maxfield with their children.

[658] Information disclosed in a private E-mail correspondence between June Pearce and the author on June 16, 2013. Eileen Maxwell must have died some time between 1950 and 1953 (latest) as June Pearce confirmed during a personal meeting on September 22, 2013 in Clowne. The Parish Marriage Registers for Harthill, 1940-1959 reveal that Mr Maxfield of Clowne, here noted as "Master Joiner" and aged 48, had married a second time on April 20, 1957, a certain Alma Booth from Harthill, aged 39; cf. Hinson, *Harthill*. June Pearce remembers that Alma Maxfield passed away sometime in the 1980s (reported September 22, 2013).

[659] Cf. The Edinburgh Gazette, April 29, 1960; The London Gazette, June 15, 1965 and May 6, 1969, cf. http://www.london-gazette.co.uk/issues/44842/pages/4807/page.pdf (viewed 16/05/2013), http://www.london-gazette.co.uk/issues/43685/pages/5754/page.pdf (viewed 16/05/2013) and http://www.edinburgh-gazette.co.uk/issues/17817/pages/263/page.pdf (viewed 16/05/2013).

Some changes have occurred over the course of the following years: on April 21, **1980** Southgate Stables became a listed building by English Heritage. According to the Electoral Rolls of the same year, the inhabitants of what they list as "Southgate Cottages" are Vincent and Nora Fullwood and their new neighbours are Roy Clarke, Mavis Clarke and Antoni S Clarke. In **1984** Worksop artist Graham Duckmanton made a pencil drawing of the building which shows it apparently inhabited and in comparatively good condition (see image on back cover), even though it has remained more or less unaltered over the years. In **1985** (Electoral Rolls) the neighbours of the Fullwood family are still Roy and Mavis Clarke and Antoni S Clarke.

The next ten years brought more modifications: it was not until **1990** when, with financial aid of English Heritage, extensive renovation work was carried out on Southgate Stables.[660] The owner of the building received a Building at Risk Grant from English Heritage; this was offered on 22 January 1990 and was for £17,566. This was later increased to £19,427 in April 1991. The grant was for structural repairs to the building. The house seemed to have been empty at that time as shown by photographs from 1990.[661] It can be assumed that the building complex was put up for sale after renovation and changed hands a couple of times over the course of the following decades.

According to the Electoral Rolls, John R Struggles shares the residence in **1995** with Alexander, Ann and Samantha Birch. In **1999** the Struggles family (John R, Tussanee, Gladys and Stanley W) are the only inhabitants of the cottages of Southgate Stables.

Southgate Stables is still in private hands today. Current public directories (2013) list a company called "Southgate Estate (UK) Ltd Property Leasing" for 1, Southgate Cottages, Worksop Road, Chesterfield, Derbyshire S43 4TB, and "Pictures to Canvas" for 2, Southgate Cottages, Clowne, Derbyshire S43 4TB.

There was a drover's path, leading up from Harlesthorpe to Southgate House, recalls June Pearce: "The drovers used the stables across the road from Southgate House, then continued their journey crossing the road into the wood and used this path down to Manor Farm." The path passes to the right of the house as viewed from the stables.[662]

Hermann Muthesius adds another interesting detail: "Stables such as these - there is an example at Welbeck Abbey, seat of the Duke of Portland - often have a sizeable covered riding school. Welbeck Abbey has stalls for one-

---

660 Information according to an E-mail correspondence between Sheena Charrett, Business Officer at English Heritage and the author on November 4, 2013.

661 Picture The Past, *Southgate Stables (103754)*; Picture The Past, *Southgate Stables (103755)*; Picture The Past, *Southgate Stables (103756).*

662 Information obtained during a personal meeting on September 22, 2013 in Clowne and further details by E-Mail between June Pearce and the author in September 25, 2013. The path is referred to as "Park Lane" sometimes.

hundred horses most luxuriously appointed."[663] It would not be surprising if the Butler-Bowdons had maintained respective business relationships, perhaps buying their horses from Welbeck Abbey stables.

14.2.2. "Farewell! Old Cottage"[664] – The Occupants of Toll Bar Cottage

The Derbyshire Record Office in Matlock holds a handwritten correspondence regarding the purchase of Southgate tollhouse by Major John (6) Butler-Bowdon, dated **1883/1884**.[665] The correspondence comprises of six handwritten letters composed between October 10, 1883 and January 3, 1884 by George Unwin, land agent and employee of Messrs. Shipton of Hallewell House of Whitwell, Chesterfield (a law firm established in 1756 which still exists today in the city of Chesterfield).[666] The recipient of the letters remains unnamed but it must be assumed that it was a clerk of the "Chesterfield to Worksop Turnpike Trust Fonds" (1741-1884).

During the 18th and early 19th centuries tollhouses were an integral part of turnpike trusts in England, Wales and Scotland.[667] Among the houses listed for Whitwell in the 1841 census of England and Wales, which today have all been demolished, are four toll bar houses.[668] Toll Bar Cottage was originally the toll gate to the Dukeries, an area taking in Worksop Hall, Welbeck Abbey, Thoresby Hall and Clumber Park.[669]

A list which can be retrieved from the website of Whitwell Local History Group lists all burials of Whitwell through the centuries.[670] According to this list, a lady named Ann Cordale was a resident of "Southgate Bar" until she died in **1835**. Her occupation or position is not stated.

---

663 Muthesius, *English House*, p. 105.

664 "Farewell! Old Cottage" was composed by Stephen C Foster for voice and piano in G major in 1851.

665 Derbyshire Record Office, *Ref. No. D3/ATC/317-322.*

666 http://www.shiptonhallewellsolicitors-chesterfield.co.uk/ (viewed 10/05/2013). For Mr Unwin see Chapter 8.

667 The set-up of turnpike trusts began at the rate of less then 10 a year around 1750; between 1750 and 1770 the rate quadruplicated; canals did not have any significance until 1760. Turnpike roads as well as canals as transport routes were favoured by local nobility and gentry, "due not merely to the hope of opening wider markets to agricultural produce, but to the anticipated advantages of better and cheaper transport for local mines and manufactures." But "Canals and turnpike trusts were rarely expected to do more than pay for themselves with perhaps a modest return on capital.", cf. Hobsbawm, *Industry and Empire*, p. 8. The spreading network of turnpike roads contributed to better access to country houses as well and made the landed gentry appear less provincial by connecting them to the amenities of high society in the cities; cf. Girouard, *English Country House*, p. 218.

668 Hopkins, *Census Returns.*

669 Information disclosed by Derek Bower in a personal E-mail correspondence on May 20, 2013 based on the recollections of his sister, Jean Elizabeth Bower.

670 Ann Cordale (b. 1794, d. 15/10/1835); cf. Hopkins, *Graves Index.*

The **1841** census of England and Wales names Henry Steel as keeper of the toll bar house of Southgate (listed for the parish of Whitwell).[671] He acted as toll barkeeper and turnpike road labourer, and lived there for over forty years with his wife Mary and his son George.[672]

The **1851** census of England and Wales attests Henry Steel, aged 48, born in Barlbro (*sic!*), Derbyshire as "Tollbar Keeper & Turnpike labourer". Living with him under the address of "Chesterfield and Worksop Turnpike Road" were his wife Mary, aged 52, born in Chesterfield, Derbyshire and their three children (all scholars) George, aged 19, born in Clown, Derbyshire, and Harriet, aged 13, and Charles, aged 10, both born in Whitwell, Derbyshire.

According to the ten-yearly censuses Henry Steel, now 58 years old, born in Barlbro (*sic!*), Derbyshire continued to fulfil his duties as "Turnpike Labourer" in **1861** on "South Gate Bar". Mary, his wife, now 62 years old, born in Chesterfield, Derbyshire still shared the household with him as well as two of their three children: George, aged 29, born in Clown, and Harriet, aged 23, born in Whitwell ("at home"). It is unknown what happened to son Charles. George Steel seems to have become his father's assistant because his occupation is also stated as "Turnpike Labourer".

Ten years later the census of **1871** for England and Wales lists a new small family living at "Toll Bar House" (in this case registered for the parish of Clowne). Interestingly enough it is not the head of the family, Henry Chetham, aged 47 and born in Chrich, Derbyshire, who was responsible for the payments of duty at Toll Bar Cottage. He is stated as Labourer. It is his wife, Elizabeth Chetham, aged 46, born in Scotland, who acted as Toll Collector. Together they had a son, George, aged 13, born in Hatfield, Derbyshire, who is recorded as a scholar. The census of the same year lists Mary Steel, aged 72, her son George, aged 39, and her daughter Harriet, aged 33, as occupants of "South Gate", Whitwell (registered for the parish of Whitwell). This in itself is confusing. It is hard to imagine two families living under the same roof of this comparatively small building, but I also cannot

---

[671] The other three tollhouses were situated at Hollin Hill, Whitwell High Street and at Steetley; cf. Hopkins, *Census Returns*. The source says that Southgate toll bar house was located almost directly opposite today's Springfield Farm entrance. This cannot be correct and must be due to confusion with two other cottages on the southern side of the lane, see below. A local historian reports that two old cottages near the lay-by on the southern side of A619 were always called "Toll Bar Cottages", even though one of them reportedly was a smithy (information disclosed by Tony Bak in a personal E-mail correspondence on May 17, 2013).

[672] Information disclosed by Tony Bak in a personal E-mail correspondence on May 17, 2013. See also Hopkins, *Census Returns*. A little boy called Charles Steel (b. 1835, d. 12/05/1837) and an infant named John Steel (d. 27/01/1834) appear in the list of Whitwell burials for "Southgate"; cf. Hopkins, *Graves Index*. Presumably they were sons of Henry and Mary Steel.

find another explanation, especially since in the following decade (**1881** census returns) Mary Steel, aged 82 and widowed, is again listed as "Tollgate Keeper" of "Southgate Bar, Whitwell (Derby)". Her son George Steel, aged 49 and single, assisted her as "Turnpike Lab(ourer) Road".

An entirely new family seems to have taken over Toll Bar Cottage by **1891** (as attested by the decennial census): Albert Johnson, aged 27, born in Ashover, Derbyshire. He is listed as a Coal Miner and was married to Fanny Johnson, aged 24, born in Bolsover, Derbyshire. Albeit still a very young couple they already had five children: Rosehanna, aged 7, born in Bolsover, Derbyshire; Rebecca, aged 5, born in Bolsover, Derbyshire; James, aged 3, born in Clowne, Derbyshire; Frank, aged 1, and baby boy George; both born in Whitwell, Derbyshire.

The **1901** census of England and Wales lists an "Old Toll Bar" for Whitwell with the following inhabitants: a farmer named Thomas Newton, aged 60, born in Whitwell, Derbyshire; his wife Lucy Newton, aged 60, born in Whitwell, Derbyshire; and their daughter Emma E Newton, aged 10, born in Whitwell, Derbyshire and their granddaughter Beatrice E Trueman, aged 11, born in Clown, Derbyshire. It cannot be stated with any certainty whether the house in question is identical to Toll Bar Cottage of Southgate.

The existence of the Southgate toll house building can in fact be traced much further back in time: according to Philip Riden, the Chesterfield-Worksop road (today A619) was turnpiked under an Act of 1739.[673] Nottinghamshire Archives hold a document from the so-called Foljambe Family Archives dated May 1779. This record sheds some light on the work of a turnpike labourer in the form of a first-hand report from a man named Robert Getliffe. He vividly describes his work as surveyor of the turnpike road from Chesterfield to Worksop for eight years, and as surveyor of the road from Derby to Buxton for the previous eight years where he tended to the new roads.[674] Local newspaper the Derby Mercury dated August 8, 1826 reports that the toll accrued by the several toll gates, among them "Southgate Lane Gate", upon the Chesterfield to Worksop turnpike road will be let by auction to the best bidder.[675] There is at least one other newspaper announcement with an almost identically worded text which also mentions "Southgate Lane Gate", published in The Derbyshire Times of November 12, 1881, calling for interested bidders to gather at the "Angel Inn" at Chesterfield

---

[673] Riden, *History of the County of Derby III*, p. 1.

[674] Nottinghamshire Archives, *Ref. No. DD/FJ/11/1/4/131-132*.

[675] "Whoever happens to be the best bidder, must at the same time pay one month in advance (if required) of the rent at which such Tolls may be let, and give security with sufficient sureties to the satisfaction of the trustees of the said turnpike road for payment of the rest of the money monthly, or in such other proportions as shell be directed." Information courtesy of Tony Bak of Barlborough Heritage and Resource Centre in private E-mail correspondence on May 17, 2013

and referring to an act passed by King George IV "For Regulating Turnpike Roads"[676]. The same Chesterfield and Worksop Turnpike Road is mentioned in passing in The Derbyshire Times of February 4, 1882, in a reporting on parishioners of Clowne who apparently object to proceedings by the Turnpike Trust, and calling on the Surveyor of Highways for support. The short article is titled "The Tollbar Difficulty".[677] The content of another article in The Derbyshire Times dated May 6, 1882, somehow forewarns of the impending end of turnpike roads, possibly making reference to the previously cited article.[678] Parishes in the borough of Chesterfield petitioned against the continuance of the Chesterfield and Worksop turnpike road and the case (related to the Turnpike Acts Continuance Bill, 1882) came before the Select Committee of the House of Commons as one of the creditors of the Trust feared for his income and claimed an indefinite extension of the terms. Incomes generated from tolls evidently were a profitable business. The committee however decided against the interests of the creditor and "could not recommend Parliament to grant a continuance of the Trust for above one year longer."

All ca. 5,000 British tollhouses (number according to the Turnpike Returns in Parliamentary Papers, 1840) were sold off in the 1880s when the turnpikes were closed. In most cases their fate was demolishment, but a substantial number of buildings were preserved to function as domestic dwellings, their characteristic features of once having been a tollhouse still discernible.[679] The early 19th century tollhouses often had a distinctive bay front so that the person in charge had a clear view of the proceedings on the road and the tollboard could be displayed in full view.

Below see the transcription (abstract of the record[680]) of the letters George Unwin sent to the Chesterfield to Worksop Turnpike Trust Fonds:

10th October 1883. (…)

- I am favoured with yours of 8th Inst.(ant) in reference to Southgate Toll House & Premises; and am submitting the matter to Major Bowdon, whom I hope will be inclined to purchase on terms to be arranged. –

- I am leaving home tomorrow for a short time, but on my return shall be happy to call upon you respecting the above. –

---

676 http://www.britishnewspaperarchive.co.uk/ (viewed 11/06/2013).

677 http://www.britishnewspaperarchive.co.uk/ (viewed 11/06/2013).

678 http://www.britishnewspaperarchive.co.uk/ (viewed 11/06/2013).

679 http://en.wikipedia.org/wiki/Toll_house (viewed 30/04/2013); Rosevear, *Turnpike Roads*. In a private E-mail conversation with the author on May 2, 2013 Graham Duckmanton reports that he had noticed quite a few of these types of cottages in various parts of England usually called "Toll Bar Cottage".

680 Derbyshire Record Office, *Ref. No. D3/ATC/317-322*.

- I have communicated with Mr. Turner His Grace's Agent, and hope an arrangement may be made for not only acquiring the Whitwell Toll House & Premises adjoining the Duke of Portland's Estate but also the small portion of ground in front of the Rectory Garden. - (...)

13th November 1883. (...)
- Referring to our conversation last Saturday at Chesterfield on the above subject - I now beg to repeat my offer of Thirty Pounds for the same on behalf of Major Butler-Bowdon. -
- To comprise House, Gardenground on the Eastside, space between it and Cottage, with Gates & Posts. -
- As I remarked before the House requires Repairing and Woodwork attending to and painting.
- Hoping the Trustees will agree to negotiate on the Terms stated.

22nd December 1883. (...)
- I am much obliged for Draft of Inventory Form of Conveyance, and glad to hear the Trustees have accepted my offer of £30[681] in behalf of Major Butler-Bowdon.
- As I am hoping to meet the Major at the end of next week or early in the following one, I will immediately after return you the Draft accompanied by Cheque for the purchase money. - (...)

28th December 1883. (...)
- By appointment I am meeting Major Bowdon next Monday in Manchester, and immediately on my return, shall be glad to forward Draft Conveyance for completion. -
- Trusting this short delay will not be inconvenient. (...)

29th December 1883. (...)
- Thanks for Telegram, and I have now pleasure in forwarding Draft Conveyance with Major Bowdon's homes & description inserted according to your wish. -
- After my return from meeting Major Bowdon in Manchester, I shall be glad to remit your Cheque. - (...)

3rd January 1884.

---

681 In 1895 £1 corresponded to about £55-60 today, so £30 in 1883 is equal to ca. £1,700-1,800 today; cf. http://wiki.answers.com/Q/How_much_was_a_pounds_worth_in_England_in_the_1800%27s (viewed 15/05/2013).

- I have now pleasure in forwarding Cheque Value £30 Amount of Purchase money; and shall be glad to receive the Conveyance duly executed at your convenience. – (…)

Since a building with the designation "toll house" is not mentioned anywhere else in later sources available to me, it can be assumed that after purchase John (6) Butler-Bowdon had the building converted into habitable housing for members of his staff. This theory is backed-up by Tony Bak of Barlborough Heritage and Research Centre.[682] Yet it remains unclear who lived in Southgate House at that time, as Southgate House seems to have been empty in 1881 (according to the census) and in 1891 the Fowler family are living there as tenants. I find it very difficult, if not impossible, to determine what happened during this ten-year gap. John (6) Butler-Bowdon is attested to have been living in Pleasington Hall, Lancashire, with his family in 1881 and 1891 (cf. census returns, see Chapter 21), but this clearly did not prevent him from taking care of matters in Clowne. Or was he on-site, at least temporarily? In his letters Mr Unwin mentions meeting with Major Bowdon in Manchester for further negotiations. Perhaps they agreed to meet each other halfway.

Derek Bower, a former resident of the building in question, holds a black and white photograph dated from the ca. 1940s showing a pretty, small, square house built of blocks of stone with small mullioned windows and a steep tiled roof (sloping down on the left side) and two chimneys (Figure 31).[683] According to him, the building in the picture is Toll Bar Cottage at Southgate; situated to the right of the entrance to Springfield Farm (north side of A619). Its position can be verified by the vegetation in the background: according to Tony Bak, the woods across from Southgate House are visible in the distance.[684] Derek Bower reports that he moved to Toll Bar Cottage together with his parents and his sister when he was about four years old (around 1937/1938). He left there when he was 18 years old to join the Royal Air Force (in 1950). His mother lived there for about twenty-five years, even after his father died in 1951. She moved to Clowne around 1957 because of the imminent demolition of the cottage when the A619 was widened.[685]

---

682 Information disclosed by Tony Bak in a personal E-mail correspondence with the author on May 16, 2013.

683 Information disclosed by Derek Bower in a personal E-mail correspondence with the author on May 19, 2013.

684 Information disclosed by Tony Bak in a personal E-mail correspondence with the author on May 17, 2013.

685 http://www.clownevillage.co.uk/feedback/feedback.htm (Derek Bower on January 17, 2009) (viewed 19/05/2013) and Derek Bower in personal E-mail correspondences with the author on May 19, May 20, and October 13, 2013. Between 1947/1948, when he left school and 1950 Mr Bower remembers working full time to help boost the family income, especially after his father had an accident which left him disabled.

It is interesting to note that the Land Values Map of 1909/1910 records the existence of the toll bar building, but it is not marked as Southgate property. Also Springfield Farm apparently was not part of Southgate Estate at that time, but was in 1938 according to the Sale Particulars of 1938 (and before). This concurs with the memories of Derek William Bower.[686] His memories form a valuable contribution to this book, as he is one of the few witnesses of life on Southgate Estate still alive today. He generously took the time to describe his recollections to me. His family consisted of his father, William Bower, his mother, Elizabeth Ester Bower, his sister Jean Elizabeth Bower and himself. His father was originally a coal miner but had to leave the mines for health reasons and took up working at Springfield Farm before and during WWII. He was called up for military service in 1941, but was discharged on the grounds of being unfit for service in 1943. He then worked in the Welbeck Abbey tunnels for the military and stayed in that work until about 1947, when he had to leave owing to an accident. He then returned to work at Springfield Farm until 1951, when he died following a major stomach operation. Mr Bower's mother did not work outside the home because her two children were too young for her to leave them on their own. Mr Bower's sister was employed as a confectioner with a bakery in Worksop for several years until she married in 1966. Mr Bower himself was employed as a civil servant from 1948 until September 1950, when he joined the Royal Air Force. He did some farm work in the few months prior to joining the service. His work for the RAF took Mr Bower to many places such as Singapore (until 1958), Gibraltar and various parts of the UK until he left the RAF in 1972 and he settled in Branton near Doncaster with his wife where he lives to this day.[687]

Toll Bar Cottage does not appear in the rental/tax account book of 1946-1961[688] which is kept in the archives in Matlock, but Mr Bower recalls that the rents due were paid to Mr Bertram Coupe (see Chapter 16) who was the farmer and tenant of Springfield Farm.[689] According to Mr Bower's memories, the cottage was a "tied" cottage and therefore it is safe to assume that the rent for Toll Bar Cottage was included in the farm rent.[690]

---

686 From his recollections Derek Bower could confirm that Bertram Coupe was the tenant of Springfield Farm, information disclosed by Derek Bower in a private E-mail correspondence with the author on June 12, 2013.

687 Information disclosed by Derek Bower in a personal E-mail correspondence with the author on May 20, 2013.

688 Derbyshire Record Office, *Ref. No. D6573/Box 120/5.*

689 Information disclosed by Derek Bower in a private E-mail correspondence with the author on June 12, 2013.

690 Information disclosed by Derek Bower in a personal E-mail correspondence with the author on June 12, 2013.

14.2.3. "The Avenue Story"[691] – The Occupants of Southgate Cottages/Cottages at The Avenue/Southgate Avenue

For a period of time a stretch of the main Chesterfield-Worksop road was called "Southgate Avenue" (contemporary black and white photographs, for example from the 1950s, give additional evidence of this, Figure 32), maybe in order to give the thoroughfare some (undeserved) glamour. During the middle of the last century the part of the road between the two cottages and Toll Bar Cottage resembled an s-bend and was very narrow. It ran alongside the small, square cottage building with no verge or footpath separating them.[692] The nearby crossroads that leads to Clowne is also a place with history, and in this case tells a very peculiar story. June Pearce can recall a very old man once telling her that the stagecoach used to travel along this road. It was protected by a very large stone which was rolled out to block the road, and then rolled away again to allow the stagecoach to continue down Rotherham Road through the village of Clowne.[693]

The question regarding the location and history of Southgate Cottages (named "Southgate Cottages Whitwell" in the 1901 and 1911 censuses, "Southgate Cottages" on the Land Values Map of 1909/1910), "Cottage at The Avenue" in the rental/tax account book of 1946-1961[694] and "Southgate Avenue" in the Electoral Rolls from 1930 onwards) can be outlined in little more detail: the so-called Land Values Map[695], produced in 1909/1910, shows two adjacent buildings on that spot: one largish rectangular and one smaller square building with an a slightly irregular layout on the south side of what today is Worksop Road (A619), ca. 500 m to the east of Southgate House (see above Chapter 9 and Figure 33), denoted as "Southgate Cottages". It is interesting to see that the rectangular building only partly belonged to Southgate Estate, as it is divided in two: a square annex on its western narrow side was at that time owned by another proprietor. The related Reference Book list however, does not name any inhabitants for the buildings, which is quite curious.

Near the spot today is a lay-by. The derelict ruins of the buildings are hidden in copsewood and trees. Nothing substantial remains which could remind passers-by of the chequered history of the "Cottage at The Avenue". Only a few walls made of sandstone ashlars and brick have survived, which

---

691 "The Avenue Story", novel by R F Delderfield (1964), the saga of a suburban avenue between 1914 and 1947.

692 Information disclosed by Derek Bower in a personal E-mail correspondence with the author on May 23, 2013.

693 Information disclosed by June Pearce in a personal E-mail correspondence with the author on May 24, 2013.

694 Derbyshire Record Office, *Ref. No. D6573/Box 120/5*, page in book dated December 9, 1947.

695 Land Values Map (Duties on Land Values), Derbyshire Record Office, *Ref. No. D595.*

are not higher than about 50 cm. Scattered fragments of roof tiles can also be found lying around.[696] It does not seem that any archaeological research has ever been undertaken; the buildings must simply have been deserted and were left to fall to ruins or were demolished. The last mentioning of these cottages in official records is in 1947. June Pearce remembers seeing the old cottages in the mid to late 1950s when they were still standing, and also when the cottages were in ruins and all the stones lay scattered around before the site was cleared.[697] I could not find any verified pictures or photographs to give the reader an impression of how the buildings must have looked like when they were still standing. This leaves the history of both houses open to interpretation. I would like to assume that one of the cottages was home to a number of inhabitants over the years; whilst the other was reportedly always used as a smithy workshop. Tony Bak says that the latter is backed-up by later Ordnance Survey maps. He attended a history fair a few years ago, and while talking to one of the stall holders about the buildings that were near the lay-by, a man standing close by overheard and said that his grandparents were the last people to live there.[698] Confusingly, a local historian reports that the old cottages near the lay-by on A619 were always called "Toll Bar Cottages"![699] The bigger, rectangular house was used for living (as proved by the various census returns, see below); so the smaller, foursquare building was very likely the home of the smithy. In the Sale Particulars of 1938 a pair of cottages are offered as Lot 20: "A Pair of Cottages known as Avenue Cottages, with Blacksmith's Shop and Good Gardens, situated on Whitwell Road, containing: - Living Room, Scullery and Pantry, 3 Bedrooms and outside Coal House; one has additional Sitting Room, producing a Annual Gross Rental of £26 0s 0d. The Landlord paying Rates amounting to £9 4s 4d." The quantity in decimal acreage for gardens and buildings was estimated at 0.413. Last but not least, the rental/tax book of 1946-1961 names the places as "Cottage at The Avenue" in 1947.

Pigot & Co.s National Commercial Directory of Derbyshire lists a blacksmith in Clowne in **1828/1829** named Abel Littlewood.[700] Could he be the smithy from our cottage?

A John Gunby is attested as blacksmith for "South gate" in Pigot & Co.s National Commercial Directory of **1835** and when looking for further leads in

---

696 Site visited personally by Graham Duckmanton and the author on April 22, 2013.

697 Information disclosed in a private E-Mail correspondence between June Pearce and the author on January 10, 2014.

698 Information disclosed by Tony Bak in a personal E-mail correspondence with the author on May 17, 2013.

699 Information disclosed by Tony Bak in a personal E-mail correspondence with the author on May 16, 2013.

700 Pigot & Co.s *1828-29*, p. 112. According to this source Abel Littlewood simultaneously kept one of the local inns in Clowne, "The Anchor".

the **1861** census for Whitwell I detected two families living in a place "South Gate" which I would identify with the "Cottage at The Avenue" for the simple reason that the head of one household was John Gunby, aged 58, born in Eckington, Derby, and described by the census as "Blacksmith".[701] His wife was Sarah Gunby, aged 52, born in Creswell. Their two children Thomas, aged 14, and Amy, aged 11, were both born in Whitwell, Derby and were both scholars. The second household in **1861** was that of George Richardson, aged 56, born in Elmton, Derby(shire). He was married to Mary Richardson, aged 55, also from Elmton, Derby(shire), and together they had a son named George, aged 21, born in Whitwell, Derby(shire), working as farm servant.[702] In the same household lived Joseph Wragg, aged 16, born in Bolsover, Derby(shire), also listed as a farm servant. Mr G Richardson's profession is interesting: the census describes him as "Farm Bailiffe".[703] Since a farm bailiff was the man who collected the rent from the tenant farmers for the Lord of the manor, Mr Richardson surely executed his work by order of the Bowdon family.[704]

"South Gate" is still home to the Gunby family in **1871**. John Gunby, aged 69, lives there with his 23-year old son Thomas, his daughter-in-law Caroline, aged 23, and their infant son John T. The same constellation of Richardsons still inhabits the other cottage.

In **1881** an impressive number of people can be found as occupants of the two cottages: a coal miner named Robert Heeley, aged 25, born in Whitwell, Derbyshire now lives there together with his wife Maria, aged 23, born in Barlbro (*sic!*), Derbyshire (stated as "Coal Miners Wife") and their daughter Ada Buxton[705], aged 5, also born in Barlbro (*sic!*), Derbyshire, and infant daughter Sarah Heeley, born in Whitwell, Derbyshire. George Richardson, now aged 76, and Mary Richardson, now aged 74, are still there. Mr Richardson is listed as "Farm Labourer", Mrs Richardson as "Farm Labourers Wife". John Gunby, blacksmith and widower, aged 81 shares the household with his son Tom Gunby, aged 35, now too working as blacksmith, and his wife Caroline, aged 30 and "Blacksmith Wife". The younger Gunby

---

[701] Pigot & Co.s *1835*. The Whitwell burial list supports my theory by naming John Gunby (b. 1800, d. 25/10/1882) as resident of "Southgate Cottages" together with his family; cf. Hopkins, *Graves Index*.

[702] "The traditional farm-servant was hired annually, at the great hiring-fairs, and if unmarried, lined in and ate at the farmer's table. A large part of his income was in kind. He earned little, but enjoyed at least the security of regular employment."; cf. Hobsbawm, *Industry and Empire*, p. 81.

[703] A farm bailiff usually belonged to the staff of the home farm of a large estate; cf. Horn, *Victorian Country House*, p. 69.

[704] Information on the occupational image of a farm bailiff disclosed by Tony Bak in a personal E-mail correspondence with the author on July 2, 2013.

[705] She is the later Adelaide Buxton, housekeeper of Barlborough House (see Chapter 22).

generation adhered to the Christian principle of being fruitful and multiplying, they were parents to five children by then: John Thomas, scholar, aged 10; Mary Olive, scholar, aged 8; Sarah Ann[706], aged 5; Tom, aged 3; and Francis, aged 1, all born in Whitwell Derbyshire. Two more members of the household live under the same roof as boarders: coal miner William Browne, aged 45, and his wife Harriet, aged 45, "Miner Wife"; both born in Sheffield, Yorkshire. The cramped conditions of living together in the two cottages are almost unimaginable and such crowded arrangements certainly could not have lasted very long.

For the year **1885** another blacksmith of Clowne is attested: Albert Draper. He belonged to a group of three people who drowned in the pond of Southgate Estate in 1885 as a result of an accident on the ice (see Chapter 11). Was he a successor to the building in question?

By **1891** a new blacksmith has taken up work at "Southgate Cottages": Charles Smith, aged 50, born in Creswell Derbyshire. He was married to Lillah Smith, aged 76 (!), born in Scarcliffe Lanes (near Nether Langwith), Derbyshire. A very interesting press release in The Derbyshire Times and Chesterfield Herald of August 28, **1897** publicises the auction of the household furniture and effects of a Mrs C Smith (I suppose this means Mrs Charles Smith) of Southgate Cottages, who retires from her work after fulfilling her duty as housekeeper at Southgate House (having worked for the Fowler family which resided there at that time and reached a great age in that position, Figure 19). The occupants of the second cottage are two miner families: head of one family is the colliery labourer George H Woolley, aged 30, born in Clowne, Derbyshire. He was married to Hannah M Woolley, aged 24, born in Clowne Derbyshire, and they had two little sons: George W, aged 2, born in Clowne, Derbyshire, and infant Arthur, born in Whitwell, Derbyshire. He of the second family is that of the Learys: head of household is the coal miner Smith Leary, aged 26, born in Riseholme, Lincolnshire. He was married to Elizabeth A Leary, aged 26, born in Clowne, Derbyshire, and they also had two children: Bertha, aged 2, and infant Arthur L(eonard)[707], both born in Whitwell, Derbyshire.

The picture changes slightly in **1901**. A new class of people has moved into one of the two cottages: John Doherty, aged 33, born in Ireland is listed as "Butler (Domestic)". It is not to great a leap top assume that he was in employment at the Butler-Bowdon household at Southgate House at that time. He was married to Annie Doherty, aged 25, born in Swansea, South Wales; they had a baby daughter together: Lilian A, born in Urchfont Devizes,

---

[706] Ten years later Sarah Gunby, then aged 16, is attested as General Domestic (Servant) of the Warrener family on Hickingwood Farm; cf. 1891 census returns (the census denotes Hickinwood Farm as "Southgate Farm, Whitwell").

[707] According to the Whitwell burial list Arthur Leonard Leary died as a young boy, see Chapter 14.

Wiltshire. Their neighbour was the coal miner (hewer) Charles Kirby, aged 32, born in Blackenall, Staffordshire; married to Mary Kirby, aged 23, born in Methley Junction, Yorkshire. They had three daughters: Alice M, aged 5, Violet, aged 3, and infant Ethel M; all born in Clown (*sic!*), Derbyshire. On the day the enumerator passed by the family had a little visitor: Florrie Barker, aged 8, from Clown, Derbyshire. The forge at that time was run by Richard Close, aged 25, born in Oundle, Northamptonshire. He lived there with his wife Gertrude W Close, aged 21, born in Manchester, and his sister-in-law Lottie Bonsall, aged 9, born in Heage, Derbyshire. Mr Close apparently was a man who one should not cross: a short newspaper announcement in the Derbyshire Times and Chesterfield Herald dated February 15, **1902** reports that a John William Glossop, miner, Clowne, sued a Richard Close, blacksmith, of Southgate.[708]

The census of England and Wales of **1911** lists a new blacksmith ("Shoeing and General Smith") and his family as occupants of Southgate Cottages: Arthur William Palmer, aged 36, born in Burton Coggles, Lincolnshire , Anne Louise Palmer, aged 30 and married for 7 years, born in Old Somerby, Lincolnshire. Together they had 5 children: Winifred Mary, aged 6, Margaret, aged 5, Dorothy Ellen, aged 4, all three girls were born in Burton Coggles Lincolnshire; Amelia, aged 2, and Leslie Parker, aged 1, were both born in Whitwell, Derbyshire. The number of rooms in their house is recorded as four (including the kitchen; sheet signed by Arthur William Palmer's signature). The second family that inhabited the cottages were the Gullifords: head of household was Walter Charles Gulliford, aged 32, born in Thurluxton, Somerset. His profession is stated as "Gardener Domestic". He was doubtlessly employed by the Butler-Bowdons to take care of the gardens of Southgate House. He was married to Elizabeth Ann Gulliford, aged 39, born in Somerby (?), Leicestershire. They had two daughters: Lucy Jane, aged 9, born in Bakewell, Derbyshire, and Malees (?) Noemi, aged 7, born in Clowne, Derbyshire. Both girls were pupils. The number of rooms of their living quarters is also recorded as four (including the kitchen; sheet signed by Charles Gulliford's signature).

The census of England and Wales of **1911** records a third party of inhabitants at "Southgate Avenue Clown": John Liddy, aged 29 and born in Newmarket, County Clare (Ireland). He is denoted as head of household and his profession is stated as Butler (Domestic). One cannot rule out the possibility that many (but not all[709]) of the inhabitants of the various cottages on Southgate Estate in the first half of the 20th century were members of the

---

708 http://www.britishnewspaperarchive.co.uk/: "Rabbit Shooting at Clowne - Man hit instead - Heavy Damage in the County Court" (viewed 25/06/2013).

709 For example Annie and Henry Ives who according to Tony Bak ran the "Dusty Miller" public house in Barlborough somewhere along the line (information revealed in a personal E-mail correspondence with the author on October 13, 2013).

domestic staff at Southgate House (mentioned in the censuses for the House, see Chapter 14) who may not have all lived together under one roof with the Bowdon family in the manor house. It is quite safe to assume that John Liddy was the Butler-Bowdon's Butler at that time. John's wife for many years to come (attested by the Electoral Rolls until 1945) was Teresa, aged 28, born in Uttoxeter, Staffordshire. Two children lived with them: daughter Eileen, aged 3, and son Cyril, aged 2, both born in Clowne. Like for the other cited censuses of 1911, the census sheet for "Southgate Avenue" gives us valuable information about the living quarters of the Liddy family: the apartment consisted of five rooms (including the kitchen; sheet signed by John Liddy's signature). John Liddy was attested as living in a cottage with garden at Whitebrick Moor in **1909/1910** (cf. Land Values Map, see Chapter 9), so he possibly moved into "Southgate Cottages" only shortly before the annual electoral register was compiled.

The Liddys (of partially Irish origin) presumably were Catholics as were their employers. Peter Hopkins reports on a small group of Catholic worshippers from Whitwell who used to walk from Whitwell "in all weathers" in order to attend Mass at the chapel of Southgate House. On their way there they often called on Mr and Mrs Liddy, "who would always greet them with a welcome cup of tea; no one was ever turned away."[710] Derek Bower remembers two specific people who came past Toll Bar Cottage every Sunday to attend Mass at the chapel: a father and his daughter, both school teachers from Whitwell Junior School.[711] And people also came from further afield: local Catholics from Elmton went to Southgate Chapel for service in the 1930s.[712]

The Electoral Rolls of **1912** attest the presence of John Liddy and Anthony Taylor (the presence of family members not eligible to vote can be considered as verified). In **1913** Anthony Taylor is listed as sole occupant. In **1915** the electoral registers state the presence of John Liddy and Harry Cottram. From **1918** onwards the residents professionally attached to Southgate are John Liddy and his wife Teresa Liddy and they possibly had some short-terms neighbours: from 1920 onwards Charles Andrews and from 1924 his wife Lily Andrews. This constellation remains until ca. **1928** when the Liddys apparently move across the road to Southgate Stables, swapping their home with the Garfitts and the Hardwicks. If we can place confidence in the records of the Electoral Rolls, whose information is astonishingly variable, for the years following **1930** the new inhabitants of the cottages at "Southgate Avenue" are Henry and Annie Ives, Roger, Mary, Kate and Esther Garfitt, and

---

710 Hopkins, *Churches and Religion.*

711 Information disclosed in a private E-mail correspondence between Derek Bower and the author on October 10, 2013. See also Riden, *History of the County of Derby III*, p. 192.

712 Riden, *History of the County of Derby III*, p. 160.

Mary and John Joseph Hardwick (son?). This constellation is attested until **1934**. In **1935** the Hardwick family seems to have moved away and has also Kate Garfitt, the remaining inhabitants are Henry and Annie Ives and Roger, Mary and Esther Garfitt. Henry and Annie Ives's son Cyril is listed in **1936** as inhabitant for the first time (and for the last time in **1937**), and Roger, Mary and Esther Garfitt are still there (also in **1937**). Two years later the Ives' have left. The occupants of "Southgate Avenue" in **1938** are Roger and Mary Garfitt and their daughter Esther and Arthur and Eileen Maxfield (née Liddy). Because of the gap owing to the lack of Electoral Rolls during WWII, we do not know how the inhabitants of "Southgate Avenue" fared during that period of time.

For the year **1945** and **1947** the Electoral Rolls list Teresa Liddy (apparently widowed and back from Southgate Stables), Arthur and Eileen Maxfield as sole inhabitants of the address "Southgate Avenue". This is contradicted by the rental/tax book of 1946-1961 which lists two tenants with other surnames of "Cottage at The Avenue" for 1947.[713] According to this list, each party paid a half years rent of 6 pounds, 6 shillings and 6½ halfpence for their accommodation. The rent from all tenants was collected monthly. **1948** is the last year in which the Electoral Rolls inform us about the presence of Arthur and Eileen M Maxfield as Southgate Avenue, but there is no Teresa Liddy anymore. Derek Bower has no recollection of the presence of a smithy at Southgate Cottages while he lived at Toll Bar Cottage between ca. 1937 and ca. 1950[714], but he remembers that the families who lived there until demolition were the Naylors and the Simms.[715] He reports that both cottages were demolished at the time when the road was widened which took place around 1957.[716]

14.2.4. "Folks round here all know one another"[717] – The Occupants of Cottage at Harlesthorpe Dam

"Cottage at Harlesthorpe Dam" (named "Lake View" in the lists of Reference Book of the Land Values Map of **1909/1910**)[718] was situated on the eastern side

---

713 These two persons do not appear in the Electoral Rolls, but both persons are remembered by Derek Bower as disclosed in a private E-mail correspondence with the author dated May 20 and May 23, 2013.

714 The Sale Particulars of 1938 explicitly list a blacksmith's shop in Lot 20 for "Avenue Cottages".

715 Information disclosed by Derek Bower in a personal E-mail correspondence with the author on May 20, 2013.

716 Information disclosed in a private E-mail correspondence between Derek Bower and the author on May 23, 2013.

717 Quote from the song "Davis & Golightly" written by Jez Lowe, from the album "Briefly on the Street" (Jez Lowe and the Bad Pennies, 1990).

718 Mary Jones informed me that sometime along the way the address was changed to "Lake View" because there had been some confusion with the post when a new estate

of Harlesthorpe Dam, at the end of what today is Harlesthorpe Lane, overlooking the lake from north, in close proximity to today's Manor Farm (the latter was not part of Southgate Estate during the time these maps were produced). The Book of References indicates nine different house numbers with the respective number of occupants for that time[719]: lodger of 1, Lake View was Henry S Froggatt; lodger of 2, Lake View was Tom Reynolds; lodger of 3, Lake View was William Tomlinson; lodger of 4, Lake View was Charles Rowland; lodger of 5, Lake View was William Bestall; lodger of 6, Lake View was Joseph Davenport; lodger of 7, Lake View was Charles P Glossop; and lodger of 8, lake View was George William Windle (a relative of Thomas Windle of 101, Rotherham Road?). 9, Lake View was shared by Harry Milner and James Dalwin (a relative of Joseph Dalwin of 45, Station Road?).

The occupants of Harlesthorpe Cottages were also recorded by the Electoral Rolls. Spot-check inspections yielded the following results: in **1914** 8 (10) families/inhabitants shared the now ten houses[720]: lodger of 2, Harlesthorpe was Joseph Hill, lodger of 3, Harlesthorpe was John Arthur Redfearn; lodger of 4, Harlesthorpe William James Heath; lodger of 5, Harlesthorpe was William Bestall; lodger of 6, Harlesthorpe was Charles Glossop[721]; lodger of 7, Harlesthorpe was John Joseph Haywood; lodger of 8, Harlesthorpe was George William Windle; and lodger of 10, Harlesthorpe was Frank Featherstone. Ten years later, in **1924**, the picture has changed: occupants of 1, Harlesthorpe are Albert (only spring 1924, not listed for autumn 1924 anymore) and Elizabeth Froggatt; occupants of 2, Harlesthorpe are Noah and Rhoda Ellen Plumb; occupants of 3, Harlesthorpe are James and Mary Plumb with James jnr. Plumb; occupant of 4, Harlesthorpe is Joshua Swift Medlam; occupants of 5, Harlesthorpe are William and Elizabeth Bestall and James John Albert (in autumn 1924); occupants of 6, Harlesthorpe are Charles Peter and Constance Glossop and Maxwell Wood (in autumn 1924); occupants of 7, Harlesthorpe are Charles and Gladys Jepson (Gladys Jepson and Albert Nicholson in autumn 1924); occupant of 8, Harlesthorpe is William Sim(m)s[722]; occupants of 9, Harlesthorpe were Henry and Ada Milner and their son (?) Thomas Ithran Milner; and occupant of 10, Harlesthorpe was Martin Fahey. The year **1931** shows the following constellation: Elizabeth and

---

was built and they named one street Harlesthorpe Avenue and one Harlesthorpe Lane (information by E-mail on June 1, 2013).

719 Derbyshire Record Office, Ref. No. D595.

720 The inhabitants of 1, and 9, Harlesthorpe seem to be missing in that year. According to the recollections of Ruby Thorpe, former inhabitant of 10, Harlesthorpe and home to the Woolley family, the house belonged to Manor Farm and the rent was paid to the farmer (information disclosed during a personal meeting in Clowne on April 27, 2014).

721 C P Glossop becomes tenant of Eastwood Farm later on, as attested by the Sale Particulars of 1938 and for the year 1948 by the rental/tax book of 1946-1961.

722 A relative of Mr Simms at "Cottages at The Avenue"?

Lilian Froggatt for 1, Harlesthorpe; Noah and Rhoda Plumb for 2, Harlesthorpe; Wilmer and Alice Thompson and Frank Cantrill for 3, Harlesthorpe; Harold and Hetty Whitehead for 4, Harlesthorpe; William and Elizabeth Bestall for 5, Harlesthorpe; Joshua Swift and Mary Medlam for 6, Harlesthorpe; George Harold and Lilian Birkett for 7, Harlesthorpe; Neville and Jessie Jarvis for 8, Harlesthorpe; Henry and Ada Milner for 9, Harlesthorpe; John Henry and Annie Woolley for 10, Harlesthorpe.[723] According to June Pearce, Number 10 was the larger house at the side of the row of cottages belonged to Manor Farm and was home to Ruby Thorpe, whose mother died giving birth to her. She was cared for by her maternal grandmother, Mrs Woolley, who insisted on taking her.[724] Ruby Thorpe has vivid and fond memories of her childhood home ("It was lovely in that cottage.")[725]: the cottage had thick stone walls, about 50cm wide, a wooden door with a large key and a lock which did not leave much room for privacy. There was no water, no bathroom, and no electricity. Warm water came of the fire and the bath was in a tin in front of the fireplace. It happened that a visitor called through the closed door that Mrs Woolley was not to bother getting out of the water as he could see her through the keyhole anyway. The cooking range was equipped with only one gas ring. In the night they took the warm shelves out, wrapped them in blankets and took them to bed, or put their clothes in the oven to warm them up. The bedroom where little Ruby slept had a big wooden beam across. Apparently there was a resident ghost in the house named "Lady Harlesthorpe" who occupied herself banging doors in the cottage.[726]

Another interesting detail is the occasional presence of travellers at Harlesthorpe. Little Ruby observed them well and tried to learn from them. They could read people's fortunes accurately and precisely and made secret signs on house walls, things that fascinated Ruby immensely.

Some inhabitants seemed to have been very bound to Harlesthorpe Cottages, whereas a few others did not last long which can be seen in the data of the following year (**1932**, listed without house numbering): Elizabeth and Lilian Froggatt, Frederick and Rose Emma Brown with Robert Arthur Brown and Frederick junr. Brown, Wilmer and Alice Thompson, Frank Cantrill, Benjamin and Ellen Mosley, William and Elizabeth Bestall with Eva Bestall,

---

723 In the field next to the pond, cf. Mary Jones in an E-mail to the author dated March 28, 2014.

724 Information disclosed in personal E-mail correspondences dated March 26 and May 5, 2014.

725 She shared her memories with me her during a personal meeting in Clowne on April 27, 2014.

726 Lady Harlesthorpe was a real person who used to live at Manor Farm who turned into a ghost and was seen riding across the pond in a chariot, but probably that was only fog collecting across the lake.

Harlesthorpe, John William Goodall, Harlesthorpe, Thomas Ithran and Hilda Milner, Albert Victor and Phyllis Allison, Neville and Jesse Jarvis, and Henry and Ada Milner. The occupants of the cottages present themselves in **1937** as follows: Lillian Froggatt at 1, Harlesthorpe Cottages; Frederick, Rose Emma and Robert Arthur Brown at 2, Harlesthorpe Cottages; William and Edith Grant at 3, Harlesthorpe Cottages; Wilfred and Janet Childs at 4, Harlesthorpe Cottages; William and Elizabeth Bestall at 5, Harlesthorpe Cottages; Thomas Ithran and Hilda Milner at 6, Harlesthorpe Cottages; John William and Eva Goodall[727] at 7, Harlesthorpe Cottages; Wilfred Leonard and Beatrice Wool(l)ey at 8, Harlesthorpe Cottages; Henry and Ada Milner at 9, Harlesthorpe Cottages; and John Henry and Annie Wool(l)ey at 10, Harlesthorpe Cottages.

In the Sale Particulars of 1938 Harlesthorpe Cottages are offered as Lot 17, "Nine Freehold Stone Built Cottages (…) with Good Gardens and Main Gas and Water, producing a Gross Annual Rental of £190 0s 4d., the Landlord paying General and Water Rates amounting to about £57 15s 0d." The quantity in decimal acreage of buildings and gardens was estimated at 1,818.

During the Second World War apparently no significant changes took place, the picture remains astonishingly homogenous in **1947** (according to the Electoral Rolls): Lilian and Leslie G Froggatt live at 1, Harlesthorpe Cottages; Frederick Rose E, Robert and Frederick Brown, live at 2, Harlesthorpe Cottages; Walter F and Millicent Charlesworth with Edna M, Ada and John T Charlesworth live at 3, Harlesthorpe Cottages; Albert A Ellis, Wilfred and Janet Child live at 4, Harlesthorpe Cottages; William and Elizabeth Bestall live at 5, Harlesthorpe Cottages; Thomas I and Hilda Milner live at 6, Harlesthorpe Cottages; Eva Goodall lives at 7, Harlesthorpe Cottages; Elizabeth Clarke and Stanley Shaw live at 8, Harlesthorpe Cottages; Thomas and Nellie Sharpe live at 9, Harlesthorpe Cottages; and John H Wool(l)ey lives at 10, Harlesthorpe Cottages. The list in the rental/tax book of 1946-1961 informs us about the rents due at that time[728]: varying from flat to flat the inhabitants paid a half years rent of 8 pounds and 9 shillings; of 12 pounds, 11 shillings and 4 halfpence; of 12 pounds, 4 shillings and 10 halfpence; of 8 pounds, 4 shillings and 12 halfpence, of 7 pounds, 11 shillings and 8 halfpence and of 9 pounds, 8 shillings and 6 halfpence. The rents were paid to the Renishaw Hall Estate owned by the Sitwell family.[729]

The last sample I have taken from the Electoral Rolls for "Lake View, Harlesthorpe Cottages" is the year **1949** when the inhabitants consist of the following group of people (again listed without house numbering): Lilian and

---

[727] Née Bestall?

[728] Derbyshire Record Office, Ref. No. D6573/Box 120/5.

[729] Information disclosed in a private E-mail correspondence between Mary Jones and the author on June 1, 2013. Renishaw Hall Estate is still owned by the Sitwell family which owns many properties in Eckington, Barlborough and Renishaw.

Leslie Froggatt; Frederick, Rose E, Robert and Frederick Brown, Walter T, Millicent, Edna and John T Charlesworth; Janet and John F Child; Harry Heath; Denzil Griffith; William and Elizabeth Bestall, Thomas I and Hilda Milner; Eva and John W Goodall; Elizabeth Clarke; Thomas and Nellie Sharpe; and John H and Annie Woolley.

Mary Jones of Clowne, daughter of Thomas (Tom) and Nellie Sharpe, lived with her parents at Cottage number 9 from when she was born until in her early 20s (during the 1940s and 1950s). She describes the place as two rows of cottages, five near the pond and four behind (in which her family resided), so "Cottage at Harlesthorpe Dam" ("Lake View") was a quite big dwelling. An old photograph provided by Mary Jones unit (Figure 34) shows the rear building; a low terraced house built of stone and amended with red brick, two storeys high and with a red-tiled roof. Green painted woodwork surrounded pretty mullioned windows. She reports that the buildings were old and crumbly at the time they lived there, "but they were so cosy inside and nothing beats stone" to live in.[730] When the cottages were condemned unfit to be lived in, a councillor bought them and converted them into two mansions (today called "Harlesthorpe Lodge"). People who lived in the cottages wanted to buy them themselves and update them but the council refused permission.[731]

June Pearce adds to the observations of Mary Jones that Monday was the traditional "washday" at Harlesthorpe Cottages. Visits were not paid on that day because doing the washing was a hard and tedious chore and normally took all day to be complete. The women did not want the added nuisance of visitors. The facilities for the washing process were located in the bigger building of the "outhouses" which were in the yard of the cottages (together with the toilets for each cottage). The "wash-house" was equipped with several sinks as, and far as Mrs Pearce remembers with cold water only. There was a purpose-built copper container (called "copper") encased in brick for boiling really dirty clothes and bed sheets. There was also ample space to hang the washing to dry if it was raining. Mrs Pearce also remembers the "mangle" consisting of two rubber rollers which were turned by a handle. The clothes were put through to squeeze out some of the excess water.[732]

It must have been a sworn community at Harlesthorpe where problems were often solved with a very pragmatic approach and among the inhabitants

---

730 Information disclosed in a private E-mail correspondence between Mary Jones and the author on May 29, 2013 and May 30, 2013.

731 Information disclosed in a private E-mail correspondence between Mary Jones and the author on May 31, 2013.

732 Information disclosed in a private E-mail correspondence between June Pearce and the author on June 28, 2013. The progress of this kind of work had not much altered during the preceding 100 years, especially the boiling "copper" played a predominant role in the washing cycle; cf. Ferry, *Victorian Home*, p. 53f.

themselves, as Ruby Thorpe recalls.[733] Like her Mary Jones has very fond memories of the cottages and can recall all the families who lived there at that time. She could only remember two changes to the properties before they were demolished. She says that everyone loved living there and she finds it quite striking how moderate the rents of Harlesthorpe Cottages were in 1947.[734]

Furthermore Mrs Jones recalls that Harlesthorpe Dam was locally known as "Bumpmill Pond" back then. The name can be explained by the fact that dam and pond were purpose-built around 1800 to power a local cotton (spinning) mill which in later years was said to be making "bump sheets", meaning candlewick, sacking and sailcloth.[735] Mary Jones also remembers that Southgate House could be reached by a lovely walk from their cottage, up a leafy lane, through a small wood which ended behind the house ("Park Lane", the drover's path, see Chapter 14.2.1). As a child she used to play in the wood and field nearby with the other children from the cottages, if one of the older girls agreed to take them with them. According to Mary Jones, a tunnel was said to run from Southgate House to the pond.[736] When asked, Ruby Thorpe said that she never saw a tunnel herself but remembers her grandfather talking about it.[737] Tom White who used to spend time at Southgate Stables as a young boy said that he watched the soldiers of the Cheshire Yeomanry building a drain at Southgate Stables. This could have been mistaken for being an old tunnel.[738] Tony Bak of Barlborough Heritage and Resource Centre reports that the only tunnel in the area which they can be certain of was from the Old Hall in Barlborough to the church[739], so the existence of a tunnel of Southgate House will have to remain a mystery for the time being.

---

[733] Information disclosed by Ruby Thorpe during a personal meeting in Clowne on April 27, 2014.

[734] Information disclosed in a private E-mail correspondence between Mary Jones and the author on June 1, 2013.

[735] Riden, *History of the County of Derby III*, p. 110f., p. 118. The cotton mill existed until ca. 1850. In her personal recollections Teresa Staples mentions that the pond measured six acres and was in extend stocked with trout, carp, eels, tench, bream and perch. It also was the resort of wild fowl (addendum to Staples, *My Parish*, information by kind courtesy of Father Peter D McGuire in a private E-Mail correspondence with the author on May 18, 2014).

[736] Information communicated by Mary Jones during a personal meeting in Clowne on September 22, 2013.

[737] Information communicated per E-mail by June Pearce following a personal meeting with Ruby Thorpe on March 25, 2014.

[738] Information disclosed in a private E-mail correspondence between June Pearce and the author on December 31, 2013.

[739] Information disclosed in a private E-mail correspondence between Tony Bak and the author on September 28, 2013.

14.2.5. "Although the Cottage-Rose is Fair!"[740] – The Occupants of Cottage at Rotherham Road

"Cottage at Rotherham Road" (or "101, Rotherham Road" and "103, Rotherham Road" in the lists of Reference Book of the Land Values Map of 1909/1910) was positioned north of the Western pool of Harlesthorpe Dam, ca. 200 m north of where Harlesthorpe Lane meets Rotherham Road (A618). Today no architectural remains can be detected.[741] This feature is confirmed by Mary Jones: "The cottages were demolished I think in the mid 50s. There's no sign of them now apart for a gap in the hedge of the field."[742] Evidently no further research has been undertaken regarding the history of the building. Following the lists in the Reference Books of the Land Values Map, "Cottage at Rotherham Road" ("101, Rotherham Road" and "103, Rotherham Road") was home to two separate of tenants in **1909/1910**: Thomas Windle and James H Pearce. The Electoral Rolls offer some more information for the years that followed: in **1918** Thomas and Elizabeth Windle inhabited 101, Rotherham Road; James Herbert and Bertha Pearce lived at 103, Rotherham Road.[743] In **1920** and **1921** the situation is unchanged for 101, Rotherham Road, but 103, Rotherham Road is now home to four occupants: next to James Herbert and Bertha Pearce there are now Leonard and James Pearce.[744] The years **1923** and **1924** attest Thomas Windle as now living on his own at 101, Rotherham Road whereas 103, Rotherham Road is still home to all four members of the Pearce family. In **1926** Bertha Pearce is not there anymore and in **1928** it is only Thomas Windle, James Herbert and James Pearce who live in the Cottages at Rotherham Road, Leonard has gone, too. This situation changes over the course of the next two years: 101, Rotherham Road has new inhabitants in

---

740 Quote from the poem "British Rural Cottages in 1842", written by Rotherham poet Ebenezer Elliot.

741 Information according to an on-site inspection by Graham Duckmanton on May 13, 2013.

742 Information disclosed in a private E-mail correspondence between Mary Jones and the author on May 30, 2013. Indeed the gap in the hedge is still visible today as viewed by June Pearce, Graham Duckmanton and the author on September 22, 2013.

743 James Herbert Pearce was the great-grandfather of June Pearce. From the personal recollections of June Pearce (by E-mail correspondence with the author on October 7, 2013): "(…) James Herbert worked at the coal mine but also he had a business selling firewood. He paid the Forestry Commission an annual fee to chop down trees in Whitwell Wood. He then sawed it and bundled it up into smaller pieces and sold it around the village using his horse and cart. It was a family concern (…)".

744 According to June Pearce, Leonard Pearce was one of the brothers of her grandfather Ernest Sr.. She does not think he was married and recalls that he lost a leg in a mining accident (information disclosed in a private E-Mail between June Pearce and the author on October 8, 2013). James Pearce was June Pearce's father's "Uncle Jim" (information disclosed in a private E-Mail between June Pearce and the author on October 7, 2013).

1930: John and Edna Wilson. 103, Rotherham Road is still home to James Herbert and James Pearce. In **1932** the latter two men have found a new cohabitant, Sarah Shimwell, and John Wilson now lives together with Emma Wilson in 101, Rotherham Road. For **1934** and **1936** the constellation presents itself as follows: Emma Wilson lives alone 101, Rotherham Road and Clara Beardmore lies together with James Herbert and James Pearce.

In the Sale Particulars of **1938** the cottages at 101, and 103, Rotherham Road are offered as Lot 18, "a Pair of Stone Built Cottages (...) each Cottage contains: - Living Room, Kitchen, 2 Bedrooms, and Pantry, also Good Back Gardens, producing a Gross Annual Rental of £35 10s 8d., the Landlord paying General and Water Rates amounting to about £10 10s 4d." The quantity in decimal acreage of garden and buildings was estimated at 0.190.

According to the rental/tax book of 1946-1961, Rotherham Road Cottages housed two households in 1947. The rent at that time was 8 pounds and 15 shillings for one of them; the other one paid 9 pounds, 4 shillings and 2 halfpence.

Mary Jones relates that one of Rotherham Cottages was the home of her grandfather's family. A large family was brought up here and the last person living in the cottage was her grandfather's brother James H Pearce who never married but spent his life there.[745] An old black-and-white photograph from Mrs Jones' possession, taken after Uncle Jim had died, shows a house built very similarly to "Cottages at Harlesthorpe"/"Lake View": erected of blocks of stones with a mullioned window and a coarsely timbered wooden porch. Next door to Uncle Jim lived Clara (Tomlinson) and her son Laurence who Mrs Jones describes as a lovely old-fashioned man who looked after his mother and Uncle Jim. The presence of the Tomlinson family is confirmed by the Electoral Rolls of **1947** and **1948** when Clara M Tomlinson and Laurence Tomlinson inhabited 101, Rotherham Road and James Pearce 103, Rotherham Road. This is the last time the cottages at Rotherham Road are mentioned in the documents available to me.

14.2.6. "Whitebrick-moor consists of several scattered farms"[746] - The Occupants of The Hermitage

"The Hermitage" exists up to the present day: it is located at White Brick Moor, in direct proximity to what is today called Eastwood Farm. Evidently no further research has been carried out regarding its history. The Reference Book of the **1909/1910** Land Values Map lists two occupants for that time: Henry Edward Weaver and Charles Wenham. When the parents of Teresa Staples came to Southgate in **1907**, there was a resident priest at the house who had his living quarters at "The Hermitage". According to her, was a

---

[745] Information disclosed in a private E-mail correspondence between Mary Jones and the author on May 30, 2013. Mrs Jones grandparents were Ernest and Alice Pearce.
[746] White's *1875*, p. 732.

Belgian and his name was Father Keetles.[747] In the Sale Particulars of **1938** "The Hermitage" is offered as Lot 19 and appears as a stone built "Small Holding", "approached from Wall's Lane, near Whitwell, and containing Sitting Room, Kitchen, Scullery, 3 Bedrooms, also Loose Box and Barn." The building at that time was let to Mr R(oger) Garfitt on a monthly tenancy, "producing a Gross Rental of £27 6s 0d., the Landlord paying Rates amounting to £5 5s 4d." From at least 1920 until 1938 Roger Garfitt used to live at the Cottages as Southgate Avenue (according to the Electoral Rolls), so in March 1938, the date of the Sale Particulars, he must have just moved into "The Hermitage". The quantity in decimal acreage of grass and garden of "The Hermitage" was estimated at 1.035. According to the Electoral Rolls of **1947** and **1948**, a Malinder[748] M Garfitt lives at "The Hermitage". According to the rental/tax book of 1946-1961, the rent of "The Hermitage" at that time (**1947**) amounted to 26 pounds rent per half year. In **1949** Melinder[749] M Garfitt shares her quarters with George and Elsie Goddard. In **1966** Miss Garfitt must have married; she is listed as Melinda M Bates and still lives at "The Hermitage", together with John W Bates.

When looking at the amount of the rent per person in 1938 and 1947 compared to that of the other cottages it can be assumed that "The Hermitage" was by far the best-equipped cottage of that time. The building as it presents itself today is quite large. I did not delve any further into the history of this building as to go into too much detail would take us too far afield.

14.3. "Where the Present and the Past will make Connection"[750] - The Diary of Henry (5) Bowdon

There is evidence that Henry (5) Bowdon kept a journal which spanned at least a couple of years. Until this book went to print in summer 2014 I was not able to discover today's whereabouts of this diary, but in his book on the Church of the Immaculate Conception at Spinkhill, art and design historian Paul D Walker quotes some extracts from the journal. Henry (5) Bowdon apparently found it noteworthy to record the occasion when the new organ of Spinkhill Church, the Brindley, was played for the first time on April 1, 1866. In the entries for January 20, 1867 and January 22, 1868 Mr Bowdon complains of the cold inside the church which always forced him to leave mass early. A burglary of a substantial number of ecclesiastical goods, which took place on March 26, 1867 in Spinkhill, is likewise noted in the diary: five sets of

---

[747] Staples, *My Parish*, p. 1.
[748] Misspelling for Melinda.
[749] Another misspelling for Melinda.
[750] Line from "Home to a Million Thoughts" by Show of Hands from their album "Wake the Union" (2013).

vestment, a silver-gilt chalice, a spoon, an alb, surplices, a funeral pall, lace and other items were stolen from the sacristy.[751]

15. "She works hard for the Money"[752] – Domestic servants and their origins

Keeping domestic servants was one of the most significant features of the British middle class of the mid-Victorian era.[753] The number of such servants in middle class households rose from 900,000 in **1851** to 1,4 million in **1871** (peak amount). The number of female cooks is put to at 90,000 in 1871 and the number of housemaids was not very different. According to Eric J Hobsbawn, this allows an estimated measure of the size of the middle (and perhaps of the lower middle) class. One of the many outcomes of the evaluation of the **1881** census of England and Wales is that in that particular year 6% of Derbyshire's female population were employed as indoor domestic servants; and more than five times as many females were working as domestic servants than males.[754] Domestic service was far and away the biggest industry in which women were employed; the other option for females in the Victorian era and the time of industrialisation was of course to work in a factory (mainly as textile employees).[755] There was a wealth of people prepared to take posts in domestic service, and the census of **1901** census shows that one in ten women over the age of ten were employed as servants.[756]

I cannot say with any certainty whether the number of domestic personnel at Southgate House is in any way representative of above mentioned findings. The ratio of 5:1 (female:male) of domestic personnel recruited in Clowne or its immediate vicinity however does not apply for Southgate House, neither

---

751 Walker, *Church of the Immaculate Conception*, p. 51. Paul D Walker quotes from Mount St. Mary's College's in-house journal "The Mountaineer" (NN, "Diary of Henry Bowdon", p. 136); information by kind courtesy of Paul D Walker in a personal E-mail correspondence with the author on July 4, 2014).

752 "She works hard for the Money" by Donna Summer was released on the album with the same title in 1983.

753 Eric J Hobsbawn defines Victorian "middle class" as a "relatively small community" within British society, including ca. 17,000 merchants and bankers in 1871, 1,700 ship-owners, an unknown number of factory and mine-owners, ca. 15,000 doctors, 12,000 solicitors, 3,500 barristers, 7,000 architects, 5,000 civil engineers and not many intellectuals or people with "creative" occupations (2,148 authors, editors and journalists are recorded for that time). "Lower middle class" comprised of the labour aristocracy, small shop keepers, innkeepers, small employers, and the thin layer of white- collar and clean-hand workers such as ca. 100,000 commercial and bank clerks (hardly more than a third of the number of those working in the coalmines); cf. Hobsbawm, *Industry and Empire*, p. 134f.

754 Office for National Statistics, *Derbyshire Area Monitor*.

755 Hobsbawm, *Industry and Empire*, p. 37, p. 96.

756 Ferry, *Victorian Home*, p. 45. Contrary to this is Horn, *Victorian Country House*, p. 47 who says that a working life in domestic service became less and less attractive to younger people, "even in the comparative comfort of a country house".

between 1841 and 1911 taken together nor for 1881 taken separately. In all cases the percentage distribution lies at a ratio of 2:1 (30 local persons: 18 x female, 9 x male, 3 female children without occupation). What interferes with this data further is the possible presence of staff who only came to the house to work on a daily basis and lived in one of the neighbouring villages. Moreover the turnover rate of domestic staff was high, especially among younger servants who seeked to change their jobs frequently. They were keen on making a career in domestic service, and moving around meant adding to their experience which in turn increased the changes of promotion, better payment and a position in a more desired household.[757] So the numbers given below can only be seen as a tentative attempt at a statistic; the total number of persons is anyway far too small to constitute reliable and serious statistical data.

F / Bradfield, South Yorkshire
F / Bradfield, South Yorkshire
F / Brimington, Derbyshire
F / Calow, Derbyshire
F / Clowne, Derbyshire
F / Clowne, Derbyshire
F / Clowne, Derbyshire
F / Derby, Derbyshire
F / NN, Derbyshire
F / NN, Derbyshire
F / North Wingfield, Derbyshire
F / Oldcotes, Nottinghamshire
F / Pilsley, Derbyshire
F / Ruddington, Nottinghamshire
F / Staveley, Derbyshire
F / Staveley, Derbyshire
F / Whittington, Derbyshire
F / Whitwell, Derbyshire
F / Whitwell, Derbyshire
F / Whitwell, Derbyshire
F / Whitwell, Derbyshire
M / Barlborough, Derbyshire
M / Clowne, Derbyshire
M / Elkesley, Nottinghamshire
M / NN, Derbyshire
M / NN, Derbyshire
M / NN, Derbyshire
M / Radford, Nottinghamshire
M / Whitwell, Derbyshire

[757] Horn, *Victorian Country House*, p. 43.

M / Brackenfield, Derbyshire

For domestic personnel originating from places further away the ratio of 5:1 also does not apply to the situation at Southgate between 1841 and 1911 taken together and also not for 1881 taken separately. In all cases the percentage distribution lies at a ratio of about 3:1. The number of people whose origins are very far away from Clowne is quite impressive, in particular among the women, whereas the distances for men are not quite as large (24 non local persons: 19 x female, 5 x male):

F / Bloxwich, Staffordshire
F / Burton, Staffordshire
F / Candroom, North Wales
F / Cheltenham, Gloucestershire
F / Ireland
F / Lamesley, Durham
F / Leyburn, North Yorkshire
F / Liverpool, Merseyside
F / London, Middlesex
F / Newton Hall, Durham
F / NN, County Durham
F / Overbury, Worcestershire
F / Padbury, Buckinghamshire
F / Plymouth, Devonshire
F / Porthantwich, Cheshire
F / Rochdale, Lancashire
F / Shenfield, Essex
F / Tinham, Lincolnshire
F / Weybridge, Surrey
M / Huntington, North Yorkshire
M / Inskip, Lancashire
M / Malpas, Cheshire
M / Markington, North Yorkshire
M / Stapleton, North Yorkshire

Without differentiating between local and non local persons the ratio female/male remains about 3:1. Not one of the registered servants was married; apparently working as servant domestic in a household of the landed gentry was linked to being in an unmarried state. Once a female got married she left domestic service (in general single women were expected to give up work after marriage).[758] A few of the employees were alarmingly young and

[758] During the first phase of industrialisation (textile industry) many women and children worked in the underpaid sector of the "sweated industries", in 1851 for example 75% of married women were employed in some form or another. During the second phase of industrialisation (coal, iron and steel industry, railway) the workforce was made up almost exclusively of men; in 1913 only 10% of the female part of the

by modern standards of compulsory school age. Yet the most striking feature, and also the most affecting one for me, is the presence of two widowed females, one very young (29), the other a bit older (46).[759] One tends to forget just how high the mortality rate was until not so long ago, and not only among newborns, children and females (often in child-birth), but also among men, who where more likely to fall victim to accidents during hard physical labour.[760]

Just for comparison: only ca. 8 km kilometres to the east of Southgate House and Estate, on the southern outskirts of the town of Worksop, is located the large country house residence of Welbeck Abbey, home of the Dukes of Portland. Their household represented the other end of the scale. A description made by a footman from the early 20th century reveals that there were so many people employed as domestic staff at Welbeck Abbey that he, the footman, could not recall the number of people working together with him there.[761] Pamela Horn states that at that time the number of staff comprised of ca. 320 persons, among them 14 housemaids, and 38 male and female servants working in the kitchens and adjoining sectors.[762] She also discusses the question of local and non local staff: according to her, there were several reasons why senior indoor staff was rarely recruited locally. Firstly, the required high standards of skill and efficiency could not be found everywhere, and secondly it was to be avoided that the internal affairs of the employer's families became subject to gossip among the local villagers. Personnel normally was recruited through personal recommendations or through tradesmen/household suppliers, newspaper ads or specialised

---

British population was employed; cf. Hobsbawm, *Industry and* Empire, p. 14, p. 77ff., p. 36, p. 96, p. 146. See also the recollections of Margaret Powell (Powell, *Below Stairs*). She stresses the fact that marriage always was a means to escape the hard working conditions of being in service. In addition to it "Working class husbands bitterly resented the very thought that their wives should have to work outside the home. It seemed to cast a slur on the husband and implied that he wasn't capable of keeping you. If a man was unemployed, well that was a different thing. Then you had to." (p. 194).

759 A third widow aged 37 is listed in the 1881 census for Pleasington New Hall (see Chapter 21).

760 Infantile mortality rate was the highest of all three. It remained at a high level until the 1900s and fell steadily and quickly afterwards. Male mortality was always slightly higher than the female death rate, but both fell gradually and became parallel after the 1870s and remained at a stable level after 1921; cf. Hobsbawm, *Industry and Empire*, p. 329, diagram 3 (Mortality rates in England and Wales, 1840-1991); see also Horn, *Victorian Country House*, p. 49.

761 Horn, *Victorian Country House*, p. 11.

762 Horn, *Victorian Country House*, p. 11.

agencies.[763] For the employees of Southgate House a clear distinction in the sense of senior domestic staff = non local persons and ordinary staff = local people can not be made, but a certain swing into that direction seems to be discernible.

16. "Living off the Land"[764] - The Farms of Southgate Estate

Until the middle of the last century England was largely a country of landowners who owned large estates which were managed by tenant farmers who cultivated the land with hired help. The farmland was not only a means of income for its owners, but was for more a way of life.[765] Money earned from the land in turn allowed social conventions and cultural practices connected to the English country house and underpinned society at the time.[766] From the social point of view, agriculture "was the foundation and framework of an entire society, rooted in remotest antiquity, which rested on the man who made the land produce, and was governed by the man who owned the land. While the former was not of great political importance (...) the latter was. The political and social structure of Britain was controlled by landlords, and what is more by a rather small group of perhaps four thousand people who between them owned something like four sevenths of the cultivated land, which they let to a quarter of a million farmers who in turn employed (...) about a million and a quarter labourers, shepherds, and so on. Such a degree of concentrated landownership was unparalleled in other industrial countries."[767] The system however was limited as pre-existing farming methods and land management systems curbed any growth or change. The more estates were split into smaller portions of productive land such as smaller farms or tenancies, the more the scope for economies of scale and the

---

[763] Horn, *Victorian Country House*, p. 31f, p. 43f.: well-trained upper servants were also in demand by the newly rich country house owners as they could profit from their knowledge regarding the subtleties of domestic life in upper-class circles.

[764] Quote taken from Arnold, Dana, "9 Living off the Land: Innovations in Farming Practices and Farm Design", in: Arnold, *Georgian Country House*, p. 152.

[765] Hobsbawm, *Industry and Empire*, p. 76f., p. 136: In 1851 2 million of 9 million employed Britons were engaged in agriculture, by 1881 the figure was 1.6 of 12.8 million, and before the outbreak of WWI the number was fewer than 8%.

[766] Arnold, Dana, "9 Living off the Land: Innovations in Farming Practices and Farm Design", in: Arnold, *Georgian Country House*, p. 152.

[767] Hobsbawm, *Industry and Empire*, p. 173f., his numbers are based on the census returns of 1851. Another interesting approach to this subject from the archaeologist's view is given by Oliver, *Ancient Britain*, p. 38 (transferring the transition of Mesolithic hunters and gatherers to Neolithic farmers into the 19th century): "Aristocratic landowners do not soil their hands with the work of farming - they have tenant farmers for that. And while the farmers grow the crops and tend the animals, those richest landowners don crimson coats and black hats and gallop across the land on horsebacks as ... hunters."

adoption of new farming techniques was reduced, in particular if productivity could not be increased, then money earned from farming remained stalled.[768] The relationship between landlord and tenant was a key element in the practice of farming practices as well as the social make-up of life in the countryside.[769]

Southgate Estate was certainly no exception to this rule, and therefore to include the farmhouses, which were a vital element of the estate, is essential in this context, albeit to describe every single farm of the estate and its function and its inhabitants would go beyond the scope of the present research. Consequently, I did not try to find any contracts of purchase or any other proof that the farms were bought between 1909/1910 (the years the Land Values Map and its related documentation were drawn up) and the Sale Particulars of 1938. Therefore it has to remain as an assumption when it was exactly that the Butler-Bowdons added these farms to their domain, and exactly how the farms functioned within the framework of Southgate Estate. However, the farms deserve some mention they formed another integral part of Southgate Estate. The Sale Particulars of Southgate Estate from 1938 give a good overview of sizes and features of all the farms which were arranged in a semicircle around Southgate House.

According to the Book of Reference of the Land Values Map of 1909/1910, agricultural land at Southgate was given to Bryan (Brian) Woodhead and Anthony and John Warrener. Benjamin James Davies is tenant of agricultural land and a house (?) at 262 Creswell Road, Hollin Hill[770], and Henry Davenport is tenant of four patches of agricultural land at Harlesthorpe (west of North Road and north of Womble Hill). Not all tenants of land can be counted as proper inhabitants of Southgate Estate as they may have lived somewhere else and not on the grounds of Southgate Estate. The Electoral Rolls of 1912 also list Brian Woodhead as holding land at "Southgate Whitwell, Clown", but I could not in all confidence assign one of the estate's farms in particular to him.

---

768 Arnold, Dana, "9 Living off the Land: Innovations in Farming Practices and Farm Design", in: Arnold, *Georgian Country House*, p. 153.

769 Arnold, Dana, "9 Living off the Land: Innovations in Farming Practices and Farm Design", in: Arnold, *Georgian Country House*, p. 153f.: "This land-owning class formed a kind of paternalistic oligarchy which had a slightly ambiguous relationship with the lower orders. (...) the emphasis being on the loss (without choice) of freedom and rights in exchange for a sense of responsibility and benevolence on the part of the landowner. The country house and its estate is a focal point of these social contracts." Only with the advancing industrialisation and its economic rationalisations did these bonds as an economic system and method of social control slowly become watered down.

770 A ligature in the Reference Book in front of 262 Creswell Road could be read as "Hse" for house or "Res" for residence and was added by another hand at a later date.

Lot 2 of the auction catalogue of 1938 is **Springfield Farm**. Apparently, it was the biggest of all farms of Southgate Estate; a stone built house, evidently of considerable size as it contained not only sitting and living rooms, a kitchen and a scullery, but also five bedrooms, a bathroom and a larder. Several outbuildings belonged to the farm: two pig cotes, two calf sheds, a cow house for six bovines, two barns and a granary, stabling for four animals and a chop chamber above, another brick-built cow house for twelve bovines, cart sheds, two implement sheds, two bullock sheds, a loose box, a turnip house, an engine house and last but not least a "Labourer's Cottage" which was without doubt Toll Bar Cottage. Various plots of arable land, spinney, grass land and the old quarry formed the ground on which Springfield Farm was situated. The decimal acreage was estimated at 92.957; tenant in 1938 was Mr R Coupe and he paid £250 of rent *p.a.*. The rental/tax account book of Renishaw Hall Estate, executed between the years 1946 and 1961, attests in **1948** the presence of a tenant farmer of Springfield Farm which according to the book had ca. 126 acres of land; the annual rent was 100 pounds. Springfield Farm was not part of Southgate Estate at the time the Land Values Map was drawn up (1909/1910).

Lot 3 of the auction catalogue is **South Walls Farm**. Built of stone it contained sitting and living rooms, a kitchen, a cellar, a pantry, four bedrooms, three attics, and a "range of stone buildings" which comprised of a feeding house for four animals, two calf sheds, a pig cote, four horse stables, a cow house for eight bovines, a barn with a chamber above, two loose boxes, two implement sheds, a poultry shed, a barn and a covered yard. Arable and grass land formed the ground on which Springfield Farm was situated. The decimal acreage was estimated at 121,274; Mr T Morris was the tenant in 1938 and he paid a yearly rent of £128. The rental/tax account book of Renishaw Hall Estate attests in **1948** the presence of a tenant farmer of South Walls Farm which according to the book had ca. 121 acres of land; the annual rent was 77 Pounds and 10 Shillings.

Lot 4 of the auction catalogue is **North Walls Farm**. The farmhouse was built of stone and contained an entrance hall, two sitting rooms, a living room, a scullery, a pantry and cellars, three bedrooms, two box rooms and two attics. The agrarian useful space included a horse stable for five animals with a chamber above, two barns (one with a granary), two pig cotes, implement and cart sheds, a feeding house for six animals, two open sheds, a cow house for six bovines, three loose boxes (one with a chamber above). The agricultural production land comprised of arable land, spinney, grass land, Walls Holt and Walls Plantation and a fish pond. The decimal acreage was estimated at 121,089; in 1938 Mr E S Bennett was the tenant and he paid £198 of rent per year. The 1911 census returns lists William Woombell, Dairy Farmer, and his family (his wife Mary, his stepdaughter Mary Platts and a Thomas Seyland, a boarder and labourer from Lathom, Lancashire) for "Walls Farm, Southgate", which in all probability was North Walls Farm. Mr Woombell is also attested as inhabitant of a dwelling house at Southgate in the Electoral Rolls of 1912. From 1921 onwards (until 1938) Edwin Simpson Bennett is listed in the Electoral Rolls as holding "land Southgate, abode Southgate, Whitwell". The rental/tax account book of Renishaw Hall Estate attests in **1948** the presence of a tenant farmer of North Walls Farm which, according to the book, had ca. 132 acres of land; the annual rent was 81 pounds, 17 shillings and 6 halfpence. Today a G Platts owns North Walls Farm.[771]

According to the Land Values Map of 1909/1910 both South and North Walls Farms seem not to have been part of Southgate Estate at the time the data was collected, they are colours other than violet on the map sheet and are not mentioned in the Book of References.

Lot 5 of the auction catalogue is **Manor Farm**. The two-storeyed dwelling house, originally Harlesthorpe Manor House[772], was built of limestone and contained on two sitting rooms, a kitchen, a dairy, a wash house, four bedrooms, a cellar and a coal house. The farm buildings comprised a barn and a granary, a feeding house for four animals and a loose box for four horses (with a chamber above), a stable for three horses, a cow house for eight bovines, three more loose boxes (with chamber above), five pig cotes with a loose box, a poultry house, a implement shed and a turnip house. Arable land, spinney, grass land and an orchard and a garden formed the productive land. The decimal acreage was estimated at 122,276; tenant in 1938 was Mr H(orace) V(ictor) Widdowson and he paid an annual rent of £178 10s and 0d. According to Robert Innes-Smith the building was purchased by Sir Osbert Sitwell when the Butler-Bowdons dissolved their estate.[773] The rental/tax account book of Renishaw Hall Estate attests in **1948** the presence of a tenant farmer of Manor Farm which, according to the book, had ca. 120 acres of land; the annual rent was 68 pounds and 10 shillings. In spring 1924 the tenants of Manor Farm were Thomas and Harriet Truman and George Truman (source: Electoral Rolls). Half a year later, in autumn 1924, Horace Victor and Kenneth

---

771 http://www.yell.com/ucs/UcsSearchAction.do?keywords=farmers&location=clowne &scrambleSeed=61856656&searchType=&M=&bandedclarifyResults=&ssm=1 (viewed 16/10/2013).

772 Riden, *History of the County of Derby III*, p. 113: a C17 house with alterations in C19 and later, possibly on the site of a mediaeval predecessor building. One of its main architectural features is a wooden beam *in situ*, perhaps a spolia, with carvings. These carvings consist of various heraldic symbols such as the royal arms (*fleurs de lys* and the three lions of England as used by Henry IV), perhaps a Tudor rose, a Catherine wheel and a (Lancastrian) eagle, a shield bearing a chevron (symbol of the Stafford family?), a mason's mark (or a symbol against witchcraft?), a talbot (symbol of the Talbot family?) and are published by Robert Innes-Smith (Innes-Smith, "Plantagenet or Tudor" , p. 124f., with photographs).

773 Innes-Smith, "Plantagenet or Tudor", p. 124; Riden, *History of the County of Derby III*, p. 113.

Figure 2
Old black and white photograph depicting Southgate Colliery (undated)

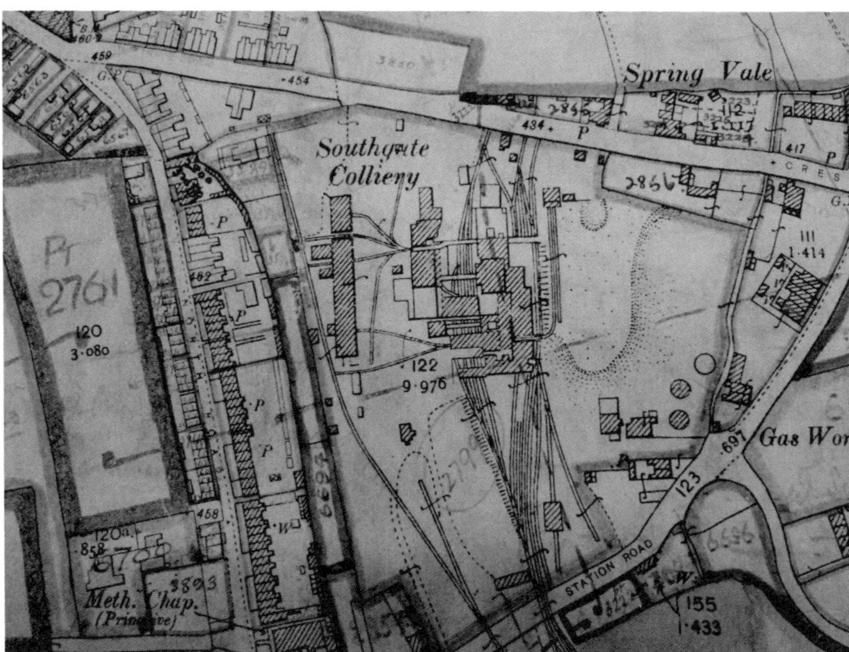

Figure 3
Land Values Map depicting Southgate Colliery

Figure 4
Southgate House/1900s

Figure 5
Southgate House/1900s

Figure 6
Southgate House/1900s

Figure 7
Southgate House/1900s

Figure 8
Foundation plaque with inscription *Ad maiorem dei gloriam*

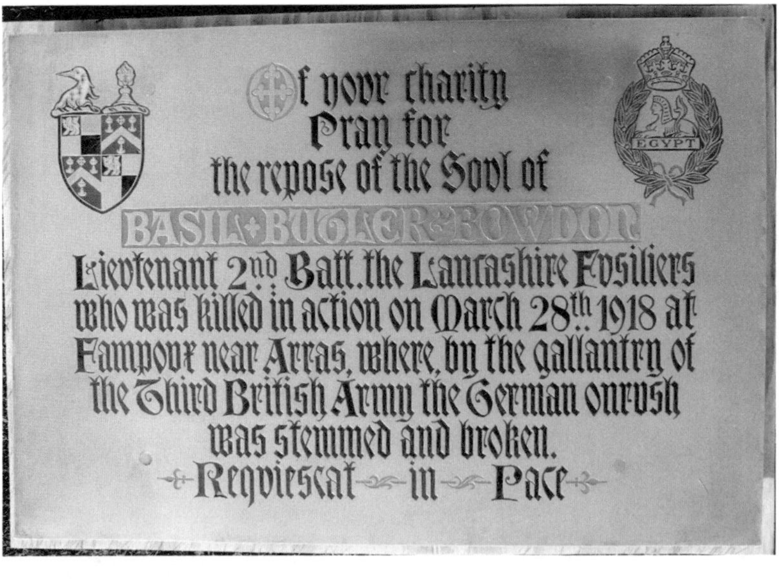

Figure 9
Memorial plaque of Basil Butler-Bowdon

Figure 10
Cover photograph of Sale Particulars of Southgate House (1938)

Figure 11
A soldier of the Cheshire Yeomanry (undated)

Figure 12
Land Values Map depicting Southgate House and Stables

Figure 13
Fire place in Barlborough House displaying family motto *Vanus est honor*

Figure 14
Fire place in Barlborough House displaying

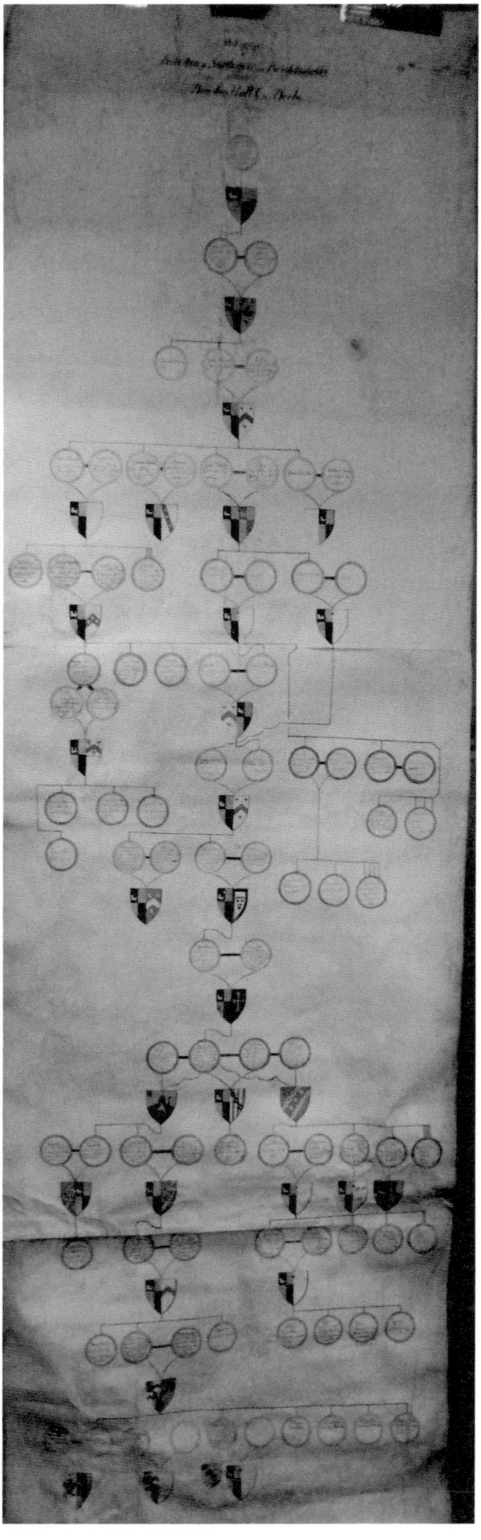

Figure 15
The copy of the Bowdon family tree on parchment in possession of Barlborough Heritage and Resource Centre

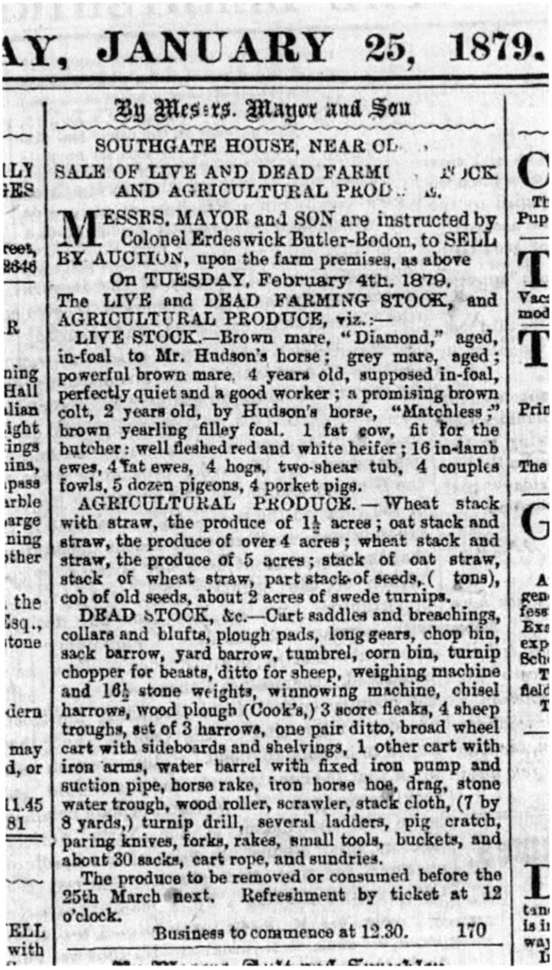

AY, JANUARY 25, 1879.

By Messrs. Mayor and Son

SOUTHGATE HOUSE, NEAR CL[illegible]

SALE OF LIVE AND DEAD FARM[illegible] [illegible]OCK AND AGRICULTURAL PROD[illegible].

MESSRS. MAYOR and SON are instructed by Colonel Erdeswick Butler-Bodon, to SELL BY AUCTION, upon the farm premises, as above

On TUESDAY, February 4th. 1879.

The LIVE and DEAD FARMING STOCK, and AGRICULTURAL PRODUCE, viz.:—

LIVE STOCK.—Brown mare, "Diamond," aged, in-foal to Mr. Hudson's horse; grey mare, aged; powerful brown mare, 4 years old, supposed in-foal, perfectly quiet and a good worker; a promising brown colt, 2 years old, by Hudson's horse, "Matchless;" brown yearling filley foal. 1 fat cow, fit for the butcher: well fleshed red and white heifer; 16 in-lamb ewes, 4 fat ewes, 4 hogs, two-shear tub, 4 couples fowls, 5 dozen pigeons, 4 porket pigs.

AGRICULTURAL PRODUCE.—Wheat stack with straw, the produce of 1½ acres; oat stack and straw, the produce of over 4 acres; wheat stack and straw, the produce of 5 acres; stack of oat straw, stack of wheat straw, part stack of seeds, (tons), cob of old seeds, about 2 acres of swede turnips.

DEAD STOCK, &c.—Cart saddles and breachings, collars and blufts, plough pads, long gears, chop bin, sack barrow, yard barrow, tumbrel, corn bin, turnip chopper for beasts, ditto for sheep, weighing machine and 16½ stone weights, winnowing machine, chisel harrows, wood plough (Cook's,) 3 score fleaks, 4 sheep troughs, set of 3 harrows, one pair ditto, broad wheel cart with sideboards and shelvings, 1 other cart with iron arms, water barrel with fixed iron pump and suction pipe, horse rake, iron horse hoe, drag, stone water trough, wood roller, scrawler, stack cloth, (7 by 8 yards,) turnip drill, several ladders, pig cratch, paring knives, forks, rakes, small tools, buckets, and about 30 sacks, cart rope, and sundries.

The produce to be removed or consumed before the 25th March next. Refreshment by ticket at 12 o'clock.

Business to commence at 12.30. 170

Figure 16
The Derbyshire Times and Chesterfield Herald announcing an auction sale dated January 25, 1879

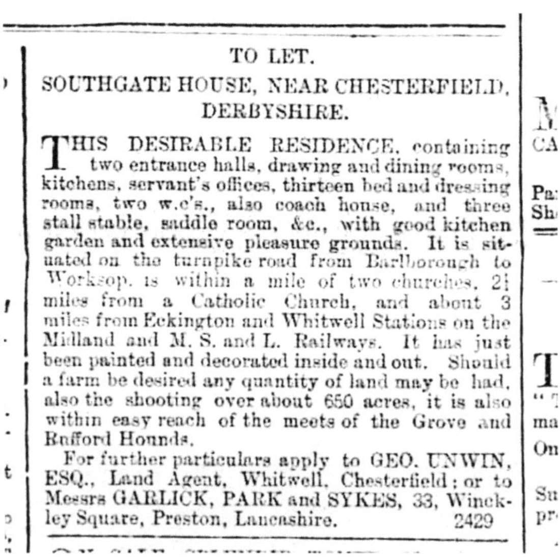

TO LET.

SOUTHGATE HOUSE, NEAR CHESTERFIELD, DERBYSHIRE.

THIS DESIRABLE RESIDENCE, containing two entrance halls, drawing and dining rooms, kitchens, servant's offices, thirteen bed and dressing rooms, two w.c's., also coach house, and three stall stable, saddle room, &c., with good kitchen garden and extensive pleasure grounds. It is situated on the turnpike road from Barlborough to Worksop, is within a mile of two churches, 2½ miles from a Catholic Church, and about 3 miles from Eckington and Whitwell Stations on the Midland and M. S. and L. Railways. It has just been painted and decorated inside and out. Should a farm be desired any quantity of land may be had, also the shooting over about 650 acres, it is also within easy reach of the meets of the Grove and Rufford Hounds.

For further particulars apply to GEO. UNWIN, ESQ., Land Agent, Whitwell, Chesterfield; or to Messrs GARLICK, PARK and SYKES, 33, Winckley Square, Preston, Lancashire. 2429

Figure 17
Advertisement in The Derbyshire Times and Chesterfield Herald dated December 27, 1882

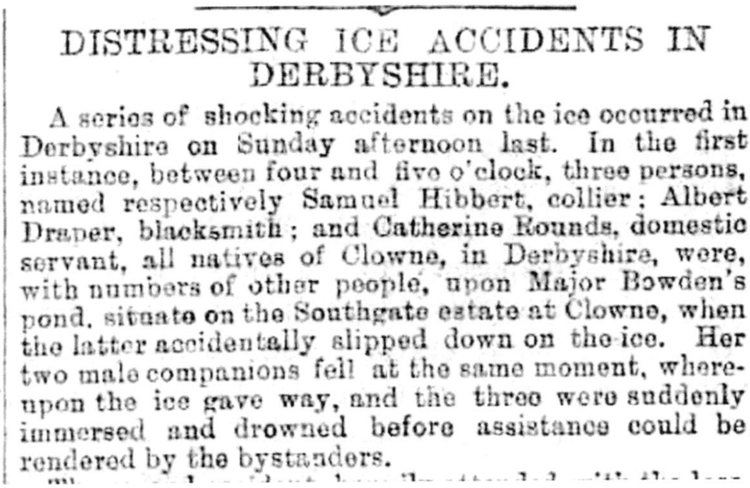

DISTRESSING ICE ACCIDENTS IN DERBYSHIRE.

A series of shocking accidents on the ice occurred in Derbyshire on Sunday afternoon last. In the first instance, between four and five o'clock, three persons, named respectively Samuel Hibbert, collier; Albert Draper, blacksmith; and Catherine Rounds, domestic servant, all natives of Clowne, in Derbyshire, were, with numbers of other people, upon Major Bowden's pond, situate on the Southgate estate at Clowne, when the latter accidentally slipped down on the ice. Her two male companions fell at the same moment, whereupon the ice gave way, and the three were suddenly immersed and drowned before assistance could be rendered by the bystanders.

Figure 18
Manchester Courier and Lancashire General Advertiser reporting on an accident on ice dated January 21, 1885

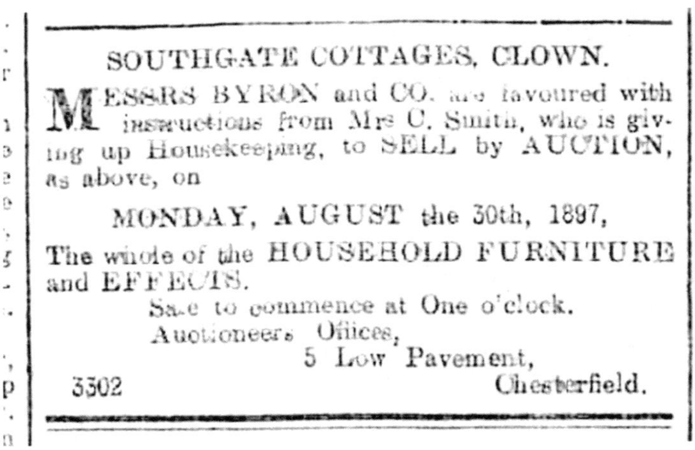

SOUTHGATE COTTAGES, CLOWN.

MESSRS BYRON and CO. are favoured with instructions from Mrs C. Smith, who is giving up Housekeeping, to SELL by AUCTION, as above, on

MONDAY, AUGUST the 30th, 1897,

The whole of the HOUSEHOLD FURNITURE and EFFECTS.

Sale to commence at One o'clock.
Auctioneers Offices,
5 Low Pavement,
3302 Chesterfield.

Figure 19
Household goods are announced to be sold by auction in The Derbyshire Times and Chesterfield Herald dated August 28, 1897

FUNERAL OF H. BOWDEN, Esq., J.P.

The remains of the late Henry Bowdon, Esq., were interred on Friday in the private burial ground of the family, at Beighton Fields Preory, near Barlborough. The funeral *cortege* left Southgate House at half-past ten and reached Spinkhill Church an hour later, when solemn high mass was celebrated. The procession then reformed, and proceeded slowly to Beighton Fields, which was reached about one o'clock. The Body of the deceased gentleman was enclosed in three coffins, the second being a lead one. The outer one bore the following inscription:—"Pray for the soul of Henry Bowden, of Southgate House, born 1814, died 1875." The Requiem having been sung by the choiristers the body was lowered to the grave. The procession was a very large one, and was preceded by twenty constables of the Eckington division, under the command of Superintendent Cruitt. The chief mourners were Colonel and Captain Bowdon of Pleasington Hall, Lancashire, Captain Blunt, Reading; and J. Carrington Wright, Esq., of Kelvedon Hall, Essex. There was five mourning coaches and many private carriages. Amongst those in the procession we noticed the Rev. E. B. Estcourt, Eckington; the Rev. M. Stapylton, Barlborough; Dr. Fleming, Harthill, &c. A vast concourse of people had assembled to pay their last tribute of respect to the deceased gentleman —Beighton Fields Priory as its name implies, was at one time a monastery, and has been in the Bowdon family for many generations. The burial ground is in the garden, and tablets are erected to those buried there. The following inscription is to be seen:— "Through all adversity they ever remained steadfast to the faith of their forefathers." The undertaker was Mr. Ald. Grundy, of Sheffield, and the carriages supplied by the Sheffield Carriage Company.

Figure 20
The Derbyshire Times and Chesterfield Herald reporting on the funeral of Henry (5) Bowdon on May 12, 1875

Figure 21
Gravestone of Eliza Jemima Bowdon
at Spinkhill cemetery

Figure 22
Gravestone of Alice Del Monaco at Spinkhill cemetery

Figure 23
Gravestone of Ireneo Del Monaco at Spinkhill cemetery

Figure 24
Gravestone of Enrico Del Monaco at Spinkhill cemetery

Figure 25
Gravestone of Corona Del Monaco at Spinkhill cemetery

Figure 26
Gravestone of Lancelot George B Butler-Bowdon and Ella Cicely Mary Butler-Bowdon

Figure 27
Gravestone of John (6) Erdeswick Butler-Bowdon, Monica Mary Petre Butler-Bowdon, Isabel-Mary Helena Butler-Bowdon and Mary Monica Butler-Bowdon at Spinkhill cemetery

Figure 28
Commemoration plaque for Constance Bowdon at Spinkhill cemetery

Figure 29
Gravestone of John Joseph Baldwin Young and his wife Margarita at Spinkhill

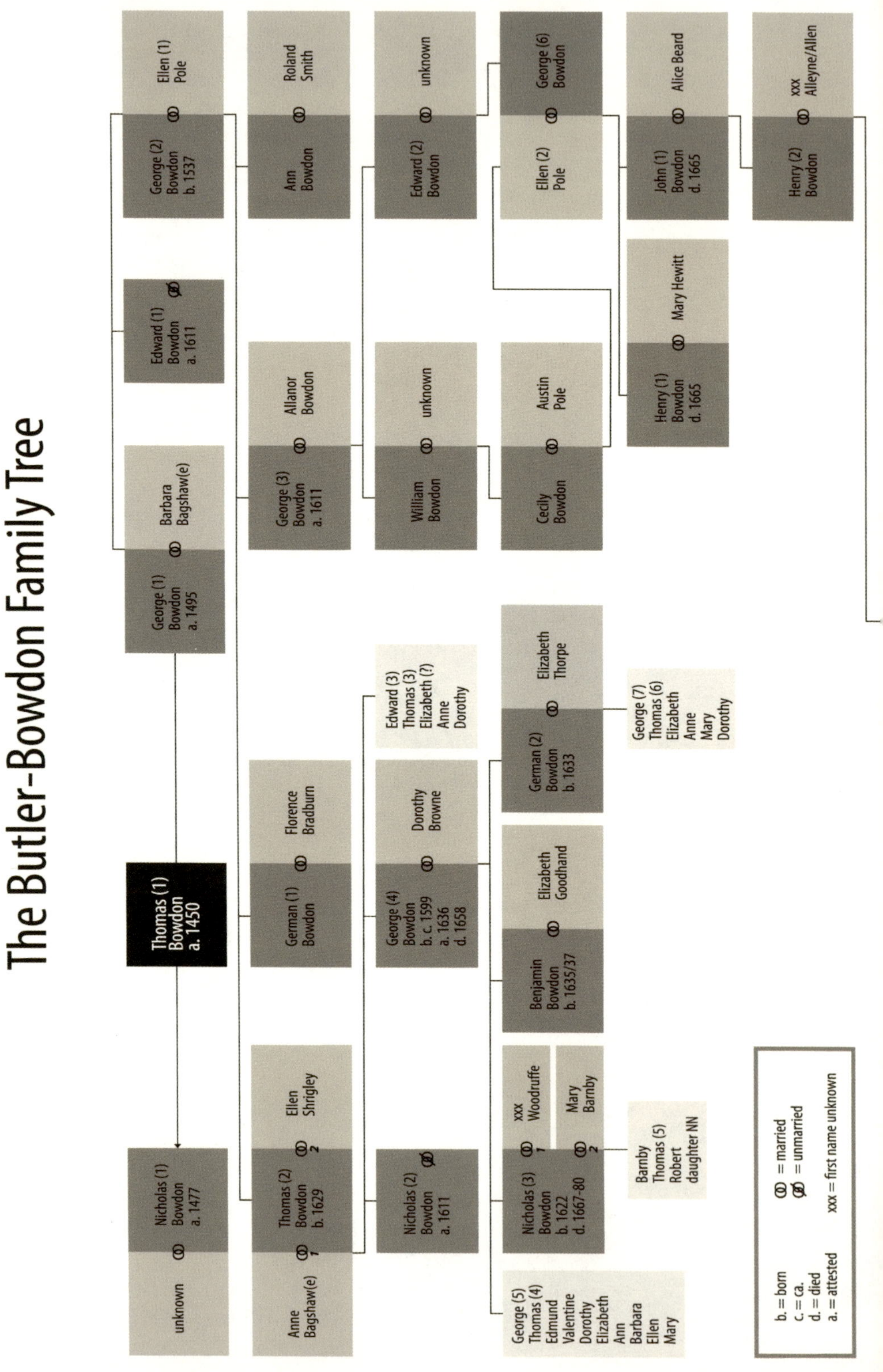

Figure 30
Family tree of the Butler-Bowdon family

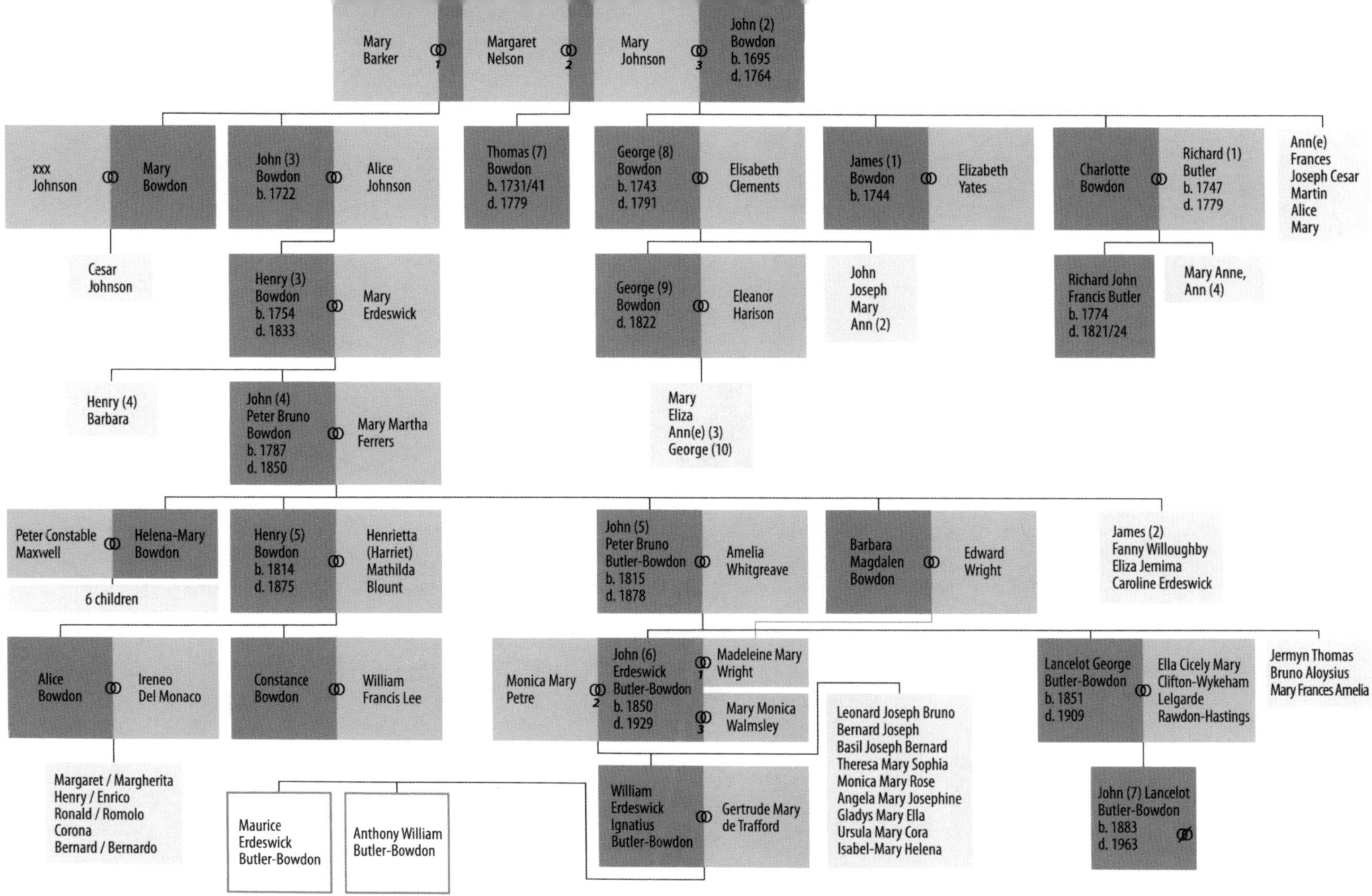
Mary Barker
Margaret Nelson
Mary Johnson
John (2) Bowdon b. 1695 d. 1764
xxx Johnson
Mary Bowdon
John (3) Bowdon b. 1722
Alice Johnson
Thomas (7) Bowdon b. 1731/41 d. 1779
George (8) Bowdon b. 1743 d. 1791
Elisabeth Clements
James (1) Bowdon b. 1744
Elizabeth Yates
Charlotte Bowdon
Richard (1) Butler b. 1747 d. 1779
Ann(e) Frances Joseph Cesar Martin Alice Mary
Cesar Johnson
Henry (3) Bowdon b. 1754 d. 1833
Mary Erdeswick
George (9) Bowdon d. 1822
Eleanor Harison
John Joseph Mary Ann (2)
Richard John Francis Butler b. 1774 d. 1821/24
Mary Anne, Ann (4)
Henry (4) Barbara
John (4) Peter Bruno Bowdon b. 1787 d. 1850
Mary Martha Ferrers
Mary Eliza Ann(e) (3) George (10)
Peter Constable Maxwell
Helena-Mary Bowdon
6 children
Henry (5) Bowdon b. 1814 d. 1875
Henrietta (Harriet) Mathilda Blount
John (5) Peter Bruno Butler-Bowdon b. 1815 d. 1878
Amelia Whitgreave
Barbara Magdalen Bowdon
Edward Wright
James (2) Fanny Willoughby Eliza Jemima Caroline Erdeswick
Alice Bowdon
Ireneo Del Monaco
Constance Bowdon
William Francis Lee
Monica Mary Petre
John (6) Erdeswick Butler-Bowdon b. 1850 d. 1929
Madeleine Mary Wright
Mary Monica Walmsley
Lancelot George Butler-Bowdon b. 1851 d. 1909
Ella Cicely Mary Clifton-Wykeham Lelgarde Rawdon-Hastings
Jermyn Thomas Bruno Aloysius Mary Frances Amelia
Leonard Joseph Bruno Bernard Joseph Basil Joseph Bernard Theresa Mary Sophia Monica Mary Rose Angela Mary Josephine Gladys Mary Ella Ursula Mary Cora Isabel-Mary Helena
Margaret / Margherita Henry / Enrico Ronald / Romolo Corona Bernard / Bernardo
Maurice Erdeswick Butler-Bowdon
Anthony William Butler-Bowdon
William Erdeswick Ignatius Butler-Bowdon
Gertrude Mary de Trafford
John (7) Lancelot Butler-Bowdon b. 1883 d. 1963

Figure 31 Toll Bar Cottage/1940s

Figure 32 Southgate Avenue/1950s

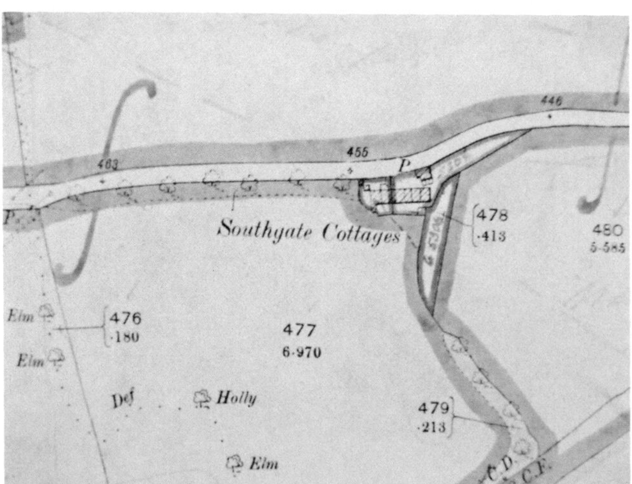

Figure 33 Land Values Map displaying Southgate Cottage

Figure 34
Harlesthorpe
Cottages

Figure 35
Walled enclosure
in the garden of
Beighton Fields
Priory

Figure 36
Gravestone of
Henry (5)
Bowdon at
Beighton
Fields Priory

Figure 37
Gravestone of
Harriet
Bowdon at
Beighton
Fields Priory

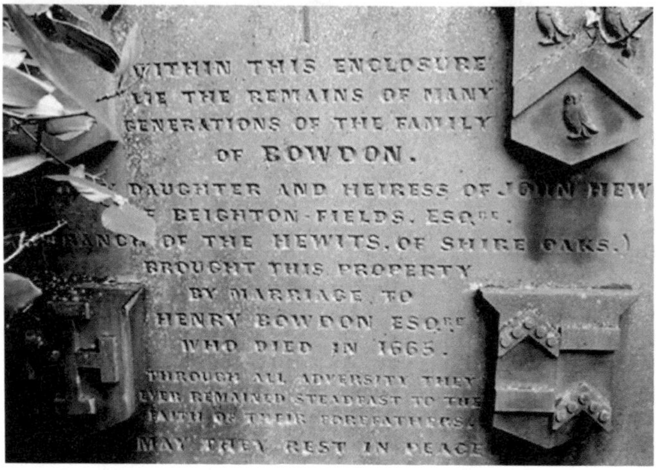

Figure 38
The inscription plaque at Beighton Fields Priory

Figure 40
Comparison of stained glass window of Southgate Chapel 1901 and 2014

Figure 43
Pleasington New Hall, Blackburn

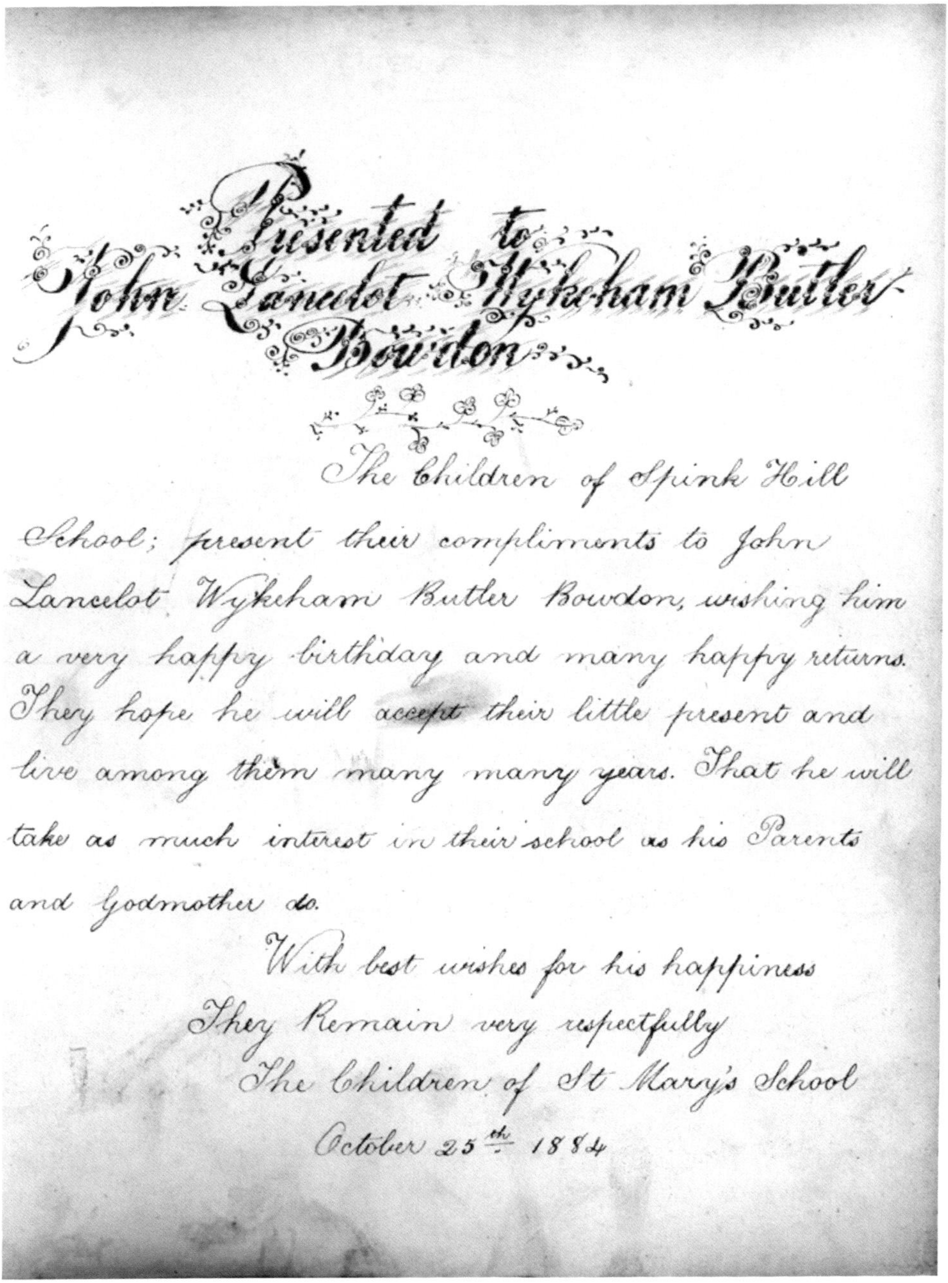
Presented to
John Lancelot Wykeham Butler
Bowdon

The Children of Spink Hill School; present their compliments to John Lancelot Wykeham Butler Bowdon, wishing him a very happy birthday and many happy returns. They hope he will accept their little present and live among them many many years. That he will take as much interest in their school as his Parents and Godmother do.

With best wishes for his happiness
They Remain very respectfully
The Children of St Mary's School
October 25th 1884

Figure 46
Page from scrapbook made for Lancelot Butler-Bowdon's first birthday

Figure 47
Pencil drawing of an American B-17 Flying Fortress by Erich Siegel (undated)

Figure 48
Five German POWs at Barlborough Farm

Figure 49
The Nissen Huts of Southgate Camp

Figure 39
Detail of the Butler-Bowdon cope depicting St Thomas and St Andrew

Figure 41
The stained glass window from Southgate Chapel at Pleasington Priory today

Figure 44 "Laying of the Foundation Stone", painting by Vladimir Osipovich Sherwood (1852)

Figure 45
Detail from "Laying of the Foundation Stone", painting by Vladimir Osipovich Sherwood (1852)

Bennett Widdowson are the new and lasting tenants of Manor Farm. The years 1931 and 1937 attest the presence of Amy Widdowson (K B Widdowson is not listed at this address anymore). Manor Farm was not part of Southgate Estate at the time the Land Values Map was drawn up (1909/1910). Cottage number 10, Harlesthorpe belonged to Manor Farm.[774] According to the recollections of Ruby Thorpe, the farm house had a big fireplace in one of the upstairs rooms and there was a discernible angle painting on the wall, extremely faint and possibly painted over. She says that the farm house "was weird to be in"; it was illuminated only by candles and gas lights.

At some point in time Manor Farm was home to two curious characters. According to the memories of Ruby Thorpe, there were two "tramps" who lived in an abandoned cottage across the fields. They worked for the farmer at Manor Farm when he needed them and generally lived off the land and were either given or stole anything else they needed. Everyone in the village of Clowne knew them. They were known as Singing Billy and Crony and no-one ever knew their real names. The story goes that when the war horses[775] were in the stables at the farm some of the soldiers called at the farm asking for Crony in Colonel Butler-Bowdon's name. The farmer, Horace Widdowson, was puzzled and asked them why. The reason for this was that the Colonel wanted to borrow a horse and that he had known Crony from when he was a boy. He had been a duke who had left his family and given up his life to roam free and live as he liked. He was a very good horseman, a marvellous rider and well known for his skills at "breaking-in" and training horses.[776] Also the soldiers needed Crony's help with a horse that was proving very difficult to train.[777] Ruby Thorpe is in possession of a very old aerial photo which shows all the old buildings of Manor Farm, one of which was the "powder house" situated near the farmhouse. This building functioned as a store for the dynamite used for blasting down the pit (Southgate Colliery).[778]

Lot 6 of the auction catalogue is **Little Walls Farm**. It was considerably smaller than the other farmhouses, built of stone and containing a sitting room, a living room, a kitchen and a diary, three bedrooms, a box room and a coal house. A cow house for four bovines, a stable for three horses (with a chamber above), a loose box, a pig cote and a turnip house were the

---

774 Information disclosed by Ruby Thorpe during a personal meeting in Clowne on April 27, 2014.

775 According to Ruby Thorpe, they were ginger coloured; information disclosed by her during a personal meeting in Clowne on April 27, 2014.

776 Information disclosed by Ruby Thorpe during a personal meeting with the author in Clowne on April 27, 2014.

777 Information communicated by E-mail by June Pearce following a personal meeting with Ruby Thorpe on March 25, 2014.

778 Information communicated by E-mail by June Pearce following a personal meeting with Ruby Thorpe on March 25, 2014.

outbuildings erected in stone. Arable and grass land formed the base of agriculture of Little Walls Farm. The decimal acreage was estimated at 22,290; tenant in 1938 was Mr H Morris and he paid an annual rent of £41 12s and 0d. The rental/tax account book of Renishaw Hall Estate does not mention the farm in 1948.

Lot 7 of the auction catalogue is **Eastwood Cottage Farm**. The dwelling house itself was a stone built cottage with a living room and a kitchen, two bedrooms, a washhouse and a dairy. The farm buildings nonetheless included two cow houses, two turnip sheds, a loose box, piggeries, a food chamber with a loft above, a stable for two horses (with a chamber above). Arable and grass land formed the base of agriculture of Eastwood Cottage Farm. The decimal acreage was estimated at 44,786; tenant in 1938 was Mr C(harles) P(eter) Glossop and he paid a rent of £68 per year. According to the Electoral Rolls, Charles Peter Glossop and his wife Constance belonged to the inhabitants of Harlesthorpe Cottages (house number 6) in 1924. Evidently, they moved to Eastwood Cottage between 1924 and 1938 and took up a farmer's life. The Electoral Rolls list Bertrand Coupe for Eastwood Farm in 1924, together with Henry Coupe (father? brother?). The rental/tax account book of Renishaw Hall Estate attests in **1948** the presence of a tenant farmer of Eastwood Cottage Farm which, according to the book, had ca. 44 acres of land; the annual rent was 28 pounds and 10 shillings.

Lot 8 of the auction catalogue is **Hickinwood Farm**. This was another quite ample farmstead. The stone built farm house consisted of a sitting room, a dining room, a kitchen and a pantry, a wash-house, four bedrooms and a bathroom, a coal house and four poultry houses. The agricultural buildings comprised of a cow house for twelve bovines (with a chamber above), a barn, a loose box, a turnip shed, an open shed with a loft above, two pig cotes and an open shed, two more loose boxes, a stable for six animals with a chop chamber above. A so-called "Dutch Barn" with bathroom fittings and two cart sheds belonged to the tenant and completed the farmstead. Hickingwood Farm was surrounded by arable land, spinney and grass land. The decimal acreage was estimated at 102,194; tenant in 1938 was Mr George Warrener and he paid a rent of £175 *p.a.*. The Electoral Rolls of 1912 to 1915 list Anthony Warrener (junior) as holding land at "Southgate Whitwell, Clown"; he was William Warrener's brother (cf. census return 1881, 1891, 1901). In 1920 William and Anthony Warrener are listed for that address, but from 1921 onwards it is William Warrener alone (until 1925).[779] The rental/tax account book of Renishaw Hall Estate does not make mention of this farm in 1948. The

---

[779] The Whitwell burial list names among others two Anthony Warreners, one b. 1878, d. 02/11/1962, married to Ethel Warrener (b. 1887, d. 24/07/1976), the other b. 1832, d. 14/10/1903. The latter is listed as resident of "Southgate" and was married to Amy Warrener (b. 1846, d. 08/10/1932). Another Amy Warrener (b. 1870/1871, d. 06 or 08/09/1885), their daughter, is also listed for "Southgate"; cf. Hopkins, *Graves Index*.

book does however inform us that some land of Southgate Estate at Gapsick Lane/Creswell Road was rented out for a semi-annual rent of 12 pounds in **1947** and **1948**. According to the decennial census returns Anthony Warrener (senior), his wife Amy, their children Mary E, John H, George, Amy, Anthony (junior), William and Lily, and his servants are attested as residents of Hickinwood Farm at least since 1871 (the farm is denoted as "South Gate" in 1871, as "Southgate Farm" in 1881 and 1891, and as "Whitwell Common Southgate" in 1901).

16.1. Other Observations on the Cottages and the Farms of Southgate Estate

Apparently, a majority of the inhabitants of the various Southgate cottages and farms were quite rooted to their native soil and evidently content with their landlords and their living conditions. A few tenants listed in 1909/1910 and their respective descendants can still be found to be living in the same place for many years later. The personal recollections of Mary Jones from "Cottage at Harlesthorpe Dam" confirm this impression. All in all, when looking at the occupants of Southgate Estate outbuildings it almost seems as if we are viewing a small self-contained universe that existed for almost a century with only few connections to the outside world.[780]

17. Bowden Hall / Chapel-en-le-Frith

According to Humphrey Butler-Bowdon, the Bowdon family originates from Bowdon in the south west of Manchester[781], but apparently moved to Chapel-en-le-Frith in the High Peak at an undeterminable point in time. There a street named "Bowden Lane" can be found, which perhaps commemorates their time there.[782] There is also the impressive building of Bowden Hall just outside the town, towards the north east. Like all the other mansions mentioned in this book, Bowden Hall is a Grade II listed building. The house as it presents itself today is a two-storey building with three bays in Tudor Gothic style built of Kinderscout grit ashlar. The architect was Richard Lane from Manchester; he designed the house in 1844. English Heritage states that the interior of the house reflects the exterior in style; the most striking element is a cast iron cusped baluster staircase and a fireplace with a four-centred arch and cusped panels to the sides.[783]

This house stands on the foundations of a predecessor building commissioned by the Bowdon family sometime in the middle of the 15th

[780] This phenomenon seems not to be unusual; cf. Horn, *Victorian Country House*, p. 69.

[781] Information disclosed in a personal E-mail correspondence with the author dated November 25, 2013.

[782] "Bowden" could also refer to the place name of Bowden Middlecale, today the villages of Hayfield and New Mills, north of Chapel-en-le-Frith, see Chapter 10.

[783] English Heritage, *Bowden Hall*.

century.[784] Although the Bowdons have their origins in Bowdon near Altrincham, sources reveal that the family resided in Chapel-en-le-Frith from 1317 onwards, and built their chancel of the local church, commonly known as "Chapel Bowden".[785] The first historically confirmed member of the Bowdon family is Thomas (1) Bowdon of Bowden Hall near Chapel-en-le-Frith, who is attested to have lived there in 1450.[786] One Nicholas (1) Bowdon was owner of Bowden Hall in ca. 1477.[787] The Bowdon family possibly held this estate as freehold from the time of the Black Death (1348) until the middle of the 17th century.[788] The reasons for the loss of the estate are not entirely clear. It possibly passed from the family through an heiress in 1680[789]. Other sources say when Robert Bowdon died in 1681 the estate passed to his uncle George (5) Bowdon (son of George (4) Bowdon and Dorothy Brown) who was the last to live at Bowden Hall.[790] According to a third source, it was sold in 1677 or 1680 to a Sir Simon Degge by Thomas (3) Bowdon, son of Nicholas (2) Bowdon, grandson of Thomas (2) Bowdon and his first wife Anne Bagshaw.[791] There seems to be gap of 40 years from the time when the Bowdon family left Chapel-en-le-Frith ca. 1650 until 1690 when they appear in Beighton Fields.[792] Also the reasons for their removal to a village thirty-five miles further to the East and across the Peak District could not be determined.

Bowden Hall however, continued to exist through the centuries, changing hands several times. Bulmer's Derby mentions a Samuel Wood of Bowden Hall for 1764.[793] After his death the house was sold to a Robert Hibberson in 1765 and it remained in his possession until it was bought by a John Sla(c)k(e)[794], who demolished the old house and replaced it with a new

---

[784] According to Chris Bowden (Bowden, *Bowdon Marriage*), parts of the old Bowden Hall still stand adjacent to the Victorian building.

[785] White's *1875*, p. 732.

[786] White's *1875*, p. 732.

[787] Craven, "Southgate House, Clowne", p. 57 mentions 1477 as the first documented date of the Bowdons inhabiting Bowden Hall, probably referring to Nicholas (1) Bowdon.

[788] Craven, Stanley, *Derbyshire Country House*, p. 38f.

[789] White's *1875*, p. 732. Possibly responsible for this was one of the two daughters of George (5) Bowden; cf. Bowden, *Bowdon Marriage*.

[790] Bowden, *Bowdon Marriage*.

[791] Craven, Stanley, *Derbyshire Country House*, p. 38f.; Bowden, *Bowdon Marriage*.

[792] Bowden, *Bowdon Marriage*.

[793] Derbyshire County Council, *Bulmer's Derby 1895*, p. 135: "Samuel Wood, of Bowden Hall, died 15th April, 1764, and left £200 to be put out to interest for charitable purposes, yearly, for ever (...)" to those of Chapel-en-le-Frith who are in need of help.

[794] John Slacke is attested for Bowden Hall in various legal documents such as a trust deed relating to a free school for the children of the poor and its premises in the parish of Chapel-en-le-Frith dated August 1841 and the Bowden School Agreement dated 1866, in which he offers to contribute a substantial amount of money under certain

building in 1844 (see above) which still stands today.[795] It was mostly tenanted during the years and remained in the ownership of the Sla(c)k(e) family until at least the First Word War. Bowden Hall was then bought by a structural engineer named Dr Dennis Matthews in 1963 who restored the building, thus saving it from collapse. In 1979 it was sold to a G E Roberts from Manchester.[796]

18. Beighton Fields Priory

Beighton Fields Priory, about five km to the east of Southgate House and off Barber's Row/Barlborough[797], is a typical late 17th/early 18th century edifice, two storeys high, built of coarse ashlar, and with attics under end gables. Like several others houses of that particular time and in that particular region, it was built with a more or less symmetrical ground plan and a central entrance hall. The front exterior shows a strikingly generous entrance and the façade is punctuated with a considerable number of windows under continuous bands.[798] It is positioned at the end of a long drive that branches off Barber's Row on the south-eastern outskirts of Renishaw, and still today overlooks the surrounding countryside.

An extract from a Sale Particulars (cover sheet) dating from the late 1940s describes the house as a "Charming XVIIth Century Residence" which is "easily run and not too large", with five principal bedrooms, fine oak doors, completely modernised and "tastefully decorated and ready to occupy without further expense". A black-and-white photo of the fully furnished Entrance Hall gives a good impression of the state the house was in during that particular year.[799]

The mansion house was homestead to the Bowdons ever since it had come into the family by the marriage of Henry (1) Bowdon with Mary Hewitt in 1665/on November 4, 1691 (?).[800] The early history of the place is not easy to

---

conditions to have a new school built in Chapel-en-le-Frith, cf. http://www.chapel-en-le-frithparishcouncil.gov.uk/history.htm (viewed 16/07/2013).

795 Bowden Hall featured in the BBC TV series "The Village" (2013) and "The Secret of Crickley Hall" (2006).

796 Craven, Stanley, *Derbyshire Country House*, p. 38; http://www.bowdenhall.co.uk (viewed 12/07/2013).

797 Beighton Fields belongs to the parish of Barlborough; cf. Riden, *History of the County of Derby III*, p. 13 and p. 25.

798 Craven, Stanley, *Derbyshire Country House*, p. 12, p. 32; Riden, *History of the County of Derby III*, p. 25.

799 Information by kind courtesy of Tony Bak of Barlborough Heritage and Research Centre in April 2013 (photocopy of Sale Particulars possibly obtained from the actual owner of Beighton Fields Priory).

800 For the accuracy of the statement see above and Chapter 10.

disentangle [801] and goes back to the 11th century when the estate was an element of the inheritance of Wulfric Spott's (see Chapter 7) nephew and heir, Morcar, in 1002.[802] Apart from a record in Domesday Book in 1086 nothing is known about the property situation. The record includes three entries, two of which mention one owner for one manor each for Beighton, one belonging to a person named Lewin/Leofwin, the other to Roger de Poitou.[803] Beighton Fields Priory as it presents itself today is the building related to the Lewin/Leofwin manor. It is said to have been at some stage a hospice (infirmary) to Welbeck Abbey where old and sick monks and aged poor were sent to spend their last days in peace[804], however it was most likely a grange belonging to the Abbey as monk's cells have been said to be seen there.[805] There also was a priest's hiding hole from the days of religious persecution.[806] The remaining cellars of the building hint to foundations of a 12th century structure. There is a Chapter House as well as farm buildings adjacent to Beighton Fields Priory which date from the 14th century.[807] Craven/Stanley state that Beighton Fields Estate came into the hands of the Hewitt family in the course of the Dissolution of Monasteries which took place between 1536 and 1541 under Henry VIII (1491-1547).[808] This is contradicted by historical

---

801 The park of Beighton Fields Priory for example is purportedly the site of a battle between the Saxons and the Danes. Information by kind courtesy of Tony Bak of Barlborough Heritage and Resource Centre in September 2013, also based on the text written in 1938.

802 Morcar inherited several local estates from his uncle such as Clowne, Whitwell, Barlborough, Wales and Eckington; cf. NN, "Focus on: Clowne", p. 24.

803 Craven, Stanley, *Derbyshire Country House*, p. 32; Domesday Book, Folio 273v (holder of one manor: Roger de Poitou), 277r, 278r (owner of other manor: Lewin under Roger de Bulli); cf. The National Archives, *Domesday*.

804 Among other sources information obtained from undated typed notes (p. 2 of six pages) which Paul D Walker made available to me in an E-mail correspondence dated May 9, 2014. He says that in the last line on p. 6 there are the letters „E & O E." - presumably the initials of the authors. Below them are the letters L.D.S. which in all probability stand for *laus deo semper*, Praise to God always. This phrase is associated with the Jesuits. According to Mr Walker, the notes were copied from an unknown earlier source.

805 Information by kind courtesy of Tony Bak of Barlborough Heritage and Resource Centre in September 2013, based on a text written in 1938 by "the last member of the Bowden (*sic!*) family to have an interest in the house", presumably William Erdeswick Ignatius Butler-Bowdon (1880-1956); see also Derbyshire County Council, *Bulmer's Derby 1895*, p. 208; Craven, Stanley, *Derbyshire Country House*, p. 32.

806 According to Derbyshire County Council, *Bulmer's Derby 1895*, p. 208 a part of the priest's hiding hole and chapel are said to remain at Barlborough House in 1895.

807 Information by kind courtesy of Tony Bak of Barlborough Heritage and Resource Centre in September 2013, based on the text written in 1938 (see above).

808 Craven, Stanley, *Derbyshire Country House*, p. 32. According to Bob Clarke, the Catholic church Priory was built in 1398. It was dissolved in 1536 by Henry VIII and

research carried out by a tenant of the property, Mr Roy Cressy Besch, in the late 1930s (evidence from local archives). During the reign of Henry VI (1412-1471) the Ince family (Sir Robert Sytwell) obtained Beighton Fields by the marriage of Henry Ince of Spinkhill to the daughter of John Beighton of Beightonfields in 1453. A Henry Ince (d. 1553) married a female named Merielle related to the Hewets/Hewitts around 1520/1530, legacies proved in his will of 1553 to all of Nicholas Hewet's children.[809] A lease dated October 20, 1606 by Henry Hewett of Beightonfields to a Barton Allot of Bentley, South Yorkshire (near Doncaster) establishes the Hewetts as owners, if not occupiers, of Beighton Fields Priory at that time.[810]

Beighton Fields Priory was rebuilt in 1603 and has been the dower house of the Butler-Bowdon family ever since. Very interesting additional information could be obtained from an essay by Richard H Turner: "In his will of 1666 (Beightonfields) Priory's owner, John Hewitt gentleman, named his son Henry heir both to the house, and with his brother Thomas, to significant coal mining assets once they reached 21. Their elder sister Mary was to have £400 from mining proceeds, and a nephew, John Hewitt £100. However, Mary had in the preceding year married Henry Bowden (sic!) of Bowden Hall in the north-west of Derbyshire, and in the event the Priory passed into their hands."[811]

Henry (2) Bowdon of Beighton Fields, yeoman, held the property as life estate; John (2) Bowdon (1695- 1764) was yeoman and freeholder of Beighton Fields Priory.[812] Philip Riden contributes an interesting detail: the Bowdon

---

became home of the Bowdon family, who was owner of a colliery to the rear of the building; cf. Clarke, "From Riches to Rags", p. 14.

809 For the Ince family see Riden, *History of the County of Derby III*, p. 25 and footnotes 4 and 5: "A freehold estate at Beightonfields may have originated with the purchase of land in Barlborough and elsewhere in 1426 by Richard Ince. Another Richard Ince, presumably his descendant, was of Beightonfields in 1548."

810 Information by kind courtesy of Tony Bak of Barlborough Heritage and Resource Centre in September 2013, based on the text written in 1938 (see above).

811 Turner, "A More Unobserved and Convenient Location", p. 186. Information by kind courtesy of Paul D Walker in a personal E-mail correspondence on June 17, 2014.

812 Estcourt, Payne, *Catholic nonjurors*, p. 30f., p. 32, p. 34. The authors list both men in their treatise on English Catholic non-jurors (together with their ancestor John Alleyne of Whetstone). By definition non-jurors are persons refusing to make an oath to a certain religious denomination (or a monarch or a civil constitution). During the 18th century "Non-Jurors began to consider the history of the Church of England and redefined its identity as a Catholic church purified by returning to the beliefs and practises of the apostolic and patristic period. Some saw the Orthodox Church as the inheritor of this authentic church and attempts were made by some Non-Jurors (…) to unite with the Greek Patriarchate of Constantinople. Non-Jurors became scholars of the early church" (… and …) "preserved high church spirituality (…) Unfortunately, the Non-Jurors themselves were split by internal differences and steadily dwindled in numbers. Furthermore, many returned to the official Church of England after the death

family of Beighton Fields were one of the most influential Catholic families in the parish and the Catholic congregation met at Beighton Fields Priory under a priest (attested for 1772).[813]

According to the Craven/Stanley, John (4) Peter Bruno Bowdon's (1787-1850) estate comprised of 56 acres in **1831** and was let at that time to a William Potter. The **1841** census of England and Wales lists a couple named John and Hannah Widdowson as occupants (tenants?) of Beighton Fields House, which directly presents us with a problem: does the term "house" refer to the Priory? No other available sources reveal the existence of a building under the name of Beighton Fields House in propertyship of the Bowdon family and the census returns of the following decennia do not always use the auxiliary word "Priory" for the building possibly in question in Beighton Fields. The Widdowsons are again listed as residents of "Beightonfields House, Barlborough" in the **1851** census returns, meanwhile with six under-aged children. John Widdowson's occupation is that of a "Farmer of 73 Acres, 1 Labourer".[814] Bob Clarke states that Henry (5) Bowdon and his wife Harriet (Henrietta Matilda) Bowdon took up residence at Beighton Fields Priory after their marriage which took place in **1853**. According to the 1851 census returns, Henry (5) Bowdon is attested for Southgate House and in 1861 he lives there again together with his wife and their two daughters (see Chapter 14). If Bob Clarke's assumption is correct, Henry (5) and Harriet cannot have lived at Beighton Fields Priory for very long.[815] The Bowdons had already used Southgate House as their principal residence for a long time, so perhaps the small family moved back there after Henry's mother, Mary M Bowdon, had passed away.

The **1861** census of England and Wales reveals the presence of two of the daughters of John (4) Peter Bruno Bowdon and Mary Martha Ferrers, Barbara Magdalen and Eliza Jemima, at Beighton Fields House (*sic!*). Head of household of Beighton Fields House in that year was Barbara M Wright (née Bowdon), aged 42, widow and gentlewoman, born in Parkgate, Cheshire. Next on the list is her sister Jemima Bowdon, aged 35, unmarried, born in Barlbro (*sic!*), Derbyshire. Two daughters of Barbara live with the two sisters: Mary B Wright, aged 9 and scholar, and Madiline (Madeline) Wright, aged 8 and scholar; both girls born in Richmond, Yorkshire. The only male relative in the house was Frederick Maxwell, aged 22, unmarried and stated as nephew,

---

of Charles III in 1788 (…)"; cf. The Jacobite Intelligencer, *Non-Jurors* (Charles III = Charles Edward Stuart, 1720-1788, son of James II).

813 The parish comprised of ca. sixty Roman Catholics at that time. A private census dated 1792 shows that the religious community had dwindled to sixteen persons including James (1) Bowdon and John (3) Bowdon; cf. Riden, *History of the County of Derby III*, p. 42.

814 Is one of the (younger) sons the later farmer Mr Widdowson of Manor Farm?

815 Clarke, "From Riches to Rags", p. 14.

with no rank, profession or occupation, born in Pontefract, Yorkshire - and "Dumb from b." (birth). The household had three female servants: Rose M Shoot, aged 28, unmarried, born in Co. Longford, Ireland, working as Ladies Maid; Mary Coburg, aged 27, unmarried, born in Stockport, Cheshire, working as Cook, and Ann Branagan, aged 16, born in Ireland, was the House Maid. Thomas Smith, aged 35, unmarried and from Lancashire was the household's Butler.

The **1871** census of England and Wales reveals that Jemima Bowdon, aged 44 and unmarried, born in Barlbro (*sic!*), Derbyshire, had taken over the role of Head of household of Beighton Fields House. She lived on "Money from dividends" and evidently took care of her nephew Frederic Maxwell, aged 30, unmarried and listed as Annuitant, born in Pontefract, Yorkshire. His terrible fate becomes even clearer now as the enumerator listed him as "Imbecile from Birth". Jemima had three persons who assisted her in her household: Mary A Gots, aged 54 and unmarried, "domestic Servant", born in Leeds, Yorkshire; Mary Hodgkinson, aged 16 and unmarried, "Kitchen Maid", and William Burgin, aged 55, unmarried and from Ireland, worked as gardener.

Harriet Bowdon moved back to Beighton Fields Priory with her two daughters, Alice and Constance, after the demise of Henry (5) Bowdon (see Chapters 11.1 and 14, **1881** census of England and Wales). Not very long after Harriet's death in 1885 it seems that Alice, finding herself alone with only a younger sister as next of kin, decided to take up action by grabbing the bull by the horns and moving to Italy where she met her future husband, Ireneo Del Monaco and decided to stay. Maybe Alice initially embarked on a kind of "Grand Tour" for young Victorian ladies, an endeavour not unusual for spinsters at that time.[816] It is at least tempting to make such deductions from the scarce information available. She seems to be the typical phenomenon of her times. She, like her sister Constance and her aunts Barbara Magdalen and Eliza Jemima, evidently belonged to "a class of *rentiers*, who lived on the profits and savings of the previous two or three generations' accumulations. By 1871 Britain contained 170,000 persons of rank and property' without visible occupation - almost all of them women, or rather 'ladies'; a surprising number of them unmarried ladies. Stocks and shares (...) were a convenient way of providing for widows, daughters and other relatives who could not - and no longer needed to be - associated with the management of property and enterprise. The comfortable avenues of Kensington, the villas of spas and the growing seaside resorts of the middle class, and the environs of Swiss mountains and Tuscan cities welcomed them. The era of railway, iron and foreign investment also provided the economic base for the Victorian spinster (...)."[817] However, Alice and Ireneo were married on February 13, 1890[818] and

---

816 Arnold, Dana, "6 The Illusion of Grandeur? Antiquity, Grand Tourism and the Country House", in: Arnold, *Georgian Country House*, p. 104.

817 Hobsbawm, *Industry and Empire*, p. 97f.

started a family in Rome where they lived at the Del Monaco family estates[819] - until they all moved back to Beighton Fields Priory together (sometime after 1898 and before 1911).

The life of Alice's sister Constance must have been a quiet one compared to that of her sister. She inhabited Beighton Fields Priory alone according to the **1891** census of England and Wales: for "Beighton Fields House" she is registered as Constance Bowdon, Head of household, aged 33, single[820], "living on own means" and born in Barlbro (*sic!*), Derbyshire. On the day the enumerator passed by she had a visitor: Agnes Waterton, aged 24, single and also "living on own means" and born in Walton, Yorkshire. Two servants were part of the household: Annie Fiddes, aged 28 and single, from Alnham, Northumberland, fulfilled her duties as Cook Domestic Servant, Annie Walker, aged 27 and single, from Newcastle, Northumberland was the Parlour Maid. One year later, in 1892, Constance married a William Francis Lee of whom nothing is known.

From the **1901** census returns we are informed that a Mrs Alice Swift resided in Beighton Fields (without any further specification). She is stated as Head of household, married, aged 49 and born in Barlborough, Derbyshire and her profession is that of a "Housekeeper Domestic". Tony Bak concludes from her occupation that she may have been residing at Beighton Fields Priory as the following entry in the census is "Beighton Fields Farm" (part of the Priory) as the neighbouring building.[821] This leaves us with the question as to who were the ladies and the gentlemen of the house and where they had been on the day the census was conducted (March 31, 1901). A commemoration plaque on the outer wall of Spinkhill Church positioned directly behind the gravestone of Eliza Jemima Bowdon gives the sad answer: Constance passed away at Mill Hill (Hendon, Middlesex, London) the very day before the survey was taken, so the house stood empty, only the housekeeper was still there, most likely taking care of matters and preparing the mourning.

We do not know what happened in Beighton Fields over the next decade but ten years later the Bowdon occupancy of Beighton Fields Priory[822] is attested by the **1911** census of England and Wales. It lists the Del Monacos at "Beighton Fields, Renishaw, Chesterfield" (filled in and signed by Alice Del

---

818 De La Caille Ruvigny and Raineval, *Plantagenet roll*, p. 41; Clarke, "From Riches to Rags", p. 14.

819 Clarke, "From Riches to Rags", p. 14.

820 Constance married William Francis Lee a year later (19/07/1892).

821 Information disclosed in a private E-mail correspondence between Tony Bak and the author on August 12, 2013.

822 Preston, Clarke, Hulls, *Derbyshire War Memorials Project* explicitly say "(...) late Ireneo Paolo de Monaco and Alice Elizabeth Del Monaco (nee (*sic!*) Bowden (*sic!*), of Beightonfields Priory (...)".

Monaco) as follows: Ireneo Del Monaco, aged 59, "Retired Officer Italian Army", born in Rocaraso (*sic!*)[823], Italy and of Italian nationality; Alice Del Monaco, aged 56, born in Renishaw, Clowne, Derbyshire, England (her nationality wrongly stated as "Italian" had been deleted at a later date and by a different hand); Margherita Del Monaco, aged 20, single; Enrico Del Monaco, aged 18, still attending school like his younger brother Romolo Del Monaco, aged 17. In the list he is succeeded by his sister Corona Del Monaco, aged 14, scholar, and his younger brother Bernard, aged 13, also attending school.[824] All five children were born in Rome (except Corona who was born in a place noted as "Christo"[825]) and all five of them were of Italian nationality.[826] The household had two employees: Rose Anna Hazlehurst, aged 17, single and Housemaid Domestic, born in Barlbro (*sic!*), England and Grace Hibberd, also aged 17, single and General/Domestic, likewise born in Barlbro (*sic!*), Derbyshire, England. For reasons unknown name and details of Corona Del Monaco had been deleted from the census sheet at a subsequent date and by another hand. Maybe she was absent on the day the census was carried out. Finally the census sheet provides us with more valuable information: apart from utility rooms and other useful spaces, Beighton Fields Priory offered five rooms (including the kitchen) - not very spacious for eight inhabitants!

---

823 Roccaraso, small village near L'Aquila in the Abruzzi.

824 The school in question is Mount St. Mary's Catholic School in Spinkhill. I owe this information to Toy Bak (disclosed in a private E-mail correspondence dated August 7, 2013). A school list from the 1911 census returns shows that the names of Henry, Bernard and Romolo have been deleted, possibly it had been realised that they had left school when the census was carried out. Another explanation might be that all three young men are mentioned in the same census for their home they were possibly there and not at school on the day of the census. All three entries are augmented with the word "resident". The school was founded in 1842 as "The College of the Immaculate Conception at Spinkhill" by the Provincial Superior of the Society of Jesus and is still today under the trusteeship of the Jesuits; cf. http://www.msmcollege.com/msm-school/the-school (viewed 31/10/2013).

825 There are four settlements named Cristò in Italy (Reggio Calabria/Calabria, Padova/Veneto, Cuneo/Piemonte and Verbano-Cusio-Ossola/ Piemonte).

826 Information courtesy of Tony Bak of Barlborough Heritage and Resource Centre (by personal E-mail correspondence on August 7, 2013); see also http://search.ancestry.co.uk/cgi-bin/sse.dll?gl=ukicen&rank=1&new=1&so=3&MSAV=0&msT=1&gss=ms_f-80&gsln=De%20monaco&uidh=000 (viewed 05/08/2013). This source (transcription of 1911 census of England and Wales) states the siblings of the marital union of Ireneo and Alice Del Monaco: Margherita, born ca. 1891 in Rome, Italy; Enrico (Henry), born ca. 1893 in Rome, Italy; Romolo (Ronald), born ca. 1894 (correct would be 1893) in Rome, Italy; Corona, born ca. 1897 in Italy (place name transliterated distorted) and Bernard, born ca. 1898 in Rome, Italy.

During the time of Alice's absence however Beighton Fields Priory was the home to a certain Arthur Keen Smith, CE (attested for 1895).[827] For **1914** and **1915** Alice Del Monaco is attested as inhabitant of Beighton Fields Priory by the Electoral Rolls. A "List of Aliens to whom Certificates of Naturalization have been granted by the Secretary of state, and whose Oaths of Allegiance have been registered in the Home Office during the month of October, 1916" was published in the London Gazette dated November 3, **1916**. This list includes the names of Alice Del Monaco (whose naturalisation was the reacquisition of British citizenship, so Alice evidently had previously emigrated to Italy), Bernard Del Monaco and Corona Del Monaco (both naturalised) as children of Alice. The date of their oath of allegiance was September 25, 1916 and all three are listed as inhabitants of Beighton Fields Priory, Renishaw, Derbyshire.[828] For the years between 1916 and **1918**, after Ireneo had passed away in 1912 in Worksop[829] (comparatively young, having just reached the age of 60), the house must have been inhabited by "Henry Del Monaco, son of the late Ireneo and Alice Elizabeth Del Monaco née Bowdon, of Beightonfields Priory, Renishaw, Derbyshire" before he emigrated to Canada in 1919.[830] It did not take him long to follow his brother Bernard who had emigrated to Canada with his brother Ronald four years earlier: Bernard's name could be found on a passenger list of the steamer "Transylvania"[831] which left Liverpool on March 27, 1915 with New York as its destination; the county of intended future residence is stated as Canada (ticket number 38838; Bernard's profession is stated there as "Mil" (= Military), his nationality as

---

[827] Craven, Stanley, *Derbyshire Country House*, p. 33; CE = Civil Engineer.

[828] http://www.london-gazette.co.uk/issues/29812/supplements/10656/page.pdf (viewed 17/10/2013).

[829] Information courtesy of Tony Bak of Barlborough Heritage and Resource Centre, in a private E-mail correspondence dated August 8, 2013.

[830] Information from a Canadian attestation paper on Ronald Del Monaco reveals the presence of Henry (Enrico) Del Monaco, his brother, as resident at Beighton Fields Priory at the time of Ronald's death in 1916; cf. Preston, Clarke, Hulls, *Derbyshire War Memorials Project*. Henry Del Monaco emigrated to Canada in 1919. This is attested by a "Naturalisation Certificate: Enrico del Monaco (known as Henry del Monaco). From Italy. Resident in Sheffield. Certificate A3986 issued 29 May 1919"; cf. The National Archives, *Ref. No. HO 334/83/3986, Naturalisation Certificate: Enrico del Monaco*. Henry must have returned to England however. He is noted for 1983 in Brighton (information by Tony Bak of Barlborough Heritage and Resource Centre, in a private E-mail correspondence dated August 8, 2013).

[831] The "SS Transylvania" is quite a famous vessel: it was brought into service in 1914 (launching date May 23, 1914, home harbour Glasgow) and was designed as a passenger ship and mail steamer, but adapting to the political situation at the time, being used as an allied troopship. It sunk in the Gulf of Genoa on May 4, 1917 after being torpedoed by a German U-boat; cf. http://www.clydesite.co.uk/clydebuilt/viewship.asp?id=19107 (viewed 05/03/2014).

Italian).[832] Bernard arrived in New York on April 6, 1915 with further destination Dunrea, Manitoba where he intended to work as farmer.[833] At this point we lose track of him for a while, until he appears again having travelled with the steamship "SS Montcalm" (Canadian Pacific Ocean Services, CPOS) from Liverpool to Québec between July 17 and July 26, 1927; this time accompanied by his mother Alice. In the document of the Canadian Immigration Service, Canadian Government Return, Bernard's profession is given as "Poultry Farmer" with a land settlement in Winnipeg, Manitoba .[834]

But what had happened to Alice after this journey? A probate to Henry Del Monaco dated April 6, 1934 gives some background information: Alice Elizabeth Mary Del Monaco of Chesham Bois, Buckinghamshire, widow, died on October 4, 1933. Her estate comprised of 3,588 pounds, 15 shillings and 5 halfpence.[835] The same document notifies the death of Margaret (Margherita) Del Monaco of "Beightonfields Priory near Chesterfield", spinster, on November 21, 1916 in Bournemouth. She left behind the sum of 831 pounds.[836] Another probate to Henry Del Monaco dated February 28, 1961 reveals that his sister Corona, having remained unmarried, died on December 7, 1960 in Horsham, Sussex. Her effects amounted to 10,566 pounds, 15 shillings and 7

---

832 Information courtesy of Teresa Bak in a private E-mail correspondence dated August 8, 2013 (information retrieved from http://www.ancestry.co.uk). Together with his brother Romolo/Ronald Bernardo/Bernard he enlisted into the 79th Battalion Canadian Infantry, Manitoba Regiment, becoming 152910 Private Bernard Bowdon (see Chapter 12 and Appendix 7); cf. eMedals, *A 1916 Canadian Memorial Cross*). I could not detect Ronald's name on the passenger list, perhaps he travelled on another ship.

833 According to "Instruction to Pursers" spreadsheet; information courtesy of Tony Bak in a private E-mail correspondence dated August 9, 2013.

834 Information courtesy of Tony Bak in a private E-mail correspondence dated August 9, 2013.

835 Information courtesy of Tony Bak in a private E-mail correspondence dated August 8, 2013. An obituary on the demise of Alice Del Monaco was published by the Catholic newspaper The Tablet (London), dated October 14, 1933: "Death. Del Monaco: - On October 4th, in her 80th year, at Coombe Lodge, Chesham Bois, Alice del Monaco, late of Beightonfields Priory, Renishaw, Chesterfield, widow of Don Ireneo del Monaco, daughter of the late Henry Bowdon, J. P., Southgate House, Clowne, Derbyshire, and Harriet Blount, of Mapledurham. R. I. P."; cf. The Tablet, *Births, Marriages and Deaths, 14th October 1933.*

836 Eric J Hobsbawn states that during the reign of King Edward VII (d. 1910) only 6% of the British population left any property when they died and only 4% left more than £300 (Hobsbawm, *Industry and Empire*, p. 144). Both quoted probates state Henry Del Monaco as "accountant" (information courtesy of Tony Bak in a private E-mail correspondence dated August 8, 2013).

halfpence.[837] Henry/Enrico himself died at the grand old age of 90 years in Brighton in 1983.[838]

Unlike the fate of Southgate House, the loss of one of the male heirs of the Del Monaco family in the war, two sons who emigrated to Canada and the premature death of one daughter apparently sealed the fate of the Bowdon family as owners of Beighton Fields Priory. I cannot say with certainty when exactly the family finally decided to give up the house[839], but for the year **1918** the Electoral Rolls name William Nesfield Fowler as sole inhabitant, a name attested in connection the Butler-Bowdon family from previous census returns.[840] He did not stay long at Beighton Fields however. The Electoral Rolls for Derbyshire list a succession of families for the following years, such as James Frederick and Bertha May Robertson from **1920** onwards, and in **1925** James Fredrik Robertson still lived in Beighton Fields Priory.[841] The Robertsons were followed by Robert Sykes Bingham, his wife Adelaide Bingham and their son Philip (attested in **1926**). A Henry Butler is attested in **1928**. His successors were William Good Rogers and his wife Margaret Ann, attested for **1930** until **1934** in the Electoral Rolls. In **1932** Georgina Jenkins and Edith Maria Swallow lived with them (as domestic staff?). From **1936** to **1937** Frank Flint and Lilian Beaumont-Flint inhabited Beighton Fields Priory. Roy Cressy and Annie Gwendoline Besche are attested for the year **1938** (according to Tony Bak they still lived there in 1939 prior to WWII[842]). In **1945** the inhabitants were William and Edith Heyman together with Richard Wright and Edward Woosey (the latter two persons living as workers on the estate?). For **1947** and **1948** the Electoral Rolls name Anthony C M B and Mary Scott as residents. The year **1950** saw the first long-term inhabitants moving in to Beighton Fields Priory: Norman V J and Gladys M A Craig are the

---

837 This probate states Henry Del Monaco as "registration clerk", information courtesy of Tony Bak in a private E-mail correspondence dated August 8, 2013.

838 http://www.london-gazette.co.uk/issues/49692/pages/4761/page.pdf dated March 30, 1984 (viewed 04/09/2013). Here Henry's profession is stated as "Registration Officer (retired)". He passed away in a Convalescent Home. Father Peter D McGuire of Spinkhill Church of Immaculate Conception remembers that he buried Henry Del Monaco at Spinkhill; information disclosed in a personal telephone conversation with the author on November 14, 2013.

839 Undated typed notes (p. 2 of six pages) reveal that the Bowdons and the Del Monacos owned the Priory until about 1946; information by Paul D Walker in an E-mail correspondence with the author dated May 9, 2014.

840 According to the 1891 census returns William E Nesfield Fowler, aged 14 at that time, lived at Southgate House with his parents and siblings (see Chapter 14) and he is cited in an article in Derbyshire Times and Chesterfield Herald on November 8, 1899 as inhabitant of Southgate House (see Chapter 11), at that time being 22 years of age.

841 Craven, Stanley, *Derbyshire Country House*, p. 33.

842 Information disclosed in a private E-mail correspondence between Tony Bak and the author dated July 14, 2013.

inhabitants until at least **1966**. From **1969** until at least **1975** James M W and Rosalind Pridham occupied the house. It is striking feature for Beighton Fields Priory that it changed hands very frequently and in short intervals during the first half of the 20th century whereas everywhere else at Southgate Estate the inhabitants of the various residential houses and tenements formed a quite stable and constant group of residents. Today's owners however have lived at Beighton Fields for almost forty years.

18.1. The Burial Ground of Beighton Fields Priory

In the garden of Beighton Fields Priory, at the back of the house, there is a walled enclosure[843] where many generations of the Bowdon family lie buried (Figure 35). Today the freestanding, cross-shaped headstones of Henry (5) and Harriet Bowdon are the most prominent remainders of this burial site. Also buried in Beighton Fields Priory are Henry (1) Bowdon[844], his wife Mary Hewitt, Henry (2) Bowdon and his wife with unknown first name of the Alleyne family, John (2) Bowdon, his second wife Margaret Nelson and his third wife Mary Johnson (see Chapter 22.1), John (3) Bowdon and his wife Alice Johnson, as well as Henry (3) Bowdon and his son Henry (4) Bowdon. A rectangular stone plaque on the wall gives an additional dedicatory inscription (see Chapter 18.1.3). A third, freestanding, rectangular, and much eroded gravestone stands a couple of metres to the right of the inscription plaque. This gravestone is decorated with some kind of arrangement of folds or drapery.[845] It remains unclear who it belonged to, but it must have had a plaque or something similar attached to it originally, which is now long lost.
The enclosure, whose present structure dates back to the 19th and 20th century, is a little overgrown. A pond dug in the middle of the enclosure by the owners of Beighton Fields Priory at an unknown point of time in the past has disturbed the mortal remains of some of the Bowdon family members.[846]

In the garden of Beighton Fields Priory there is also a shed and a Coffin Pond. Tony Bak of Barlborough Heritage and Resource Centre pointed out to me that the coffins for the family members were made in the shed and that the

---

[843] British Listed Buildings, *Beighton Fields Priory, Barlborough*; English Heritage, *Beighton Fields Priory*.

[844] Information according to Chris Bowden in a correspondence on http://archiver.rootsweb.ancestry.com/th/read/CHESHIRE/2007-12/1196623064 (viewed 14/06/2013); information on the other burials could be retrieved from the Bowdon family tree on parchment in possession of Barlborough Heritage and Research Centre.

[845] The representation of a drapery on a gravestone symbolises sorrow and mourning. The drape can also be interpreted as the "veil" between this world and the next; cf. http://www.colorado-cemeteries.com/symbols.html (viewed 10/04/2013); http://exhibitsonline.org/tombstone-art-and-symbolism.htm (viewed 10/04/2013).

[846] Information according to Graham Duckmanton who visited Beighton Fields Priory on January 7, 2013.

pond was used to soak the wood for the coffins to make it more durable. Coffin ponds in general are a very rare occurrence and, according to Mr Bak, the one of Beighton Fields Priory is unique as it is the only known one in England.[847]

Even though it was common practice during the 19th century to bury the deceased in churchyards, from the mid 19th century on burials were relocated to joint-stock cemeteries and municipal cemeteries, often in the outskirts of the town or village, because of urban expansion and for reasons of hygiene (e.g. Burial Acts of 1853 and 1855).[848] However, private burials on family homesteads were not uncommon, landed gentry in particular chose to bury family members this way.[849] Private Catholic burial grounds were common during the Reformation throughout the reign of Henry VIII.[850] It was during the Victorian era that general cemeteries in the style of a park became popular. As a result of the Burial Acts landscaped cemeteries open to public cropped up which reflect Victorian attitudes to death. The ornate gravestones and flowery epigraphs served as means for family and friends to express both their love and grief for the deceased.[851]

Large parts of the Bowdon and Butler-Bowdon family were of Catholic faith and recusants which seems to play an important role in the whole setting for several reasons: the time span in which the Bowdon family lived is one which marks a general low point for Catholicism in English history,

---

[847] Information disclosed by Tony Bak of Barlborough Heritage and Resource Centre in a personal conversation on April 20, 2013 in Barlborough, additionally in a private E-mail correspondence with the author on July 9, 2013. Ingeborg Pietschmann (Bremerhaven) informed me in a private E-mail correspondence on June 4, 2013 that it needed about one to two years to conserve wood in water. Alternatively wood could be made durable by soaking it in liquid manure or in water to which extract of oak apple had been added. Also there was conservation with tar or copper sulphate. The best way to conserve and harden oak wood was by desiccation or torrefaction. See also Cook, *English House*, p. 26: Soaking stripped oak trees in running water over a period of several months reduced shrinkage of the material.

[848] 1853: http://www.legislation.gov.uk/ukpga/Vict/16-17/134/section/1 (viewed 04/06/2013): "(...) burials in any city or town, or within any other limits, or in any burial grounds or places of burial, should be wholly discontinued, or should be discontinued subject to any exception or qualification (...)" and 1855: http://www.legislation.gov.uk/ukpga/Vict/18-19/128 (viewed 04/06/2013).

[849] Based on a 2005 report by Ken Worpole (Worpole, "Cemeteries, Churchyards and Burial Grounds", p. 2); additional input by Father Peter D McGuire in a personal telephone conversation with the author on November 14, 2013. He mentions that the Sitwells also buried members of their family on their own grounds in Renishaw.

[850] There is a similar burial ground at Mount St. Mary's in Spinkhill, now a Catholic school. The ground belonged to the Pole family of Barlborough who were staunch Catholics; information disclosed by Tony Bak of Barlborough Heritage and Resource Centre in a private E-mail correspondence dated July 9, 2013.

[851] http://www.avictorian.com/mourning.html (viewed 11/06/2014).

characterised by the constant up and down of the competing faiths of Anglicanism and Catholicism. Members of the Catholic faith found themselves once again under persecution, their civil rights being cut back, their rights to own land or property limited and burdened by extra taxes. As a consequence, the influence and visibility of Catholics in English society almost disappeared completely. Some left England and followed James II (1633-1701), the last Roman Catholic monarch, into exile in France, others conformed to Anglicanism, which compounded the loss of influence of Catholic communities were experiencing. Many others withdrew from Protestant mainstream entirely. The 1778 "Catholic Relief Act" helped to restore civil rights and the canon law of Catholics in England, leading to revolts by Protestants in 1780. In addition Catholic refugees fleeing the French Revolution (1789–1799) found safety in England and helped to increase the number of members of the Catholic faith as did the merging of Great Britain with the Catholic Kingdom of Ireland in 1801. During the Great Famine in Ireland (1845–1852) more Catholics migrated to England. Catholic families finally experienced substantial relief in the form of the Roman Catholic Belief Act of 1829 which abolished the most severe restrictions on Roman Catholic believers in the United Kingdom.[852]

It has proved impossible to gain detailed information in this regard on the Bowdon family "... for the loss of many papers which were lost or destroyed by the persecutions frequently carried on against catholic families."[853] But what is known, is that at the beginning of the 18th century John (3) Bowdon lost possession of his estates due to the claim by a Protestant relative named John Freeman. His claim was that as a Catholic John (2) Bowdon was not entitled to inherit the estate: "John Freeman seized Whetstone estate as protestant heir. John registered his estates as a catholic recusant 1715 The King granted his protection to him 1716".[854] The Catholic Emancipation Bill of 1829 surely also helped the Bowdons to reclaim their possessions and once again gain a foothold in society. The "Declaration of the Roman Catholic Laity of England" dated 1851[855], signed by Henry (5) Bowdon and his brother John (5) Peter Bruno Butler-Bowdon, shows the involvement of the family in recusancy and how firmly connected the old recusant English families were. Roman Catholic worshippers congregated in a little chapel (built originally in 1901 as the private chapel for its Catholic owners) at the Bowdon's second

852 http://www.legislation.gov.uk/ukpga/Geo4/10/7/contents (viewed 05/03/2014); http://www.britannica.com/EBchecked/topic/99817/Catholic-Emancipation (viewed 05/03/2014).

853 Glover, *History*, p. 305.

854 Quote from Bowdon family tree, Barlborough Heritage and Research Centre; see also Glover, *History*, p. 305; Estcourt, Payne, *Catholic nonjurors*, p. 32.

855 Catholics (England), *Declaration*, see also Chapter 20.

homestead next to Beighton Fields Priory, Southgate House, during the first half of the 20th century (see Chapter 8).[856]

The erection of a Catholic church in Clowne (near Creswell Road[857]) is announced in the "Catholic Herald" on December 30, 1938. The site was endowed by Colonel Butler-Bowdon, late of Southgate House, who also donated the fittings of his private chapel at Southgate.[858] And the family had dreamt even bigger before that date: (Richard) John Francis Butler was responsible for building Pleasington Priory (St. Mary and St. John the Baptist[859]) on Pleasington Road between 1816 and 1819 as an offering of thanks. The "tall and prominent building" was built in a mixed Gothic style and is said to have in its day cost the tidy sum of £23,000.[860] Building work was carried out by John Palmer (architecture) and Thomas Owen (carving and sculpture).[861]

Against this background it can be assumed that the Bowdon family formed a close-knit community within their surroundings which could be one explanation for burying some of their ancestors on their private grounds in Beighton Fields Priory. Secondly, Catholic faith, until recently, disapproved of cremation so burial on their private grounds was the most obvious solution to keep the deceased as close by as possible without having them interred at the next available public cemetery. The walled enclosure of Beighton Fields Priory and its graves was probably planned in the sense of a Victorian cemetery as part of the park-like gardens of the manor. Such cemetery grounds were often "designed and laid out by established park designers" and functioned as burials sites as well as "places for visiting and promenading of a more dignified and morally uplifting kind".[862]

---

856 Picture The Past, *Southgate House (000405).*

857 The church is named "The Sacred Heart and Our Lady of Victories".

858 Catholic Herald Archive, "Tee Church moves on". The source refers William Erdeswick Ignatius Butler-Bowdon.

859 Pleasington Priory is the burial place of several members of the Butler-Bowdon family such as Amelia Catherine Frances Butler-Bowdon (née Whitgreave), Mary Frances Amelia Butler Bowdon, Madeleine Mary Butler Bowdon, John (6) Butler-Bowdon, and Jermyne Thomas Butler-Bowdon (see Chapter 10). Outside the sacristy a tombstone in honour of the Butler-Bowdon family decorated with a crucifix, the *Nomina sacra* (monograms) of the Blessed Virgin Mary and Jesus Christ, and two family coats of arms marks the burial vault of these persons ("In this vault lie the remains of …"). The dedication inscription is almost identical to the inscription on the floor outside the sacristy (see Chapter 10). For a photograph of the tombstone and the epitaph see Child, *Pleasington Prior*, p. 54.

860 This sum equals to £1.48 million as of 2013; cf. Williamson, *MeasuringWorth.*

861 Pleasington Priory is a Grade I listed building; cf. English Heritage, *Roman Catholic Church of St Mary and St John the Baptist* (Pleasington Priory). According to this source (Richard) John Francis Butler was "then owner of Pleasington township".

862 Worpole, "Cemeteries, Churchyards and Burial Grounds", p. 6.

More insight into Catholic family life in the English modern era can be obtained from Evelyn Waugh's novel "Brideshead Revisited".[863] Every member of the Roman Catholic Marchmain family has their own issue with this faith (mostly on conversion and vocation) and their role in society during the first half of 20th century.

18.1.1. The Final Resting Place of Henry (5) Bowdon

Henry Bowdon's final resting place (Figure 36) is marked by a freestanding headstone made of sandstone in shape of a cross. The cross is decorated at the centre with floral elements which are entwined together as a garland or wreath in the centre. The headstone has a stepped lower part on a plinth which bears an epitaph which reads: "IHS[864] / Of your charity /pray for the Soul of / Henry Bowdon Esq. / (of Southgate House) / Born August 7th 1814. / Died May 3rd 1875. / R. I. P."

In the Victorian era the design of headstones and graves was very symbolic. The choice of symbols used provided information about the deceased. Emblems such as floral wreaths were seen as allegories of death and reveal something about Victorian attitudes to death.[865] The floral decoration on Henry Bowdon's grave cross can most likely be identified as forget-me-nots (*Myosotis sylvatica*). These flowers symbolised the yearning for faithfulness in love, a farewell and tender eternal remembrance.[866] There are many examples of this plant in Victorian funerary architecture. I cannot safely rule out that the depicted flowers could also be common periwinkle (*Vinca minor*[867]), but as far as I can see there are no similar examples of this type of flowers carved on headstones, so this is a bit of a wild guess. However, periwinkles are evergreen, creeping vine plants which could be used to make garlands - just like the floral wreath on Henry's headstone (the garland being the symbol for victory in death). Living Periwinkle flowers are used for grave decoration, symbolising eternal life, the circle if life, devotion, pleasures of memory and remembrance, the virtue of the Virgin Mary, and memorial to the "dearly departed", and therefore also a symbol of the dead. The leaves

---

863 Waugh, *Brideshead Revisited*.

864 *Nomen sacrum* (monogram) of Christ: Ιησους (Χριστος) / *in hoc signo (vinces)*, "By this sign you will conquer", also *iesus hominum salvor*, "Jesus, the saviour of mankind". IHS is also the Jesuit emblem which indicates the adoption from ancient Greek (*Iesus hominum salvator*, "Jesus, saviour of men" or *Iesum habebus socium*, "We have Jesus as companion").

865 http://www.avictorian.com/mourning.html (viewed 11/06/2014).

866 Thanks to Elke Müller (Bremerhaven) and Barbara and Graham Duckmanton (Worksop) for this suggestion. This assumption is supported by Robert Vogt of the Botanisches Museum Berlin-Dahlem (Berlin) in an E-mail correspondence with the author on May 15, 2013.

867 Thanks to Elke Müller (Bremerhaven) for this suggestion.

with their glossy touch can withstand extreme temperatures, which also explains why this flower is considered as a symbol of eternity.

It is noticeable that all capital letters and numbers of the inscription seem to contain traces of red, maybe the remains of pigments of what was once a golden colour. The carving is fine but a little weather-worn towards the right upper part of the inscription and there is some moss and lichen growing on the stone. The height of the headstone is about 1 m.[868]

The Derbyshire Times and Chesterfield Herald reports on May 12, 1875 on the funeral of Henry Bowdon (see Chapter 11.1). A larger number of local people gathered to express their condolences and bear witness to his remains being transferred first from Southgate House to the Church of the Immaculate Conception at Spinkhill where a High Mass was celebrated and then on to the garden of Beighton Fields Priory. A funerary cortège consisting of five mourning coaches and several private carriages and a large procession escorted the body of the deceased which was encased in three coffins on his last journey. The proceedings as described in the announcement mirrored typical Victorian burial customs, as was common at that time.

18.1.2. The Final Resting Place of Harriet Bowdon (née Henrietta Mathilda Blount)

Harriet Bowdon was the last Bowdon family member to be buried at Beighton Fields Priory. Her final resting place (Figure 37) in the garden of Beighton Fields Priory is also marked by a freestanding headstone made of sandstone in shape of a cross. The cross is decorated at the centre with floral elements which are entwined together as a garland or wreath in the centre (differently from the decoration on Henry Bowdon's headstone). The headstone has a stepped lower part on a plinth which bears an epitaph which reads: "IHS / Of your charity / pray for the Soul of / Harriet Bowdon / (wife of Henry Bowdon) / Born Sept. 30th 1832. / Died March 31st 1885. / R. I. P."

The inscription - though remarkably similar to her husband's headstone - does not show any traces of colour. The carving is very fine and the stone is clean of any growth.

The floral decoration on the cross can also be identified as either forget-me-nots (*Myosotis sylvatica*) or common periwinkle (*Vinca minor*) like on Henry's headstone, in this case possibly used to commemorate Harriet as a beloved wife and mother.

Both Harriet and Henry Bowdon's headstones are comparatively well preserved which is partly due to the fact that they are close to the enclosure

---

[868] Information according to Graham Duckmanton who visited Beighton Fields Priory on January 7, 2013.

wall, and are thus sheltered from the worst of the weather. The height of the headstone is about 1 m.[869]

18.1.3. The Inscription Plaque

Near the headstones of Henry and Harriet Bowdon there is an inscription plaque made of sandstone with four shields or coat of arms which flank a dedicatory inscription (Figure 38). The plaque is today partially obscured by a large shrub.[870]

The inscription reads: "Within this enclosure / lie the remains of many / generations of the family / of Bowdon. / Mary, only daughter and heiress of John Hewit / of Beighton Fields, Esq. / (A branch of the Hewits, of Shire Oaks.) / brought this property / by marriage to / Henry Bowdon Esq. /who died in 1665. / Through all adversity they / ever remained steadfast to the / faith of their forefathers. / May they rest in peace."[871]

The four shields show (clock-wise) four empty squares, three owls separated by a chevron, a bipartite geometrical design (dotted chevrons and rectangular blocks) and a cross. The carving is very fine and the plaque is well preserved. The top left shield is that of the Bowdon family, the top right is that of the Hewitts of Shireoaks. The bottom right one belongs to Lampson Erdeswick of Sandon Hall, Staffordshire, and the bottom left one represents the Alleyne (Allen) family of Whetstone.[872]

This inscription is mentioned in a newspaper article in The Derbyshire Times and Chesterfield Herald on May 12, 1875 reporting on the funeral of Henry (5) Bowdon: "The following inscription is to be seen: - "Through all adversity they ever remained steadfast to the faith of their forefathers."[873] Neither the size of the plaque nor the exact date and origin of the inscription could be established. The stone used for the plaque looks identical to the material of the head stone of Henry (5) Bowdon therefore a possible date could be around 1875. The font also looks quite "modern", so I would not put the date much earlier, even though earlier burials at Beighton Fields have taken place (for example that of Henry (1) Bowdon).

---

[869] Information according to Graham Duckmanton who visited Beighton Fields Priory on January 7, 2013.

[870] Information according to Graham Duckmanton who visited Beighton Fields Priory on January 7, 2013.

[871] White's *1875*, p. 733; Riden, *History of the County of Derby III*, p. 25, footnote 13 (referring to a source held by Sheffield Archives, Ref. No. JC 1105, p. 421f., original document not viewed personally).

[872] Information courtesy of Tony Bak of Barlborough Heritage and Resource Centre, by private E-mail correspondence on July 14, 2013.

[873] http://www.britishnewspaperarchive.co.uk/ (viewed 29/10/2013).

19. The Butler-Bowdon Cope

The manuscript of "The Book of Margery Kempe" apparently was not the only precious ecclesiastical object in the possession of the Butler-Bowdon family. A richly adorned and embroidered cope from the early 14th century, a ceremonial cloak worn by priests on the occasion of the celebration of the Holy Mass or on processions, was acquired by the Victoria and Albert Museum for £33,000 on July 1, 1955 (Inv. No. T36-1955) according to the "Catholic Herald".[874] This semi-circular cope with a wide orphrey (width: 165,5 cm along top, circumference: 345 cm) had been owned by the Butler-Bowdon family, latterly by William Erdeswick Ignatius Butler-Bowdon.[875] Supposedly, it is one of the finest specimen of English needlework and only few other examples are known, one is kept at the Vatican[876], another in the church of San Giovanni in Laterano in Rome and one in Pienza.[877] A similar chasuble is in possession of the Metropolitan Museum of Art in New York (the "Chichester-Constable Chasuble").[878] The Victoria and Albert Museum owns another specimen however, the so-called "Syon Cope".[879]

In his diary Henry (5) Bowdon notes on April 12, 1857 that the Butler-Bowdon Cope, apparently kept at Mount St. Mary's College, Spinkhill at that time, was to be sent to the Art Treasures Exhibition in Manchester which took place between May 5

[874] Catholic Herald Archive, "£33,000 Cope to stay in England"; Victoria & Albert Museum, *Cope*: "At that time it was considered 'undoubtedly the most important English vestment ever to come to the market.' (Minute of C.E.C. Tattersall, Keeper of Textiles to the Director, 1 March 1938)."

[875] Catholic Herald Archive, "£33,000 Cope to stay in England". Note that Lt.-Col. William Erdeswick Ignatius Butler-Bowdon at that time lived in Dapsland, Mayfield, Sussex.

[876] Cope with scenes of Christ, Virgin Mary, saints, and seraphim, Bibliotheca Apostolica Vaticana, Museo Sacro, Inv. No. 2447, manufactured in England ca. 1280-1300. Unlike many other examples of this type of garment it does not depict specifically English saints, the representations however seem do seem to display a distinctive English character; cf. Gómez-Moreno, Drake Boehm, *Cope*, p. 38f. (catalogue number 9).

[877] Gómez-Moreno, Drake Boehm, *Cope*, p. 39.

[878] The cope shows the annunciation, the three kings, the coronation of Our Lady, saints, kings and angels, animals, floral elements, crowns and stars; MMA, Fletcher Fund, 27.162.1, English, ca. 1330-1350; cf. http://www.metmuseum.org/Collections/search-the-collections/466660 (viewed 31/10/2013); Young, "Opus Anglicanum", p. 291f.

[879] Victoria & Albert Museum, *Syon Cope*, Inv. No. 83-1864. The cope takes its name from the Bridgettine convent of Syon, Middlesex, ca. 1300-1320. It shows scenes from the Life of the Virgin, the Life of Christ and the Apostles, winged seraphim, angels holdings crowns, and two kneeling clerics, "possibly the priest for whom the vestment was made".

and October 17, 1857.[880] According to notes from Mount St. Mary's, the cope was discovered[881] by two prefects from the College in 1870. It was then part chasuble, and part *antependium* (altar drape). The two prefects restored the textile completely. The notes say that the work of these two prefects was at no time mentioned save in the in-house journal called "The Mountaineer" (Volume I).[882]

The high-quality embroidery employed on the Butler-Bowdon Cope is called *opus anglicanum* (Latin for "English work(manship)" as these vestments were primarily produced in London, the centre of *opus anglicanum* manufacture from the middle of the 13th century on. The textile originates from Italy, and the embroidery was made in England between 1330 and 1350 by an unknown artist and executed by using silver thread and silver-gilt thread on a ground of red silk velvet (camaca), with details in silk and stitched on pearls, beads and small metal rings. The needlework displays various stitching techniques.

Garments like these were highly coveted by European princes and popes and typify the lavish and expensive cloth favoured by members of the Christian church, and which were frequently donated by generous patrons, who wished to make a conspicuous show of both their mortal riches and their religious devotion.[883] The Vatican inventory of 1295 for example records 113 pieces of *opus anglicanum*, which were acquired as commissions by the pope, gifts to Rome made by English priests, royals and nobleman. The Archbishop of Canterbury and the Bishop of Ely both sent copes to Pope John XXII (1245/1249 - 1334) in the 1320s and 1330s.[884]

The Butler-Bowdon Cope shows the following decoration scheme: three concentric rows of Gothic arches depict the Life of the Virgin, figures of apostles and saints with crouching lions, lion masks, angels, a pair of birds and details of plants. The top row of the arcaded imagery depicts four saints: Saint Laurence, Mary Magdalene, Saint Helen and Saint Stephen. The central row depicts eight saints: Saint Edward the Confessor, a mitred bishop (possibly Saint Nicholas), Saint Margaret, Saint John the Evangelist, Saint John the Baptist, Saint Catherine of Alexandria, a mitred archbishop (possibly Saint Thomas of Canterbury) and Saint Edmund of Bury. The bottom row consist of depiction of the following apostles (all barefoot): Saint Matthew, Saint Simon,

---

880 NN, "Diary of Henry Bowdon", p. 136 (see also Chapter 14.3).

881 Rediscovered?

882 Information obtained from undated typed notes (p. 2 of six pages) which Paul D Walker made available to me in an E-mail correspondence dated May 9, 2014.

883 Victoria & Albert Museum, *Cope*: "The use of such rich decoration (…) must have made the garment very heavy to wear, imposing a stately gait for processions; it would also have been particularly impressive to a viewing public for whom such showiness was the preserve of Church and Court (…)."

884 Gómez-Moreno, Drake Boehm, *Cope*, p. 39; Young, "Opus Anglicanum", p. 291.

Saint Thomas, Saint Andrew, Saint James the Great, Saint Peter, Saint Paul, Saint Mathias, Saint James the Less, Saint Philip, Saint Jude and Saint Bartholomew. In the middle of the vestment is a vertical column with representations of the Annunciation, the Adoration of the Magi and the Coronation of Our Lady. The image on Figure 39 stands *pars pro toto* for all depicted figures on the cope and shows Saint Thomas and Saint Andrew under convoluted arches with spandrels, holding their respective iconographic objects. The two apostles are divided by a twisted branch that rests on the back of a recumbent lion on a flower-strewn grassy mound. The intertwined limbs of the plant are sprouting acorns and oak leaves. The twisted branch is crowned by a lion's mask and a winged angel.

The orphrey, the ornamental border of an ecclesiastical vestment, is made up of architectural niches which contain kings and bishops, surrounded by a rich variety of heraldic and vegetal ornaments. The depicted persons (four crowned kings, two bishops, two archbishops) can unfortunately not be identified by names or symbols. They are placed in a way that when the cope is worn a king and bishop always face each other. The horizontal panels separating the niches each contain a rose which is flanked by two heraldic lions of England, arranged in an antithetical symmetrical composition.

The base of the cope is lined by a narrow border decorated with herbaceous ornaments and two angels.[885] Creating such a vestment was a time-consuming task: according to a record referring to payments and labour incurred when producing a famous embroidered frontal made for the high altar of Westminster Abbey around 1271 (now lost), it took four women almost four years to complete the work.[886]

Bonnie Young believes that the so-called "Chichester-Constable Chasuble", which is conspicuously close "both in style and subject matter" to the Butler-Bowdon Cope, came from the "same set (or chapel) of vestments" and that both objects were made between 1330 and 1350. "Although there are no documents tracing the early history of these vestments, the chasuble, from at least the sixteenth century, is believed to have belonged to the Chichester-Constable family of Burton Constable in Yorkshire, while the cope belonged to another important Catholic family, the Butler-Bowdons of nearby Derbyshire, for generations. For many years each vestment has been known by the name of the family that formerly owned it."[887] Another clue to the possible connection of both garments is the depiction of Saint Edward the Confessor holding a model of Westminster Abbey on the Butler-Bowdon Cope. According to Bonnie Young, the inclusion of the model in the depiction could indicate "that the cope and the chasuble were made for use in the

---

[885] Description of decoration according to the on-line catalogue of Victoria and Albert Museum, London; cf. Victoria & Albert Museum, *Cope*.
[886] Young, "Opus Anglicanum", p. 291.
[887] Young, "Opus Anglicanum", p. 293.

Abbey."[888] Based on Francis Morris' research on the Chichester-Constable Chasuble in 1927, Bonnie Young dates chasuble and cope to the reign of King Edward III (reigned 1327-1377), and states that "they may well have come into the possession of the Chichester-Constable and Butler-Bowdon families either by gift or inheritance".[889] And there is further proof for these assumptions: "The earliest known mention of what is probably the Chichester-Constable chasuble is the will (1559) of Lady Margaret Scrope, wife of Sir John Constable, in which she bequeaths 'ye ancient vestment' to 'ye fair chapelle' (...) Her ancestor Lord Henry Scrope and other members of that family served both Edward II and III in important capacities, and the chasuble might well have been a royal gift. In a 1945 letter, Colonel W. Butler-Bowdon, who at that time still owned the cope, mentioned another mediaeval vestment in is possession that had coats of arms referring to the 1398 marriage of the Earl of Stafford to Anne Plantagenet, a granddaughter of Edward III. Since that vestment had come to his family by direct inheritance, it is possible that the Victoria and Albert cope did too."[890]

20. "... that would be expecting a miracle!"[891] - The Stained Glass Window of Southgate Chapel

The Sale Particulars of Southgate Estate dated March 1938 make mention of a "stained-glass window" as a decoration element of Southgate House chapel.[892] Along with the "memorial brass" made by John Hardman & Co. in the memory of Basil Butler-Bowdon (see Chapter 8), the window is another outstanding feature of the chapel of Southgate House, which must have been quite spectacular in its original surrounding. It is still remembered by the local people of Clowne today. June Pearce refers to it as "lovely stained glass window".[893] An old black and white photograph of Southgate House from the 1900s (Figure 6) shows a Gothic style window with a decorated frame. The glass panes form a tripartite lancet window.

Mark Girouard writes: "(...) gothic was increasingly associated both with Christianity and truthfulness. A gothic house stood for good principles as well as good cheer. Especially pious families could give their gothic houses and extra flavour of religion by an admixture of tracery and stained glass - or by building a chapel (...)."[894] Its chapel apart, Southgate House certainly does not

---

888 Young, "Opus Anglicanum", p. 296, text to image 10.

889 Young, "Opus Anglicanum", p. 294, p. 296.

890 Young, "Opus Anglicanum", p. 297.

891 Graham Duckmanton in an E-mail to the author on the chances of finding the stained glass window (October 7, 2013).

892 Derbyshire Record Office, Ref. No. D1300/11/1, p. 5.

893 Information disclosed in a private E-Mail correspondence between June Pearce and the author on May 24, 2013.

894 Girouard, *English Country House*, p. 273.

display any Gothic architectural elements. The Butler-Bowdons, however, had evidently found elements of the style attractive, and the name John Hardman may be a clue to this: the Hardmans, like the Pugins and the Butler-Bowdons, were steadfast Catholics, and just like the Butler-Bowdons the Hardmans originated from Lancashire. Their company, John Hardman & Co., flourished during the Victorian era, chiefly because it was based in Birmingham which at that time had a Catholic community (the Hardmans played an important role in religious and civic life of Birmingham as the most prominent Catholic family in the city) and because it cooperated with the architect, designer and artist A W N Pugin, a recent convert to Catholicism, and his son Edward Welby Pugin (1834–1875).[895] One of the reasons why Pugin's work was so successful in religious circles was that he associated the Classical Order of architecture during the preceding Georgian Era with Paganism, the Gothic style by contrast reflected Christian values and was therefore the only acceptable style for Christians.[896]

Later Pugin's two younger sons Cuthbert Welby Pugin (1840–1928) and Peter Paul Pugin (1851–1904), as well as Pugin's grandson Sebastian Pugin Powell (1866–1949) contributed their designs and artworks.[897] Their company was called "Pugin & Pugin", and was founded in the Westminster office of A W N Pugin in 1851. It lasted until ca. 1928.[898]

Head of the original Hardman family business was John Hardman senior (1767-1844), who specialised in designing and manufacturing metalwork such as buttons, tokens and medals (until 1800 operating as "Hardman and Lewis" in Paradise Street, Birmingham).[899] His son from his second marriage, John Hardman junior (1811-1867), withdrew from the family business and set up on his own under the name John Hardman & Co., in 1838. In cooperation with his close, lifelong friend A W N Pugin, who was responsible for most of the designs, his company first specialised in all kinds of ecclesiastical fittings and ornaments (made of stone, wood, leather, textiles) and later in stained glass production, the first stained glass window was completed in November 1845.

---

[895] Suggested reading: Doolan, Brian, *The Pugins and the Hardmans*, Birmingham 2004; Cheshire, Jim, *Stained Glass and the Victorian Gothic Revival*, Manchester 2005; Shepheard, Mathé, *The Stained Glass of John Hardman and Company under the Leadership of John Hardman Powell from 1867 to 1895*, Vol. I, Birmingham 2010; Ferry, Kathryn, *The Victorian Home*, Oxford 2012, p. 67f.; The Library of Birmingham, *Rewriting the Book, MS 175*; Muthesius, Hermann, *The English House* (edited by Dennis Sharp), Oxford 1979 , p. 155ff.

[896] Cook, *English House*, p. 80, p. 276.

[897] http://www.birminghamheritage.org.uk/pugin.html (viewed 02/11/2013).

[898] Nisbet, Garner, *Glasgow*.

[899] John Hardman senior was the driving force behind the replacement of the old chapel of St. Chad's in Birmingham, which later was to become St Chad's Roman Catholic Cathedral; cf. Banerjee, *John Hardman & Co.*; further reading: The Library of Birmingham, *Rewriting the Book, MS 175*.

Detailed studies of mediaeval stained glass windows in England and in Northern Europe formed the basis of Pugin's Gothic Revival/Neo-mediaeval artwork. He saw glasswork as a key element of a church's interior. The majority of his drawings were made at his home in Ramsgate, Kent.[900]

Over the decades John Hardman & Co. set up factories at numerous sites in Birmingham's Jewellery Quarter, e.g. at Newhall Hill.[901] A showroom designed by Pugin was opened in Great Charles Street, Birmingham, which also housed one of the workshops.[902] It displayed the complete range of Hardman's works. Additionally, the company produced printed catalogues to enable customers to order the merchandise by mail.[903] Mathé Shepheard, who has made an exhaustive study on John Hardman & Company under the Leadership of John Hardman Powell between the years 1867 and 1895, made a stocktaking of the firm's output as part of her research and states that "it becomes evident that the windows were individually designed with no repeats".[904]

John Hardman junior's nephew John Hardman Powell (1827-1895)[905] joined the business after having studied under Pugin together with Pugin's own son Edward Welby at the Pugin's home in Ramsgate, Kent from the end of 1844 onwards. Powell became chief designer at John Hardman & Co. about 1849, in 1850 he married A W N Pugin's daughter Anne, and became artistic head of the firm after A W N Pugin's death in 1852. After 1852 both, Hardman and Powell, resumed their collaboration with Pugin's son E W Pugin.[906] The

---

900 The Library of Birmingham, *Rewriting the Book, MS 175.*

901 In 1979 the firm transferred to Lightwood Park. An additional London based office in Piccadilly was established at the beginning of the 20th century; cf. The Library of Birmingham, *Rewriting the Book, MS 175.*

902 http://www.birminghamheritage.org.uk/pugin.html (viewed 02/11/2013).

903 Banerjee, *John Hardman & Co.*; Fisher, "John Hardman and Company: Pugin's glasspainters"; Shepheard, *Stained Glass of John Hardman and Company*, p. 12ff., p. 15ff.

904 Shepheard, *Stained Glass of John Hardman and Company*, p. 12.

905 He was born in Birmingham as son of the brass founder and manufacturer William Powell (1789-1861). John Hardman Powell's stained glass designs in particular are considered to be original innovative examples of the Gothic style, which go beyond merely imitating and recreating 13th and 14th century art, e.g. the large window at Pugin's St. Chad's Cathedral in Birmingham which depicts the Immaculate Conception and was designed in 1868 in memory of John Hardman junior; cf. http://www.pugin-society.1to1.org/JHPowell.html (viewed 21/10/2013).

906 The larger part of stained glass orders which the company received were from churches and convents, but they also took a number of orders from non-religious organisations. Along with the many glass windows the Hardmans created for churches in England, Ireland, the United States, South Africa and even Australia, probably the most famous of all was for new Houses of Parliament in London, for which A W N Pugin was responsible for the interior design. Although he employed the company Ballantine and Allan from Scotland to produce the windows that he had himself designed for the House of Lords, all the remaining glass artworks were made by

Hardman firm continued to cooperate with the Pugins after E W Pugin's death in 1875 in the form of London-based company of "Pugin & Pugin". In 1883 the metalwork design department of the company split from the stained glass department and operated under the name of Hardman, Powell & Co.; the stained glass unit continued to trade under the name John Hardman & Co. with John Hardman Powell as principal designer until his death in 1895. His second son, Dunstan John Powell (1861–1932), succeeded him as partner and the company's principal designer.[907] After John Hardman Powell's death control of the company passed to John Hardman's son John Bernard Hardman (1843–1903)[908] who was head of the business until 1903. Two of his sons, John Tarleton Hardman (1872-1959) and Gerald James Hardman (ca. 1875-xxxx) joined the company. John Tarleton worked as a stained glass artist, and Gerald James was an art metal manufacturer. This constellation, which spanned three generations, has a profound influence not only on Catholic ecclesiastical architecture and interior design, but also on the Gothic Revival period as a whole. John Hardman & Co. continued to produce stained glass well into the 21st century (including the lean years during WWI and during the 1970s and 1980s), but the influence which the Hardman family once wielded came to an end in 1936 when John Tarleton Hardman retired, and directors Patrick A Feeny (see below Chapter 20.1) and Tom Farrell took over the running of the company.[909]

The way stained glass windows were manufactured by Hardman's (in this case for customers in the United States, but the procedure would have been the same for all other clients) is described by Michael Fisher, consultant historian and archivist for Pugin, Hardman and Powell and author of the first full history of John Hardman & Co.: "The commissioning of windows from Hardman's was initiated directly by the client, who would submit the project's requirements to the firm in England. Hardman's would then provide a watercolour of the proposed window for approval. When the client was satisfied with the design, a full-size cartoon would be made, and the glass cut,

---

Hardman's, who continued to take care of them over the years by repairing and replacing glass which had either been damaged or destroyed during the Second World War; cf. The Library of Birmingham, *Rewriting the Book, MS 175*; University of Glasgow, *John Hardman Powell*; Fisher, "John Hardman and Company: Pugin's glasspainters", p. 1; Muthesius, *English House* , p. 55f. (who does not mention Hardman's at all). Pugin and Hardman also exhibited their works at the Great Exhibition at Crystal Palace in London in 1851 when "Pugin was particularly keen to promote the Gothic Revival style for domestic as well as ecclesiastical purposes."; cf. Banerjee, *John Hardman & Co.*

907 University of Glasgow, *John Hardman Powell*; The Library of Birmingham, *Rewriting the Book, MS 175.*

908 University of Glasgow, *John Bernard Hardman.*

909 Banerjee, *John Hardman & Co.*; Fisher, "John Hardman and Company: Pugin's glasspainters"; University of Glasgow, *John Bernard Hardman.*

painted, and assembled in panels ready for export to the United States, normally through the port of Liverpool."[910] In order to create stained glass separated mosaic glass pieces must be fitted together, which themselves are taken from the cartoons of the original design.[911] Mathé Shepheard adds: "Before stained glass manufacture was capable of meeting the demands of the Gothic revival and the renewed religious fervour, the craft had to be relearnt, for the legacy of the Reformation and the systematic iconoclasm that followed, with only a few pockets of resistance, had very nearly annihilated the art of stained glass. The technical basis for the rediscovery of old skills came about through the persistent research by a number of inquiring minds."[912]

In my opinion it is not hard to imagine that, just like the memorial brass, the stained glass window from Southgate Chapel stems from Hardman manufacture. Since the window in question is a Gothic lancet window the connection to Gothic Revival can be quickly made. Apparently, a John Hardman Trading Company Ltd., originally recorded as manufacturer and processor of glass and the successor of John Hardman & Co., went of out business in 2008[913], hence it proved difficult to find out more about the origins of the Southgate Chapel window. Tim Williams of Pugin Hardman & Powell Ltd (Reclaimed Building Materials, Lichfield) informed me in October 2013 that they still keep the majority of the Hardman archive, including the logbooks detailing all windows that were made by John Hardman & Co.[914], but apparently nothing there could be related to the Butler-Bowdons as Mr Williams did not come up with any results. Birmingham Museums and Art Gallery holds some of the company's full-size drawings for artworks which

---

[910] Fisher, "John Hardman and Company: Pugin's glasspainters", p. 2. His treatise on John Hardman & Co. was published in 2008 (Fisher, Michael, Hardman of Birmingham: Goldsmith and Glasspainter, Ashbourne 2008).

[911] The Library of Birmingham, *Rewriting the Book, MS 175.*

[912] Shepheard, *Stained Glass of John Hardman and Company,* p. 22f. Names are Eugene Bontemps and Charles Winston. The first manufacturers to recreate antique glass were James Powell and Sons of Whitefriars, London. In the 1850s and 1860s, Hardman purchased the material he needed for work from them, and also from Chance Brothers, leading suppliers of glass to Hardman during the 1860s, known for their meticulous dealings regarding the choice of colours. More details on coloured glass in metal windows cf. Muthesius, *English House*, p. 192f.

[913] http://companycheck.co.uk/company/05119198 (viewed 15/10/2013).

[914] Information by E-mail correspondence dated October 25, 2013; http://www.construction.co.uk/company_515210.htm (viewed 31/10/2013). Apparently most of the records in the Hardman archive apart from business records, letters, drawings, and cartoons for stained glass windows, covering the entire period of the company's history, are daybooks related to the trade with customers in the United States, (artworks for each of the windows made for more than 130 American churches between 1882 and 1935); cf. Fisher, "John Hardman and Company: Pugin's glasspainters", p. 2, p. 4.

survived a devastating fire at the firm's main workshop at Newhall Hill Studio in Birmingham in 1970, and Birmingham City Archives at the Birmingham City Library hold the business records.[915] When taking into account the time when Southgate Chapel was possibly built (around 1901), it is also interesting to note that at the same time the younger generations of Pugin and Hardman such as Cuthbert Welby Pugin, Peter Paul Pugin, Sebastian Pugin Powell, and Dunstan John Powell as well as John Tarleton Hardman and Gerald James Hardman could be credited as the artistic originators of the stained glass window, rather than the first generation of the Pugin-Hardman enterprise. The same applies for the making of the brass plaque commemorating Basil Butler-Bowdon (see Chapter 8) in 1920.

If we start from the assumption that the Pugins, Hardmans and Butler-Bowdons were privately linked[916], all being Catholic and recusant families, it is not impossible that the window of Southgate House chapel was made as a friendly turn by John Hardman & Co., and therefore does not appear in the firm's books. Martin Ellis, curator at Birmingham Museums and Art Gallery, informed me that there is also no reference to either Southgate House or the Butler-Bowdon family in the Hardman firm's warehouse books which are in possession of the museum and which record completed windows and their related design index. According to Mr Ellis, this does not necessarily mean that the window in question was not manufactured by Hardman. He adds that the documentation, at least the visual material, for domestic commissions is only partial. If a window was commissioned by the Butler-Bowdons Birmingham City Archives should hold the respective correspondence.[917] There is, however, a document held at the archives of Birmingham City Library. It is a correspondence between Hardman Studios and Rev. A I Whittet of Mount St. Mary's College, Spinkhill, referring to "Clowne, Catholic

---

[915] Birmingham City Archives at the Birmingham City Library, *Ref. No. MS 175A*, the major series covers accounting (glass sales ledger, metal sales ledgers, decoration sales ledger) and operational matters (brasswork, decoration, glasswork, metalwork, general) records; cf. The Library of Birmingham, *Rewriting the Book, MS 175*; Banerjee, *John Hardman & Co.*; Fisher, "John Hardman and Company: Pugin's glasspainters", p. 4. Additional information was kindly provided by Martin Ellis, Curator (Applied Art), Birmingham Museums Trust, Birmingham Museums and Art Galleries, via personal E-mail correspondence on January 21, 2014.

[916] This is supported by the concurrent appearance of names from the Butler-Bowdon family together with Charles Hansom, John Hardman and William and James Powell in the list of signatories in the so-called "Declaration of the Roman Catholic Laity of England" dated 1851 (cf. Catholics (England), *Declaration*, p. 9f., p. 12, see also Chapter 20). Thanks to Paul D Walker for pointing out this document to me (in a personal E-mail correspondence dated June 16, 2014).

[917] Information disclosed in a personal E-Mail correspondence between Martin Ellis, Curator (Applied Art), Birmingham Museums Trust, Birmingham Museums and Art Galleries, and the author on January 21, 2014.

Church, 1952/1953".[918] Unfortunately the correspondence does not make mention of the window in question, but refers to other furnishings from Hardman manufacture for the newly built church in Clowne (see Chapter 20.1) and the chapel of Southgate House (see Chapter 8).

So where is the stained glass window of Southgate Chapel today? I followed several leads in the hope of finding out. I started with a very brief and inconspicuous paragraph in the Catholic Herald dated December 30, 1938 to see if it would reveal the origin and today's whereabouts of the window. The text was regarding the Catholic church which was to be newly built around that time on Creswell Road, Clowne as the Church of Sacred Heart and Our Lady of Victories: "Work will begin in the near future on a new church near Creswell Road, Clowne. The site was given by Colonel Butler-Bowden (*sic!*), late of Southgate House, who also has given the fittings of his private chapel at Southgate."[919] The last part of the second sentence refers in all probability to the sale or auctioning of Southgate House and Estate earlier in 1938 when William Erdeswick Ignatius Butler-Bowdon said he would claim the "memorial brass" and the stained glass window from the chapel if Southgate Chapel were to be converted or demolished. It seemed only natural to suppose that Mr Butler-Bowdon may have had both objects transferred to the new church in Clowne. Unfortunately this proved to be nothing more than a red herring - there is no such window at the Church of Sacred Heart in Clowne.[920]

The next lead was a report by Peter Hopkins on Whitwell Local History Group's website that Southgate Chapel only fell from favour as a place of worship as recently as 1950[921], and that the window had remained in place until then. This fits with June Pearce's recollections of seeing the window as a very young girl. Born in 1949 she remembers the window clearly. According to her, it was made of beautiful colours, but unfortunately she does not remember the motif. She remembers parts of it were a very pure white, and that all the other colours were rich and vivid. Mrs Pearce has vague memories of noticing that the window had gone after some alterations had been made to Southgate House. She thinks it could possibly have been there when the Van Dyks first bought the estate (in 1955).[922]

---

918 Birmingham City Archives at the Birmingham City Library, *Ref. No. MS 175/A/4/5/3/67, File 67 (C).*

919 For more information on the founding of the Church of Sacred Heart and Our Lady of Victories and the fittings of Southgate Chapel see Appendix 8 and Chapter 20.1.

920 Information disclosed in a private E-Mail correspondence between Father Peter D McGuire and the author on January 10, 2014.

921 Hopkins, *Churches and Religion*.

922 Information disclosed in a private E-Mail correspondence between June Pearce and the author on January 10, 2014.

Geoffrey Holdsworth can remember certain details of the interior of the chapel of Southgate House. The Van Dyks had to gain the approval and permission of the church authorities for all work carried out inside the building. According to Mr Holdsworth, the ceiling of the chapel was painted dark blue with gold stars and there also was a picture of Christ on the ceiling. The Van Dyks were not allowed to alter this; they were allowed only to cover it with a false ceiling. Mr Holdsworth thought that there was a chance that the stained glass window might still be in its original place, just covered up as happened with the ceiling.[923] When comparing the black and white photograph of Southgate House with the chapel annex at the front of the building with how it appears today (Figure 40), it becomes clear that the window frame has been shortened on its lower end to make room for two modern windows on the ground floor, thus the stained glass window must have been removed at some point after the early 1950s.

But what has really happened to the window after the chapel was desecrated? According to the old black and white photograph (Figure 6), it was of considerable size and therefore certainly heavy and unwieldy. Removing the window without causing it serious damage must have been a very difficult task.

In her personal recollections on the history of the parish of the Sacred Heart, Clowne, Teresa Staples writes that after the Butler-Bowdons left Southgate in 1938, the stained glass window was indeed removed and sent to Pleasington (New) Hall for safe keeping[924], but this observation does not fit with those of the local inhabitants who remember the window still in place in the 1950s (see above). Aside from this, the Butler-Bowdons gave up Pleasington New Hall a few years before they gave up Southgate House, and Pleasington New Hall had already been demolished by Blackburn Council in 1932 (see Chapter 12).[925]

Consequently the only possibility remaining I saw was that after its removal the window had been incorporated into the architecture of Pleasington Priory, but since the Bishop refused to allow Basil Butler-Bowdon's commemoration plaque to be re-hung there (see Chapter 8), it did not initially seem very likely. It turned out that I was completely wrong, and that it was there that the window had found a new home. Martin Child, the parish historian of Pleasington, informed me that when walking down the south aisle of Pleasington Priory, the first stained glass window to be seen commemorates the Butler-Bowdon family. The family had requested that the window of Southgate Chapel be re-erected to Pleasington Priory. Their wish

---

923 Information disclosed via personal communication between June Pearce and Geoffrey Holdsworth and communicated to the author via E-mail by June Pearce on January 15, 2014.

924 Staples, *My Parish*, p. 5.

925 Pritt, *Pleasington New Hall.*

was carried out in 1953.[926] Mr Child also reports that the window was originally given to the family when Southgate Chapel was built by Bernard Henry Philip Petre, 14th Baron Petre (1858-1908[927]), brother of Monica Mary Butler-Bowdon (née Petre) and brother-in-law of John (6) Erdeswick Butler-Bowdon.

The window is thirteen feet high and six feet wide and in excellent condition (Figure 41). Even after more than a hundred years the colours have not lost their radiance and one can see that the workmanship is of the finest quality. The pointed arch bears six cruciform flowers: four with red crosses in their centres, arranged in a circle, and two green crosses in their centres to each side. The layout of the window must have been altered after it was removed from Southgate Chapel. The structure of the pointed arch as it is today differs noticeably from the configuration of the top section of the window when it was still part of Southgate Chapel (compare to Figures 6 and 40).[928] The cruciform flower patterns are therefore to be viewed as secondary additions to the original features, as the builders must have had to alter the window to fit into one of the already existing window frames of Pleasington Priory.

The central scene is spread out over the tripartite glass panel. The middle pane depicts Jesus Christ as the Sacred Heart in the traditional way with the heart visible. He wears a bright red cloak whose colour outshines all other colours of the window. He sits on a beautifully adorned throne with a crown on top and looks lovingly down onto the Blessed Virgin Mary, who leans or kneels in front of him, looking up. She is clad in a bright blue dress and a black cape. Beneath her feet lies a loose bundle of white lilies, these flowers being the symbol of light and purity, of innocence and virginity, and often found in connection with images of the Virgin Mary.

The scene is crowned by three coats of arms, one for each pane. The one to the left is the armorial of the Petre family made up of a golden band between two silver-coloured shells on a red background. The banner beneath the shield bears the family motto: "*Sans Dieu rien*", without God nothing.[929] The middle pane is crowned by the Butler-Bowdon shield and motto (see Chapter 10 and Appendix 6), and the pane to the right is crowned by the crest of the de Trafford family, a rampant red griffin on a silver background. The banner beneath reads: "Gripe, Griffin, hold fast".

---

926 Information disclosed via a personal E-mail communication between Martin Child and the author on May 8, 2014. Also see Child, *Pleasington Priory*, p. 54f.

927 Lundy, *Peerage* (Person Page 3621).

928 Thanks to Tony Bak for drawing my attention to this in a personal E-mail correspondence on June 2, 2014.

929 This motto can also be found underneath a one-handed clock on the clock turret of the gatehouse of Ingatestone Hall, Essex, the Petre's family seat.

Eleven saints are grouped around Jesus Christ and the Blessed Virgin Mary.[930] Two winged angels, one on the left panel, and one on the right, form canopies over them. The back row (from left to right) shows a mitred saint, Saint William of York[931], holding a book (the Holy Bible?) and a staff. Next to him stand Saint Helena[932] (with an empress crown on her head and holding up a massive cross), Saint Bernard of Clairvaux[933] (identifiable by his tonsured head), and Saint Basil the Great (in Eastern attire)[934]. The front row depicts, on the left, Saint John the Baptist in a burgundy cloak and with bare feet, holding a cross, and on the very right Saint Angela Merici[935]. Both saints parenthesise the scene in the foreground: to the left a kneeling and praying saint, most likely Saint Gladys[936] with a crown on her head, dressed in a diaphanous black gown and with a very bright halo is escorted by two other haloed female saints without recognisable attributes (possibly Saint Monica of Tagaste[937] and Saint Ursula of Cologne[938]). Both female saints look down upon Saint Gladys as does Saint William of York. To the right a tonsured male, in all

---

930 Child, *Pleasington Priory*, p. 55. Paul D Walker comments on the depiction of Mary: "(...) The Virgin figure might have been St Margaret Mary, the habit of the Visitation sisters (the order StMMA belonged to) is not blue. Nevertheless there is something unusual about the length of The Virgin's veil; and awkward about the figure's posture."; information disclosed in a personal E-mail correspondence with the author on June 2, 2014.

931 Saint William of York is a late 11th century saint (d. 08/06/1154) and member of the FitzHerbert family. He was born in York and was twice bishop there (information by kind courtesy of Father Peter D McGuire in a personal E-mail correspondence with the author on May 30, 2014). He is buried in York Minster. In the depiction on the stained glass window embroidered across his chest on his cope are the letters EBOR, the abbreviation of the word *Eboracum*, the Latin name for the town of York. According to Paul D Walker, the archbishops of York still sign themselves with their first name and then "*Ebor*" to this day (information disclosed in a personal E-mail correspondence with the author on May 3, 2014).

932 Saint Helena (ca. 250 – ca. 330), mother of Emperor Constantine the Great; cf. The Original Catholic Encyclopedia, *Helena, Saint*.

933 Saint Bernard of Clairvaux (1090-1153), greatest exponent of the Cistercian Order; cf. The Original Catholic Encyclopedia, *Bernard of Clairvaux, Saint*.

934 Saint Basil the Great of Caesarea, Cappadocia (330-379), ascetic, bishop, Doctor of the Church; cf. The Original Catholic Encyclopedia, *Basil the Great, Saint*.

935 Saint Angela Merici (1474-1540), religious leader and founder of *Ordo Sanctae Ursulae* (Order of the Ursulines); cf. The Original Catholic Encyclopedia, *Angela Merici, Saint*.

936 Saint Gwladys ferch Brychan is a 11th/12th century Welsh saint; cf. Catholic Online, *St. Gladys*.

937 Saint Monica of Tagaste (ca. 332-387), mother of Saint Augustine; cf. The Original Catholic Encyclopedia, *Monica, Saint*.

938 Saint Ursula of Cologne (dates uncertain), a Romano-British virgin and martyr; cf. Catholic Online, *St. Ursula*.

probability Saint Leonard of Noblac/Limousin[939], with an equally bright halo is escorted not only by Saint Angela Merici, but also by Saint Teresa of Ávila[940] holding an arrow in her right hand and a crosier in her left. Both Saint Angela Merici and Saint Leonard, who is clad in a richly embroidered brown monk's habit, hold their hands out in an intercessory gesture. Saint Angela Merici is looking down on her charge. Saint Helena, Saint Bernard and Saint Teresa of Ávila seem to be looking at the Virgin Mary, whereas Saint Basil and Saint John are looking at the Sacred Heart of Jesus. It cannot not be excluded that the respective viewing directions have a certain meaning or pursue a purpose. Further examination would be required.

Underneath the scene runs a banner with an inscription in mediaeval Latin: *Placare / Christe, servulis, Quibus / Patris clementiam Tuae ad Tribunal / gratiae Patrona Virgo / postulat*. This can be translated as "Bring peace to your servant, O Christ, with the mercy of your father, as the Virgin patroness pleads at your tribunal of grace".[941] The text is the first stanza of an early mediaeval hymn, in its original form attributed to Rabanus Maurus (776-856) as *Christe, Redemptor omnium*. It was revised by Pope Urban VIII (1568-1644) and later used in the Roman Breviary for Matins and Vespers on the occasion of the Feasts of All Saints (November, 1).[942]

The key question in this context is (as Paul D Walker frames it): are the saintly figures related to the general promotion of a devotion to the Sacred Heart or are they a manifestation of the Butler-Bowdon family's devotion?[943] As the window came from the private chapel of Southgate House, the latter suggestion could well be correct. According to Mr Walker, "the subject of the window is very Catholic, but of a Church of a very different era. The hagiography it uses would have been more generally familiar, especially in the élite company of the Jesuits with whom the Butler-Bowdons associated".

Ultimately, it remains difficult to define the proceedings in the scene (is there an underlying message?) or identify all those depicted with absolute certainty. Martin Child says that "the person dedicating the window needs to leave a written record of the meaning of the window, unfortunately this is not always done."[944] Perhaps such a text was composed at the time when the

---

939 Saint Leonard of Noblac/Limousin is a 6th century French saint; cf. The Original Catholic Encyclopedia, *Leonard of Limousin, Saint*.

940 Saint Teresa of Ávila (1515-1582), founder of the Reformed Carmelites and Doctor of the Church; cf. The Original Catholic Encyclopedia, *Teresa of Jesus (Avila), Saint*.

941 Translation by Father Peter D McGuire in a personal E-mail correspondence with the author on May 30, 2014.

942 Martin, *Thesaurus Precum Latinarum* offers a more poetic translation: "To Thy poor servants reconciled / show mercy, Christ, for whom the mild / and Virgin patroness this grace / implore before Thy Father's face", or: "O Christ be reconciled to Thy servants ..."

943 Discussed in a personal E-mail correspondence with the author on June 2, 2014.

944 Disclosed in a personal E-mail correspondence with the author on June 1, 2014.

window was commissioned and manufactured, but any respective documents are possibly lost today. It is, however, certainly no coincidence that the names of the saints correspond to the names of the members of the Butler-Bowdon family at the time the window was commissioned. I would attribute the depicted saints to the following Butler-Bowdon family members:

Saint William of York = William Erdeswick Ignatius Butler-Bowdon, first son
Saint Helena = Isabel-Mary Helena Butler-Bowdon, sixth daughter
Saint Bernard of Clairvaux = Bernard Joseph Butler-Bowdon, third son
Saint Basil the Great = Basil Joseph Bernard Butler-Bowdon, fourth son
Saint John the Baptist = John (6) Erdeswick Butler-Bowdon, father
Saint Monica of Tagaste = Monica Mary Rose Butler-Bowdon, second daughter
Saint Ursula of Cologne = Ursula Mary Cora Butler-Bowdon, fifth daughter
Saint Gladys = Gladys Mary Ella Butler-Bowdon, fourth daughter
Saint Teresa of Ávila = Theresa Mary Sophia Butler-Bowdon, first daughter
Saint Leonard de Noblac/Limousin = Leonard Joseph Bruno Butler-Bowdon, second son
Saint Angela Merici = Angela Mary Josephine Butler Bowdon, third daughter

This leaves us with a crucial question: where is Monica Mary Butler-Bowdon, John (6) Erdeswick Butler-Bowdon's wife and mother of the children in this tableau? Is she (as the mother) visually equated with the Blessed Virgin Mary? As there are thousands of women with Mary in their name, Paul D Walker adds, they can be equated with Mary, mother of Christ.[945]

Taking all uncertainties into consideration, I would like to dare two interpretations of the tableau which are, however, equations with n unknowns. On the condition that 1907 (instead of hitherto assumed 1901) is the year engraved on the AMDG plaque at Southgate Chapel[946], which would be identical with the year of Monica Mary's death, it perhaps becomes explicable why the stained glass window had been given to the Butler-Bowdons for their chapel at Southgate House by Monica Mary's brother Bernard - meant for a memorial for his recently deceased sister. Certainly the Butler-Bowdons would have been affluent enough to pay for such a window themselves any time.

However, the scene on the window to me somehow conveys an indistinct sense of mourning or grief. If we put aside what is visible on the tableau on first sight (the interacting saints and their conduct towards the Blessed Virgin Mary and the Sacred Heart) and assume that there is a second, underlying

---

[945] Information disclosed in a personal E-mail correspondence between Paul D Walker and the author on June 2, 2014.

[946] As suggested by Paul D Walker in a personal E-mail correspondence with the author on June 3, 2014. See also Chapter 8.

level of depiction where all saints have their worldly counterparts, then we possibly see a widowed husband and the family's children, recommending their deceased wife and mother to Christ by means of prayer, protective postures and with intercessory gestures. This is visibly underlined by the triangular structure of the picture. Unfortunately this interpretation has at least one deficiency as we come into problems with the dates. According to the sources, John (6) and Monica Mary Butler-Bowdon commissioned the building of Southgate Chapel when they moved to Southgate House, most likely at the end of the 1890s. Following the deductions made from the images on the stained glass window a possible *terminus post quem* for this could be the year their last child, Basil, was born: 1898. But if the window in question had indeed been manufactured at a later date, viz on the occasion of Monica Mary's death in 1907, and perhaps in parallel with the commencement of construction of the chapel, this would ultimately mean that pious Monica Mary never had a chance to attend mass at the family's personal place of worship - a highly unlikely thought. John, 18th and present Baron Petre of Ingatestone Hall, Essex, however, carefully confirmed my assumption of 1907 being the year of origin of the window.[947]

There is room for a second presumption: another possible reading of the year on the foundation plaque is 1904. Leonard Joseph Bruno Butler-Bowdon died in South Africa in December 1904. What I find striking when looking at the window is that the scene renders Saint Leonard and Saint Angela Merici with identical intercessory gestures, and while Saint Angela Merici looks down on him benevolently, she also has an extraordinarily sad face. In turn Saint Leonard's somewhat brighter face colour seems to differ ever so slightly from the complexions of all other depicted persons which make him stand out. Can we assume that the window then perhaps commemorates Leonard Butler-Bowdon's death? In this case the Butler-Bowdon family members would present him to the Sacred Heart, supported by recommendation of his mother in prominent position. But was Southgate Chapel really erected as late as 1904? This seems even more improbable than the previous assumption.[948]

If we continue to believe that the chapel had been built around 1901 and the window commemorates either Monica Mary's or Leonard's death, this

---

[947] "I imagine that the 14th Lord Petre commissioned it in memory of his sister, Monica, who died in 1907."; information disclosed in a personal E-mail correspondence with the author on June 17, 2014. However, according to Lord Petre, his branch of the family does not hold any information on Pleasington Priory (he is not a direct descendant of the 14th Lord Petre, who died without a male heir, so the title passed to his younger brother, the present Baron Petre's grandfather).

[948] This assumption is even shakier when taking Leonard Butler-Bowdon's date of death into consideration: 30/12/1904. It is improbable that the family will have heard about his death immediately, also building a chapel and commissioning a window on the last remaining day of the year 1904 is more than impossible.

leaves us with a time gap of about three and six years respectively in which Southgate Chapel must have had another window (perhaps a plainer and simpler one?[949]). For practical reasons this does not seem very logical. Further studies on the subject could bring light into the darkness.

Regarding the age determination of the window (1901?), Paul D Walker adds that it could tie in with the Encyclical of Pope Leo XIII (1810-1903) consecrating the human race to the Sacred Heart, promulgated in 1899.[950]

The extraordinary quality of the workmanship of the window in Pleasington Priory, its stylistic execution and its religious contents suggest that it was created by Hardman Studios, but my theory is to be understood as an assumption only. According to Paul D Walker in his book on Spinkhill Church, there was a stained glass artist who worked locally in the 19th century, a Joseph Goodwin of Barlborough (the 1851 census returns list him as "plumber, glazier and glass-stainer"). He was reported for producing two small windows for the Church of the Immaculate Conception at Spinkhill (their allocation unknown today[951]). A second stained glass artist who contributed to the windows of Spinkhill Church was a Mr Snow of London, of whom nothing further is known.[952] Yet Spinkhill Church also boasts a window of Hardman productions. To mark the centenary of the church in 1946 a new stained glass window was fitted in 1947. It was designed by Patrick A Feeny (see Chapter 20.1) who was the brother of one of the teachers at Mount St. Mary's in the 1940s, which is again evidence of the close connection Hardman Studios had to area.[953] According to Mr Walker, there is even more evidence for Hardman windows in the area: the Jesuits at Spinkhill established several missions in the vicinity of Spinkhill in the mid to late 19th century. One was located at Staveley. Here a church, St. Joseph's, was built in 1933, which contains windows by Hardman from that date and the 1950s.[954]

---

[949] Is this the explanation for the divergent lay-out of the window as depicted in the black and white turn-of-the-century photograph (Figures 6 and 40)?

[950] Information disclosed in a personal E-mail correspondence between Paul D Walker and the author on June 1, 2014.

[951] The only surviving original window at Spinkhill church is the east window of 1846, but its creator is unknown, see Walker, *Church of the Immaculate Conception*, p. 39 and footnote 4.

[952] Walker, *Church of the Immaculate Conception*, p. 39. In a personal E-mail correspondence with the author on July 5, 2014 Paul D Walker adds that he thinks that neither Mr Goodwin nor Mr Snow were the actual designers or makers of the windows in question. He assumes that Mr Goodwin, especially, was a local glazier who helped to install them.

[953] Walker, *Church of the Immaculate Conception*, p. 58.

[954] Information disclosed in a personal E-Mail correspondence between Paul D Walker and the author on July 5, 2014. Mr Walker reports that for another Jesuit mission in Chesterfield a new church, the Annunciation, was built in 1854. It had been designed by the same architect as for Spinkhill, Joseph Aloysius Hansom, and enlarged by him

Also St. Marie's Cathedral at Sheffield is home to a substantial number of stained glass windows from Hardman & Co., Birmingham.[955]

20.1. Excursus on the furnishings of Southgate Chapel and the Church of Sacred Heart and Our Lady of Victories, Clowne

There is correspondence between Hardman Studios, Birmingham and Rev. A I Whittet[956] of Mount St. Mary's College, Spinkhill from the years 1952 and 1953 regarding the possible renovation works on some plaster statues. The correspondence is held by Birmingham City Archives at the Birmingham City Library and sheds some interesting light on the furnishings of Southgate Chapel and the Church of Sacred Heart and Our Lady of Victories, Clowne.[957] According to these documents, alongside the stained glass window and the metal commemoration plaque for Basil Butler-Bowdon, Southgate Chapel must also have been home to a statue of St Joseph, which is today seemingly lost.

Hardman Studios Memo dated November 10, 1952: (...)
Recipient: John Hardman Studios, 43, Newhall Hill, Birmingham
Dear Sirs, I have three plaster statues, roughly from 3′ 6″ - 4″ in height, which I would like to have repainted. Also a crucifix figure (about 5′). Would it be possible for you to send a representative to see the statues and to give an estimate of the cost of re-painting? Yours faithfully (Rev.) A. I. Whittet

Note in pencil on lined paper, written by an unnamed person at Hardman Studios and dated February 6, 1953:

---

in the 1870s. While it has a number of stained glass windows, he does not know their makers, but according to him, none are like the original windows at Spinkhill.

955 These windows can be found in the Baptistery, the West End Nave (here: A W N Pugin and Hardman & Co.), the North Transept, the Lady Chapel, and on the South Aisle; information by kind courtesy of Paul D Walker in a personal E-Mail correspondence on July 5, 2014.

956 In 1948 Father Whittet was appointed as priest solely for Clowne by Mount St. Mary's College. According to the recollections of Teresa Staples, he inherited the use of Southgate Chapel and tried to hold meetings there but it became clear very quickly that by then the chapel was no longer in any fit state to celebrate masses as it was too damp, cold and dilapidated. The "Nag's Head" in Clowne (North Road) became a temporary quarters for meetings and Sunday mass in winter; cf. Staples, *My Parish*, p. 5f.

957 Birmingham City Archives at the Birmingham City Library, Ref. No. MS 175/A/4/5/3/67, File 67 (C).

FB Whittet from Mount St. Marys, Spinkhill, would like a confirmed estimate for redecoration 2 3feet Statues of B.V.M. and S.H.[958] told him between £30 - £35 the two.
The Crucifix is O.K. + agreed to leave it.
There is also a Statue of St Joseph - about same size in the disused Chapel of Southgate House. I couldn't get in to see it.
Reynolds is the architect of the new church here - quite small but pleasing.

Hardman Studios Memo dated December 24, 1953: (...)
Recipient: Patrick A Feeny, Esq., John Hardman's Studios, 43, Newhall Hill, Birmingham
Dear Mr. Feeny,
Thank you for your letter of 17th February and quotation. I am sorry to say that the Committee feels that at present we cannot tackle the work of the painting of the Statues. It is a question of expense, of course. We should like to get them done, but it cannot be at present.
I will keep this matter in mind, and will again apply to you when it is possible for us to meet the expense.
Thank you for your kindness in coming. I was very happy to meet you and hope to see you again soon.
Yours sincerely, A. I. Whittet S. J.

Whether any work was ever carried out at a later date, we do not know. Teresa Staples in her book recalls a Presider's Chair which bore the initials of the Butler Bowdon family and says that most of the fittings transferred from Southgate Chapel to Clowne were still in use in 1999 when she wrote down her memories.[959] At the time of writing the chair is stored at the church of the Sacred Heart and Our Lady of Victories, Clowne, but is not presently in use (Figure 42).[960] The initials are carved into the backrest which is adorned with two impressive lion's heads. The backrest not only shows the Butler-Bowdon initials, but also the letter C which is formed in the shape of a pretty little fish complete with tailfins. We can therefore understand the letter as an abbreviation of the Ancient Greek word Χριστος (= Christ). At the same time

958 The abbreviations of B.V.M. and S.H. stand for "Blessed Virgin Mary" and "Sacred Heart".
959 Staples, *My Parish*, p. 8.
960 Information disclosed in a private E-Mail correspondence between Father Peter D McGuire and the author on May 13, 2014. Father McGuire also contributed the photograph. The chair mimics the mediaeval (and antique) paragon of a foldable chair ("scissors chair") when society was a mobile one and things by definition had to be portable. The Presider's Chair from Clowne is a typical exponent of its time when historic furniture was rediscovered by Gothic Revival and the Arts and Crafts Movement.

the fish, Ιχθυς in Ancient Greek, is a symbol of Christ, the single letters standing for Ιησους Χριστος θεου υιοσ σωτηρ, Jesus Christ, son of God, saviour. It is remarkable how tenderly and delicately the letter C symbolically embraces the two Bs. Nothing can be said about the manufacturer of the chair, but it clearly is a very fine specimen of Gothic Revival art. Tony Bak reports that the Bowdons possessed two carved chairs, both privately purchased at auction. According to Mr Bak, the design is very elaborate, but unfortunately they do not bear any coat of arms.[961] Peter McGuire thinks he might have heard about the crucifix mentioned in the Hardman correspondence.[962] In personal notes collected by local parishioners Mrs Staples recalls further furnishings that came from Southgate to the new church in Clowne: the seats, a large crucifix over the altar, a large statue of Our Lady, and a vestment press (now in the sacristy).[963] The Nottingham Diocesan Yearbook of 1953 mentions that even the altar itself was transferred from Southgate Chapel to the new church in Clowne.[964]

21. Pleasington (New and Old) Hall, Lancashire

The oldest part of Pleasington **Old** Hall was built in 1587 by the de Houghton family[965], and it is said that a Mr E Pawson lived there for 56 years.[966] The style of the house is described as Elizabethan.[967] Between 1870 and 1872 it was converted into a farmhouse.[968] It is a Grade II* listed two-storey house flanked by two-storey crosswings. It is built of sandstone blocks and some old bricks, and is partially rendered (rear and right side). It has a roof of slate tiles and three chimneys. A two-storey lean-to porch has a moulded Tudor-arched doorway whose lintel bears carved panels with crests and an abbreviated inscription: "RH 1587 TH LA IS". The initials RH stand for Richard Houghton, TH for Thomas Houghton and IS for John Southworth; only traces of the initials LA can be made out.[969] The panel in the middle shows the crests of the

---

961 Information disclosed in a private E-Mail correspondence between Tony Bak and the author on May 6, 2014.

962 Information disclosed in a private E-Mail correspondence between Father Peter D McGuire and the author on May 5, 2014.

963 Information by kind courtesy of Father Peter D McGuire in a private E-Mail correspondence with the author on May 18, 2014.

964 "New Church-Hall at Clowne" by Fr A J Whittet, in: Nottingham Diocesan Yearbook 1953, p. 160f.; information by kind courtesy of Canon Anthony Dolan by E-mail on May 19, 2014.

965 http://www.blackburncitizen.co.uk/touristguide/947207.Tourist_guide_to_Pleasington/ (viewed 16/06/2013)

966 BBC, *Domesday Reloaded, Pleasington Old Hall.*

967 BBC, *Domesday Reloaded, Pleasington Old Hall.*

968 Wilson, *Imperial Gazetteer of England and Wales (1870-72).*

969 Abram, *Parish of Blackburn*, p. 80.

three families whose initials are inscribed: Ainsworth, Houghton and Southworth, who were all chief landowners at Pleasington when the Hall was built in 1587.[970] As tradition has it that the front door of the house was made of two inch thick oak with 365 metal studs - one for each day of the year. A door of this dimension was difficult to be breached and saved the Hall from attacks.[971] The living room is said to have been adorned with an Inglenook fireplace behind which a priesthole was hidden where monks could hide in times of danger.[972] The windows of the house, some old, some 19th century alterations, feature a great variety of shapes and dècor. The building's interior has been mostly altered over the years, but the right wing has two original beams supported by stone corbels and a rectangular fireplace. The left wing has two modernised cross-corner fireplaces.[973] Belonging to the Hall there were seventy acres of land under which, allegedly, a tunnel lead to another hall nearby and which was used to escape from Pleasington Old Hall unobserved.[974]

After centuries of ownership by the Ainsworth family, Pleasington **Old** Hall passed into the hands of the Butlers in 1777 when Richard Butler (b. 17/11/1747[975]) bought the Hall and Manor.[976] The connection between the Bowdons and the Butlers was established by the marriage of John (2) Bowdon's daughter Charlotte (from his third marriage to Mary Johnson) to Richard Butler in his second marriage on October 2, 1771 in Barlborough.[977] Together they had three children: (Richard) John Francis Butler, Mary-Anne and Ann Butler. (Richard) John Francis Butler was the heir to Pleasington Estate and was responsible for building **New** Hall of Pleasington in 1805-1807 and the Roman Catholic church of St. Mary and St. John the Baptist in Pleasington.[978] The New Hall building superseded the old manor house as a residential mansion and in descriptive terms can be considered as a large manor house with something of a stately home character (Figure 43).[979] Although married, (Richard) John Francis *decessit sine prole* / died childless in 1821/1824, as did his sisters. When Mary-Anne passed away in 1840 she left

---

970 Abram, *Parish of Blackburn*, p. 80; Farrer, Brownbill, *History of the County of Lancaster*, p. 266-269.

971 BBC, *Domesday Reloaded, Pleasington Old Hall.*

972 BBC, *Domesday Reloaded, Pleasington Old Hall.*

973 English Heritage, *Old Hall Farm House* (formerly listed as Pleasington Old Hall).

974 BBC, *Domesday Reloaded, Pleasington Old Hall.*

975 Cf. Bowdon family tree, Barlborough Heritage and Research Centre.

976 Kelliher, "Rediscovery of Margery Kempe", p. 261; Abram, *Parish of Blackburn*, p. 80; Burke, Burke, *Genealogical and Heraldic History*, p. 125.

977 FamilySearch, *England Marriages.*

978 Pritt, *Pleasington New Hall*, also see above.

979 For contemporary photographs of the building see Pritt, *Pleasington New Hall* and Figure 43.

Pleasington Estate to her cousin, John (5) Peter Bruno Butler-Bowdon who later extended the house (at an unrecorded date).[980]

According to The Imperial Gazetteer of England and Wales dated 1870-1872, Pleasington **New** Hall in Lancashire is "a modern mansion in the Grecian style".[981] At that time the manor, including both Pleasington Halls, belonged to John (5) Peter Bruno Butler-Bowdon, Esq. (1815-1878) who succeeded to the manorial estate of Pleasington by above mentioned legacy of his cousin Mary Anne Butler in 1840. By sign manual dated 28/01/1841 he assumed her surname of Butler and added it to his own.[982] Mary Anne was the only surviving child and heir of Richard and Charlotte Butler (the daughter of John (2) Bowdon and Mary Johnson).[983] A short announcement in the London Gazette dated January 12, 1841 reports the following: "Whitehall, January 11, 1841 The Queen has been pleased to grant unto John Bowdon, of Pleasington-hall, in the township of Pleasington, in the parish of Blackburn, in the county palatine of Lancaster, Esq. Her royal license and authority, that he may (in compliance with a condition obtained in the last will and testament of Mary Ann Butler, of Pleasington-hall aforesaid, spinster, deceased) henceforth taken upon himself and use the surname of Butler, in addition to and before that of Bowdon, and bear the arms of Butler quarterly with those of Bowdon; and that such surname and arms may, in like manner, be taken, borne, and used by his issue; such arms being duly exemplified according to the law of arms, and recorded in the Herald's Office, otherwise Her Majesty's said licence and permission to be void and of none effect: And also to command, that the said royal concession and declaration be recorded in Her Majesty's College of Arms."[984]

When searching for more information on this the period, the **1841** census of England and Wales reveals that the Styche and Hart family and their six servants were occupants of "Pleasington Hall" (without indication of **New** or **Old** Hall). It seems as if the Butler-Bowdons had themselves not yet taken up residence at Pleasington at that time. Things look differently ten years later. The **1851** census of England and Wales attests that the Butler-Bowdon family now inhabits "Pleasington Hall", in this case clearly the **New** Hall, as Pleasington **Old** Hall has an entry of its own (see below). The owners are recorded as John (5) Butler-Bowdon as "Landed Proprietor and Magistrate", aged 35 and born in Derbyshire, and his wife Amelia Bowdon, aged 30 and born in Staffordshire. They lived at Pleasington with their two infant sons, Erdeswick (= John (6)), aged 1, born in Staffordshire, and Lancelot, aged 0,

---

980 Abram, *Parish of Blackburn*, p. 80.

981 Wilson, *Imperial Gazetteer of England and Wales (1870-72)*.

982 Riden, *Barlborough*, p. 37; Abram, *Parish of Blackburn*, p. 80.

983 Riden, *Barlborough*, p. 37.

984 http://www.london-gazette.co.uk/issues/19940/pages/112/page.pdf (viewed 16/06/2013).

born in Pleasington, Lancashire. Six servants were responsible for running the household: Eli Petty, unmarried, aged 26, born in Southampton, was the Coachman; John Leston, aged 19, unmarried, born in Derbyshire, was the Footman; in the hands of Elizabeth Lewes, aged 28, unmarried, born in Staffordshire, lay the care of the two little boys as Nurse Maid; Elizabeth Perkes, aged 22, unmarried, born in Staffordshire, was the Amelia Butler-Bowdon's Ladies Maid; Elizabeth Taylor, aged 25, unmarried, born in Staffordshire, was the Cook and Elizabeth Ross, aged 21, unmarried, born in Staffordshire, was the House Maid.

John (5) Peter Bruno Butler-Bowdon appears as a subject in a painting by the Russian-British artist and architect Vladimir Osipovich Sherwood[985], entitled "Laying of the Foundation Stone". Painted in 1852 it is today stored in the Blackburn Museum and Art Gallery, Blackburn. It depicts well-known local dignitaries at the time[986] such as councillors, mayors, Members of Parliament and significant manufacturers as well as military commandos firing a volley on the occasion of the opening of the cotton exchange in Blackburn. Hats are thrown aloft and the gathered crowd in the background cheers (Figure 44). The names of each man in the picture have been recorded and one of them is John (5) Peter Bruno Butler-Bowdon (Figure 45).[987] Vladimir Sherwood, the artist, was brought to England specifically to do this painting and it can be assumed that the depicted persons sat with him for their individual portraits.[988]

Vinai Solanki, History Curator of Blackburn Museum and Art Gallery, contributed some valuable additional background information on the painting: Blackburn belonged to the biggest cotton weaving towns in England.[989] This branch of industry was flawed, as cotton which was brought into England (via Liverpool) from its originating countries such as India, Sudan or the United States, was then sold back to the same countries after weaving as entrepot trade (via the cotton exchange in Manchester). It was therefore decided that establishing a cotton exchange of its own in Blackburn would be a good idea for the town, in order for it to be able to sell the end product directly and n that way gain more profit. But at that time the cotton industry in Lancashire was already on the decline as the last great recipients

---

985 Vladimir Osipovich Sherwood (30/08/1832-27/07/1897); cf. http://shelf3d.com/Vladimir%Osipovich%Sherwood (viewed 05/03/2014).

986 Information disclosed by E-mail by Vinai Solanki, History Curator of Blackburn Museum an Art Gallery on April 4, 2013.

987 Interesting observation: the names of the depicted females attending the occasion were not recorded.

988 Information disclosed by E-mail by Vinai Solanki, History Curator of Blackburn Museum an Art Gallery on April 4, 2013.

989 Between 1867 and 1869 textile goods formed 72% of Britain's manufactured exports (and dropped to 51% at the eve of WWI); cf. Hobsbawm, *Industry and Empire*, p. 121.

of manufactured cotton goods (India, Japan and China) began developing their own textile industries. For example, all political attempts to prevent industrialisation in India failed, "though as late as the 1890s the Lancashire pressure-group had prevented the imposition of duties to protect the Indian cotton industry."[990] Consequently the cotton exchange in Blackburn did not last many years.

At that time Pleasington **Old** Hall was inhabited by the large Hothersall family and their staff (according to the **1851** census returns). William Hothersall was a farmer, married to Mary, and together they had seven children (all boys). Their staff consisted partly of farm labourers and partly of house servants. A third element of Pleasington Estate in that period was "Pleasington Hall Stable House", home to the gardener of Pleasington grounds and his family: Robert and Elizabeth Price and their four sons. An interesting little detail about farm life at Pleasington Estate was found on-line: "In the late 18th and early 19th century it was not unusual for large Halls and country houses to have a resident donkey - as a beast of burden, a donkey was invaluable. Pleasington **Old** Hall, for example, had a donkey amongst whose tasks it was to pull the lawnmower to keep the grounds tidy. (...)."[991]

The **1861** census of England and Wales shows a steadily growing family at Pleasington **New** Hall: John B Bowdon, aged 45, born in Barlbro (*sic!*), Derbyshire, stated as "Landed Proprietor" and his wife Amelia, aged 40, born in Busberry (= Bushbury[992]), Staffordshire, are now parents to four sons: Erdeswick, aged 11, Lancelot, aged 10, Jermyn, aged 7 and Bruno, aged 3, all born in Pleasington, Lancaster. Four servants are part of the household: Thomas B Bowdon (*sic!*[993]), aged 33, born in Wexford, Ireland was the family's Domestic Servant. The four boys had a governess, Veronica Sillyman (?), aged 21, unmarried and born in Lancaster. Ellen Webster, aged 21, unmarried, born in Lancaster, Liverpool, and Mary McGuarty, aged 18, unmarried, born in Ireland, Caven (?), were the household's Domestic Servants. Pleasington **Old** Hall was still inhabited by the Hothersalls, their children, farm hands and servants. The following censuses no longer mention any residents at the stables building.

John (5) Butler-Bowdon seems to have been a fearless character. Clive Emsley cites an incident in November 1862 when ca. 400 people marched on the Bowdon's residence, throwing stones, after the prosecution of four men

---

[990] Hobsbawm, *Industry and Empire*, p. 129.

[991] According to Roberts, Harriet, http://poundday.org.uk/tag/orphanage/, in a blog dated May 11, 2012 (viewed 06/09/2013). A picture of the legendary donkey with the lawnmower on the banked gardens in front of Pleasington **New** Hall can be viewed at Pritt, *Pleasington New Hall* (image 3).

[992] This possibly is an auditory misunderstanding by the enumerator; cf. Parker, *Wolverhampton History and Heritage Website.*

[993] This is either a coincidence or another slip of the pen made by the enumerator.

for night poaching on the land of John (5) Butler-Bowdon after evidence was given by the estates' gamekeepers at the town hall. Mr Bowdon himself and his servants drove the trespassers off by firing two or three shots over their heads and a military unit of the local constabulary were rushed into Blackburn to re-establish order.[994]

Lancashire Record Office holds a document dated September 1, 1864 which gives evidence that land in Birkdale (near Southport, ca. 30 km north of Liverpool) was given from a Thomas Weld Blundell (of Ince Blundell Hall[995]) to John (5) Butler-Bowdon for the erection of a battery for artillery practice.[996]

For **1871** the census of England and Wales reveals a new feature: John (5) and Amelia Butler-Bowdon are seemingly no longer inhabitants of Pleasington **New** Hall - or were absent the day the enumerator came by. The only Butler-Bowdon present was their son, (John (6)) Erdeswick Butler-Bowdon, aged 21, apparently unmarried and born in Staffordshire. Five servants of unspecified duty were with him: John Owen, aged 29, born in Montgomeryshire; Henry Firkins, aged 33, born in Herefordshire; Isabella Sandwell, aged 22, born in Lancashire; Catherine Mallen, aged 27, from Ireland, and Elizabeth Sherwin, born in Cambridgeshire. Pleasington **Old** Hall had found new residents over the past years: Christopher and Alice Wood, their son and their daughter and two servants. Another building is listed in the 1871 census as part of Pleasington Estate: Pleasington Hall Lodge, which at that time was inhabited by the Kenyon family and presumably let by the Butler-Bowdons to them as people professionally tied to the Butler-Bowdon household. In all probability Mr Kenyon was the gardener at Pleasington Estate.

Not much could be found about the goings on at Pleasington Estate over the following years in the sources available to me, but a "Trap Accident at Blackburn" is the headline in Manchester Courier and Lancashire General Advertiser on October 18, 1880. "On Saturday afternoon a somewhat serious

---

994 Emsley, *Crime and Society*, p. 185 and footnote 8. This incident found repercussion in the national press, for instance in the Dundee, Perth and Cupar Advertiser (Tayside, Scotland) dated November 7, 1862 or the Newcastle Guardian and Tyne Mercury dated November 8, 1862; cf. http://www.findmypast.co.uk (British Newspapers 1710-1965) (viewed 04/09/2013).

995 Ince Blundell Hall today is a care and nursing home and is a Grade II* listed building. Its former owner was Henry Blundell (1724-1810), a collector of Roman and Greek antiquities and Renaissance art. Between 1802 and 1810 he built a miniature version of the Pantheon in Rome adjacent to the Hall to appropriately house his collection (the contents have since been dispersed and are today kept at World Museum and Walker Art Gallery in Liverpool); cf. English Heritage, *Ince Blundell Hall*; English Heritage, *Pantheon Adjoining Ince Blundell Hall*; Girouard, *English Country House*, plate 105 and p. 179; Jenkins, *Best Houses*, p. 440f.

996 Lancashire Record Office, *Ref. No. DDIN 66/40* (from The Blundell of Ince Muniments, original document not viewed personally).

trap accident occurred at Blackburn. Colonel Butler Bowden (*sic!*), J. P., of Pleasington Hall, and his wife were driving up Lord-street when the horse fell and both were thrown out of the trap and received a severe shaking. Mrs. Butler Bowden (*sic!*) who alighted on her head on the pavement received a bad wound on the forehead and was taken into a neighbouring shop where she was attended to."[997]

According to the **1881** census of England and Wales, John E Butler-Bowdon, aged 31, born in Rugeley, Staffordshire as "Landed Pror (= Proprietor) and Magistrate County Lancaster" was owner of Pleasington New Hall. He is listed as married to Monica Butler-Bowdon, aged 20, born in London, Portland Place, London Middlesex. Together they had two sons: William E, aged 1, born in London, Manchester Square, London, Middlesex, and baby Leonard J, aged 0, born in Pleasington, Lancashire. Coresidents were Mary B Wright, cousin, aged 29, single, born in Richmond, Yorkshire, and Philip B Petre, brother-in-law, aged 16, single and scholar, born in Thorndon Hall[998], Essex. Seven servants completed the household: Conrad J Edney, aged 18, single, born in Buckland Faringdon, Berkshire[999], was Footman (Domestic); Charlotte A Mirley, aged 28, single, born in Farlington, Yorkshire, was the household's Cook (Domestic); Isabella Wearden, aged 25, single, born in Pilling, Lancashire, assisted as Kitchen Maid (Domestic); Emma Budd, aged 18, single, born in Haslemere, Surrey, acted as Under Housemaid (Domestic); Elizabeth Gegan, aged 29, single, born in Everton, Lancashire is listed as Housemaid; Catherine Bastock, aged 37, widow, born in Tavistock, Devon, held the important position of being the children's Nurse (Domestic); she was assisted by Fanny Barwell, aged 16, single, born in Herongate, Essex, who worked as Under Nurse (Domestic). Another family lived together with the Butler-Bowdons and their staff under the same roof: Jane Baker, her brother Thomas Baker, her sister Alice Baker and three under-aged nephews. They belonged to a farmer's family; Jane, Thomas and Alice are recorded as the farmer's children, and the nephews were the respective grandsons. Pleasington **Old** Hall again had new occupants: the Noblett family, listed as farmers, Joseph Noblett and his wife Amy and their five children. The 1881 census recorded Pleasington Hall Lodge and Pleasington Lodge as additional once again inhabited houses. Just as ten years previously, Pleasington Hall Lodge was home to gardener Richard and his wife Agnes Kenyon. Richard

---

997 http://www.findmypast.co.uk (British Newspapers 1710-1965) (viewed 04/09/2013). Mrs Butler-Bowdon is John (6) Erdeswick's second wife, Monica Mary Petre (year of marriage: 1879).

998 Thorndon Hall in Essex was the seat of the Petre family along with Ingatestone Hall, Essex where the family resides today (cf. Ingatestone Hall, *Story of the House*; Thorndon Hall Management Company Ltd., *History of Thorndon Hall*).

999 Buckland Faringdon was part of Berkshire until 1974 when boundary changes relocated the village to Oxfordshire.

Welland, a 13-year old boy, who worked as Groom (Servant Domestic) lived together with them as a boarder.

A few years later a tragic and mysterious accident took place on the grounds of Pleasington Estate. The Manchester Courier and Lancashire General Advertiser reports on May 24, 1888 that "The body of a respectably-dressed young woman, 24 years of age, has been found floating in Pleasington Reservoir by Major Butler Bowden (*sic!*). In the young woman's pocket were found letters by which the body was identified as that of Bella Leigh, Short-street, Blackburn. She disappeared from home a month ago. She had been in a desponding state of mind."[1000]

Towards the end of the 19th century John (5) Peter Bruno Butler-Bowdon's son, John (6) Erdeswick Butler-Bowdon (1850-1929), still owned the manor and the **New** Hall at Pleasington.[1001] The **1891** census of England and Wales gives the following information on the household of Pleasington Hall: John (6) E Butler-Bowdon, aged 41, born in Rugeley, Staffordshire was Head of household, his occupation is listed as "Gentleman J.P. Lieut Col 3rd East Lanc Regt" and he is an employer to ten domestic servants. His (second) wife Monica, aged 30, born in Portland Pl (Place), London 35, has no occupation. The enumerator lists seven children: William, aged 11, Leonard, aged 10, Theresa, aged 8, Angela, aged 7, Monica, aged 5, Gladys, aged 4, and infant Ursula, aged 1 - all children born in Pleasington, Lancashire. Helen M G Shean, aged 27, single, of Seymour Street, London was the Governess (the word "School" added by a later hand) of the children at that time. Jane Mitchell, aged 51, single, from Enzie, Banffshire (Scotland); Andrew Botts, aged 27, single, from Nairn, Nairn(shire, Scotland); Martha Pearson, aged 33, single, from Kentchurch, Hereford(shire); Hanna L Davis, aged 29, single, from Swindon, Wiltshire; Rita Prichard, aged 18, single, from Coleford, Gloucestershire; Frances Arundell, aged 27, single, from Belgravia, London; Sophia Foster, aged 22, single, from Ilmington, Warwickshire; Maria Wilks, aged 21, single, from Westminster, London and Ellen O'Brien, aged 17, single, from Southbank, Yorkshire were working as Domestic Servants (without further specification) for the household. Later in life Theresa remembers her childhood fondly growing up in the circle of her brothers and sisters (who just like her all later became nuns save one sister) – "if not for the series of governesses employed to teach them", one of whom was French.[1002]

Other than the decennial census returns, the bulk body of source material which is directly accessible regarding basic information on the estate of

---

1000 http://www.findmypast.co.uk (British Newspapers 1710-1965) (viewed 04/09/2013).

1001 Kelliher, "Rediscovery of Margery Kempe", p. 261.

1002 Boscombe Catholics, *Past Pupils' Association*; http://www.angelfire.com/realm/gotha/Part15.htm (viewed 15/08/2013).

Pleasington Hall is not very substantial.[1003] Generally, the available sources convey very little in the way of information on the individual characters of the Bowdon family members. But for John (6) Erdeswick Butler-Bowdon however, we are lucky enough to find some more detailed information, although the circumstances are rather sad. In an obituary for his daughter Theresa Mary Sophie, who became a nun in a convent in Bournemouth (d. 28/03/1963) he is cited as "a born comedian and entertainer".[1004]

John (6) also acted as one of the trustees of Great Harwood Memorial Park, a recreational area with a war memorial, ca. 50 km north of Manchester between Blackburn and Burnley and not very far away from Pleasington Hall. His name is mentioned in the indenture made on July 25, 1921, he being the trustee in the contract.[1005] There must be an inherent connection between him and the park, but it was not possible to find out any more than this.

For some obscure reason Pleasington **Old** Hall could not be traced in the census returns of 1891 (maybe it stood empty at that time), but Pleasington Hall Lodge could however. The inhabitants of the latter are recorded as John Crawley, head of household, aged 30, born in Malvern, Worcestershire. His profession is given as Coachman Domestic Servant; a later hand added the word "Groom". He was married to Annie Crawley, aged 30 and born in Hereford. Together they had a daughter: Mary A, aged 2 and born in Pleasington

William Erdeswick Ignatius Butler-Bowdon remembers that the manuscript of "The Book of Margery Kempe" lay on a bookshelf in the library of Pleasington **Old** Hall (next to a missal of 1340 in the rite of York).[1006] This possibly is a small fallacy in allocation, as Hilton Kelliher also states *expressis verbis* that John (6) Erdeswick Butler-Bowdon was the owner of **New** (and not **Old**) Hall at Pleasington along with Southgate House at Clowne. This gives us some clue as to the time when the Butler-Bowdons moved out of their Lancashire property: "long before" the time of the discovery of the "The Book of Margery Kempe" which took place in 1934 (the house was vacated by John (6) Erdeswick Butler-Bowdon and his family around 1891, the reasons for this are unknown).[1007] In 1894 the family is attested to have lived in the south of England temporarily (see Chapter 14), before they moved north again to

1003 The Lancashire Archives in Preston, Lancashire apparently hold a lot of records, but it would have gone beyond the scope of this project to carry our further research here.

1004 Boscombe Catholics, *Past Pupils' Association.*

1005 Robinson, *Friends of Memorial Park Great Harwood.*

1006 Account published in "The Times" on 30/09/1934; cf. Kelliher, "Rediscovery of Margery Kempe", p. 260.

1007 Kelliher, "Rediscovery of Margery Kempe", p. 261; Pritt, *Pleasington New Hall.*

Derbyshire and took up residence at Southgate House[1008] around the year 1900.

The last inhabitant of Pleasington **New** Hall was Sir William Henry Hornby (also known as Harry Hornby)[1009], 1st Baronet and Member of Parliament in Blackburn with his family (as tenants).[1010] The presence of the Hornby family is attested from **1891** onwards[1011], and in the **1901** census of England and Wales. This list shows the picture-book household of late Victorian era, therefore worth mentioning in this context. William H Hornby, aged 59 and born in Blackburn, Lancashire and his wife Letitia G Hornby, aged 40, born in New Zealand were the householders. They had three children at that time: daughter Olive L, aged 11, son William R, aged 7, and infant daughter Margaret, aged 0, all born in Blackburn, Lancashire. On the day the enumerator visited by the Hornby family had two visitors: a German governess named A W Schlesinger, aged 34 and single, from Bavaria, Germany, and Nigel V Combe, aged 28 and single, a gentleman living on his own means from London. It is not inconceivable that the Hornbys invited Ms Schlesinger for a job interview as the otherwise substantial household staff was missing someone like a teacher or governess at that point in time, and Pleasington **New** Hall was apparently equipped with a school room and an appendant maid (see below). Isabella Porter, aged 40, single, born in Scotland, was the Housekeeper Domestic; Mary Bryan, aged 41, single, born in Newport, Shropshire, was Ladies Maid Domestic; Sarah A Picking, aged 28, single, born in Ashton-in-Makerfield, Lancashire, was Housemaid Domestic; Helen K Mackay, aged 24, single, born in Scotland, was Laundry Maid Domestic; and Isabella Mackenzie, aged 18, single, born in Scotland, was another Laundry Maid Domestic. Hester N MacDougall, aged 26, single, born in Scotland was Kitchen Maid Domestic; and Elizabeth Bradshaw, aged 21, single, born in Etwall, Derbyshire, was School Room Maid Domestic. Louisa M Blake, aged 23, single, born in Stroud, Surrey, and Sarah Sibley, aged 19, single, born in Morley, Yorkshire, were the Housemaids Domestic.; Florence V Henderson, aged 18, single, born in Chelsea, London, was Scullery Maid Domestic; Emily Ashley, aged 51, single, born in Icklingham, Suffolk, was the Monthly Nurse. The only male servant amongst all the female personnel was George W Haslam, aged 20, single, born in Bakewell, Derbyshire. He worked as Footman Domestic. Living under the same roof at Pleasington New Hall

---

[1008] Child, *Pleasington Priory*, p. 54.

[1009] Pritt, *Pleasington New Hall.*

[1010] Sir William Henry Hornby (29/08/1841-22/10/1928), English industrialist, Mayor of Blackburn (1876-1879, 1901-1902), Justice of the Peace and Deputy Lieutenant for Lancashire and MP for Blackburn (Conservative Party, 1886-1910); cf. Lundy, *Peerage* (Person Page 24361).

[1011] According to Kelly's Directory of Lancashire; cf. Kelliher, "Rediscovery of Margery Kempe", p. 263, footnote 10.

were two families, the one was the family of Luke James, aged 41, born in Hope under Dinmore, Herefordshire. He worked as Coachman Domestic. With him were his wife Elizabeth M James, aged 30, born in Moor, Worcestershire, and their four under-aged children (all born in Worlston, Chester). The other was the family of John T Eddleston, aged 27, born in Darwen, Lancashire and stated as Farmer. He lived there with his 29-year old wife and a male boarder named William Hampson, aged 30, single, born in Bolton, Lancashire, who worked as General Farm Labourer.

Pleasington **Old** Hall was inhabited in **1901** by the Alty family. Ormerod Carr Alty, aged 56, born in Clitheroe, Lancashire was Coal Merchant and Farmer. He was married to Agnes Alty, aged 57, born in Blackburn, Lancashire. Together with them in their household lived their son George, aged 29, also born in Blackburn, Lancashire, with his wife Harriet, aged 32, born in Ribchester, Lancashire, and their daughter Clara, aged 18, single and born in Blackburn, Lancashire. They must have been relatively well-off since they could afford to have a servant who worked as "General Worker on Farm": Thomas H Robinson, aged 21, single and born in Blackburn, Lancashire as well. The 1901 census additionally mentions buildings named Cottage at Pleasington Hall and Lodge House Pleasington Hall. Their occupants have not been traced in this research.

Pleasington **New** Hall was occupied by the Hornby family right up until 1914.[1012] The Manchester Courier and Lancashire General Advertiser reports on May 13, 1913: "Sir Harry Hornby may leave Blackburn for the South. There is a possibility that Sir Harry Hornby, Bart., may leave Blackburn, as his lease of Pleasington Hall and grounds, owned by Mr. Butler Bowden (*sic!*), expires next year, and it is understood the family have now under consideration a suggestion to remove to one of the Southern resorts. Should this occur it will mean a break in the family association with Blackburn, which has lasted for nearly a century and a half, and that Blackburn will lose its popular baronet and one of its first freemen."[1013]

In 1918 the house was - according to Kelly's Directory of Lancashire - unoccupied.[1014] It suffered the same fate as so many other manor houses in England: over the following eighteen years it stood empty and subsequently fell into disrepair and was finally demolished in 1932 by Blackburn Council. The estate which at that time comprised of 170 acres of land was purchased by Blackburn Corporation in 1931 to make way for a new cemetery and crematorium.[1015] Pleasington **Old** Hall still stands to this day.[1016]

1012 Pritt, *Pleasington New Hall.*

1013 http://www.findmypast.co.uk (British Newspapers 1710-1965) (viewed 04/09/2013).

1014 Kelliher, "Rediscovery of Margery Kempe", p. 261 and especially footnote 10.

1015 Pritt, *Pleasington New Hall.*

1016 Pritt, *Pleasington New Hall.*

Although the Butler-Bowdon's time at Pleasington is now in the distant past, the family has left their marks on the estate: in 1881 there was a "Butler-Bowden Avenue" which I gather is what today is called "Bowden Avenue" (as very short lane ca. 500m south of Pleasington **Old** Hall). Also I cannot leave out the local pub "Butler's Arms" which perhaps owes its name to the Butler family.

What caused me quite a headache is that the ten-yearly censuses mention another bigger building at Pleasington named "Pleasington Lodge". A house with this name survives until this day in Pleasington. It was erected around 1870 as a Victorian villa in Palladian style as a square single-floor house in the centre of the village, ca. 1 km south of Pleasington **Old** Hall.[1017] I cannot say for sure whether this house was part of Pleasington Hall Estate and therefore belonged to the property of the Butler-Bowdons, but the name of the house hints to that. They could have let it to independent families on lease. According to the census, it was inhabited by the Stott family and their servants in 1871. In 1881 it was still occupied by the Stott family and their household. The censuses state James Stott as a Cotton Manufacturer. Ten years later, in 1891, Pleasington Lodge was home to the family of Frederick Thomas Marwood and his wife Mary Agnes and their three children and domestic staff. The Marwood family were cork merchants.[1018] Confusion is caused by the fact that there is another cluster of buildings named "Pleasington Lodge and Gateway to Woodfold Park" at Billinge End Road in Pleasington, ca. 1.5 km north of Pleasington Old Hall. According to English Heritage these lodgings were built in ca. 1800, so they do not fit with regard to the dates.[1019]

22. Barlborough House, Barlborough

Barlborough is described in Pigot and Co.s National Commercial Directory as "Nothing calculated to arrest the attention of the tourist, or man of business is connected with this village.", which does the pretty village severe injustice. The directory does at least find friendly words for the most notable building: "The hall of Barlborough, about a mile hence, is pleasantly situated."[1020] And right inside the village another gem is hidden: Barlborough House, property of the Butler-Bowdon family for many years.

Before Barlborough House, a late Georgian building formerly known as Barlborough Gates, was purchased by the Bowdon family (namely John (6)

1017 http://www.mortimers-property.co.uk/property/residential-sales/pleasington-lane-pleasington-blackburn-62205_1396.html (viewed 07/09/2013).

1018 More about the Marwood family: Maclaren, *Maclarens, Birtwistles and Many Other Families*; Kirby, *Pleasington Lodge*.

1019 English Heritage, *Pleasington Lodge*.

1020 Pigot & Co.s *1828-29*, p. 112.

Erdeswick Butler-Bowdon, brother of Lancelot George Butler-Bowdon[1021]). It was previously owned by a Quaker family in the 17th century, namely Samuel Barker and his wife Elizabeth (née Shaw). Samuel's granddaughter Mary Barker married John (2) Bowdon of Beighton Fields Priory (see Chapter 22.1), hence the Bowdon family connection to the house.[1022]

According to the census of England and Wales in **1891** Southgate House was rented out to the Fowler family; the same census (**1891**) lists John (6) Erdeswick Butler-Bowdon and his family living in Pleasington Hall, Lancashire (see Chapter 21). Barlborough House was inhabited by John's brother Lancelot George B Bowdon, aged 40, born in 1851 in Pleasington Hall, Lancashire.[1023] His occupation is stated with "P C O Derby Mgs Batt in Staff Management".[1024] He is listed as "employer" and was married to Ellen C M Bowdon (née Clifton Wykeham (?) Lelgarde Rawdon-Hastings), aged 34, born in Keith, Aberdeenshire. Together they had one son: John Lancelot Bowdon, aged 7, born in London.[1025] Little John evidently had his own teacher: Margaret H(elen) Hughes, aged 30, born in Preston, Lancashire is listed as School Governess. Margaret Helen Hughes must have played an important role in the Butler-Bowdon family. An inscription dedicated to her is engraved on the left hand side of Lancelot George B Butler-Bowdon's gravestone on Spinkhill Cemetery.[1026] Ms Hughes' closeness to the Butler-Bowdon family bears a certain semblance to Nanny Hawkins of Evelyn Waugh's "Brideshead Revisited", the governess to the four Marchmain children who stayed at Brideshead after her retirement. A teacher or governess' predominant role within a family of nobility is also attested for the Grimshaw family of

---

1021 According to the recollections of Teresa Staples. Information by kind courtesy of Father Peter D McGuire in a private E-Mail correspondence with the author on May 18, 2014.

1022 Barlborough Heritage and Research Centre, *Interesting Facts*.

1023 British Listed Buildings, *Barlborough House, Barlborough*.

1024 The job description is inexplicable and possibly not related to military ranks and titles: "The only part of this abbreviated census entry that looks vaguely military is the 'Mgs Batt' bit. Up to and including the First World War they used to talk about Machine Gun Batteries but since this is from 1891 and before the British Army's adoption of the Maxim Machine Gun in 1895 I do not think that this is relevant (and it doesn't really fit from the context either). I do not think there is any reason to believe that P C O Derby has any military connection." Information disclosed by Alastair Massie of the National Army Museum (London) by E-mail on March 28, 2013. In modern times PCO is an abbreviation for Public Carriage Office, but also for Primary Components Operations (for example at Rolls Royce Derby). The abbreviation "Mgs Batt" remains unclear.

1025 Lundy, *Peerage* (Person Page 3446).

1026 Information according to Graham Duckmanton who visited the cemetery on August 23, 2013 (disclosed in a personal E-mail correspondence between Mr Duckmanton and the author on August 26, 2013). Gravestone viewed by the author on a by personal visit to Spinkhill Cemetery on September 21, 2013.

Errwood Hall near Buxton in the Peak District.[1027] Further members of the Butler-Bowdon household in 1891 were Theresa Webster aged 24, born in St. Helens, Lancashire was the Cook, Selina Barbridge, aged 22, born in Northampton was the Barlborough Houses Parlourmaid and Agnes D Avil, aged 24, born in Shropshire was the Housemaid.

At the end of the 19th and the beginning of the 20th century, Lancelot George B Butler-Bowdon lived at Barlborough House together with his wife Ella Cicely. The house remained in Bowdon hands by inheritance until its last inhabitant, John (7) Lancelot Wykeham Butler-Bowdon, 25th and last Lord Grey de Ruthyn, son of Lancelot George B Butler-Bowdon and Ella C M Bowdon, a very well-liked member of Barlborough village community, died in 1963 without issue. Thus this collateral line of the Butler-Bowdons became extinct and the title of nobility fell abeyant.[1028] John (7) Lancelot Butler-Bowdon was often called "Bibby" and according to Mona Ives, he was a "real gentleman".[1029] His outstanding role in the community of Barlborough is underlined very early in his life. For his first birthday on October 25, 1884 he (or in this case his parents) received a scrapbook, made by the children of Mount St. Mary's School in Spinkhill written in fanciful letters and elaborate cursive handwriting (Figure 46)[1030]: "Presented to John Lancelot Wykeham Butler-Bowdon / The Children of Spink Hill School; present their compliments to John Lancelot Wykeham Butler Bowdon, wishing him a very happy birthday and many happy returns. They hope he will accept their little present and live among them many many years. That he will take as much interest in their school as his Parents and Godmother do. With best wishes for

---

1027 Information by Alan Taylor during a personal meeting on September 20, 2013 in Chapel-en-le-Frith. According to the website of Merilyn Tarplees and Dorinda Boags (Tarplees, Boag, *Grimshaw's Origin and History*) there was a private school belonging to Errwood Hall which was attended by about 30 local children. Their teacher was a member of Spanish nobility named Dolores de Bergrin, who died on a visit to Lourdes. Because of the strong Roman Catholic faith of the family they built a shrine to her memory in 1889 on the moor below Foxlow Edge. The Grimshawes apparently met "Miss Dolores" during their world travels in the family yacht. She returned to England with the Grimshawes and lived out her life there.

1028 Lundy, *Peerage* (Person Page 3446): he succeeded to the title of 25th Lord Grey, of Ruthyn in 1940, when the barony was called out of abeyance. On his death, his barony fell into abeyance between the 22nd Baroness's sisters; see also http://www.derbyshireheritage.co.uk/Menu/Townsandvillages/Barlborough.php (viewed 27/03/2013).

1029 Reported by Mona Ives during an interview given to the author on September 21, 2013 in Barlborough.

1030 This book was on display during an exhibition on the Butler-Bowdon family at Barlborough Heritage and Research Centre in September 2013. Apart from the personal dedication on the frontispiece, it also contains cuttings from magazines and books and little colourful collector's ornaments.

his happiness /They remain very respectfully / The Children of St. Mary's School / October 25th 1884".[1031]

Whilst being the 25th baron of Britain's 7th oldest barony since 1940 and bearer of the Golden Spurs, John (7) Lancelot Butler-Bowdon lived under modest conditions. He could not afford to attend the coronation of the Queen in London in 1953 and was subsequently dubbed by the newspapers "the Poorest Peer" of England. Sylvia Linacre remembers him as an "eccentric gentleman who lived in reduced circumstances. He was very kind and was in great affection by the people in the village. (...) He was a familiar sight in the village in his navy blue suit, shiny brown boots and bowler hat, greeting everyone he saw courteously." Nonetheless, he was always generous towards his fellow people in his home village. At Barlborough Fair he paid the first ride for the children of the village[1032] and bought them sweets in the local shop when he was there[1033]. On May 20, 1974 a portrait of Lord Grey de Ruthyn was published in a book of essays written by Sir Osbert Sitwell.[1034] Here, the author describes more quirky details of the life of Barlborough's most eccentric inhabitant who rarely left the village, and when did so only reluctantly. At the time of the coronation not only could he afford a trip to London, but he also turned down a fund opened by the Barlborough bus company to pay his expenses for the journey and decided to watch the ceremony on a neighbour's TV set.[1035] John (7) Lancelot Butler-Bowdon received things in very British manner. Tradition has it, that when meeting up as chairman of Renishaw magistrates with his fellow magistrates his reaction to the bombings at the time of the Sheffield blitz was that of cool understatement: "Good morning. I don't know what you all felt last night, but I was absolutely terrified - and I can tell you so were my geese. They gave the alarum (*sic!*); such intelligent birds."[1036] His flock of geese meant a lot to him.

[1031] There is every likelihood that John (7) Lancelot Butler-Bowdon' godmother was the cousin of Ella Cicely Butler-Bowdon, Lady Flora Abney-Hastings, the Duchess of Norfolk and first wife of Henry Fitzalan-Howard, the 15th Duke of Norfolk (1847-1917); cf. Lundy, *Peerage* (Person Page 1123) (see Chapter 11.1). Tony Bak supplied this information in a personal E-Mail correspondence on October 23, 2013, and added that the Duke of Norfolk donated the clock on top of the old coach house at Barlborough House. He also informed me that his housekeeper's daughter holds quite a few personal artefacts and jewellery originally belonging to John (7) Lancelot Butler-Bowdon and his mother.

[1032] Reported by Mona Ives during an interview given to the author on September 21, 2013 in Barlborough.

[1033] Linacre, *How it was*, p. 64.

[1034] Sitwell, Osbert, *Queen Mary and Others*, London 1974. Review by Peter Harvey in Sheffield Morning Telegraph on May 20, 1974; newspaper article by kind courtesy of Tony Bak of Barlborough Heritage and Research Centre on September 21, 2013.

[1035] Peter Harvey in Sheffield Morning Telegraph on May 20, 1974.

[1036] Peter Harvey in Sheffield Morning Telegraph on May 20, 1974.

He had one goose named after himself, Goosey Grey, and another one was christened Rosa and obviously a pet. It upset him a lot when Rosa was stolen one Christmas.[1037] The geese and also his beloved dogs prevented him from leaving Barlborough for longer periods of time; the latter animals were the chief reason why he did not take his seat in the House of Lords. As a fervent defender of animal's rights, he made it into the German press as president of the League against Cruel Sports. The weekly magazine "Der Spiegel" reports in 1959 on the annual meeting of the League: "Lord Grey de Ruthyn, 75, Mitglied des britischen Oberhauses und Präsident der Liga gegen grausame Sportarten, warf auf der Jahresversammlung seiner Liga dem britischen Königspaar vor, einen außergewöhnlichen Gefallen am blutigen Sport - gemeint ist die Jagd - zu haben. Besonders dem als Nimrod bekannten Prinzgemahl müsse es übelgenommen werden, so führte Lord Grey aus, dass er seinen Sohn Charles, 10, den Prinzen von Wales, zum blutigen Sport und nicht im Sinne humanitärer Ideale erziehe. Die Versammlung beschloss unter großem Applaus, eine entsprechende Protestschrift an den Buckingham-Palast abzusenden."[1038] His political engagement went even further: he also served as chairman of Barlborough parish council for a number of years, as well as for the rural district council in the 1930s.[1039]

He had a shrewd sense of humour ("I like listening to one of those Beethoven sympathies.") and had a carrying and booming voice, quite sure of himself when speaking. "(...) once, when he had opened a garden fete for charity at Barlborough, after his speech was over, he asked one of the committee whether his speech had been audible. He received the enthusiastic reply, "Yes, they loved every word of it, and so they did at Clowne - some two miles away."" He was a fervent philanthropist and people could come to him at all hours with their concerns, even a burglar who one night broke into Barlborough House was not spared Lancelot Butler-Bowdon's boundless kindness.[1040] His further eccentricities included, when travelling by bus, offering conductor and driver cigarettes even though he himself did not smoke. His typewriter had two coloured ribbons, one red and one blue which enabled him to type capital letters in red.[1041] John (7) Lancelot Butler-Bowdon

---

1037 Linacre, *How it was*, p. 64.

1038 "Lord Grey de Ruthyn, 75, member of the House of Lords and president of the League against Cruel Sports, accused the British royal couple at the annual meeting of his league of taking an extraordinary pleasure in the bloodthirsty sport - by which he means the hunt. The prince consort in particular, also known as „Nimrod", Lord Grey goes on to explain, has to be resented for the fact that he educates his son Charles, 10, on the bloodthirsty sport and not in the sense of humanitarian ideals. To great applause the assembly decided to send a letter of protest to Buckingham Palace."; cf. Der Spiegel, *Lord Grey de Ruthyn* (issue 14/1959).

1039 Riden, *History of the County of Derby III*, p. 43 and footnotes 17 and 18.

1040 Peter Harvey in Sheffield Morning Telegraph on May 20, 1974.

1041 Linacre, *How it was*, p. 64.

was either a superstitious man, or indeed a psychic. He believed that Barlborough House was haunted and often told that his mother had several times seen a ghost whose chief object was apparently to forewarn the death of members of the family. Lancelot's mother claims to have seen the ghost the night his father died suddenly. Lancelot also often saw, strange apparitions such as floating figures.[1042]

Another detail of Mr Butler-Bowdon's eccentricity can be found in the Electoral Rolls, where from ca. 1921 until 1940 he becomes "John L W Grey de Ruthyn (Baron, Barlborough House)" he is listed as "John Lancelot Bowdon-Butler"! Since this word constellation does not appear only once but continually over the years I presume that this was not some kind of singular erroneous recording, but that there was some intent behind this. The reasons for this can only be speculated. The Electoral Rolls tell us that in addition to this from ca. 1930 on John (7) Lancelot Butler-Bowdon shared Barlborough House with Adelaide Buxton who was his housekeeper (her name is attested on a sample basis until 1949).[1043]

To sum up, Sir Osbert Sitwell describes John (7) Lancelot Butler-Bowdon as "a fascinating human being to explore, a man of warm and kindly nature, of a simple character, albeit with many fantastic traits and convolutions enough to make him of continual interest."[1044]

After John (7) Lancelot Butler-Bowdon's demise in 1963 Barlborough House was purchased by a Mr and Mrs Smith.[1045] They demolished the annexe housing the servant's quarters. Today Mrs Smith lives in the old Coach House.[1046]

Today the exterior of the house (a Grade II listed building) shows components from three centuries: 17th, mid 18th and mid 19th. It is built of squared sandstone, has two storeys, five symmetrical bay windows on the first floor and two canted bay windows flanking the central doorway on the ground floor. The roof is steep and tiled with Welsh slate. The interior is mostly 18th century (e.g. a closed string staircase with turned balusters, an

---

[1042] Peter Harvey in Sheffield Morning Telegraph on May 20, 1974.

[1043] So was Mary Crooks, whose granddaughter possesses many pieces of the Bowdon family jewellery and personal belongings of Lord Grey de Ruthyn (according Tony Bak in a personal E-mail correspondence with the author on October 12, 2013).

[1044] All information following the review by Peter Harvey in Sheffield Morning Telegraph on May 20, 1974.

[1045] A "Catalogue of Sale by Auction of the Contents of the House" dated December 11, 1963 was on display during an exhibition on the Butler-Bowdon family at Barlborough Heritage and Research Centre in September 2013 ("By order of the Executors of the Late Right Honourable the 25th Lord Grey de Ruthyn (…) Henry Spencer & Sons, Auctioneers/Worksop, Retford, Sheffield, Scunthorpe, Brigg, Winterton".

[1046] Information disclosed by Tony Bak of Barlborough Heritage and Research Centre in a private E-mail correspondence with the author on July 9, 2013.

eared chimneypiece with Hopton Wood stone and relief carving) but the entrance hall has 16th century panelling.[1047]

Apart from the corner chimney with the family motto (see Chapter 10 and figure 13), another open-hearth fireplace in Barlborough House is decorated with six coats of arms, five in a row on the chimney breast, and one attached to the centre of the stepped overmantel (that one being the crest of the Butler-Bowdon family, and containing unknown elements, see figure 14).[1048] Only one of these five coats of arms match with those on the inscription plaque on the wall of the enclosure of Beighton Fields Priory (see Chapter 18): the inscription plaque shows one crest with dotted chevrons, this pattern is also depicted on one of the six coats of arms. Tony Bak of Barlborough Heritage and Research Centre did some research on these emblems but could not determine all elements.[1049] However, one of the heraldic devices (three red stars on a white diagonal stripe on a black background) belong to the Clifton family who actually descended from the Anglo-Saxon king Alfred the Great (849-899).[1050]

22.1. The Will of Mary Bowdon of Barlborough

A handwritten document written in Secretary Hand or Court Hand has been preserved and is currently kept at the National Archives in Kew.[1051] The document is the last will and testament of Mary Bowdon of Barlborough, widow of John (2) Bowdon, late of Beighton Fields, and is dated 22/08/1782, annexed with a codicil likewise dated 22/08/1782, and proved in London on 15/03/1785. This text provides some revealing insights into this branch of the Bowdon family.[1052]

In the Name of God Amen

[1047] Description according to British Listed Buildings, *Barlborough House, Barlborough*; English Heritage, *Barlborough House*.

[1048] Cf. photo by kind courtesy of Tony Bak of Barlborough Heritage and Research Centre.

[1049] Result of a personal conversation in Barlborough on April 20, 2013.

[1050] Information disclosed in a private E-mail correspondence between Tony Bak and the author on September 2, 2013.

[1051] The National Archives London, *Ref. No. PROB 11/1127/218*. All wills that are kept at the National Archives in Kew are registered copy wills. This means they are the copies of the original probates written into volumes by clerks at the church courts. The National Archives state on their Website that "until 12 January 1858 all wills had to be proved by the church and other courts."; cf. The National Archives, *Wills 1384-1858*.

[1052] A comprehensive analysis of the role of women in regard to the country house and how they exerted influence on economic as well as domestic matters is provided by Arnold, Dana, "5 Defining Femininity: Women and the Country House", in: Arnold, *Georgian Country House*, p. 79ff.

I Mary Bowdon of Barlbrough (*sic!*) in the County of Derby Widow and Relict of John Bowdon late of Beighton Fields in the said County Gentleman deceased being of sound and disposing mind memory and understanding do make public and declare this my last will and testament in manner following, that is to say first it is my will and desire and I do direct that all my Household Goods Furniture Implements of Household and Pictures which shall be in my Mansion House at Barlbrough (*sic!*) wherein I now dwell at the time of my decease my plate China and Linen excepted shall be considered as Heir Looms and be constantly used and enjoyed together with my said Spouse by such person and persons as shall be intithed to the possession thereof under this my will and I give and devise my said = = Mansion House and the furniture therein with all the Lands Tenements and Hereditaments thereunto belonging

and all other my Lands Tenements Hereditaments = and real Estate within the parish of Barlbrough (*sic!*) = = aforesaid to my eldest Son George Bowdon and his Assigns for his Life without Impairment or waste and I do earnestly request and desire my said Son George Bowdon to make his Mansion House the place of his Chief Residence during his Life and from and after the determination of that Estate I give and devise the same to my son in Law John Bowdon of Beighton Fields aforesaid Gentleman and his Heirs during the Life of my said Son George Bowdon In Trust to preserve the Contingent Remainders herein after limited from being defeated or destroyed and for that purpose to make Entries or bring actions as the Case shall require yet nevertheless to permit and suffer my said Son George Bowdon and his Assigns During his Life to receive and take the Houses Funds (?) and Profits thereof to and for his and their own use and benefit and from and after the decease of my said Son George Bowdon I give and devise the same to my Grandson George Bowdon Eldest son of my said Son George Bowdon and his Assigns for his Life without Impairment or Waste and from and after the determination of that Estate I give the same unto my said Son in Law John Bowdon and his Heirs during the Life of my said Grandson In Trust to preserve the Contingent Remainders and from and after the decease of my said Grandson George Bowdon I give the same to the first son of his Body lawfully to be begotten and the Heirs Male of the Body of such first Son lawfully Issuing and in default of such issue to the second third fourth fifth and all and every other Son and Sons of the Body of my said Grandson George Bowdon lawfully to be begotten severally and successively in Tail Male and for default of = such Issue I give and devise the same to my = = = Grandson John Bowdon second Son of my said Son George Bowdon and his Assigns for his life without = = = = Impairment or Waste Remainder to my said Son in Law John Bowdon and his Heirs during the Life of my said Grandson John Bowdon In Trust to preserve the Contingent Remainder(s) <*unreadable*> to the first Son of the Body of my said Grandson John Bowdon lawfully to be begotten and the Heirs Male of the Body of such first Son lawfully Issuing Remainder to the second third fourth fifth and all and every other: the Son and Sons of the Body of my said Grandson lawfully to be begotten severally and successively in Tail Male and for default of such Issue I give and devise the same to my Grandson Joseph Bowdon third Son of my said Son George Bowdon and his Assigns for

his Life without Impairment or Waste Remainder to my said Son in Law John Bowdon and his Heirs during the Life of my Grandson Joseph Bowdon In trust to preserve the Contingent Remainders; = Remainder to the First Son of the Body of my said Grandson Joseph Bowdon lawfully to be begotten and the Heirs Male of the Body of such first Son lawfully Issuing Remainder to the second third fourth fifth and all and every other the Son and Sons of the Body of my said Grandson Joseph Bowdon lawfully to be begotten severally and successively in Tail Male = and for default of such Issue I give and devise the same unto the fourth fifth sixth and all and every other the Son and Sons of the Body of my said Son George Bowdon lawfully begotten or to be begotten severally and successively in Tail Male and for default of such Issue I give and devise the same to my second Son James Bowdon his Heirs and Assigns for ever and I give unto my said Son George Bowdon and all and every other person or persons who shall be Tenants for Life of my said Messuages Lands and Hereditaments at Barlbrough (*sic!*) aforesaid under this my Will full power to Grant Leases thereof or of any part thereby Except of my said Mansion House with the appurtenances from time to time for any term or number of years not exceeding twenty one years to commence in possession and not in(xx)eversion and so as the best and most improved yearly Rents be thereby reserved Also I give and devise all and every my Messuages Lands Tenements and Hereditaments whatsoever as well Freehold as Leasehold situated and being in the County of Warwick Except the Moiety of the Estate there which I have herein after otherwise disposed of And also my Moiety or half-part of the Farm and Lands in the Parish of Sheffield and said county of York in the possession of Amos Meymott and also of my Farm and Lands at Sutton in Ashford in the County of Nottingham unto my said Son George Bowdon his Heirs Executors = = = Administrators and Assigns for over subject and - chargeable with the payment of one hundred Pounds to his Daughter Ann Bowdon on her attainment of the age of twenty one years with Interest for the same in the mean time after the rate of four Pounds per centum per annum and Subject and chargeable also as herein after is mentioned Also I give and devise to my said Son James Bowdon all my Messuages Lands Tenements and Hereditaments as well Freehold as Leasehold situate lying and being in the Parishes of Sheffield and Handsworth in the said County of York and at Bolo Hill in the Parish of Eckington in the said County of Derby Except the

Moiety of the Farm and the Lands in the Parish of Sheffield which I have herein before devised to my said Son George Bowdon and also my Copyhold Estates within the Manor of Bolsover in the County of Derby and also all my

Messuages Lands Tenements and Hereditaments situated and being at Edale in the Parish of Castleton in the said County of Derby now or late in the respective possessions of John T(?)imms, Robert Howe and John Denham And also all that my undivided Moiety or half part of the Messuage Farm and Lands situated and being at Burton near Barnsley in the said county of York called Ganberhall Farm now or late in the possession of Mr. Thorpe To hold the same to my said Son James Bowdon, his Heirs Executors = administrators and Assigns for over subject nevertheless to and charged with the payment of five hundred Pounds which I hereby direct shall be applied by my = = Executors towards the discharge of my debts and legacies and subject also as herein after is mentioned And I give and devise all that my Messuage Farm Lands and Hereditaments at Edale Head in the parish of Castleton aforesaid which I purchased of my said Son George Bowdon to my Daughter Ann Bowdon her Heirs and Assigns for over on Condition that the Purchases the Legacies of three hundred Pounds and nine hundred Pounds given to her by the Will of my said late Husband deceased but in case my said Daughter Ann shall prefer the said Legacies to the said Estate and shall signify the same in writing under her Hand to my said Son James Bowdon within six months after my decease = Then I give - and devise - - - the same Estate unto my said Son James Bowdon his Heirs and Assigns for over he or they paying unto my said Daughter Ann the said Sums of three hundred Pounds and nine hundred Pounds and also the further Sum of forty Pounds within twelve - - - - - - - - months next after my decease with Interest for the same respective Sums after the Rate of four Pounds per centum per annum from the time of my decease until the time of payment and in that case I do - hereby charge all my said Estates herein before - given to my said Son James Bowdon with the payment of the said Sums making together the Sum of one thousand two hundred and forty Pounds and the Interest thereof accordingly also I give and devise to my Grand Daughter Mary Bowdon Daughter of my said Son George Bowdon and her Heirs all that my Moiety or half part of the Messuage Farm and Lands situate at Preston Baggott (*sic!*) in the said County of Warwick and I also give unto my said

Grand Daughter Mary Bowdon my Gold Watch and my square Diamond Ring and I give unto my said Grand Daughter Ann Bowdon my Purple Diamond Ring and whereas my said Son in Law John Bowdon is indebed (?) to me for principal Money upon Bond in the Sum of four hundred and twenty Pounds = besides a considerable Arrear of Interest for the = same and also in the Sum of ninety Pounds forthwith (?) paid for his use on account of a Colliery in Yorkshire And whereas my said late Husband was Indebted to my said Son in Law John Bowdon in a considerable Sum of Money for his share of a certain Fire Engine at – - Rotherham Mew I do hereby direct that my Executors shall on Receipt of the said ninety Pounds Release and Discharge the said John Bowdon his Heirs = = Executors and administrators from the Payment of the said Bond Debt and Interest and I do direct my Executors to control and deliver up the said Bond to my said Son in Law John Bowdon his Heirs Executors or Administrators as soon as conveniently may be after my decease But I do declare that the same shall be in Discharge of all Money due and owing to him on account of the said Fire Engine I also give unto my Grand Children Richard Butler, Mary Butler and Ann Butler the Sum of fifty Pounds each to be paid to their Mother[1053] and for their use within twelve Months after my decease to my Servant Elizabeth Ferguson the Sum of three Guineas and to my Servant John Godwin the Sum of ten Pounds to be paid to them respectively within twelve months next after my decease I give the sum of ten Pounds to the Poor of the Parish of Barlbrough (*sic!*) aforesaid to be distributed among them at the Discretion of my Executors within one Month after my decease. Also I give to my said Sons George Bowdon and James Bowdon all my Silver Plate and China to be divided equally between them share and share alike and all the rest of my Jewells (*sic!*) Trinkitts (*sic!*) Cloaths (*sic!*) and wearing apparel I give to my Daughter Ann Bowdon and I give my Household and Table Linen to my said Sons and Daughter George James and Ann Bowdon equally divided between or amongst them share and share alike and all the rest residue and remainder of my Real and Personal Estates of what nature or kind soever (?) and wheresoever I give devise and bequeath unto my said Sons George Bowdon and James Bowdon their Heirs Executors and administrators they paying satisfying and Discharging all my just Debts Financial Expenses and the several Legacies - herein by me given and bequeathed provided always and I do declare that in case the said Sum of five hundred Pounds herein before directed to be applied

by my Executors towards the discharge of my Debts and Legacies and the residue of my said Real and Personal Estate shall not sufficient to pay satisfy and discharge my said debts, funeral Expenses and Legacies then I will that such deficiency - shall be paid and made good by my said Sons George Bowdon and James Bowdon in equal shares and proportions and I do accordingly charge and make chargeable my said Estates in Warwickshire devised to my said Son George Bowdon with one Moiety of such deficiency and my said several Estates in the Parishes of Sheffield, Handsworth and Eckington devised to my said Son James Bowdon with the - other Moiety thereof. And lastly I do hereby nominate constitute and appoint my said Sons George Bowdon and James Bowdon joint Executors of this my last Will and Testament and hereby - revoking all former Wills declare this to be my last Will and Testament and I desire my friend Sir Anthony Sax of Chesterfield with aid and assist my said Executors in the Execution of this my Will and see that the same be duly performed and I give unto him the said Anthony Sax the Sum of fifty Guineas for his trouble therein and to buy him a piece of Plate

[1053] This must be Charlotte Butler, née Bowdon. It remains open to speculation why she does not partake from the general legacy and why she does not even gets mentioned with her full name.

and a Ring In Witness whereof I the said Mary Bowdon have to this my last Will and Testament to contained in four sheets of paper in my hand to the first three sheets and my hand and seal to the last sheet thereof this - - - twenty second day of August in the twenty = second year of the Reign of our Sovereign Lord George the Third by the Grace of God Kind of Great Britain and so forth and in the year of our Lord one thousand seven hundred and eighty two *Mary Bowdon* Signed sealed published and declared by the above named Testatrix Mary Bowdon as and for her last Will and Testament in the presence of us who at her earnest (?) and in her presence and on the presence of each other have subscribed our Names as Witnesses of the one Execution thereof, *Wm. Paitson, Elizabeth Hall, Mary Bottom*

This is a Codicil to the last will and = = = Testament of me *Mary Bowdon* of Barlbrough (*sic!*) = = Widow and Relict of John Bowdon laid (*sic!*) of Beighton Fields in the said country Gentleman I give and = devise unto my son George Bowdon all my share and Interest in the Copper Work at Brimington in the said county of Derby. To hold to him his Heirs and Assigns for ever I give to my Sister Elizabeth

Johnson one Amenity of five Pounds for her Life to be paid by equal half yearly payments at Lady Day and Michaelmas Day in every = year to be paid her by my said Son George Bowdon out of and I do hereby charge the Estates devised to him by my said Will with the payment thereof - - accordingly and I also give unto my said sister one other amenity of five pounds for her Life to be = paid her in the same manner and at the same times as the other amenity abovementioned by my Son James Bowdon and I do hereby charge the Estates devised to him by my said Will with the payment thereof and do give unto my said sister power of distress and Entry in case of non payment of the said Amenities I give unto my Daughter Ann Bowdon twenty Ponds exclusive of what I have given = her by my Will for that that purpose of buying for Mourning And I do thereby revoke the Legacy of three Guineas given to my Servant Elizabeth Ferguson and do only give to my Servant John Goodwin a Legacy of five Guineas instead of the Legacy of ten Pounds given to him by my said Will and I do hereby ratify and confirm my said Will in all other aspects as witnesses my hand and seal the twenty second day of August one thousand seven hundred and eighty two *Mary Bowdon*. This writing was signed sealed published and declared by the said Mary Bowdon as and for a Codicil to her Last Will and testament after she has executed the said Will and Testament in the presence of = *Wm. Paitson, Elizabeth Hall, Mary Bottom.*

I give for Prayers 10L.0.- To be given to Lady Abbis (= Abbess?) = at Gant (?) for prayers 5. 5.– I give five Pounds to the poor where ye think proper 5-0-0 In my Will I have left to my Sister Betty Johnson ten Pounds a year for her Life But if she insists of that left by Miss An(n)e (?) Bowdon I only give five for Life I would not have my Son Mr George Bowdon to meddle with the Estate in Oxcroft which I have given to my Son Mr James Bowdon I wish to be buried privately only my own Servant to attend – *Mary Bowdon.*

This Will was proved at London with two Codicils the fifteenth Day of March in the year of our Lord one thousand seven hundred and eighty five before the Right - Worshipful Peter Calvert Doctor of Law Master Keeper or Commissary of the Prerogative Court of Canterbury lawfully constituted by the oaths of George Bowdon and James Bowdon the Sons of the Deceased and Executors which in the said Will to whom - - Administration of all and singular the Goods.

Chattels and Credits of the Deceased was = = = granted their having been first sworn by = = commission Duly to administer. <*Ligature*>

The testament of Mary Bowdon provides us with a substantial amount of information. Firstly, she gives detailed instruction as to the distribution of her estate including her mansion and all property belonging to her in Barlborough, making sure that everything was to remain in the family for generations to come, which included Joseph Bowdon[1054] and the rest of her numerous grandsons as well as her son-in-law John Bowdon. Secondly, the will reveals the extent of this branch of the Bowdon family's wealth accumulated during the mid 18th century through estates and properties dotted all over Derbyshire, Yorkshire, Nottinghamshire and Warwickshire. In addition there were substantial amounts of money to be inherited as well as interest and shares in raw materials (copper).

Aside the house in Barlborough, Mary bequeathed family land and estates in Warwickshire and in the parish of Sheffield, as well as lands in Nottinghamshire along with the interest she earned and shares in a copper work in Derbyshire to her first-born son George (8), who appears to have lived in Wootten Wawen, Warwickshire at the time of his mother's demise.[1055] Her two granddaughters, the daughters of George (8), Ann and Mary, are also included: Ann was to receive money and Mary both the estate and land in Warwickshire. Ann was also to inherit a diamond ring; Mary was to receive her grandmother's golden watch and a diamond ring.

1054 Joseph Bowdon took holy orders and became a clergyman, He became a "wealthy gentleman and a zealous ecclesiastic", cf. Dolman Stapleton, *Catholic missions in Oxfordshire,* chapter on Radford Chapel/correspondence between a Mr Charles Browne-Mostyn and a Mr Heffernan dated November 23, 1839.

1055 Dolman Stapleton, *Catholic missions in Oxfordshire.* According to a valuation drawn up in a sales offer in 1787, the estate mentioned in the will appear to be manor house and priory of Wootten Waven. The other estate mentioned in Warwickshire is Preston Bagot. George (8) Bowdon sold Wootten Waven for 21,000 pounds in 1787. He bought the estate of Towersey, Buckinghamshire in 1788 and held court lee there until 1791 (the year of his death), but moved to live in Radford/Oxfordshire with his wife Elizabeth Clements/Tufton and their five children. Towersey remained in the family until sold by George Bowdon's great grandson.

Mary's second son James, who seemingly resided in Staveley, was to inherit the properties in Derbyshire and Yorkshire, with the exception of specific shares (moieties) going to his brother George.

It is striking that Mary's daughter Charlotte (who married Richard Butler of Pleasington Hall) is not once named or is mentioned in any way in the testament, whereas the grandchildren Richard (John Francis), Mary Anne and Ann Butler were all to receive the sum of 50 pounds each. By contrast, Mary's other daughter, Ann, was to receive payments of 1,220 pounds, or optionally land in Derbyshire. Cloths and garments were also bequeathed to her, plus extra 20 pounds in order to buy a mourning outfit. Mary also intended Ann to inherit her jewellery and clothes.

Valuable household goods and jewellery were to be divided equally between Mary's three children. Neither was Mary's sister Elizabeth overlooked. Some money was also intended for the poor of the parish of Barlborough and for the church.

A serious matter is the true identity of Mary's son-in-law John Bowdon. A son-in-law with an identical surname and in the constellation as cited by Mary is naturally cause for suspicion. As there was no other "suitable" John Bowdon in that particular time, we seemingly have to assume that Ann was married to her elder half-brother John (3) Bowdon of Beighton Fields, the son of John (2) Bowdon and his first wife Mary Barker. In all probability this was a strategic union: to ensure that the family's wealth stayed in the family, and could therefore be seen as marriage of convenience ("marrying for England"). It seems that he and Ann did not have any children. Alas, I have no further source to support this theory. Throughout the available literature John (3) is always stated as married to Alice Johnson (the sister of Mary and his father's third wife) with whom he only had one son, Henry (3) Bowdon (born in 1754). But it cannot be excluded that John (3) Bowdon married for a second time (Ann) after his first wife died.

The relationship between Mary's two sons appears not to have been the best, and it is not hard to imagine that money was the root of the bad feeling. The line "I would not have my Son Mr George Bowdon to meddle with the Estate in Oxcroft which I have given to my Son Mr James Bowdon" is evidence of this. This flaw, which seemed to run in that part of the family, was not unbeknownst to Mary. George (9), son of George (8), seemingly too did not have a way with money, as a bankruptcy note from the "London Gazette" from April 1827 proves along with another from July 15, 1828.[1056] The profession of this "George Bowdon, late of Barlborough" (d. 1822) is stated as candlewick and sacking manufacturer. In order to satisfy the creditors parts of

---

[1056] http://www.london-gazette.co.uk/issues/18349/pages/779/page.pdf (viewed 08/06/2013), issue 18349 dated April 3, 1827, p. 779, right column; http://www.london-gazette.co.uk/issues/18487/pages/1381/page.pdf (viewed 10/12/2013), issue 18487 dated July 15, 1828, p. 1381, right column.

the family silver had to be sold off. A subject of negotiation in 1827 was the family's estate at Ganber Hall in the parish of Darfield, Yorkshire and the coal underneath it (the other family's estate at Towersey, Buckinghamshire could not be sold). In 1828 the creditors agreed that the estate of Ganber Hall including the coal seam was to be put to private auction or private contract in order to be sold. Philip Riden adds[1057] that between 1809 and 1814 a company called "Bowden (*sic!*), Malkin & Co." (or "Bowden (*sic!*) & Co.") manufactured sailcloth and sacking at Harlesthorpe (later also candlewick), the firm possibly being a partnership between Henry (3) Bowdon and a Robert Malkin, apparently a wholesale mercer of Chesterfield.[1058] A half-share in the mill was advertised for sale in 1820, which could have coincided with George (9) Bowdon's bankruptcy.

Mary Bowdon's testament leaves the impression that she took a very pragmatic view with regard to her offspring and her keen observation skills left her bitter, mistrustful and disappointed. That she requested a private funeral and only wished her servant to attend, seems to speak volumes. Along with her daughter Charlotte, who she left out of her will, John Bowdon, husband of Ann, had seemingly also fallen out of favour because of his debts.

Also, we will never know what occurred on August 22, 1782 between Mary Bowdon and her two servants that was grave enough for her to cut Elizabeth Ferguson out of her will forthwith and only leave John Godwin a fraction of what she originally intended.

A fundamental stocktaking and appraisal of the total amount of estates, land and minerals owned by the Bowdon family over the centuries would undoubtedly be very revealing, but unfortunately cannot be carried out within the confines of this book. Original documents and records are scattered throughout various libraries and archives in England, and to search all files in this context would be to get off track. Research for this book did, however, yielded a few interesting by-products: the University of Nottinghamshire holds a file containing miscellaneous memoranda and reports related to the Duke of Portland (the records are evidently in a rather fragile condition, stated as "unfit for production"), and among them correspondence between Thomas (3) Bowdon, Mary Bowdon's stepson from her husband's second marriage, with the 3rd Duke of Portland, relating to Shuttlewood/Oxcroft collieries (dated January 9, 1777). The bundle also contains memoranda of lands held by the Bowden family of Beighton Fields and Southgate House between the years 1731 and 1845 arranged as a schedule of surrenders and

---

[1057] Riden, *History of the County of Derby III*, p. 118.

[1058] Clowne parish Settlement Examinations list a number of workers of "Bowden (*sic!*) Malkin& Co. Mill at Harlesthorpe": William Eadson (weaver, 1813), John Humphries (bleacher, 1816), George Bullock (weaver, 1818), John Wigley (labourer, 1818 and 1829), John Smith (weaver, 1818); list published on-line by Spencer, *Yesterday's Journeys, Settlement Examinations.*

admittances.[1059] Documents of Younge Wilson, solicitors of Sheffield, and Taylors, solicitors of Sheffield, stored in the Sheffield Archives[1060] give further indication of the riches and holdings of John (2) Bowdon, his wife and descendants. On March 23, 1784 Mary Bowdon and others leased land in Little Sheffield to Henry Tudor of Tudor, Leader and Nicholson for a year.[1061] A grant dated September 30, 1793[1062] was given by James (1) Bowdon and another person of noble rank to a silversmith of Sheffield, a grinder, a button manufacturer and a pewterer, regards the exploitation of coal beds in the parish of Handsworth and the respective rents depending on quality and quantity of coal raised. Land in Edale, Derbyshire was rented out for 700 pounds by Mary's son James to a nobleman from Derbyshire, an iron monger and a linen draper, lease documents date June 02 and 03, 1797.[1063] An assignment of mortgage was made to a stocking maker of Tideswell, Derbyshire for 700 pounds he still owed regarding a lease on the family's estate at Edale Head and land in Barlborough on January 24, 1804.[1064] In 1830 an abstract of title of Mary's grandchildren Rev. Joseph Bowdon and Miss Mary Bowdon was rendered in regard of several closes of land called the Gill Carrs in the parish of Sheffield.[1065] A conveyance for 250 pounds dated December 30 and 31, 1830 refers to the same place: a piece of land at the corner of Bowden Street and Wellington Street, part of the Gill Carrs in Sheffield, by Rev. Joseph Bowdon of Sedgley Park in the parish of Sedgley, West Midlands (historically Staffordshire) and the spinster Mary Bowdon of Radford in the parish of Enstone, Oxfordshire.[1066] Another document from the collection of the University of Nottingham dated November 11,

---

1059 University of Nottingham, *Ref. No. PI E12/10/1/26/1-12* (original documents not viewed personally).

1060 "The documents reflect the firm's work for many local families in Sheffield, south Yorkshire and north Derbyshire. They include records of property dealings, including involvement in the building development of Sheffield in the mid-nineteenth century, and records relating to several businesses and partnerships dealing mainly with cutlery and associated activities and with coalmining.", documents dating between 1603 and 1941; see Sheffield Archives, *Ref. No. YWD*.

1061 Sheffield Archives, *Ref. No. YWD 1013/4* (original document not viewed personally).

1062 Sheffield Archives, *Ref. No. YWD 870 1793* (original document not viewed personally).

1063 Sheffield Archives, *Ref. No. YWD 923/14a-b* (original document not viewed personally).

1064 Sheffield Archives, *Ref. No. YWD 923/15a-b* (original document not viewed personally).

1065 Sheffield Archives, *Ref. No.* YWD 1047/1 (original document not viewed personally).

1066 Sheffield Archives, *Ref. No. YWD 1047/3a-b* (original document not viewed personally).

1823/September 24, 1835 refers to legacies charged on lands in Whitwell under the last will of a certain Elizabeth Sissons. Henry (3) Bowdon purchased part of the lands of one of the devisees, paying him a moiety of 200 pounds, and in doing so adding the lands of Southgate Estate (maybe Wall's Plantation or Wall's Holt?). The legal document was signed *inter alia* by John (4) Peter Bruno Bowdon on September 24, 1835, on condition that he would deliver the underlying document to the Duke of Portland.[1067]

A house let to Mary Bowdon and her two sons between 1762 and 1767 is mentioned in the so-called "Spinkhill Papers", a collection of more than 100 documents dating from 1711 to 1840 and kept in the Archives of the British Province of the Society of Jesus in London. The building in question was located north of the "Guest House" ("Tailor's Shop") in Spinkhill in 1951[1068] and is described several times as a house "made out of a barn", or "made out of a barn or a cowhouse". Spinkhill Papers n. 74 is a four-yearly account rendered to the trustees of the property. The credit side of above mentioned account reads: "By allowance made to Mrs. Bowdon for repairing and changing a Barn into an (*sic!*) house……£40."[1069] Did Mary or one her children ever live in that house?

23. 66 Southgate, Eckington

Eckington is a small town south east of Sheffield and north east of Chesterfield. It was home to a Mr Staniforth, who, according to Tony Bak, was a scythe and sickle manufacturer during the middle of the 18th century.[1070] His impressive residence, Southgate Old House, was located in the Southgate district of Eckington which has been attested as early as the beginning of the 14th century.[1071] The mediaeval town of Eckington must have had a city wall or some other kind of surrounding fortification with several gates as along with Southgate there is also a Northgate district attested in Eckington as well as Towngate.[1072]

1067 University of Nottingham Archives, *Ref. No. PI E12/6/26/6/10* (original document not viewed personally).

1068 NN, "Sodality Chapel", p. 61f. and footnote 14. Information by kind courtesy of Paul D Walker by E-Mail on May 9, 2014.

1069 "A close inspection of this old building will show definitely that it was once a barn or cowhouse. By adding a gabled attic and inserting what looks like a Tudor window in the west wall, the "changing" was so effectively achieved that a tradition has grown up that it was a relic or portion of a previous dwelling house pre-existing the Guest House. (…)"; cf. NN, "Sodality Chapel", p. 62.

1070 Barlborough Heritage and Research Centre, *Interesting Facts.*

1071 Court rolls of 1431, cf. Stroud, *Derbyshire Extensive Urban Survey*, p. 4.

1072 Stroud, *Derbyshire Extensive Urban Survey,* p. 4, p. 13f.. Streets with the element "gate" in their name normally refer to old city walls and usually lead to the former gates; information according to David Hawkins by telephone on April 4, 2013.

Southgate is the name of a street which crosses the old town centre of Eckington diagonally from the north west to the south east. It is also the road linking the seat of the Sitwell family from Renishaw Hall and Eckington town centre.[1073] According to a source quoted by Gill Stroud, the houses on Southgate belonged to the best in the village of Eckington during the 15th century.[1074] Southgate was the namesake of George Staniforth's newly acquired estate in Clowne, and which later became home to his son Charles. When George Staniforth bought the estate and mansion of Southgate House and part of his family moved there they evidently took the name of their provenance with them, the reasons for this are unknown. It leastwise explains, however, how the large country house got its name despite being far from the village centre of Clowne, on a busy thoroughfare almost in the middle of nowhere where no "north", "south" or any other cardinal direction can be defined by landmarks or any other noticeable buildings in the vicinity.

After the Staniforth family left Eckington and George, his wife Hannah and their children Charles, Jeremiah, Hannah and Sarah moved to live in Southgate, Clowne during the first third of the 18th century, Southgate Old House evidently changed hands; whether it was sold or let to tenants I cannot say. The material available on this matter was very scarce. The earliest possibilities to find out more were, of course, the ten-yearly censuses of England and Wales again. For **1841** there is no "Southgate House" on record, only the street Southgate is listed with 41 entries. Members of a Staniforth family are attested for various areas of Eckington. None of this information could be related to the matter in hand. The results of the search in the data of the **1851** census yielded even less fruitful information. Things start to assume shape in **1861**. Here the census provides us with details for "South Street, Eckington", where, among a long list of entries, the Wells family could be found. George Wells, aged 38, was a Colliery Owner and lived at the above mentioned address with his wife Jane, aged 36, and their eight children (all scholars or infants) and two servants (one a House Maid, the other one a Nurse Maid). The **1871** census unfortunately shows almost the same features as the one of 1841: a street named Southgate is recorded with 57 results for residents. But in **1881** we meet the Wells family again: at the address of "Southgate House, Eckington" lives widow Jane Wells, meanwhile aged 55 and Annuitant, together with three of her eight children and three Domestic Servants. Son William E, aged 29, is listed as "Colliery Manager (Mine?)", son George, aged 28, was a Brick Manufacturer. More people are listed at the same address: the Hayes and the Pattinson family. John Hayes, head of household, aged 60, and married to Ann, aged 51, was Farm Labourer, one his two sons was a Groom and the daughter worked as General Servant. Thomas O

1073 http://planningdesignpractice.blogspot.de/2009/10/october-2009-newsletter_30.html (viewed 27/03/2013).

1074 Stroud, *Derbyshire Extensive Urban Survey*, p. 14.

Pattinson, aged 30, was an Engine Fitter. He lived at Southgate House with his wife Selina E, aged 28, and their three under-aged sons (all scholars) and Thomas' sister Harriet, aged 16 and working as General Servant. I am under the impression that these two families lived in a separate outbuilding (for its presence see below) which was not recorded by the enumerator. But the 1881 census returns also list a building called "Southgate House Lodge, Eckington" which was home to Gardener William Comer, aged 38, and his wife Harriet, aged 38, and her nephew George Taylor, aged 6 and scholar. So the grounds of Southgate House were possibly equipped with more than one outhouse. "Southgate House, South Gate, Eckington" was in **1891** home to George H Wells, aged 38 and second eldest son of George Wells the Elder. He had carved out quite a career for himself: the census lists him as "Colliery Proprietor, Brick Manfr (= Manufacturer) also Wesleyan Local Preacher". He was married to Isabella Lewis Wells, aged 39. Together they had three daughters and one son, all under-aged, two daughters were scholars. Three servants (a cook, a housemaid and a nurse) took care of the family. Ten years later we get an entirely different picture: in **1901** Southgate House on Southgate was home to Eckington's local Medical Practitioner George H W Jones, aged 43. He lived there with his wife Ada M, aged 38, and their two daughters aged 10 and 1. Dr. Jones' Medical Assistant, Percival H Court, aged 31, had his lodgings at Southgate House as well. Four domestic servants (a nurse, a cook, a housemaid and a kitchen maid) lived under the same roof. The Jones's evidently valued consistency as in **1911** the family constellation remained unchanged, and Dr. Jones was still General Medical Practitioner, and three servants domestic still worked for the family (a cook and two housemaids). A spot-check inspection of the Electoral Rolls for Eckington still record George Henry West Jones as the occupant of Southgate Old House (copyhold house and garden) in **1914**. But some time over the course of the following six years new occupants moved in and stayed for ca. 10 years (attested between **1920** and **1930**): George and Harriet Hayes. Southgate Old House was only temporarily occupied by Cyril and Ruby Agnes Gambles (attested for **1932**). For unknown reasons there is no entry in the Electoral Rolls for **1934**, possibly the house stood empty at that time. Almost exactly 200 years after inhabitants with the surname Staniforth lived at Southgate Old House, people of the same surname are back: from at least **1936** on a Benjamin Staniforth and a Kathleen Eugenie Staniforth lived at Southgate, they are attested by the Electoral Rolls until at least **1948**. Randomised samples of the Electoral Rolls from the following decades leave a somewhat indistinct impression. In **1975** a Sheila M Sims is listed at the address, but until 1995 none of my samples record inhabitants for 66 Southgate (1966, 1970, 1980, 1985, 1990, and 1995).

The Sitwell family is the point where things finally come full circle as Sir Osbert Sitwell, 5th Baronet of Renishaw and writer of WWI prose (see Chapter 8), bought Southgate House in Clowne in ca. 1938/1939. The Sitwell family is closely connected to Eckington and Renishaw, their ancestral home has been Renishaw Hall (ca. one mile from the town centre of Eckington) for nearly four centuries and still is today.[1075] The Sitwells are considered as major benefactors of Eckington over the past centuries; their family tree can be traced back almost 800 years (first recorded in the late 13th century in the neighbouring village of Ridgeway).[1076] Sitwells were attested to have lived at Southgate, Eckington between 1431 and 1543.[1077] The foundations of the prosperity of the family were laid in 1530 when a Robert Sitwell bought land rich in coal and iron near Netherthorpe on the north-eastern outskirts of Staveley. 58 years later he was said to be one of the five richest men in Derbyshire; by the time of his death in 1599 he owned land not only in North East Derbyshire, but also in Nottinghamshire and Yorkshire.[1078] His cousin's grandson, George (1600/1601-1667), High Sheriff of Derbyshire in 1653, ironmaster and early industrial pioneer with several furnaces and forges in the area[1079], inherited the prosperous holdings and together with his eldest son Francis they became forerunners of the coming industrial revolution. By the middle of the 17th century one tenth of the nations iron trade was in their hands and Francis Sitwell was deemed the world's largest manufacturer of iron nails.[1080]

In Renishaw, at the geographical centre of their thriving businesses, George Sitwell laid the foundation for Renishaw Hall around 1625.[1081] The industrial activity led to a tripling of the local population during the early 18th century; houses, churches and chapels were erected. Large new mansions built by local industrialists swiftly followed the developments of the Industrial Revolution during the late 18th and early 19th century.[1082]

But the Sitwells withdrew from industry at the end of the 18th century when the Renishaw estate was inherited by George Sitwell's great-grandson and country squire Francis Hurt (1728-1793, who changed his surname to Sitwell, his mother Katherine Sitwell being the heiress of the Sitwell family).

1075 Jenkins, *Best Houses*, p. 171f.

1076 Bates, *Eckington*; http://www.inside-eckington.co.uk/abouteckington.html (Eckington) (viewed 27/03/2013).

1077 Bates, *Eckington*.

1078 Derbyshire County Council / Derbyshire Record Office and *Derby Diocesan Record Office, Sitwell of Renishaw: Estate Records*, p. 1. More land in Yorkshire was added to the Sitwell property when a William Sitwell married Mary Reresby in 1693.

1079 A furnace at Foxbrooke is said to have become the core of the largest ironworks in whole Derbyshire; cf. http://en.wikipedia.org/wiki/Eckington,_Derbyshire, footnote 6 (viewed 27/03/2013).

1080 Bates, *Eckington*; also sickles and scythes for local use and export were manufactured, cf. http://en.wikipedia.org/wiki/Eckington,_Derbyshire (viewed 27/03/2013).

1081 Bates, *Eckington*.

1082 Bates, *Eckington*.

His first son Sitwell Sitwell (1769-1811) became the 1st Baronet in 1808.[1083] He initiated major rebuilding activities between 1793 and 1808, enlarging Renishaw Hall.[1084] Yet already his heir, Sir George (1) Sitwell, faced financial constraints which forced him to close down Renishaw Hall and move to Scotland and later to Wiesbaden, Germany.[1085] His son, Sir Sitwell Reresby Sitwell (d. 1862), inherited Renishaw Estate, which after his death passed into the hands of his son Sir George (2) Reresby Sitwell (1860-1943, 4th Baronet), who laid out the gardens in the 1890s (in an Italianate style) and a golf course in 1911.[1086] Sir George (2) Reresby Sitwell was the father of Edith (1887-1964), Sir (Francis) Osbert and Sacheverell Sitwell (1897-1988), and like his son he was a writer, concerning himself with local and family history.[1087]

Southgate Old House at Nr. 66 Southgate was a Grade II listed building in 1967, dating back to the mid 17th century with extensions made during the 19th century.[1088] According to English Heritage, it was built of coursed coal measures sandstone and had a very elaborate façade, rich in detail, and a Roman tiled roof covering. Inside the building only a few architectural features from the previous centuries seemed to have survived when listed by

1083 The title in the Baronetage of the United Kingdom, the Sitwell Baronetcy, of Renishaw in the County of Derby was created for him on October 3, 1808; cf. Thorne, *History of Parliament*; Derbyshire County Council/ Derbyshire Record Office and Derby Diocesan Record Office, *Sitwell of Renishaw: Estate Records*, p. 1.

1084 Lysons, *Magna Britannia, Eckington*, p. 142ff.; Derbyshire County Council/Derbyshire Record Office and Derby Diocesan Record Office, *Sitwell of Renishaw: Estate Records*, p. 1.

1085 Derbyshire County Council/Derbyshire Record Office and *Derby Diocesan Record Office, Sitwell of Renishaw: Estate Records*, p. 1.

1086 Bates, *Eckington*; Derbyshire County Council/Derbyshire Record Office and Derby Diocesan Record Office, *Sitwell of Renishaw: Estate Records*, p. 1. Mary Jones contributed a few memories of Renishaw Hall (in a personal E-mail correspondence with the author dated April 5, 2014): her parents were invited to a reception along with all the tenants when Sir Reresby Sitwell inherited the Hall. The nephew of Mrs Jones, Philip Tongue, spent many hours helping out at the Hall. When Sir Reresby took over, Mr Tongue was employed to do a lot of electricity work (possibly rewiring). Unfortunately the Sitwells could not employ Philip Tongue as a full-time electrician as money was short, they did however use him whenever they needed work doing. As time went by, Mr Tongue took on other jobs at the Hall. He spent some nights as night watchman when none of the family were at home and worked as a butler when the Sitwells had banquets and other occasions. According to Mrs Jones, he once served Prince Charles.

1087 Derbyshire County Council/Derbyshire Record Office and Derby Diocesan Record Office, *Sitwell of Renishaw: Estate Records*, p. 1.

1088 A photograph of Southgate Old House from the 1970s can be viewed on Picture The Past, *Southgate Old House (203929)*; another one from the 1980s on Picture The Past, *Southgate Old House (000418)*.

English Heritage in January 1967.[1089] The Derbyshire Record Office in Matlock holds a document that contains a site plan of Southgate, Eckington (undated) as well as a proposed reconstruction (architectural drawing) of a property for Capt. Francis Osbert S Sitwell dated 1937.[1090] The site plan very clearly shows the position of Southgate Old House, but a personal visit to Eckington in April 2013 revealed that the mansion had been demolished which must have taken place after 1999, as Gill Stroud still mentions the house in his article on Eckington in that same year.[1091] In April 2013 it was nothing but an empty plot.[1092]

On the grounds of the estate was at least one outbuilding: a square, unadorned two storey house believed to date from the same period as the manor house and which has been redundant for a number of years (date of information: 2009). It contained a 17th century hearth.[1093] In April 2013 a notice attached to a tree along Southgate from North East Derbyshire District Council notifies of an application made to the North East Derbyshire District Council by Sitwell Estate for a planning permission, which referred to the conversion of an outbuilding into a new dwelling (Listed Building/Conservation Area).[1094]

24. "We are Family"[1095] - The Bowdons and the Butler-Bowdons

For centuries the Bowdon and Butler-Bowdon family had a determining influence on both the inward and outward appearance of Pleasington, Beighton Fields, Barlborough, Clowne and the surrounding villages in the district. If we give credence to the available sources such as the valuable memories of local inhabitants, the various newspapers announcements and numerous obituaries, then it seems fair to say that the Bowdons and the Butler-Bowdons were universally well-liked, and their enduring commitment to those entrusted to them, during bad times as well as in good, has been greatly acknowledged. Family values played a significant role and were prudently handed down to each and every member of the family. A sense of

---

1089 Stroud, *Derbyshire Extensive Urban Survey*, p. 14; English Heritage, *Southgate Old House*; British Listed Buildings, *Southgate Old House, Eckington.*

1090 Derbyshire Record Office Ref. No. D6573/Box 53/26-27.

1091 Stroud, *Derbyshire Extensive Urban Survey*, p. 14.

1092 Site visited personally by Graham Duckmanton and the author on April 23, 2013.

1093 http://planningdesignpractice.blogspot.de/2009/10/october-2009-newsletter_30.html (viewed 27/03/2013); British Listed Buildings, *Southgate Old House, Eckington.*

1094 Notice viewed by Graham Duckmanton and the author on April 23, 2013, the notice dates from December 7, 2012. Sitwell Estate = part of Renishaw Hall Estate that deals with the upkeep, renting and sales of their properties (confirmed by Mary Jones in a private E-mail correspondence on April 15, 2014).

1095 "We are Family" was a hit dance song performed by Sister Sledge (1979), from the album of the same name.

responsibility, attentiveness, communal spirit and charitableness were words that struck me again and again when reading and researching about the family.

From the mid 18th century on the male Butler-Bowdon's were all of military ranks and held offices in administrative bodies, which they occupied with a great earnestness and sense of obligation. An earlier occupational title attested for male members of the Bowden family is that of yeoman (at the beginning of 17th century)[1096], but as a bulletin reveals, Bowdon men could also hold quite ordinary professions: George (9) Bowdon for instance was a candlewick and sacking manufacturer, Ireneo Del Monaco worked as an accountant and later on as a registration clerk after his military service, his son Romolo was a labourer before he joined the armed forces, his other son Bernard intended to work as a farmer after emigration to Canada and his son Enrico later made a career in public service as a clerk and registration officer.

Female members of the family were committed to the principle of Christian love and cared for the less fortunate, as was expected from them in those times. Yet they seemed to fulfil their duties with a certain pride and common sense. The gravestone of Eliza Jemima Bowdon at Spinkhill Cemetery affirms her dedication ("Because of Her Charity to The Poor" which - initially together with her sister Barbara - included taking care of her gravely ill relative Fredrick Maxwell), and an obituary for Theresa Butler-Bowdon dated 1963 tells us that from childhood on she and her siblings "learned to think of others, especially the poor, and their mother obliged the girls to spend part of their leisure time making garments for the poor."[1097] But some women were a little less compliant than others and lived rather exceptional lives for their times. Alongside sharp-witted Mary Bowdon, Alice Del Monaco also leaves the impression of having been a determined and courageous young woman who was undaunted by the prospect of travelling, possibly on her own, and marrying a foreigner - unheard of in the family before.

Henry (5) Bowdon was revered by all members of the community, in particular by his tenants and the poor. His political orientation was that of a Liberal, but only in a passive manner. John (5) Butler-Bowdon was widely considered to be a kind and liberal landlord who was respected and esteemed.

[1096] Small freeholding.

[1097] Cf. Boscombe Catholics, *Past Pupils' Association*. These activities can, however, be viewed critically. At the end of the 18th century, when the French Revolution lead to social upheaval on the continent, the English upper classes were very well aware that they were also treading on the thin ice, and went to great lengths to reduce disaffection among their dependants and the less fortunate by means of entertainment and charity. Mark Girouard says: "At its best, entertaining the lower orders expressed a genuine concern for the poor and a desire to improve the relations between the classes; at its worst it showed a rather odious condescension.", cf. Girouard, *English Country House*, p. 241f. The latter certainly did not apply to the Butler-Bowdons. Their concern seemed to be genuine throughout the years.

When it came to defending his house and farm John (5) Peter Bruno Butler-Bowdon showed that he was a brave and intrepid man. He was also engaged in the economic interests of the town of Blackburn.

John (6) Erdeswick Butler-Bowdon was known for having a notable comedic talent. Also he could perform conjuring tricks such as producing rabbits and even plum puddings from his top hat.[1098] Monica Mary Petre Butler-Bowdon, his second wife, was popular for her unostentatious engagement for any advancement within the community and her thoughtful and kind acts improved the lot of many people. After her death, Mary Monica Butler-Bowdon, third wife and widow of John (6) Erdeswick Butler-Bowdon, evidently adopted her role and was equally well-liked.

The family also contributed generously to religious life: firstly, there was Richard John Francis Butler who was financially responsible for building the impressive structure of Pleasington Priory, and secondly, there were Henry (5) Bowdon and his brother John (5) Peter Bruno Butler-Bowdon, fervently advocating their belief by signing the "Declaration of the Roman Catholic Laity of England" in 1851.[1099] Thirdly, William Erdeswick Ignatius Butler-Bowdon, first son of John (6) and Monica Mary Butler-Bowdon, endowed the erection of a Catholic church on Creswell Road in Clowne. He apparently was a person with some historical appreciation as well: an enormous Art Deco silver cup, on loan by Allan Bailey, Secretary of Clowne Local History Society, as part of an exhibition of Barlborough Heritage and Research Centre in 2013 bears the following inscription[1100]: "The Poppies Cup / Presented by / Lieut. Col. W. Butler-Bowdon D.S.O. / To be held annually / by the best seller of Poppies / For Earl Haig Fund / in / Clown (*sic!*)".[1101] The inscription on the cup relates to the commemoration of WWI. The cup was manufactured in

---

[1098] According to the recollections of Teresa Staples; cf. Staples, *My Parish*, p. 2.

[1099] Catholics (England), *Declaration*, p. 8ff. Among the hundreds of signatories and alongside Henry Bowdon of Southgate House and John Butler Bowdon (*sic!*) of Plessington (*sic!*) Hall there are familiar names such as Lord Petre, Michael H Blount and Michael Blount jr. of Maple Durham and other male members of the Blount family, a Charles Cecil De Trafford, Marmion Edward Ferrers of Baddesley Clinton, Charles Hansom (Clifton), John Hardman (Birmingham), male members of the Maxwell Constable family, James and William Powell (Birmingham) and male members of the Walmsley and the Whitgreave families as well as John Francis Wright of Kelvedon Hall.

[1100] Mr Bailey recently found the cup in a skip when the Technical College in Clowne was demolished. The cup was housed in the old College prior to demolition. Information disclosed by Tony Bak in personal E-mail correspondences with the author on January 8 and 9, 2014. It could not be established who gave the cup to the College, or when and or for what reason.

[1101] The Earl Haig Fund mentioned on the cup is a charity set up in 1921 by WWI Field Marshal Douglas Haig, 1st Earl Haig (1861-1928) to assist former servicemen and which still helps war veterans today; cf. Encyclopedia Britannica, *Douglas Haig 1st Earl Haig*.

1937 (a small rectangular plaque attached to foot of the cup is engraved with "1937 Mrs E. Foye."). It was donated to the community by Lt.-Col. Butler-Bowdon on his return from WWI and was to be presented to the most successful poppy seller each year (these were volunteers who sold silk poppies worn on Remembrance Day).[1102] The cup was also likely to have been of personal significance to William Erdeswick Ignatius, who lost his brother Basil during WWI. 1937 unfortunately was the only year in which the cup was won and presented.[1103] Ruby Thorpe remembers Colonel Butler-Bowdon walking around the lanes and the gardens of Southgate Estate, but he did not talk much to her. According to her recollections, he was a very large gentleman who always wore plus fours which were very much the fashion for the country gentleman at the time, but which looked "daft" in little Ruby's opinion, almost like a skirt. He was always accompanied by a huge St. Bernard and two tiny dogs.[1104]

Lancelot George B Butler-Bowdon of Barlborough was another highly esteemed member of society, too, who was especially recognised for his discreet generosity and his love of the children of Barlborough. He was also known as a fervent Conservative. His wife Ella Cicely Mary Butler-Bowdon was noted for her many acts of charity. Their only son John (7) Lancelot, the family eccentric with a huge heart, had time for everyone in the community and was equally well remembered in the village of Barlborough.

Another striking discovery is that at least three female family members, Monica Mary Petre, second wife of John (6) Erdeswick Butler-Bowdon, Henrietta (Harriet) Bowdon née Blount, wife of Henry (5) Bowdon, and subsequently her daughters Alice (and her offspring) and Constance are said to have been of Plantagenet blood.[1105] If this is true - was their descent an underlying strategic move of the Bowdon men in choosing their wives? Further evidence for this assumption is the mentioning of Anne Plantagenet, granddaughter of Edward III, in a letter William Erdeswick Ignatius Butler-Bowdon wrote in 1945 when referring to the direct inheritance of ecclesiastical

---

[1102] Information by June Pearce in a personal E-mail correspondence with the author on November 28, 2013.

[1103] Information by Tony Bak in a personal E-mail correspondence with the author on September 28, 2013.

[1104] Information communicated per E-mail by June Pearce following a personal meeting with Ruby Thorpe on March 25, 2014 and by Ruby Thorpe during a personal meeting with the author in Clowne on April 27, 2014.

[1105] De La Caille Ruvigny and Raineval, *Plantagenet roll*, p. 41. Other sources name members of the Bowdon family such as Monica Mary and William Erdeswick Ignatius Butler-Bowdon and all their offspring as well as the Del Monacos as descendants of James I (1566-1625); cf. http://www.angelfire.com/realm/gotha/Part15.htm (viewed 15/08/2013); https://groups.google.com/forum/#!topic/alt.talk.royalty/rN-0VLYBiBE (viewed 21/05/2014).

vestments, which at that time were in the ownership of the Butler-Bowdon family.[1106]

Yet appearances can often be deceptive and not everything was in the family was always perfect. The last will and testament of Mary Bowdon shows that the neat veneer had occasional cracks and that not everything was love, peace and harmony, rather there were disagreements and black sheep in the family just like in any other. It is not only through Mary Bowdon that we receive the impression that when it came to outward demarcation and defending the interests of the family, an unrelenting steeliness manifests itself. Another example of which is the lease document regarding of Southgate Colliery. With a strong determination Henry (5) Bowdon rejected the Duke of Portland's demands. This outward differentiation, however, could become permeable for some, as the dedication to Ms Hughes, the teacher in the household of Lancelot George B Butler-Bowdon, on his gravestone at Spinkhill Cemetery shows.

Another behavioural characteristics of Henry (5) Bowdon seems to constitute a small aberration of the family's principles of beneficence: the Archives of the British Province of the Society of Jesus, London, hold some records for him relating to so-called "bench rents" (during the 1860s).[1107] "Bench rents" or "pew rents" were a system that pertained in England whereby parishioners could pay a sum of money for a seat in the church and no-one else was allowed to sit there, regardless of whether those that rented attended Mass. While this certainly formed a genuine way of supporting a church financially, it also meant that the rich had the best seats at the front and the poor had to sit or stand at the back.[1108] Yet the idea that the family

---

1106 See Chapter 19 and Young, "Opus Anglicanum", p. 297.

1107 British Jesuit Archives, ***Ref. No. MQ/1*** (n. 19 on the list of Spinkhill documents deposited at Farm Street in 1968, "Papers concerning Mr Henry Bowden's (*sic!*) acknowledgement of the justice of paying Bench Rents. 1864". The bundle of documents is very interesting as it contains a correspondence between Henry (5) Bowdon and several clergymen from Mount St. Mary's College at Spinkhill such as H Birch, George Tickell, Felix Poole S.J., Father Vaughan (the later Cardinal Herbert Vaughan (1832-1903)? Suggested by Paul D Walker in a personal E-mail correspondence with the author on July 2, 2014), Maurice Mann, John Baron (for some of the names and positions see Kelly, *Historical Notes*, p. 127 and Walker, *Church of the Immaculate Conception*, p. 84). An account reveals that apparently Mr Bowdon was considerably in arrears with payments for his bench rents. He in turn decisively tries to convince the clergymen of a payment in kind (timber/larch wood from Southgate Estate) for the Mount.

1108 This system must have lasted well into the 1940s. At Spinkhill Church there is some evidence of the floor at the back of the church being paved/stone flagged (from the porch to the west end of the church) while the rest under the benches (from the porch to the sanctuary) was a (warmer) sprung wooden floor, so people who had walked miles to church on a bad day came with muddy footwear, while those who had ridden

paid money to secure a seat in one of the first rows or any other exposed position in Spinkhill Church does not fit with the picture of the Butler-Bowdons I have in my mind. From all I could see they leave the impression of a wealthy family who was very well aware of their position in society and who would not have made use of their prosperity to their advantage. But since reserving seats in church was a common demeanour of members of the upper class perhaps the Butler-Bowdons in way felt obliged to adapt to the system.[1109]

Little could be found out about childhood life in the Butler-Bowdon family, but one newspaper article from The Western Gazette (Yeovil, Somerset) dated August 14, 1925 tells us a about pastime in the early years of Maurice and Anthony Butler-Bowdon. "Good Afternoon's Enjoyment (...) for the benefit of the local Football Club" of Chideock, Dorset included a wide variety of children's sports events for both girls and boys where Maurice Butler-Bowdon won a respectable 3rd prize for boys under 16 and the 1st prize for the mixed sack race. Anthony Butler-Bowdon was 2nd in the relay race. The grown-ups got their money's worth as well; in the couples' "thread-needle, tie, and cigarette race" M Butler-Bowdon and a Miss Weld won 3rd prize. Together with another lady Mrs Butler-Bowdon was responsible for presenting the prizes afterwards; Col. Butler-Bowdon and another gentleman acted as judges.[1110]

Sporting activities seem to have played a fundamental role in the life of the Butler-Bowdon family. Teresa Staples recalls the family having a tennis court[1111] halfway between Southgate House and the village of Clowne on "Park Lane", the footpath connecting both places. It boasted a court, a pavilion, an umpire's seat, and tea was provided every Sunday afternoon. Cricket matches were held in the park. Teams came as far away as from Derby and Nottingham.[1112]

---

or driven arrived relatively clean-shod (information disclosed in personal E-mails exchanged with Father Michael Beattie S.J. of Mount St. Mary's College, Spinkhill, Paul D Walker and the author on June 23, 2014 and with Father Peter D McGuire on June 30, 2014).

1109 At least Henry (5) Bowdon had the grace to not only reserve seats for himself and his family ("Bench 6 sittings"), but also for his servants ("servants' bench"); cf. British Jesuit Archives, ***Ref. No. MQ/1***. I doubt they were the same sets of pews though. The Bowdon family must have had seats as well at the Sodality Chapel in the old college building of Mount St. Mary's as Baines, "History of Spinkhill", p. 100 mentions "stairs to 1st floor chapel with 2nd flight to 'the tribune of the Bowden (*sic!*) family'" (thanks to Paul D Walker for this hint, disclosed in a personal E-mail correspondences with the author on July 4 and July 5, 2014).

1110 http://www.findmypast.co.uk (British Newspapers 1710-1965) (viewed 13/10/2013).

1111 See Chapter 8.

1112 Staples, *My Parish*, p. 2f.

However controversial the debate concerning the landed gentry, to me the Bowdons and Butler-Bowdons were - as characterised by Blake Morrison (see Chapter 5) - "wise custodians" of their entrusted land who managed to keep Southgate Estate together as long as it was economically possible for them - or as Mark Girouard describes the romanticised old-style English way of life, "dispensing hospitality in a great hall, with fires blazing in the great arched fireplaces, smoke rising from innumerable chimney-stacks, comfortable groups gossiping in ingles and oriels, and generous sheltering roofs over all."[1113] They leave the strong impression of having been responsible-minded people who looked after their tenants and servants well, who devoted their lives to public service and showed unfailing hospitability to friends and guests.[1114] This is mirrored in the countless obituaries and eulogies in the press, not one of which leaves an insincere or feigned impression. According to the recollections of Mona Ives, former maid of Southgate House, the Butler-Bowdons filled their galleries with beautiful pictures, and they had an extensive library of all kinds of books which also housed some rare finds, such as The Book of Margery Kempe.

25. German Prisoners of War in Britain / Southgate Camp

No successful attempt has so far been made to calculate the exact number of POW camps in the United Kingdom and even less effort has been invested to have them properly located or documented.[1115] Consequently, the list of the total number of camps in Britain is still incomplete today. German historian Renate Held made a first comprehensive synopsis on the topic of German prisoners of war in British detention in 2005 (she looked at, for example, motives, decision-making and development processes, actions of the detention powers, and impacts on soldiers).[1116]

Buildings (often disused) such as factories, colleges, schools, hotels and function rooms or purpose-built buildings, so-called Nissen huts, served as camps.[1117] Additionally semi-autonomous hostels were set up in the countryside, and a large number of POWs were billeted on farms and in

---

1113 Girouard, *English Country House*, p. 273.

1114 There were some friendly and some less friendly houses, and the rules of households could vary considerably, for some examples and descriptions see Girouard, *English Country House*, p. 285.

1115 Thomas, *Prisoner of War Camps*, p. 4 and p. 10f.

1116 Doctoral thesis by Renate Held: Held, *Kriegsgefangenschaft in Großbritannien*, p. 3. Further research on the Italian prisoners of war at Southgate and in Barlborough would have gone beyond the frame of this study. Being German myself, my main interest lay in unravelling the fates of the German prisoners.

1117 Wheeler, *German Prisoners of War in Britain*; Linacre, *How it was*, p. 71, p. 73.

country manors.[1118] The camps themselves came in a great variety of types, sizes and classes and varied throughout the war.

According to Roger J C Thomas's analysis, there were four distinct classes of POW camps during the early part of the war: command cages, interrogation centres, transit camps and internment camps, each serving its own specific purpose.[1119] In 1939 there were only two POW camps in Britain (the number of German prisoners was still low and was comprised chiefly of airmen and naval personnel[1120]), but by the end of the war there were more than 600 camps.[1121] The typical administration of a camp consisted of a British camp commandant (responsible for the complete organisation of the camp) and his staff, as well as of a German camp spokesman and his assistants (responsible for carrying out British orders and day to day running of the camp).[1122]

1940 was a crucial year for German POWs on British soil. Home Defence (Security) Executive (HD(S)E) decided to deport[1123] German prisoners, as well as so-called "enemy aliens" (German and Austrian citizens who either lived - sometimes for generations - and worked in Britain or were there as refugees), to Canada as fear was spreading that in the case of a German invasion of the British Isles, the Germans would rescue of the imprisoned Wehrmacht troops (this was based on speculations made by previous military proceedings in Norway and the Netherlands). This frequently led to the absurd situation that victims (Jewish refugees, resistance fighters) and aggressors (followers of National Socialism) found themselves penned up together on ships heading west.[1124] Paranoia within the government went as far as to imagine that in the case of a German invasion even Jewish refugees would support the attacking forces.[1125] The deportations were not without controversy within the British

---

1118 Thomas, *Prisoner of War Camps*, p. 4; Harris, *No Voice from the Hall*, p. 4f. Accommodating prisoners at manor houses (in this case Grizedale Hall) turned out to be quite pricey. An MP of the House of Commons asked in a debate on November 21, 1939: "Would it not be cheaper to keep them at the Ritz?"; cf. Held, *Kriegsgefangenschaft in Großbritannien*, p. 28.

1119 Thomas, *Prisoner of War Camps*, p. 5.

1120 Grizedale Hall (Lake District) for higher ranking officers and Glen Mill Camp (Oldham) for soldiers with lower military ranks, both camps were ignored in British public; cf. Held, *Kriegsgefangenschaft in Großbritannien*, p. 265.

1121 Wheeler, *German Prisoners of War in Britain.*

1122 Held, *Kriegsgefangenschaft in Großbritannien*, p. 137f.

1123 Contrary to the Geneva Conventions of 1929 which forbade deportment of ill detainees (article 25) and which demanded advance notification of the relocation of prisoners (article 26); cf. Held, *Kriegsgefangenschaft in Großbritannien*, p. 43f., footnote 62.

1124 Held, *Kriegsgefangenschaft in Großbritannien*, p. 29ff.

1125 Held, *Kriegsgefangenschaft in Großbritannien*, p. 38. Suspicion went even further: while German soldiers were parachuting into the Netherlands, rumour had it that they

government however: the Foreign Office feared that this strategy could lead to retaliation acts against the 44,000 British soldiers in German detention.[1126] Transports quickly proved to be too dangerous (one ship was torpedoed by a German U-boat and sank) and too complicated and the whole project was aborted shortly before the "Battle of Britain" (July - October 1940).[1127]

A change was brought about when, in the course of the success of the 8th Army's North African campaign against the Italian army (which began in September 1941), a substantial number of prisoners initially held in North African camps were transferred to the British Isles.[1128] An increasing number of camps were built (many of them by the prisoners themselves) between 1942 and 1943.[1129] After D-Day (June 6, 1944) more German captives were brought to Britain. Prior to that (in early summer 1940) Britain was disinclined to accept a greater number of German POWs, as there was the ongoing threat of a German invasion of Britain.[1130]

---

not only wore Dutch military uniforms but some were even disguised as nuns, a repeat of which in Britain was greatly feared as described by a BBC employee in 1940; cf. Held, *Kriegsgefangenschaft in Großbritannien*, p. 36 and footnote 32. A situation parodied in the BBC sitcom "'Allo 'Allo" (1982-1992)?

1126 Held, *Kriegsgefangenschaft in Großbritannien*, p. 43ff., p. 265: detainees were never safe: German POWs were used as hostages in a circle of reprisals and counter reprisals later in the war, the prisoners were abused by the demonstration of power on both sides, the Allied Forces and the Third Reich. This made an exchange of detainees impossible.

1127 Held, *Kriegsgefangenschaft in Großbritannien*, p. 51.

1128 A first contingent of about 2,000 Italian POWs, mostly farmers held in Egyptian camps, arrived in England in July 1941 and were to work under the Ministry of Agriculture (later more Italian POWs were brought to England). This appears paradoxical when looking at the great effort that was made at the same time to ship German POWs out of England and overseas; cf. Held, *Kriegsgefangenschaft in Großbritannien*, p. 56f.

1129 Thomas, *Prisoner of War Camps*, p. 5.

1130 Wheeler, *German Prisoners of War in Britain*. The presence of "enemy aliens" was considered a high risk (the so-called „Fifth Column") by the War Office; cf. Held, *Kriegsgefangenschaft in Großbritannien*, p. 3, p. 28, p. 30f., p. 33 ff. Interrogation of German POWs in December 1939 yielded confirmation of the British assumption that the German prisoners were dangerous: "Their morale is high and their attitude inclined to be defiant, not to say hostile. They have an exaggerated admiration for Hitler." (camp commanders at the same time also emphasised the discipline of the German prisoners); cf. Held, *Kriegsgefangenschaft in Großbritannien*, p. 60f. and footnote 29 (a memorandum by the Secretary of States for Foreign Affairs on December 18, 1939, The National Archives, *Ref. No. PRO ADM 1-10069*, original document not viewed personally). Already a year later interrogations showed that this statement could not be equally attributed to all German POWs, especially as the war went on. Analyses were not published however, as the British government strived to maintain the picture of the dangerous enemy in order to boost fighting morale.

In May 1945 the United States began to release prisoners of war, but also transferred large numbers to the Allied Powers because of urgent need for labour, especially in Britain which was suffering from a shortage of labour. Following the capitulation of Italy in 1943, this shortage could no longer be compensated by Italian POW labourers alone.[1131] Therefore 123,000 German POWs were sent to England.[1132] The terms of the Geneva Convention of 1929 forbade forced or compulsory labour for war captives (officers). British POW policy took a very pragmatic approach to the labour shortage however, especially towards the end of the war when the Italian POWs had already been released, and German POWs awaiting repatriation themselves preferred to work rather than doing nothing. They worked on farms[1133], in the construction and mining industry, and rebuilt homes damaged by bombing and cleared away bomb damage.[1134] They were also employed as lorry drivers.[1135] In 1946 when more than 400,000 German POWs were still being held in Britain[1136], up to one fifth of all farm work was carried out by German POWs, who were also put to work on road works and building sites.[1137]

Generally the German POWs were well treated.[1138] Re-education programmes equipped them for their new life in Germany.[1139] Many former captives looked back on their time in Britain and in British captivity with respectful sentiments, and they experienced the re-education scheme as something positive, unlike the POWs who were detained in the camps in the United States.[1140]

The principal idea of re-education rooted in Sir Robert Vansittard's (Permanent Under-Secretary at the Foreign Office) thesis that the Germans

---

1131 Held, *Kriegsgefangenschaft in Großbritannien*, p. 148.

1132 WDR, *Heimkehr mit Verzögerung*; Nix, *Situation deutscher Kriegsgefangener.*

1133 Already by the summer of 1944 German POWs worked on farms in groups of 12 people without any military supervision; cf. Held, *Kriegsgefangenschaft in Großbritannien*, p. 150.

1134 Wheeler, *German Prisoners of War in Britain*; WDR, *Heimkehr mit Verzögerung.*

1135 Held, *Kriegsgefangenschaft in Großbritannien*, p. 150.

1136 Richards, *Life in Britain for German Prisoners of War.*

1137 Richards, *Life in Britain for German Prisoners of War.*

1138 This was possibly not only due to humanitarian reasons. The British feared that not treating German POWs according to the rules of the Geneva Conventions would lead to repressive measures against British prisoners in German detention. A control and information system, monitored by the International Committee of Red Cross (ICRC), was established; based on the mechanism of reciprocity. But the resolutions did not last long as the warring parties had the right to repay unjustness by retaliatory measures and prisoners of war could easily be instrumentalised - which indeed took place and escalated during the progress of the war; cf. Held, *Kriegsgefangenschaft in Großbritannien*, p. 63ff.

1139 Wheeler, *German Prisoners of War in Britain*; Held, *Kriegsgefangenschaft in Großbritannien*, p. 94ff. (also p. 147ff., p. 155ff., p. 122ff.)

1140 WDR, *Heimkehr mit Verzögerung.*

were a nation of aggressive, militaristic and untrustworthy people, who were full of cruelty, envy and self-pity and whose values were deeply entrenched in their Prussian military history, all of which were symptoms of the "German disease" which needed to be cured (formulated in 1940/1941). British historian, diplomat and political theorist Edward Hallett Carr took a more moderate and liberal line in 1942, when he proclaimed that the mislead Germans needed a new perspective, which could be achieved by making them an integral part of the communal endeavour to reconstruct Europe. Neither the threat of punishment nor that of indoctrination could achieve deep-routed, radical changes required. Leading the Germans to democracy by example and seeking an open discussion would be the better way. Church of England bishop George Kennedy Allen Bell went a step further and proclaimed the concept of "self help under British guidance". Finally the British war cabinet came to an agreement that "Germans alone can re-educate their fellow countrymen", a German task for the Germans, with Britain in the background supervising in accordance with the colonial principle of "indirect rule". This concept formed the basis of the British post war plan.[1141] Clearly then, German POWs in Britain were therefore assigned the role of a pioneer. The inherent strategy was to segregate potential "converts" from their comrades and teach them English in order to guarantee propagandistic success.[1142] In August 1944 a special POW camp, "Camp No. 7", was established in Ascot where German opponents of the Third Reich could debate the future of their country and prepare the re-education of their fellow countrymen. Political Warfare Executive (PWE), part of Foreign Office, and Prisoner of War Division (POWD) chose ideally suited prisoners (a small number from camps in Northern Africa), who worked together with German opponents of the Third Reich. Cyrus Brooks was responsible for the planning, and later became known as the "father of re-education".[1143] One of the strategies developed in Ascot was a snowball system for a process of democratisation in which small

[1141] Held, *Kriegsgefangenschaft in Großbritannien*, p. 97, p. 100f. and footnote 32. The concept of changing people's minds under the constraint of a vested interest or general weal is not entirely new however; rather it is as old as human kind. Caesar for example demanded and was given "hostages" from British tribes when he landed in Britain in 55 BC for the first time. Called *obsides* by the Romans these were boys or young men, sons or close relations of local chieftains. They were brought to Rome where they were educated in the Roman way, allowed to mix at their will with Roman citizens and all in all encouraged to themselves become Romans in their demeanour. When this was accomplished they were sent back to Britain in the hope that they would take what they had learnt with them and would in turn teach the people back home about Rome and convince them that Roman traditions and practises were best. This strategy helped to pave the way for the Roman invasion of Britain almost 100 years later in 43 AD; cf. Oliver, *Ancient Britain*, p. 343f.

[1142] Held, *Kriegsgefangenschaft in Großbritannien*, p. 103f.

[1143] Held, *Kriegsgefangenschaft in Großbritannien*, p. 156f. and footnote 78.

groups of those convinced by the system of democracy were to visit other camps in Britain in order to educate their countrymen on democracy. The aim being that re-educated prisoners would become "democratic missionaries" upon their return to Germany. After screening the prisoners of the various camps and selecting suitable candidates[1144], nationwide re-education began in the summer of 1945.[1145]

Re-education exclusively took place in camps in Britain and Northern Africa. Camps in Europe, Canada and Australia were excluded from the scheme.[1146] The aim of PWE and POWD was to confront the POWs with the cultural aspects of their respective detention forces, making them aware of the culture and history of not only their homeland but also of other countries, and by doing so developing a new image of humanity based on democratic values. In a second step they were to turn their backs on Nazi philosophy and learn about the benefits of a democratic system of government - as independently thinking individuals and not based on group conformity. This was rooted in the firm belief that the merits of democracy could only be properly conveyed through open debates and by providing role models.[1147] Camp libraries and camp newspapers, cinema shows and lectures, radio broadcasts, exhibitions, English lessons, committees for various cultural activities and religious provision were the basic components of the re-education scheme.[1148] Varying from camp to camp, the prisoners could also attend concerts, join sports activities, and receive any medical care required and get the same food rations as British servicemen.[1149] Some camps such as "Camp Nr. 18" (Featherstone in Northumberland) offered education at university level with degree courses (which would later also be recognised in Germany) in various subjects alongside political training courses[1150]; others such as the most famous camp and training centre in Great Britain, Wilton Park in Buckinghamshire, was established "to supplement and crown the general work of re-education" and was therefore a signature project of the British endeavours towards a future democratic reconstruction of Germany.[1151] Unfortunately, as it turned out, due to the extent of the administrative side of the project, the ambitious plans could only be realised to a marginal degree.[1152] The success of the re-education

1144 Held, *Kriegsgefangenschaft in Großbritannien*, p. 163ff.
1145 Held, *Kriegsgefangenschaft in Großbritannien*, p. 181.
1146 Held, *Kriegsgefangenschaft in Großbritannien*, p. 193.
1147 Held, *Kriegsgefangenschaft in Großbritannien*, p. 179.
1148 Held, *Kriegsgefangenschaft in Großbritannien*, p. 179.
1149 Wheeler, *German Prisoners of War in Britain*.
1150 Held, *Kriegsgefangenschaft in Großbritannien*, p. 193ff.
1151 Held, *Kriegsgefangenschaft in Großbritannien*, p. 202ff. and footnote 26 (quote from a leaflet of a camp commander).
1152 Held, *Kriegsgefangenschaft in Großbritannien*, p. 226.

scheme and its influence on post-war democratic life in what later became the Federal Republic of Germany is impossible to measure.[1153]

Although POW camps were established in the vicinity of almost every major town in Britain, neither the name Barlborough nor the name Southgate appear in the available lists of POW camps in England. According to Roger J C Thomas's list, there were eight POW camps in Derbyshire and four in Nottinghamshire, mostly described as "Working Camps".[1154] All of them were comparatively close to Barlborough and Clowne (near Alfreton, near Burton-upon-Trent, just outside Derby, around Worksop and in the vicinity of Chesterfield). The German Red Cross' tracing service holds files which contain testimonials from returning German soldiers from England, but unfortunately again neither Barlborough, Clowne nor Southgate are explicitly mentioned anywhere.[1155] A "Camp Nr. 635" in Derby is mentioned a few times, this seems however to have been a mere hut camp.[1156]

At the time of the Fourth Meeting of the Council of Foreign Ministers in Moscow, from March 10 to April 24, 1947, 435,295 German prisoners were being detained in Great Britain or held by British authorities.[1157] In accordance with the agreement of the Victorious Powers from April 1947, the first POWs returned home in 1947, and the last in 1949.[1158] The key date of release of the last German war prisoners in England was July 12, 1948 (the end date for the conclusion of British repatriation was scheduled for December 31, 1948). During the first half of 1948 there were still 100,000 former Wehrmacht soldiers detained in Britain.[1159] More than a few decided to stay in England instead of returning home to Germany, for example taking jobs as civil agricultural workers (ca. 32,000 former prisoners of who 19,000 held contracts with the County Agricultural Executive Committees).[1160] Renate Held

1153 Held, *Kriegsgefangenschaft in Großbritannien*, p. 239.

1154 Thomas, *Prisoner of War Camps*, list p. 18-55.

1155 These two camps must have been rather insignificant. The databases of the Bundesarchiv - Abteilung Militärchiv (Department Military Archives) in Freiburg im Breisgau do not hold any information on camps at Southgate House or in Barlborough. Achim Koch of the archives was so kind as to search the Elsa-Brandström-Gedächtnisarchiv: Kriegsgefangenenwesen 1867 bis Gegenwart (MSg 200), the archive of the Evangelisches Hilfswerk für Kriegsgefangene e.V. (MSg 194), the documents of the Maschke-Kommission zur Erforschung der Kriegsgefangenengeschichte (B 205) and the Militärgeschichtliche Sammlung (MSg 2) for me, unfortunately without any results (information disclosed by E-Mail on August 7, 2013).

1156 Information disclosed by Eva Stoewer of the tracing service of the German Red Cross by E-mail on April 4, 2013.

1157 Held, *Kriegsgefangenschaft in Großbritannien*, p. 232, footnote 64.

1158 Wheeler, *German Prisoners of War in Britain.*

1159 Held, *Kriegsgefangenschaft in Großbritannien*, p. 232; WDR, *Heimkehr mit Verzögerung.*

1160 Held, *Kriegsgefangenschaft in Großbritannien*, p. 234.

provides a list of the number of German POWs in British hands between 1939 and 1948[1161]:

- November 14, 1939: 112 German POWs in British detention / 112 in Great Britain
- December 18, 1940: 3,594 German POWs in British detention / 401 in Great Britain
- December 31, 1941: 7,275 German POWs in British detention / 1,850 in Great Britain
- December 31, 1942: 25,930 German POWs in British detention / 550 in Great Britain
- December 31, 1943: 35,860 German POWs in British detention / 1,110 in Great Britain
- December 31, 1944: 270,535 German POWs in British detention / 144,450 in Great Britain
- December 31, 1945: 1,007,700 German POWs in British detention / 211,300 in Great Britain
- December 31, 1946: 606,805 German POWs in British detention / 355,200 in Great Britain
- December 31, 1947: 214,650 German POWs in British detention / 155,700 in Great Britain
- December 31, 1948: 1,500 German POWs in British detention / 0 in Great Britain

The esteem in which Britain was held, among the prisoners as well as the general public, for treating its POWs respectfully and the ambitious efforts of the re-education schemes became seriously threatened the longer repatriation took after the war had ended. The German prisoners played a significant role in the British post-war economy when labour was urgently needed (especially in agriculture). Italian POWs had already been repatriated and British soldiers detained abroad had yet to be returned. On top of all this, British military strategists wrestled during the last weeks of the war with the question of how to deal with resistance groups, whose presence was seen as a serious threat. Consequently, they attempted to delay the repatriation of the elite leaders of the Wehrmacht for as long as possible as well. However, the British general public soon became aware of the difficult situation and denounced the circumstances as slave labour. The government felt under pressure to finally

---

1161 Based on Wolff, S., *Die deutschen Kriegsgefangenen in britischer Hand. Ein Überblick*, (Zur Geschichte der deutschen Kriegsgefangenen des Zweiten Weltkrieges, hrsg. v. E. Maschke, Leiter der Wissenschaftlichen Kommission für deutsche Kriegsgefangenengeschichte, Bd. 11-1), München 1974, p. 3 to 24, p. 21, data compiled at the behest of the Maschke-Kommission; cf. Held, *Kriegsgefangenschaft in Großbritannien*, p. 241.

repatriate all German prisoners. Government plans regarding release were revised in favour of the prisoners.[1162]

It seemed a good idea to me to try and find German war veterans alive today who had spent time as POWs in Barlborough or Southgate. A memoir from that particular time would have made a valuable contribution to this book. Unfortunately, I was not successful in this regard although there is ample proof of the presence of German POWs in the area: Derek Bower, who formerly lived on Southgate Estate, asserts in an on-line blog that Southgate House was requisitioned for military purposes and was indeed initially a British Army camp.[1163] Towards the end of the war it housed German POWs, and later Italian POWs.[1164] The German prisoners of Southgate Camp came from Albuquerque (USA) where they were initially taken after being captured by the Americans. They came to Southgate while awaiting repatriation (also for re-education programmes).[1165] In 1945 a German POW named Erich Siegel was one of those prisoners.[1166] According to Derek Bower, his father used to work with Mr Siegel for the military in the tunnels at Welbeck Abbey.[1167] Six prisoners worked with his father there, apart from Erich Siegel Mr Bower only remembers that one was named Karl and that there were four others. To his

---

1162 "Operation Seagull" and "Operation Oberon"; cf. Held, *Kriegsgefangenschaft in Großbritannien*, p. 219ff., p. 239.

1163 http://www.clownevillage.co.uk/feedback/feedback.htm (Derek Bower on January 17, 2009) (viewed 19/05/2013).

1164 Nora and Denis Jones remember that on summer evenings Whitwellian inhabitants "could often hear the Italians singing as they walked back to their POW Camp at Southgate."; cf. Jones, *Life in the Village during World War II*. The Italian soldiers apparently were quite popular with the ladies as Sylvia Linacre recalls "Some Italians were very friendly and it was whispered that at least one dark-eyed dusky-skinned baby appeared."; cf. Linacre, *How it was*, p. 79.

1165 This was based on an agreement made in January 1943 between Great Britain and the United States. In accordance with this the United States consented to take 150,000 German prisoners into custody on trust for Great Britain. After the war London was entitled to claim them; cf. Held, *Kriegsgefangenschaft in Großbritannien*, p. 227, footnote 27.

1166 During his imprisonment in Albuquerque Erich Siegel made a couple of pencil drawings, many of them of excellent quality. He collected the drawings in a sketchbook which he gave to Derek Bower as a present before he left to return to Germany. Derek Bower treasured this little book for 60 years until it was finally returned to the children of Mr Siegel in autumn 2013. I added one of his drawings to this book (the drawing is undated, Figure 46). It shows a bomber aircraft (presumably an American Boeing B-17 Flying Fortress) dropping its deathly freight over some unspecified landscape (if the black dots underneath the aircraft are interpreted correctly).

1167 http://www.losttrekkers.com/detail.asp?iType=199&iAd=2193 (entry undated, viewed 18/05/2013) and communicated to the author in a private E-mail correspondence on May 20, 2013.

regret, Mr Bower and Mr Siegel lost contact after he was repatriated to Germany. He vaguely remembers that he lived in Southern Germany with his family and that he worked as a clerk. Attempts to find Mr Siegel proved to be somewhat painstaking, but thanks to good archival practice it was possible to trace him, alas I was a year too late to speak to him personally.[1168]

Karl celebrated his 21st birthday whilst he was at Southgate. Derek Bower recalls that his mother, Elizabeth Bower, prepared a special tea for him and his colleagues at the Bower's cottage. The Bower family and friends also attended the celebration. Erich and Karl were regular visitors to the Bower's house on Sundays for afternoon tea. They also took Derek and his sister to the Camp every Wednesday evening to watch cinema screenings, which were always films starring Deanna Durbin.

The recollections of June Pearce's father support Mr Bower's stories. He told his daughter that the prisoners were allowed to roam freely, because they enjoyed staying at Southgate. They were well treated, well fed and found there to be people friendly. The prisoners worked on local farms. Many settled in Clowne after the war ended.[1169] The photograph on Figure 47 shows five German POWs at Barlborough Farm. Madge Bunting, the owner of the photograph, remembers them coming by bus to the farm so it may be that they were billeted at Norton Camp/North Cuckney Camp (Mansfield, Nottinghamshire) and not at Southgate. "Whether the men were from Southgate or Norton I do not know", Derek Bower adds. "It is quite feasible because the six men working with my father were transported by lorry to Welbeck Abbey which was around the same distance as Norton to Barlborough. Why the authorities would want to transport men from Norton to Barlborough when Southgate was nearer. Why also would they transport men from Southgate to Welbeck when Norton was nearer. We may never know."[1170] Mrs Bunting recalls that the first batch of prisoners that came to the area worked very hard. The second batch however would not work at all. The farmer was asked to sign documents stating that he was satisfied with the

---

1168 Enquiries at Deutsches Historisches Museum (Berlin), Volksbund Deutsche Kriegsgräberfürsorge (Kassel), the Tracing Service of the German Red Cross (Munich) returned no results. But the „Deutsche Dienststelle (WASt) für die Benachrichtigung der nächsten Angehörigen von Gefallenen der ehemaligen deutschen Wehrmacht" (= German agency for the notification of next-of-kin of members of the former German Wehrmacht who were killed in action) (Berlin)", http://www.dd-wast.de/frame_e.htm (viewed 21/05/2013), held information on Erich Siegel in their written material and informed me by letter on July 16, 2013 that Mr Siegel passed away in Mutterstadt in March 2012. Personal contact could be established with Erich Siegel's son Klaus (b. 1943), his daughter Heide (b. 1950) and his son-in-law Georg Barczynski.

1169 Information disclosed by June Pearce in a private E-mail correspondence with the author on May 24, 2013; see also Bak, *Barbers Row*, p. 28.

1170 Extract from a private E-mail correspondence between Derek Bower and the author on August 16, 2013.

work carried out.[1171] Mavis and John Aston, a couple living in Creswell, described to me how the prisoners of war used to play football with the local miners and that German POWs helped with harvesting on the Platts family farm.[1172]

Another set of war prisoners were quartered at "The Prince of Wales", a public house on the crossroads of Sheffield Road (A6135) and Barbers Row, halfway between Barlborough and Renishaw. The pub, built in the 1860s and which still exists as a restaurant today, used to be the social hub of Barbers Row, a small neighbourhood which ceased to exist in 1970 when the old Victorian terraced houses were demolished as part of redevelopment plans and a functioning, close-knit community was torn apart.[1173] The prisoners reportedly lived in the rooms of the pub and worked as farm hands on the surrounding farms. The residents of Barbers Row recall that "some of the prisoners were extremely skilled craftsmen and very talented at carving".[1174] They carved toys for the children out of scraps of wood which they brought them.

At Barlborough Heritage and Resource Centre a large carved wooden sculpture is on display depicting St. George and the Dragon. The underside of the base of the large and skilfully carved sculpture is engraved with the name of the artist: F Seibel[1175] and the year it was made: 1946. According to the records, Friedrich Seibel was held as a POW at Norton Camp/North Cuckney Camp[1176] and worked on the grounds of Barlborough Hall in 1946, doing jobs

---

1171 Photograph courtesy of Madge Bunting and Tony Bak. Additional information disclosed by Tony Bak in a private E-mail correspondence with the author on August 16, 2013.

1172 Information disclosed during a chance meeting on September 21, 2013 in Clowne. As inhabitants of Creswell, I presume Mrs and Mr Aston were referring to Hazelmere Farm, Hazelmere Road, Creswell (today the farm of J and J Platts; North Walls Farm in Clowne is owned by a G Platts, and used to be let to A J Platts in 1948, see Chapter 16); cf. http://www.yell.com/ucs/UcsSearchAction.do?keywords=farmers&location=clowne&scrambleSeed=61856656&searchType=&M=&bandedclarifyResults=&ssm=1 (viewed 16/10/2013).

1173 Bak, *Barbers Row*, p. 6f.

1174 Bak, *Barbers Row*, p. 28.

1175 Friedrich Seibel was born in 1906 according to Stephan Kühmayer from „Deutsche Dienststelle (WASt) für die Benachrichtigung der nächsten Angehörigen von Gefallenen der ehemaligen deutschen Wehrmacht" (disclosed in a E-mail correspondence with the author dated June 3, 2013). It is fairly certain that Mr Seibel would not still be alive today, so no attempt was made to trace him.

1176 Shortly after the end of the war, in 1947/1948, Cuckney Camp became a RAF Maintenance Base manned mainly by civilian staff. Derek Bower worked there for a while, after leaving school, as a civil servant (information disclosed in a private E-mail correspondence with the author on June 3, 2013).

such as moving railings etc., hence the carving of St. George and the Dragon.[1177] Mr Seibel presented his sculpture to the local school.[1178]

Unfortunately, Sylvia Linacre's observations in her memoirs on her life in Barlborough are not very precise regarding the duration of the prisoners' detention.

The body responsible for maintaining the POW camp at Southgate was the Ministry of Works. This can be concluded from entries in a rental/tax account book of Renishaw Hall Estate between the years 1946 and 1961.[1179] In 1947 and 1948 the Ministry of Works paid rents to the Renishaw Hall Estate on a semi-annual basis for renting Southgate House and gardens, as well as for renting 16 acres of the estate's woodland. The rent for Southgate House and gardens was 65 pounds and due September 9, 1947, December 9, 1947, June 8, 1948 and December 7, 1948. The rent for the woodlands, due on the same dates, was 5 pounds, 2 shillings and 6 halfpence in 1947 and only 1 pound in 1948. Doubtlessly these portions of the plot were used to house the prisoners and to build Nissen huts on.

Mary Jones reports that after the war there were still Italian prisoners of war billeted at Southgate Estate (Derek Bower adds that the Italian POWs were brought into the Nissen huts following the German POWs departure[1180]). According to Mrs Jones, they may have worked on local farms. They used to come past Harlesthorpe Cottages on their way to Clowne. The children were told not to speak to them, "but they looked Ok, there was never any trouble".[1181]

The Nissen huts remained in place after the last prisoner left Southgate and were then made use of as cheap and primitive accommodation for those in dire need of shelter. In this case it was local families who moved into the huts following the closure of the camp around 1946/47. These people were known

---

1177 Information disclosed in a private E-Mail correspondence between Tony Bak and the author on August 16, 2013.

1178 Bak, *Barbers Row*, p. 28. Sculpture viewed by Graham Duckmanton and the author at Barlborough Heritage and Resource Centre on April 20, 2013.

1179 Derbyshire Record Office, *Ref. No. D6573/Box 120/5*.

1180 Information disclosed in a private E-mail correspondence between Derek Bower and the author on July 1, 2013. Italian POWs were clearly favoured as labourers by Winston Churchill - not only were they regarded as less dangerous than the purportedly hostile German soldiers but also more motivated than labour immigrants from Ireland – as described a memorandum to War Cabinet Secretary Sir Edward Bridges on May 29, 1941: "(…) it might be better to use these docile Italian prisoners of war instead of bringing disaffected Irish, over whom we have nothing like the same control.", cf. Held, *Kriegsgefangenschaft in Großbritannien*, p. 58 and footnote 22 (source: The National Archives, *Ref. No. PRO PREM 3-363*, original document not viewed personally).

1181 Information disclosed in a private E-mail correspondence between Mary Jones and the author on May 29, 2013.

as squatters. Derek Bower describes them as young families who could not find accommodation elsewhere in the area. They took over the huts and which, according to him, were eventually modernised by the local council who brought them up to a better standard by installing mains water and toilets. They also divided the huts into a living area with separate kitchen and bedrooms. Mr Bower estimates that the use of the huts as accommodation did not last longer than four or five years.[1182]

An old black and white photograph is evidence of the presence of these huts in the woods of Southgate Estate and in it can be seen the huts after the squatters had moved in (Figure 48).[1183] Mary Jones's Uncle Ernest and Aunt Maud (June Pearce's parents) moved into one of these renovated huts and she recalls that they made their home very cosy, she loved to visit them there. She cannot remember how long her uncle and her aunt stayed in that hut, but eventually all occupants were re-housed and the huts were demolished and the site cleared (according to Philip Riden in 1955[1184]). Some time later, June Pearce's father purchased one of the huts (after he started his transportation business in 1949). He removed it and re-erected it on his own land, and after some alterations used it as a garage for his first lorry. The foundations were made higher so that the lorries would fit under the roof. The hut was a good building, Mrs Pearce recalls. From the outside the hut now appeared taller, and the roofing material had to be replaced a few times. Inside the original wooden struts were still there. Mrs Pearce's grandfather also used the garage in cold weather for chopping firewood, which he sold in the local shops and door-to-door. Until recently, the hut was used as a workshop by both Mrs

---

1182 Information disclosed in a private E-mail correspondence between Derek Bower and the author on July 1, 2013.

1183 http://www.clownevillage.co.uk/feedback/feedback.htm (Derek Bower on January 17, 2009) (viewed 19/05/2013). The existence of these Nissen huts is further confirmed by the recollections of Barbara Duckmanton, disclosed in a personal discussion in April 2013.

1184 Riden, *History of the County of Derby III*, p. 134 and footnote 21: Minutes of Clowne Rural District Council from the years 1952, 1953 and 1955; cf. Derbyshire Record Office, Ref. No. D1271/1/24 (October 9, 1952, December 9, 1952), 25 (October 13, 1953) and 26 (February 8, 1955). Quote from the minutes of December 9, 1952 (#53/258): "The chairman raised the question of the derelict nature of this estate (referring to the evacuation of Southgate Camp) and suggested that as they were now only six tenants on the site, arrangements should be made for the transfer of these people to the Bevin Estate, Creswell, if they could not be otherwise re-housed, so that notice could be given to terminate the council's tenancy of Southgate Estate." Quote from the minutes of February 2, 1955 (#55/257): "The Clerk reported that the Surveyor and himself had met Mr. Ibbotson, of the Ministry of Housing and Local Government, and Mr. M. A. Hollingworth of this estate and had agreed the works to be carried out by the council before the site could be handed back to the owner. He stated that these would consist only of removing loose brick and rubble from the concrete foun(d)ations and of the demolition of the conveniences."

Pearce's brothers. Unfortunately, it was wrecked by winds and is no more.[1185] Today nothing is left of the Nissen huts in the woodland to the west of Southgate Stables apart from a few scattered moss-covered bricks in the undergrowth.[1186]

Additional information about the presence of squatters on Southgate Estate can be gained from the Electoral Rolls of Derbyshire. They mention a place named "Southgate Camp" on the grounds of Southgate Estate between the years 1948 and 1961. It offered space for 40 to 43 inhabitants (they are attested for example for the years 1948, 1949, 1955 and 1961). According to Philip Riden, after the POWs and the squatters there had been a third group of inhabitants of the Nissen huts: apparently they had been used as a miners' hostel before the site was finally vacated and cleared for demolition.[1187] From the viewpoint of the local Catholic congregation it deemed desirable as well to regain unrestrained access to Southgate House with its chapel as the parish needed a mass centre.[1188]

26. Short Synopsis on the Development of Southgate Estate

In order to better understand the growth and development of Southgate Estate I include a short a summary of the elements of the estate as mentioned in the original sources available to me. The Bowdon family belonged to a family of landowners with property in North Derbyshire. Henry (2) Bowdon and John (2) Bowdon, both of Beighton Fields, bore the title yeoman, and so already belonged to a group of small freeholders.[1189] The last will of Mary Bowdon (1782/1785) gives additional proof of a number of estates and properties owned by the Bowdons in the counties of Derbyshire, Yorkshire, Nottinghamshire and Warwickshire.

The first proof of the existence of Southgate Estate is the testament of George Staniforth dated 1757 which mentions "Southgate House and Farm (...) lying in the several Parishes of Barlbrough (*sic!*) Whitwell and Clown (*sic!*) in the County of Derby". If this is to be taken literally, which farm building Mr Staniforth might have been referring to? Furthermore, it can be concluded that the estate was already quite substantial, extending over three parishes.

The advertisement in the London Evening Post from 1787 describes the building of Southgate House in detail and lists various outbuildings such as

---

1185 Information disclosed in private E-mail correspondence between June Pearce and the author on January 31, 2014, February 2 and February 9, 2014.

1186 Observation from an on-site inspection by Graham Duckmanton and the author on September 22, 2013.

1187 Riden, *History of the County of Derby III*, p. 134.

1188 Staples, *My Parish*, p. 6.

1189 Estcourt, Payne, *Catholic nonjurors*, p. 32, p. 34.

"barn, stables, chaff-house" and "about 43 acres of included arable meadow, and pasture land adjoining the house".

The advertisement in The Derbyshire Times and Chesterfield Herald of December 27, 1882 again describes the mansion in detail, but remains comparatively vague regarding the grounds of the estate: "extensive pleasure grounds", farm and farm land to be provided on request, shooting range available.

The Land Values Map of 1909/1910 lists - apart from Southgate House - 26 separate units of Southgate Estate comprising of a substantial number of plantations, woodland and agricultural land on the grounds of Southgate Estate let to tenants, but no farm house is explicitly mentioned. All the more, the related Book of References cites a considerable number of cottages connected to the estate (a house called "Rodgwood", Harlesthorpe, a house and farm at Hickingwood, Cottages on 101 and 103 Rotherham Road, Cottages "Lake View"/Harlesthorpe Dam, a bungalow at 45 Station Road, Clowne, "The Hermitage" and another cottage at White Brick Moor).

In the Sale Particulars of 1938 Southgate Estate is offered for auction as an estate with a main building, a stable outbuilding and 16 cottages, several small holdings and seven farms: Springfield Farm, South Walls Farm, North Walls Farm, Manor Farm, Little Walls Farm, Eastwood Cottage Farm (at White Brick Moor) and Hickinwood Farm. The total amount of land is estimated at 800 acres, "Producing a Gross Annual Income of £1,436, Excluding the Residence".[1190]

1190 Derbyshire Record Office, *Ref. No. D1300/11/1.*

Appendices

Appendix 1

This period is marked by two consecutive developments, whose impact proved to be grave indeed. The first was the transferral of labour in rural areas of Britain from agricultural jobs to those the industrial sector (e.g. the looms and weaving mills in the north of England). Additionally numerous able-bodied farmers left the country in search of a better life in the United States. Thus agricultural land became underworked and what were once flourishing estates soon turned into empty acreage. As a result, tenants could no longer pay their rents and estates could not survive on a reduced income. The graveness of the situation was exacerbated when at the beginning of the 17th century (1813 in particular) a period of good harvests, which lasted for longer than usual, coupled with an increase in the population during the industrial advancement, and Britain faced to give up the export of grain and not very much later had to import grain. Over the course of the Napoleonic Wars (1803-1815) it was no longer possible for Britain to import corn from the continent. This resulted in an increase of wheat farming in Britain, and as a consequence higher bread prices. Yet, when to war ended the importation of foreign corn started up again which in turn caused prices to drop (prices halved between 1812 and 1815). Consequently, it became impossible for tenants to meet their cost of production and the landowning class had to deal with falling profits.

Landowners concerned about the future prospects of their income sought to apply pressure on the members of the House of Commons to step in, which led to the establishment of what became known as the "Corn Laws" (Importation Acts of 1815 and 1822). These were a measure of artificial protectionism which allowed the import of foreign cereal products to be free of duty only when the price of domestically harvested grain rose to 80 shillings per quarter (1815) and 70 shillings per quarter (1822). These acts were resented by townspeople who had to pay higher bread prices, and the industrial classes saw themselves economically disadvantaged by Parliament who seemed to be favouring the landowning class.

Furthermore, manufacturers were anxious that as a consequence of the Corn Laws they would have to pay their workers higher wages. The conflict intensified over the next years when, following a very poor harvest in 1816, bread prices rose rapidly which led to food riots, strikes and unrest among the working class who in the face of rising food prices demanded higher wages. Further pressure was inflicted on the people when they were in dire need of food, e.g. during the Great Famine in Ireland (1845-1852).

The Corn Laws never really had the desired effect, as prices remained low and never reached the level which would allow the admission of foreign corn, and tenants did not meet their cost of production and therefore could not come up to cover their rents. The invention of a "sliding scale" (import duty rises when domestic corn prices fall and again when they rise) did not alleviate the situation in the long run either. The Corn Laws were repealed by the Importation Act of 1846 and the introduction of free trade.[1191]

Appendix 2

"The ridgeway route ran north from Broxtowe through Hucknall to Annesley, Pleasley (Northfield) and from there to a fort at Clowne (Dambrook) (*sic!*), an Iron-Age fort built on the hills of Markland Grips. The road continued north to Rotherham where it converged with Ryknild Street."[1192] Ryknild Street, apparently also known as Icknield Street, was a Roman military road running south-north which passed through Derby and ended in Rotherham (Templeborough)[1193] According to NN, "Focus on: Clowne"[1194], "Ryknield Street" is the route still used today as Mansfield Road (B6417), in its course becoming part of the A618, northwards up to Harthill it is named "Packman Way". Mike Bishop calls the route "New Bound Mill", its northern course following modern B6417/Mansfield Road through Clowne and running towards Castleford/Doncaster.[1195] Matthew Beresford sees this ridgeway as "a road or trackway of at least Roman date and most likely earlier given the abundance of pre-Roman archaeological sites located within a mile or two of the road."[1196] The road could have been "the main track along the limestone plateau in prehistoric times."[1197]

Appendix 3

Copyhold is closely connected to the proceedings at manors. According to the article "Copyhold" in Encyclopaedia Britannica, this is a form of landholding "at the will of the lord according to the custom of the manor". The article elaborates: "Its origin is found in the occupation by villeins, or nonfreeman, of portions of land belonging to the manor of the feudal lord. A portion of the manor reserved for the lord was cultivated by labourers who were bound to the land; their service was obligatory, and they could not leave the manor. They were allowed, however, to cultivate land for their own use. This copyhold was mere occupation at the pleasure of the lord, but in time it grew into an occupation by right, called *villenagium*, that was recognized first by

---

1191 Ross, *Corn Laws;* Hobsbawm, *Industry and Empire,* p. 14, p. 77ff., p. 84; Engels, "Geschichte der englischen Korngesetze".

1192 Pearcy, *Forts.*

1193 Stock, *Roman Rotherham.*

1194 NN, "Focus on: Clowne", p. 24.

1195 Bishop, "An Archaeological Resource Assessment of Roman Nottinghamshire", p. 9.

1196 Beresford, "Scarcliffe Park", p. 10.

1197 Riden, *History of the County of Derby III,* p. 1. See also Derbyshire County Council, *Bulmer's Derby 1895,* p. 15.

custom and later by law. The records of the court baron constituted the title of the villein tenant to the land held by copy of the court roll (hence the term copyhold); and the customs of the manor recorded therein formed the real property law applicable to this case. In 1926 all copyhold land became freehold land, though the lords of manors retained mineral and sporting rights."[1198]

Appendix 4

In 1904/1905 Hermann Muthesius drew up a concise and meritorious description of the complicated circumstances of the other forms of land-tenure: freehold and leasehold.[1199] In his time (between 1896 and 1903 he lived and worked as technical and cultural attaché at the German embassy in London and wrote down his detailed observations on the English house) land in Britain was still mostly the property of the crown and was given to temporary owners who were considered tenants. If there was no heir to a piece of land when an owner died, it was returned to the crown. However, families tried to keep their leased land in the families, making it inalienable through heredity, and by doing so securing their prestige (and the base of their income, for example when the land yielded mineral resources, as we will see in our case). Therefore, when referring to the "estate" in England one has to distinguish between freehold and leasehold, or, simplified, between ownership and tenancy. According to Muthesius, in the great majority of cases the owner for the time being held a lease of land, with the result that freehold property was valued much higher. "…, freehold ownership is mostly only found in entire areas of some size. Freehold may either be absolute (…) or part of a family settlement (…), or there may merely be a life interest in an estate."

Since most of the aristocratic freeholders of land were unwilling to sell, building on leasehold land became the most common practice for those who were eager to build, and it was seen favourably, as it enabled many people to own a house without the obligation of buying expensive ground on which to build on. The agreement on leases between proprietor and leaseholder were long. There was the so-called "99-year lease" which was based on a law governing church land, meaning land could not be sold, but leased for a period not exceeding 99 years, but leases with similar conditions such as 80, 60, or 40 years were increasingly granted too. Requests from leaseholders to extend the lease up to 999 years in order to create a sort of "ownership" were not uncommon[1200]; all granted on the condition that "at termination both land and buildings were to revert to the landlord."

1198 Encyclopedia Britannica, *Copyhold.*

1199 Muthesius, *English House*, p. 71ff.

1200 Muthesius, *English House*, p. 72.

Landowners in England leased building-land in return for a variable annual rent, which never undercut 5% of the current selling value, and they had a right of co-determination regarding the buildings that were to be erected (size and quality of building, materials used, even retaining architects). This evidently deprived house owners of complete control over their property, as everything depended on the assent of the landlord. The value of houses erected on leasehold land decreased the closer the date of reversion drew, and house owners naturally did not have much interest in the proper upkeep of their houses the nearer the date came, even though the owner was obliged to hand over the building in sound condition (house owners naturally would have erected better houses if they had owned the ground on which they built). This development could be inversed when market values increased at the same time. House owners had the right to sell their houses with all their liabilities at any given time; the selling price was of course influenced by the underlying specific leasehold conditions. With the termination of the lease however, the ground was returned to the landlord together with the house, and the landlord became the new owner of the building. This did not mean that the inhabitants had to leave. The landlord could then let the house to them for a further 40 years (with subsequent reversion then), this was linked to certain conditions - for example modernisation works -, all much to the disadvantage of the inhabitants.

Appendix 5

Fampoux is a little village on the river Scarpe, to the East of Arras, Northern France (Somme area). It was taken from the Germans in the course of the "Battle of Arras" in 1917 and remained behind the Allied front line until the Germans started their final spring offensive, "Operation Michael" or "Kaiserschlacht", on March 21 of the following year. The German Army recaptured parts of the village, but under great loss of human life the British forces maintained the hold on the remainder. The battle lasted until July 4, 1918. Around the village of Fampoux there are five war cemeteries containing the graves of innumerable soldiers, some of whom will never be identified. These places are the silent witnesses of the dreadful proceedings.[1201] It seems as if the mortal remains of Basil Butler-Bowdon were never recovered and never returned home.

A probate calendar dated 1919 gives slightly deviant information about the date and place of his death (March 29, 1918 and Gavrelle, a place very near to Fampoux). It states that he died in active service (administration). His effects

---

1201 Baker, *Lancashire Fusiliers*; http://www.wintonforum.co.uk/fampoux.html (viewed 29/05/2014).

were priced at £79, 16s and 2d and according to his will dated June 5, 1917, they were left to his father John Erdeswick Butler-Bowdon, Esq.[1202]

Fampoux Gardens Memorial in Winton (a suburb of Bournemouth) was built by survivors of the Battle of Fampoux in memory of their fallen comrades. Irony of fate: Bournemouth is the birth-place of Basil Butler-Bowdon.

Appendix 6

Burke, *General Armory* gives the following description[1203]: "Butler-Bowdon (Pleasington Hall, co. Lancashire), Quarterly: 1st and 4th, quarterly sa. and or, in the first quarter a lion pass. erm. langued gu., BOWDON; 2nd and 3rd , az. a chev. betw. three covered cups or, the centre chief point a cross crosslet pf the last, BUTLER. Crests - 1st: A heron's head erased ppr., beaked and charged on the neck with three ermine spot, sa. 2nd: A covered cup, charged with an ermine spot, sa. Motto - Vanus est honor." Burke, Burke, *Genealogical and Heraldic History*, p. 126 describe the crest of (Richard) John Francis Butler of Pleasington: "Arms - Quarterly: 1st and 4th, sa. and or, in the first quarter a lion, passant, arg., langued, gu. for BOWDON; 2nd and 3rd, az, a chev. between three covered cups, or, for BUTLER. Crests - 1st, for BOWDON, 2nd, a covered cup, or, for BUTLER. Motto - Comme je trouve. Seat - Pleasington Hall, co. Lancashire." The same source describes the crest of John (4) Peter Bruno Bowdon of Southgate and Beightonfields: "Arms - Quarterly: 1 st and 4th, sa. and or, in the first quarter, a lion, passant, arg. Langued, gu., for BOWDON; 2nd, gu. A bordure, erm.; 3rd, arg., on a chev., gu., five bezants, for ERDESWICK. Crests -1st, a heron's head, erased, ppr., beaked, and charged on the neck with three ermine spots, sa.; 2nd, out of a ducal coronet, or, a demi-eagle displayed, ppr. Motto - Vanus est honor. Seats - Southgate House and Beighton Fields, co. Derbyshire." Fairbairn's *Book of Crests*, p. 92 also gives a short, very similar description: "(…) (1) A heron's head erased ppr., beaked and charged on the neck with three erm. spots (for Bowdon). (2) A covered cup or, charged with an erm. spat sa. (for Butler). Vanus est honor."

Appendix 7

A Canadian Memorial Cross for sale on-line in May 2014[1204] sheds some light on the situation: according to the description of the object, this cross was awarded in remembrance of Private Romolo Del Monaco alias Ronald Bowdon. The reverse is incised with "151547 Pte. R. Bowdon". Apparently he emigrated to Dunrea, Canada in 1915 under the alias of "Ronald Bowdon",

---

1202 Information retrieved from http://www.ancestry.co.uk and provided to me by Tony Bak during a personal visit to Barlborough Heritage and Research Centre on September 21, 2013 and in a personal E-Mail correspondence dated May 20, 2014.

1203 Burke, *General Armory*, p. 155.

1204 eMedals, *A 1916 Canadian Memorial Cross.*

giving his place and date of birth as Sheffield, October 25, 1893, and his trade as "laborer" (cf. an attestation paper of Library and Archives Canada (unspecified in the source and undated). Following the specifications he "Served as Ronald Bowden (*sic!*). Son of the late Ireneo Paolo del Monaco and Alice Elizabeth Del Monaco (nee (*sic!*) Bowden (*sic!*)), of Beightonfields Priory, Renishaw, Derbyshire." Stated as his next of kin is his brother Henry Bowden (*sic!*) of Beightonfields, Renishaw, Derbyshire, England. Romolo is described as 5 feet 11.5 inches tall, of fair complexion, with brown eyes and black hair. He was a Roman Catholic and unmarried.[1205]

Romolo/Ronald enlisted into the 79th Battalion Canadian Infantry, Manitoba Regiment on November 10, 1915, transferred to the 43rd Canadian Cameron Highlanders (Infantry, 9th Brigade, 3rd Canadian division) on June 28, 1916, and was killed in action at the battle of Regina Trench at the Ancre Heights (near Corbie, Département Somme, Arrondissement Amiens) on October 8, 1916. This battle took place between October 1 and November 11, 1916 when the Canadian armed forces assaults on Regina Trench witnessed brutal fighting and heavy loss of lives.[1206]

Ronald Bowdon was initially reported missing in action on October 8, 1916, but only on July 14, 1917 he was "previously reported missing now for official purposes presumed to have died".[1207] His mortal remains are interred in London Cemetery and Extension, Longueval (Département Somme, Picardie), Northern France (grave reference: 4 E 21).[1208]

Bob Clarke adds: "The use of an alias when enlisting into the military is not an unusual event and the Canadian Expeditionary Force certainly has a number of enlistees who, for various reasons, provided recruiters with a false name and purposely inaccurate personal details. This Memorial Cross is a prime example of this action. Born to such distinguished persons (an added photograph of a solemn declaration names Alice Del Monaco as "Countess", see below), one has to ponder why young Romolo and his brother Bernard immigrated to Du(n)rea, Manitoba to become labourers. On the outbreak of the Great War, Romolo and his brother both enlisted into the 79th Manitoba Battalion on November 1915, becoming 151547 Private R. Bowdon. On his attestation documents, Romolo identifies himself as Ronald Bowden (*sic!*), born 25 October 1893 in Sheffield, England, with his next of kin his brother Henry Bowdon. His other brother enlists as 1529190 Private Bernard Bowdon with his next of kin listed as his mother Alice del (*sic!*) Monaco. (...)" For estate purposes, she provided a solemn declaration signed at Horseferry Road Schools, City of Westminster on April 16, 1917, which reads as follows: "In the

---

1205 Preston, Clarke, Hulls, *Derbyshire War Memorials Project*.

1206 Commonwealth War Graves Commission, *The Battle of the Somme, Ancre Heights*.

1207 Clarke, "From Riches to Rags", p. 15.

1208 Preston, Clarke, Hulls, *Derbyshire War Memorials Project;* Commonwealth War Graves Commission, *Casualty Details* (Romolo Del Monaco).

matter of the estate of the late No. 15147. Private T. (sic!) Bowdon, 43rd Battalion, C.E.P. I Alice Bowdon Countess del Monaco of Beightonfields, Renishaw, Chesterfield. Hereby solemnly and sincerely declare: - (1) That I am the mother of No. 151547. Private Romolo Bowdon, 43rd Battalion, C.E.F. and that his correct name was Romolo del Monaco. (2) That he was born in Rome on the 26th October 1893. And I make this solemn declaration conscientiously believing the same to be true and knowing that it is of the same force and effect as if made under oath, and by virtye (*sic!*) of the Statutory Declarations Act, 1895. Alice del Monaco."[1209]

Why both brothers chose to go to Canada and joined in the Canadian armed forces in first place is beyond my knowledge. And why would a young man like Romolo Del Monaco obfuscate his true name and his place of birth when entering military service? Bob Clarke says: "Surely his family connections could have assisted him to obtain a commission or other considerations and Italy was an ally in the Great War."[1210] Romolo's motive will have to remain unexplained.

Romolo Del Monaco's medals and awards (British War Medal, Allied Victory Medal, Memorial Cross, Plaque and Scroll) were sent to his mother Alice who at that time resided at Coombe Lodges, Buckinghamshire. Later on she lived at 70 Oxford Terrace, Lancaster Gate, London – "a grand 19th century home across from Hyde Park", so Bob Clarke.

Appendix 8

Information according to an article in the Catholic Herald dated December 30, 1938.[1211] Responsible for the construction of the church was Frank M Reynolds (1910-1967, of Reynolds and Scott of Manchester): "Reynolds is the architect of the new church here - quite small but pleasing" an unnamed employee of John Hardman Studios, Birmingham observes in a handwritten memo.[1212] According to Mrs Staples, the Catholics started saving for a church of their own in Clowne, always supported by the Butler-Bowdon family. The foundation stone for was laid on May 17, 1952[1213] and the new church was opened for midnight mass at Christmas 1952. The church was officially opened in June 1953 by Bishop Ellis of Nottingham. John Lancelot Butler-

---

1209 eMedals, *A 1916 Canadian Memorial Cross*; Clarke, "From Riches to Rags", p. 14.

1210 Clarke, "From Riches to Rags", p. 14.

1211 Catholic Herald Archive, "Tee Church moves on".

1212 Birmingham City Archives at the Birmingham City Library, Ref. *No. MS 175/A/4/5/3/67, File 67 (C)*. See also Chapter 20.1; Walker, *Church of the Immaculate Conception*, p. 63ff. (for the church at Spinkhill); Staples, *My Parish*, p. 2 and p. 8 (for the church at Clowne).

1213 Cf. a typescript account (ca. 1955) of the Parishes of the Roman Catholic Diocese of Nottingham by Canon G D Sweeney, archivist of the diocese; information by kind courtesy of Canon Anthony Dolan by E-mail on May 19, 2014.

Bowdon, Lord Grey de Ruthyn, represented the Butler-Bowdon family on that occasion as Colonel William Erdeswick Ignatius Butler-Bowdon was too ill to attend.[1214] The same source also refers to Colonel Butler-Bowdon who, "many years ago, presented to the Catholics of the district a very fine plot of land situated at the extreme end of Clowne on the Creswell Road (...) and had it not been for the outbreak of the Second World War operations would have commenced in 1939. The upheaval consequent on the war put a stop to the project temporarily. Meanwhile, to the great regret of all, the Butler-Bowden (*sic!*) family left the district, and Southgate House passed into the possession of Sir Osbert Sitwell, of Renishaw. Happily, this did not mean the end of associations with Southgate Chapel, for Sir Osbert very kindly allowed the chapel still to be used. However, as the property was again for sale, it seemed good to His Lordship (the Bishop) to restart the project of building the church."

1214 "New Church-Hall at Clowne" by Fr A J Whittet, in: Nottingham Diocesan Yearbook 1953, p. 160f. Information by kind courtesy of Canon Anthony Dolan by E-mail on May 19, 2014.

Bibliography

Abram, William Alexander, *Parish of Blackburn, County of Lancaster, A History of Blackburn, town and parish*, Blackburn 1877

Aers, David, review on Staley, Lynn, *Margery Kempe's Dissenting Fictions*; cf. http://www.amazon.de/Margery-Kempes-Dissenting-Fictions-Staley/dp/0271025794/ref=sr_1_5?s=books-intl-de&ie=UTF8&qid=1364477697&sr=1-5 (review on Staley) (viewed 27/03/2013)

Alirangues, Loretta M, *Funerary Practices in the Victorian Era*, cf. http://www.morbidoutlook.com/nonfiction/articles/2003_04_vicdeath.html (Victorian burial customs) (viewed 06/06/2013)

Alchin, Linda, *Middle Ages*; cf. http://www.middle-ages.org.uk/margery-kempe.htm (general reading on Margery Kempe) (viewed 27/03/2013)

Arnold, Dana, *The Georgian Country House, Architecture, Landscape and Society*, Stroud 2013

Bahn, Paul, Pettitt, Paul, *Britain's Oldest Art, The Ice Age Cave Art of Creswell Crags*, English Heritage, Swindon 2009

Baines S.J., Fr Ralph, "A History of Spinkhill from the earliest times to 1842", in: *Spinkhill and its Registers 1757-1860*, unpublished, date unknown, at Mount St. Mary's College Archive, Spinkhill

Bak, Tony, *Welcome to Barbers Row*, Barlborough Heritage and Research Centre, Barlborough 2012

Baker, Chris, *The First Battles of the Somme*; in: The Long, Long Trail, The British Army in the Great War of 1914-1918; cf. http://www.1914-1918.net/bat22.htm (Operation Michael/Kaiserschlacht) (viewed 04/03/2014)

Baker, Chris, *The Lancashire Fusiliers*, in: The Long, Long Trail, The British Army in the Great War of 1914-1918; cf. http://www.1914-1918.net/lancsfus.htm (Lancashire Fusiliers) (viewed 29/05/2014)

Baker, Chris, *The Lancashire Hussars Yeomanry*, in: The Long, Long Trail, The British Army in the Great War of 1914-1918; cf. http://www.1914-1918.net/lancshussars.htm (Lancashire Hussars WWI) (viewed 04/03/2014)

Banerjee, Jacqueline, *John Hardman & Co.*, in: The Victorian Web; Literature, History & Culture in the Age of Victoria; cf. http://www.victorianweb.org/art/stainedglass/hardman (John Hartman & Co.) (viewed 02/10/2013)

Barlborough Heritage and Research Centre, *Interesting Facts about Barlborough*; cf. http://www.barlboroughrc.btck.co.uk/InterestingFacts (Barlborough House) (viewed 14/06/2013)

Barlborough Heritage and Research Centre, *Local Walks*; cf. http://www.barlboroughrc.btck.co.uk/LocalWalks (Barlborough Heritage and Research Centre) (viewed 25/05/2013)

Bates, Tom, *Eckington*; cf. http://www.aboutderbyshire.co.uk/cms/places/eckington.shtml (Eckington) (viewed 27/03/2013)

Baxter, Stephen et al., *Prosopography of Anglo-Saxon England* (Wulfric); cf. http://www.pase.ac.uk/jsp/DisplayPerson.jsp?personKey=15527 (Wulfric Spot(t)) (viewed 24/10/2014)
Baxter, Stephen et al., *Prosopography of Anglo-Saxon England* (Morcar); cf. http://www.pase.ac.uk/jsp/DisplayPerson.jsp?personKey=15290 (Morcar) (viewed 26/01/2014)
BBC, *Domesday Reloaded, Pleasington Old Hall*; cf. http://www.bbc.co.uk/history/domesday/dblock/GB-364000-426000/page/3 (Pleasington Old Hall) (viewed 16/06/2013)
Beckett, Matthew, *Lost Heritage, A Memorial to the Lost Country Houses of England*; cf. http://lh.matthewbeckett.com/houses/lh_derbyshire_derwenthall.html (Derwent Hall) (viewed 16/07/2013)
Beresford, Matthew, "Scarcliffe Park, A Journey through Time", in: *MBArchaeology* 2012; cf. http://www.mbarchaeology.co.uk/wp-content/uploads/2012/05/Scarcliffe%20Park.pdf (viewed 31/05/2013)
Birmingham City Archives at the Birmingham City Library, *Ref. No. MS 175/A/4/5/3/67, File 67 (C)* (Clowne, Catholic church, 1952/1953)
Birmingham City Archives at the Birmingham City Library, *Ref. No. MS 175/A/4/5/3/41, File 41 (B)* (Butler-Bowden brass)
Bishop, Elisabeth H, *Country House Revisited, The Economical and Cultural Impact of the English Country House as a Heritage Site*, 2011 (abstract of PhD thesis); cf. http:/collectionlinks.org.uk/attachment/article/1240/country_house_revisited.pdf (viewed 30/07/2013)
Bishop, Mike, "An Archaeological Resource Assessment of Roman Nottinghamshire", in: *East Midlands Archaeological Research Framework* 2011; cf. http://www.le.ac.uk/ulas/publications/documents/25nottrom_000.pdf (viewed 26/05/2013)
Booth, Tricia, *Belper Derbyshire*; cf. http://www.belper-research.com/records_matlock/Land%20values%20maps.pdf (Derbyshire Record Office, general information Land Values Map) (viewed 16/05/2013)
Boscombe Catholics, *Past Pupils' Association Magazine – 1963*; cf. http://www.boscombecatholics.net/boscombe/history/1963/1963-1.html (Theresa Butler-Bowdon) (viewed 31/03/2013)
Bowden, Chris, *Bowdon Marriage*, in: Cheshire L-Archives/RootsWeb; cf. http://archiver.rootsweb.ancestry.com/th/read/CHESHIRE/2007-12/1196623064 (Bowden/Bowdon family tree) (viewed 14/06/2013)
Bridgewater, A Neil, *Southgate Colliery 1877-1929*, cf. http://www.oldminer.co.uk/New/Southgate.htm (Southgate Colliery) (viewed 24/05/2013)
British Jesuit Archives, *Ref. No. MQ/1* (Bench Rents Spinkhill Church, Henry (5) Bowdon)

British Listed Buildings, *20, 21 Winckley Square, Preston;* cf. http://www.britishlistedbuildings.co.uk/en-392197-20-21-winckley-square-lancashire (Garlick, Park and Sykes) (viewed 05/06/2013)
British Listed Buildings, *Barlborough House, Barlborough;* cf. http://www.britishlistedbuildings.co.uk/en-79204-barlborough-house-barlborough-derbyshire (Barlborough House) (viewed 27/03/2013)
British Listed Buildings, *Southgate House, Clowne;* cf. http://www.britishlistedbuildings.co.uk/en-79287-southgate-house-clowne-derbyshire (viewed 17/10/2012)
British Listed Buildings, *Southgate Old House, Eckington;* cf. http://www.britishlistedbuildings.co.uk/en-79602-southgate-old-house-eckington-derbyshire (Southgate Old House, Eckington) (viewed 27/03/2013)
British Listed Buildings, *Southgate Stables, Including Wall to South Enclosing Stable Yard, Clowne;* cf. http://www.britishlistedbuildings.co.uk/en-79288-southgate-stables-including-wall-to-south (viewed 17/10/2012)
British Listed Buildings, *Walls Enclosing Burial Ground at Beighton Fields Priory, Barlborough;* cf. http://www.britishlistedbuildings.co.uk/en-79193-walls-enclosing-burial-ground-at-beighton (Beighton Fields Priory) (viewed 20/03/2013)
Brown, Richard, *Economic change: Agriculture;* cf. http://www.richardjohnbr.wordpress.com/2008/04/18/economic-change-agriculture/ (economy in the 1870s) (viewed 22/05/2013)
Bryn Mawr College Library Special Collections, *Hope Emily Allen Papers – Preliminary Guide;* cf. http://www.brynmawr.edu/library/speccoll/guides/allen.shtml (Hope Emily Allen) (viewed 05/03/2014)
Burke, Sir Bernard, *The General Armory of England, Scotland, Ireland, and Wales; Comprising a Registry of Armorial Bearings from the Earliest to the Present Time,* London 1884
Butler-Bowdon, William, *The Book of Margery Kempe 1436,* London 1936
Catholic Herald Archive, "Tee Church moves on"; in: *Catholic Herald* (30 December 1938, p. 13); cf. http://archive.catholicherald.co.uk/article/30th-december-1938/13/tee-church-moves-on (donation Col. Butler-Bowdon) (viewed 14/06/2013)
Catholic Herald Archive, "Acquittal of a Mystic", in: *Catholic Herald* (3 September 1954, p. 6); cf. http://archive.catholicherald.co.uk/article/3rd-september-1954/6/acquittal-of-a-mystic (discovery of manuscript Margery Kempe) (viewed 16/03/2013)
Catholic Herald Archive, "£33,000 Cope to stay in England", in: *Catholic Herald* (1 January 1955); cf. http://archive.catholicherald.co.uk/article/1st-july-1955/5/1233000-cope-to-stay-in-england (Butler Bowdon Cope) (viewed 14/06/2013)

Catholic Online, *St. Ursula*; cf.
http://www.catholic.org/saints/saint.php?saint_id=325 (Saint Ursula) (viewed 03/06/2014)
Catholic Online, *St. Gladys*; cf.
http://www.catholic.org/saints/saint.php?saint_id=3572 (Saint Gladys) (viewed 03/06/2014)
Catholics (England), *Declaration of the Roman Catholic Laity of England, A Protest against Interference with their Right to the Unfettered Exercise of their Religion*, London 1851
Chappell, Julie A, *Perilous Passages: The Book of Margery Kempe, 1534-1934*, Basingstoke 2013
Cherrett, Martin, *World War II Today*; cf. http://ww2today.com/23rd-may-1941-hms-kelly-sunk (Maurice Butler-Bowdon) (viewed 15/04/2014)
Cheshire, Jim, *Stained Glass and the Victorian Gothic Revival*, Manchester 2005
Cheshire Military Museum, *The Cheshire Yeomanry*; cf.
http://www.cheshiremilitarymuseum.co.uk/regimental-histories/cheshire-yeomanry.aspx (Cheshire Yeomanry) (viewed 31/12/2013)
Child, Stephen Martin, *A History of Pleasington Priory, The Parish of St. Mary and St. John*, Pleasington 2010
Clarke, Bob, "From Riches to Rags", in: *The Journal of the Military Collector's Club of Canada*, Winnipeg Spring 2010, p. 14f.
Commonwealth War Graves Commission, *Casualty Details* (Romolo Del Monaco); cf. http://www.cwgc.org/find-war-dead/casualty/2945685/DEL%MONACO%,%ROMOLO (Romolo Del Monaco) (viewed 29/05/2014)
Commonwealth War Graves Commission, *Casualty Details* (Basil Butler-Bowdon); cf. http://www.cwgc.org/find-war-dead/casualty/743291/BUTLER-BOWDON,%20BASIL%20JOSEPH%20BERNARD (Basil Butler-Bowdon) (viewed 25/05/2013)
Commonwealth War Graves Commission, *The Battle of the Somme, Ancre Heights*; cf.
http://www.cwgc.org/somme/content.asp?menuid=31&id=31&menuname=Ancre+Heights&menu=main (Ancre Heights) (viewed 26/05/2014)
Cook, Olive, *The English House through Seven Centuries*, Harmondsworth 1984
Craven, Maxwell, "Other Country Houses, 6. Southgate House, Clowne", in: *Derbyshire Life*, Derby, July 2002, p. 57f.
Craven, Maxwell, Stanley, Michael, *The Derbyshire Country House*, Derby 1991
De La Caille Ruvigny and Raineval, Melville Amadeus Henry Douglas Heddle, *The Plantagenet roll of the blood royal; being a complete table of all the descendants now living of Edward III, King of England*, London 1905 (Plantagenet, Blount, Petre, Del Monaco)
Der Spiegel, *Lord Grey de Ruthyn* (01/04/1959, issue 14/1959); cf.
http://wissen.spiegel.de/wissen/image/show.html?did=42624951&aref=ima

ge035/E0540/cqsp195914062- (Lord Grey de Ruthyn) (viewed 04/10/2013) ; identical with **Der Spiegel**, *Lord Grey de Ruthyn*; cf. http://www.spiegel.de/spiegel/print/d-42624951.html (Lord Grey de Ruthyn) (viewed 04/10/2013)
Derbyshire County Council, *Bulmer's Derby 1895: Facsimile Extracts from the History, Topography and Directory of Derbyshire*, first published by T. Bulmer & Co., Matlock 1988
Derbyshire County Council/Derbyshire Record Office and Derby Diocesan Record Office, *Sitwell of Renishaw: Estate Records* (undated)
Derbyshire Record Office, *Ref. No. 1300/11/1* (Sale Particulars of the Southgate Estate, 1938)
Derbyshire Record Office, *Ref. No. D1271/1/24, 25, 26* (minutes of Clowne Rural District Council regarding demolition of Southgate Camp)
Derbyshire Record Office, *Ref. No. D3/ATC/317-322* (Correspondence respecting the purchase of the Southgate toll house by Major Butler Bardon (*sic!*), 1883-1884)
Derbyshire Record Office, Ref. No., *D595 (*D595/R1/1/16, sheets 19/7 and 19/11, Land Values Duty, 1910: Derbyshire records including maps and "Domesday Books", c 1914 - c 1920)
Derbyshire Record Office, *Ref. No. D6573/Box53/26-27* (Proposed reconstruction of a property in Eckington for Capt. Francis Osbert S Sitwell, and site plan of Southgate, Eckington (undated) & Feb 1937)
Dictionary of Scottish Architects, *Charles Francis Hansom*; cf. http://www.scottisharchitects.org.uk/architect_full.php?id=201409 (Charles Francis Hansom) (viewed 04/03/2014)
Dictionary of Scottish Architects, *Joseph Aloysius Hansom*; cf. http://www.scottisharchitects.org.uk/architect_full.php?id=201396 (Joseph Aloysius Hansom) (viewed 04/03/2014)
Dolman Stapleton, Mary Helen Alicia, *A history of the post-reformation Catholic missions in Oxfordshire with an account of the families connected with them*, London 1918; cf. http://www.archive.org/stream/MN5023ucmf_2/MN5023ucmf_2_djvu.txt, Microform 1997 (viewed 08/06/2013)
Doolan, Brian, *The Pugins and the Hardmans*, Birmingham 2004
eMedals, Militaria & Historica, *A 1916 Canadian Memorial Cross, The Son of Count Del Monaco*; cf. http://www.emedals.com/collectors-gallery/canada/campaign-medals-pairs-groups/first-world-war-1914-18/the-memorial-cross-plaque/wwi-memorial-cross-to-the-son-of-count-del-monaco-c1487?vmcchk=1 (Romolo and Bernardo Bowdon/WWI) (viewed 06/05/2014)
Emsley, Clive, *Crime and Society in England, 1750 – 1900*, 3rd edition, Harlow 2005

Encyclopedia Britannica, *Brigantes (people)*; cf. http://www.britannica.com/EBchecked/topic/79492/Brigantes (Brigantes) (viewed 04/03/2014)
Encyclopedia Britannica, *Catholic Emancipation (British and Irish history)*; cf. http://www.britannica.com/EBchecked/topic/99817/Catholic-Emancipation (Roman Catholic Relief Act 1829) (viewed 05/03/2014)
Encyclopedia Britannica, *Copyhold (law)*; cf. http://www.britannica.com/EBchecked/topic/136950/copyhold (Copyhold) (viewed 05/12/2013)
Encyclopedia Britannica, *Douglas Haig, 1st Earl Haig*; cf. Haig; cf. http://www.britannica.com/EBchecked/topic/251766/Douglas-Haig-1st-Earl-Haig (1st Earl Haig) (viewed 05/03/2014)
Encyclopedia Britannica, *English Settled Land Acts*; cf. http://www.britannica.com/EBchecked/topic/188296/English-Settled-Land-Acts (English Settled Land Acts) (viewed 21/05/2013)
Encyclopedia Britannica, *Felicia Dorothea Hemans*; cf. http://www.britannica.com/EBchecked/topic/260695/Felicia-Dorothea-Hemans (Felicia Dorothea Hemans) (viewed 31/07/2013)
Encyclopedia Britannica, *Irish Potato Famine*, cf. http://www.britannica.com/EBchecked/topic/294137/Irish_Potato-Famine (Irish Potato Famine) (viewed 05/03/2014)
Encyclopedia Britannica, *John Wycliffe (English theologian)*; cf. http://www.britannica.com/EBchecked/topic/650168/John-Wycliffe (John Wycliffe) (viewed 05/03/2014)
Encyclopedia Britannica, *Julian of Norwich (English mystic)*; cf. http://www.britannica.com/EBchecked/topic/307843/Julian-of-Norwich (Dame Julian of Norwich) (viewed 16/03/2013)
Encyclopedia Britannica, *Sir Noël Coward*; cf. http://www.britannica.com/EBchecked/topic/141223/Sir-Noel-Coward (Sir Noël Coward) (viewed 31/07/2013)
Encyclopedia Britannica, *Sir Osbert Sitwell, 5th Baronet*; cf. http://www.britannica.com/EBchecked/topic/546881/Sir-Osbert-Sitwell-5th-Baronet (Osbert Sitwell) (viewed 14/11/2012)
Encyclopedia Britannica, *Thane (feudal lord)*; cf. http://www.britannica.com/EBchecked/topic/589973/thane (thegn) (viewed 04/03/2014)
Encyclopedia Britannica, *Wynkyn de Worde (English printer)*; cf. http://www.britannica.com/EBchecked/topic/647956/Wynkyn-de-Worde (Wynkyn de Worde) (viewed 05/03/2014)
Engels, Friedrich, "Geschichte der englischen Korngesetze", in: *Telegraph für Deutschland Nr. 193*, Hamburg 1845, p. 585ff.; cf. http://www.mlwerke.de/me/me02/me02_585.htm (viewed 18/11/2013)

English Heritage, *Barlborough House*; cf. http://list.english-heritage.org.uk/resultsingle.aspx?uid=1108968 (Barlborough House) (viewed 27/03/2013)
English Heritage, *Bowden Hall*; cf. http://list.english-heritage.org.uk/resultsingle.aspx?uid=1334796 (Bowden Hall) (viewed 15/04/2013)
English Heritage, *Ince Blundell Hall*; cf. http://list.english-heritage.org.uk/resultsingle.aspx?uid=1199254 (Ince Blundell Hall) (viewed 18/12/2013)
English Heritage, *Old Hall Farm House* (formerly listed as Pleasington Old Hall); cf. http://list.english-heritage.org.uk/resultsingle.aspx?uid=1072418 (Old Hall Farm House) (viewed 02/04/2013)
English Heritage, *Pantheon Adjoining Ince Blundell Hall*; cf. http://list.english-heritage.org.uk/resultsingle.aspx?uid=1075869 (Ince Blundell Hall Pantheon) (viewed 18/12/2013)
English Heritage, *Pleasington Lodge and Gateway to Woodfold Park*; cf. http://list.english-heritage.org.uk/resultsingle.aspx?uid=1072417 (Pleasington Lodge and Gateway to Woodfold Park) (viewed 08/09/2013)
English Heritage, *Roman Catholic Church of St Mary and St John the Baptist* (Pleasington Priory); cf. http://list.english-heritage.org.uk/resultsingle.aspx?uid=1072419 (Pleasington Priory) (viewed 16/09/2013)
English Heritage, *Southgate House*; cf. http://list.english-heritage.org.uk/resultsingle.aspx?uid=1108959 (Southgate House) (viewed 17/10/2012)
English Heritage, *Southgate Old House* (Eckington); cf. http://list.english-heritage.org.uk/resultsingle.aspx?uid=1109661 (Southgate Old House, Eckington) (viewed 27/03/2013)
English Heritage, *Southgate Stables, Including Wall to South Enclosing Stable Yard*; cf. http://list.english-heritage.org.uk/resultsingle.aspx?uid=1045918 (Southgate Stables) (viewed 17/10/2012)
English Heritage, *Walls Enclosing Burial Ground at Beighton Fields Priory* (Beighton Fields Priory); cf. http://list.english-heritage.org.uk/resultsingle.aspx?uid=1109002 (Beighton Fields Priory) (viewed 20/03/2013)
English, Peter, *Clowne War Memorial*, 2009; cf. http://www.roll-of honour.com/Derbyshire/Clowne.html (Clowne war memorial) (viewed 19/03/2013)
Estcourt, Edgar Edmund, Payne, John Orlebar (eds.), *The English Catholic nonjurors of 1715: being a summary of the register of their estates, with other genealogical notes, and an appendix of unpublished documents in the Public record office*, London (published prior to 1923); cf. http://archive.org/stream/englishcatholicn00estcuoft/englishcatholicn00estcuoft_djvu.txt (viewed 09/07/2013)

Fagan, Ged, Hogan, Anthony, *Liverpool and Merseyside Remembered*; cf. http://liverpoolremembrance.weebly.com/local-regiments.html (viewed 04/03/2013)
Fairbairn's *Book of Crests of the Families of Great Britain and Ireland*, London 1933
FamilySearch, *England Marriages, 1538-1973*; cf. https://familysearch.org/pal:/MM9.1.1/NVRV-CL3 Richard Butler and Charlotte Bowdon) (viewed 13/01/2014)
Farrer, William Farrer, Brownbill, J, *A History of the County of Lancaster: Vol. 6*, London 1911, p. 266-269; cf. British History Online, http://www.british-history.ac.uk/report.aspx?compid=53114 (general history pf Pleasington) (viewed 30/06/2013)
Ferry, Kathryn, *The Victorian Home*, Oxford 2012
Finberg, H P R (ed.), in: The Agrarian History of England and Wales: Volume I.II, Prehistory to AD 1042, Cambridge 2011
Fisher, Michael, "John Hardman and Company: Pugin's glasspainters", in: *The Magazine Antiques* (04/2009); cf. http://www.themagazineantiques.com/articles/john-hardman-and-company-pugins-glasspainters/ (04/2009) (Pugin Hardman & Powell) (viewed 30/10/2013)
Fisher, Michael, *Hardman of Birmingham: Goldsmith and Glasspainter*, Ashbourne 2008
Forces War Records, *Unit History: Middlesex Regiment*; cf. http://www.forces-war-records.co.uk/unit-info/1615/ (Middlesex Regiment) (viewed 10/05/2014)
Forces War Records, *Unit History: South Lancashire Regiment*, cf. http://www.forces-war-records.co.uk/unit-info/5024/ (South Lancashire Regiment) (viewed 10/05/2014)
Foster, George, *A Description of Mosborough, Chapter I, First Period, 1800 to 1825*, in: Mosborough Web, 2010; cf. http://www.abdecor.co.uk/mosborough/history/rem/chapter1.htm (cannons of Southgate) (viewed 05/07/2013)
Fredell, Joel W, Borchers, Charles W et al., *The Book of Margery Kempe/Online Documentary Edition*; cf. http://english.selu.edu/humanitiesonline/kempe/ (digital facsimile edition Margery Kempe) (viewed 05/03/2014)
Freer, Alan, *The Descendants of William the Conqueror*; cf. http://www.william1.co.uk/t34.htm (genealogy Bowdon family) (viewed 16/03/2013)
Fuller, John, W. H. Auden: Poems selected by John Fuller (Poet to Poet), London 2005

Ghosh, Kantik, ***The Wycliffite Heresy, Authority and the Interpretation of Texts***; cf. http://ebooks.cambridge.org/ebook.jsf?bid=CBO9780511483288, Cambridge 2001 (viewed 18/02/2014)
Girouard, Mark, *Life in the English Country House, A Social and Architectural History*, Harmondsworth 1980
Genealogical Society of Utah/Family History Library Catalog, *Erdeswick pedigree*; cf. https://www.familysearch.org/eng/library/fhlcatalog/supermainframeset.asp?display=titledetails&titleno=39952&disp=Erdeswick+pedigree (Mary Erdeswick Bowdon) (viewed 16/03/2013)
Glasby, Geoffrey P, *Mass Trespass on Kinder Scout in 1932 and the Founding of our National Parks*, Dartford 2012
Glover, Stephen, *The History, Gazetteer, and Directory of the County of Derby: Drawn up from Actual Observation, and from the Best Authorities, Part II*, Derby 1829, p. 304-305
Gómez-Moreno, Carmen, Drake Boehm, Barbara, *9. Cope, With Scenes of Christ and the Virgin, Saints, and Seraphim*, in: The Vatican Collections, The Papacy and Art, Metropolitan Museum of Art, New York 1983 (Vatican Cope), p. 38f.
Grove & Rufford Hunt, *Hunt History*, 2011; cf. http://groveruffordhunt.org.uk/page35.hmtl (Grove & Rufford Hunt) (viewed 05/06/2013)
Harris, John, *No Voice from the Hall*, London 1998
Held, Renate, *Kriegsgefangenschaft in Großbritannien, Deutsche Soldaten des Zweiten Weltkriegs in britischem Gewahrsam*, München 2008 (POW)
Hemans, Felicia Dorothea Browne, *Records of Woman, With Other Poems*, Edinburgh/London 1828, 2nd edition
Hickman, Kennedy, *World War II: Battle and Evacuation of Dunkirk*; cf. http://militaryhistory.about.com/od/worldwarii/p/dunkirk.htm (viewed 21/05/2013)
Hill, Rosemary, *God's Architect: Pugin and the Building of Romantic Britain*, London 2007
Hinson, Colin, *Harthill: The Parish Marriage Registers for Harthill, 1940-1959*; cf. http://www.genuki.org.uk/big/eng/YKS/Misc/Transcriptions/WRY/HarthillMarriages1940-1959.html (2008) (Harthill marriage register) (viewed 16/05/2013)
Hitchcock, Tim, Shoemaker, Robert, Howard, Sharon, McLaughlin, James et al., *London Lives, 1690-1800* (www.londonlives.org, version 1.1, 24 April 2012; cf. http://www.londonlives.org/static/EP.jsp (Settlement Examinations) (viewed 12/03/2014)
Hobsbawm, Eric J, *Industry and Empire, The Birth of the Industrial Revolution*, New York 1999

Hopkins, Peter, *Churches and Religion*, in: Whitwell Local History Group; cf. http://www.wlhg.co.uk/book/part5.htm (Chapel Southgate House) (viewed 14/06/2013)
Hopkins, Peter, *Census Returns*; in: Whitwell Local History Group; cf. http://www.wlhg.co.uk/book/part18.htm (Southgate Toll Bar Cottage) (viewed 18/05/2013)
Hopkins, Peter, *Graves Index*, in: Whitwell Local History Group; cf. http://www.wlhg.co.uk/Graves_index.htm (graves Whitwell) (viewed 08/01/2014)
Hopkins, Peter, *Woodhead*, in: Whitwell Local History Group, cf. http://www.wlhg.co.uk/Other_documents/woodhead.htm (baptisms Whitwell) (viewed 08/01/2014)
Horn, Pamela, *Life in the Victorian Country House*, Oxford 2010
Hull, Brian, *Parlington Hall*, 2014; http://www.parlington.co.uk/structures.lasso?process=3 (William Lindley) (viewed 01/02/2014)
Ingatestone Hall, *The Story of the House*; cf. http://www.ingatestonehall.com/about_history.php (viewed 16/06/2014)
Innes-Smith, Robert, "Plantagenet or Tudor, Clues in a Derbyshire Farmhouse", in: *Derbyshire Life*, Derby, September 2006, p. 124f.
Jenkins, Simon, *England's Thousand Best Houses*, London 2009
Johnson Lewis, Jone, *Margery Kempe*; cf. http://womenshistory.about.com/od/mediaevalchristianity/p/margery_kempe.htm (general reading on Margery Kempe) (viewed 27/03/2013)
Jokinen, Anniina, *Dissolution of the Monasteries in England*, in: Luminarium: Encyclopedia Project; cf. http://www.luminarium.org/encyclopedia/dissolution.htm (Second Act of Dissolution) (viewed 05/03/2014)
Jokinen, Anniina, *Middle English Literature: Essays and Articles/Margery Kempe*, in: Luminarium: Anthology of English Literature; cf. http://www.luminarium.org/medlit/medess.htm#kempe (list of on-line essays and articles on Margery Kempe) (viewed 16/03/2013)
Jones, Denis and Nora, *Life in the Village during World War II*; cf. http://www.whitwell.com/deniswar.html (Whitwell during WWII) (viewed 31/12/2013)
Kelliher, Hilton, "The Rediscovery of Margery Kempe: A Footnote", in: *The British Library Journal 23:2*, London 1977, p. 259-63; cf. http://www.bl.uk/eblj/1997articles/pdf/article19.pdf (viewed 16/03/2013)
Kelly, Bernard William, *Historical Notes on English Catholics Missions*, London 1907
Kelly's *Directory of the Counties of Derby, Notts, Leicester and Rutland, London*, May 1891; cf. http://www.andrewsgen.com/dby/kelly/clown.htm (viewed 11/07/2013)

Kirby, Justin, *Pleasington Lodge*; cf. http://descentfromadam.wordpress.com/2010/12/06/pleasington-lodge/ (Pleasington Lodge) (viewed 07/09/2013)

Knight, Kevin, *Confraternity (Sodality)*; cf. http://www.newadvent.org/cathen/04223a.htm (Sodality) (viewed 04/03/2014)

Knight, Kevin, *Sodality*; cf. http://www.newadvent.org/cathen/14120a.htm (Sodality) (viewed 04/03/2014)

Lancashire Record Office, *Ref. No. DDIN 66/40,* The Blundell of Ince Muniments; *cf.* http://www.nationalarchives.gov.uk/a2a/records.aspx?cat=055-ddin&cid=65-40#65-40 (The Blundell of Ince Muniments) (viewed 02/04/2013)

Lancashire Record Office, *Ref. No. DDLX 3/16*, Trappes-Lomax of Clayton-le-Moors (1633-1931); cf. http://www.nationalarchives.gov.uk/A2A/records.aspx?cat=055-ddlx&cid=-1#-1 (deeds relating to the manor of Clayton-le-Moors, Trappes-Lomax family, John (6) Erdeswick Butler-Bowdon in Bournemouth 02/02/1894) (viewed 16/09/2013)

Lancashire Record Office, *Ref. No. DDLX 3/38*, Trappes-Lomax of Clayton-le-Moors (1633-1931); cf. http://www.nationalarchives.gov.uk/A2A/records.aspx?cat=055-ddlx&cid=-1#-1 (deeds relating to the manor of Clayton-le-Moors) (viewed 16/09/2013)

Lancashire Record Office, *Ref. No. DDLX 8/32*, Trappes-Lomax of Clayton-le-Moors (1633-1931); cf. http://www.nationalarchives.gov.uk/A2A/records.aspx?cat=055-ddlx&cid=-1#-1 (deeds relating to the manor of Clayton-le-Moors, Trappes-Lomax family, John (6) Erdeswick Butler-Bowdon in Bournemouth 28/03/1894) (viewed 16/09/2013)

Linacre, Sylvia R, *How it was*, Ilfracombe 2002

Lockie, Rosemary, *The Wills of Derbyshire, Abstracts of Derbyshire Probate Records*; cf. http://willsdb.gukutils.org.uk/DBY/WillsA.html (various wills) (viewed 02/07/2013)

Longden, Deric, *I'm a Stranger Here Myself*, London/Reading 1994

Longden, Deric, *Lost for Words*, London/Reading 1998

Lundy, Darryl, *The Peerage* (Person Page 1367); cf. http://www.thepeerage.com/p1367.htm#i13665 (Parente and Cavendish) (viewed 04/03/2014)

Lundy, Darryl, *The Peerage* (Person Page 24361); cf. http://thepeerage.com/p24361.htm (Sir William Henry Hornby) (viewed 06/03/2014)

Lundy, Darryl, *The Peerage* (Person Page 3621); cf. http://thepeerage.com/p3621.htm (Petre family) (viewed 31/05/2014)

Lundy, Darryl, *The Peerage* (Person Page 6036); cf. http://thepeerage.com/p6036.htm#i60351 (Helena Mary Bowdon) (viewed 16/03/2013)
Lundy, Darryl, *The Peerage* (Person Page 961); cf. http://thepeerage.com/p961.htm (William John Cavendish Cavendish-Scott-Bentinck, 5th Duke of Portland) (viewed 04/03/2014)
Lundy, Darryl, *The Peerage* (Person Page 1123); cf. http://www.thepeerage.com/p1123.htm (Henry Fitzalan-Howard, 15th Duke of Norfolk) (viewed 06/03/2014)
Lundy, Darryl, *The Peerage* (Person Page 3446); cf. http://www.thepeerage.com/p3446.htm (Ella Cicely Mary Clifton, John Lancelot Wykeham Butler-Bowdon) (viewed 16/03/2013)
Lundy, Darryl, *The Peerage* (Person Page 7594); cf. http://www.thepeerage.com/p7594.htm (Anthony Butler-Bowdon, Maurice Butler-Bowdon) (viewed 16/03/2013)
Lundy, Darryl, *The Peerage* (Person Page 962); cf. http://www.thepeerage.com/p962.htm (William John Arthur Charles James Cavendish-Bentinck, 6th Duke of Portland) (viewed 04/03/2014)
Lysons, Daniel and Samuel, *Magna Britannia: Volume 5: Derbyshire, Clown*; cf. British History Online, http://www.british-history.ac.uk/report.aspx?compid=50725 (Magna Britannia, history of Clowne) (viewed 27/03/2013)
Lysons, Daniel and Samuel, *Magna Britannia: Volume 5: Derbyshire, Eckington*; cf. British History Online, http://www.british-history.ac.uk/report.aspx?compid=50728 (Magna Britannia, history of Eckington) (viewed 27/03/2013)
Maclaren, Hamish, *Maclarens, Birtwistles and Many Other Familys*; cf. http://wc.rootsweb.ancestry.com/cgi-bin/igm.cgi?op=GET&db=maclaren&id=I00492 (Marwood family, Pleasington) (viewed 07/09/2013)
Manco, Jean, *Researching Historic Buildings in the British Isles*, 2013; cf. http://www.buildinghistory.org/primary/grimm.shtml (viewed 01/02/2014)
Mandler, Peter, *The Fall and Rise of the Stately Home*, New Haven/London 2009
Martin, Michael, *Thesaurus Precum Latinarum*; cf. http://www.preces-latinae.org/thesaurus/Hymni/Placare.html (Placare) (viewed 30/05/2014)
McNeal Dodgson, John, *The Place-Names of Cheshire: The Place-names of Bucklow Hundred and Northwich Hundred*, English Place-Name Society Vol. 45, Cambridge 1970
Meara, David, *Victorian Memorial Brasses*, London 1983
Meech , Sanford Brown, Allen, Hope Emily, *The Book of Margery Kempe (ca 1400s), MS of Col. W. Butler-Bowdon*, Oxford 1961 (reprint)
Morrison, Blake, "The Country House and the English Novel", in: *The Guardian*, 11 June 2011; cf.

www.theguardian.com/books/2011/jun/11/country-house-novels-blake-morrison (viewed 30/07/013)
Muthesius, Hermann, *The English House* (edited by Dennis Sharp), Oxford 1979
Newbold, Paul, *Aston Hall*; cf. http://www.j31.co.uk/asthall.html (Verelst family) (viewed 21/11/2013)
Nisbet, Gary, Garner, Tim, *Glasgow - City of Sculpture*; cf. http://glasgowsculpture.com/pg_biography.php?sub=pugin-pugin# (Pugin & Pugin) (viewed 03/11/2013)
Nix, Dietmar, *Die Situation deutscher Kriegsgefangener in anglo-amerikanischer Haft*; cf. http://histor.ws/lagerecho/situation.php (German POWs) (viewed 06/03/2014)
NN, "Don't let Tesco be the death of Clowne"; in: *Worksop Guardian*, 15 August 2003; cf. http://www.worksopguardian.co.uk/news/local/don-t-let-tesco-be-the-death-of-clowne-1-636191 (Tesco/Clowne) (viewed 14/06/2014)
NN, "Extracts from the Diary of Henry Bowdon Esq. Part II.", in: *The Mountaineer*, Mount St. Mary's College, Spinkhill, Easter 1914, p. 135ff.
NN, "Focus on: Clowne", in: *Worksop Life Magazine/South Edition, Life Publications*, Retford, September 2013, p. 21ff.
NN, "How Old Is The Sodality Chapel?", in: *The Mountaineer*, Mount St. Mary's College, Spinkhill, Christmas 1951, p. 60ff.
NN, "Sewing seeds of friendship"; in: *Worksop Guardian*, 20 September 2011; cf. http://www.worksopguardian.co.uk/news/local-news/sewing-seeds-of-friendship-1-3791076 (Van Dyk's Garden Centre) (viewed 17/06/2013)
Nottinghamshire Archives, *Ref. No. DD/FJ/11/1/4/131-132* (Foljambe of Osberton (additional deposit): Deeds and Estate Papers); cf. http://www.nationalarchives.gov.uk/a2a/records.aspx?cat=157-ddfjaddit_1&cid=1-4-1-83#1-4-1-83 (turnpike labour) (viewed 20/05/2013)
Oliver, Neil, *A History of Ancient Britain*, London 2012
Palmer, John, http://www.wirksworth.org.uk/CRM16.htm (2003) (Charles Staniforth, Southgate House 1777) (viewed 14/06/2013)
Parker, Bev, *Wolverhampton History and Heritage Website*; cf. http://www.historywebsite.co.uk/articles/bushbury/families/whitgreaves.htm (Amelia Whitgreave) (viewed 08/09/2013)
Parks & Gardens UK, *Joseph Badger*; cf. http://www.parksandgardens.org/places-and-people/person/66 (Joseph Badger) (viewed 22/07/2013)
Pearcy, Grant, *Forts*; cf. http://www.stuffynwood.com/northfield/80AD.html (Roman roads) (viewed 27/05/2013)
Percival, John, *The Roman Villa*, London 1976
Perring, Dominic, *The Roman House in Britain*, London 2001
Picture The Past/Derbyshire County Council/Derbyshire Record Office, *Southgate Stables (103754)*, cf.

http://www.picturethepast.org.uk/frontend.php?action=printdetails&keywords=Ref_No_increment;EQUALS;PTPD103754&prevUrl= (Southgate Stables) (viewed 17/10/2012)
Picture The Past/Derbyshire County Council/Derbyshire Record Office, *Southgate Stables (103755)*, cf. http://www.picturethepast.org.uk/frontend.php?action=printdetails&keywords=Ref_No_increment;EQUALS;PTPD103755&prevUrl= (Southgate Stables) (viewed 17/10/2012)
Picture The Past/Derbyshire County Council/Derbyshire Record Office, *Southgate Stables (103756)*, cf. http://www.picturethepast.org.uk/frontend.php?action=printdetails&keywords=Ref_No_increment;EQUALS;PTPD103756&prevUrl= (Southgate Stables) (viewed 17/10/2012)
Picture The Past/Derbyshire County Council/Derbyshire Record Office, *Southgate Avenue (001760)*, cf. http://www.picturethepast.org.uk/frontend.php?action=printdetails&keywords=Ref_No_increment;EQUALS;DCHQ001760&prevUrl= (Southgate Avenue) (viewed 23/05/2013)
Picture The Past/Derbyshire County Council/Derbyshire Record Office, *Southgate House (000405)*; cf. http://www.picturethepast.org.uk/frontend.php?keywords=Ref_No_increment;EQUALS;DCBR000405&pos=2&action=zoom (Southgate House with chapel) (viewed 17/10/2012)
Picture The Past/Derbyshire County Council/Derbyshire Record Office, *Southgate Old House (203929)* (1970s); cf. http://www.picturethepast.org.uk/frontend.php?keywords=Ref_No_Increment;EQUALS;PTPD203929&pos=2&action=zoom&id=113192 (Southgate Old House, Eckington, 1970s) (viewed 14/05/2014)
Picture The Past/Derbyshire County Council/Derbyshire Record Office, *Southgate Old House (000418)* (1980s); cf. http://www.picturethepast.org.uk/frontend.php?keywords=Ref_No_Increment;EQUALS;DCNE000418&pos=7&action=zoom&id=22999 (Southgate Old House, Eckington, 1980s) (viewed 14/05/2014)
Pigot & Co.s *National Commercial Directory for 1828-29*, London/Manchester
Pigot & Co.s *National Commercial Directory of Derbyshire for 1835*, in: Mosborough Web, 2010; cf. http://www.abdecor.co.uk/mosborough/history/pigot.htm (Pigot, blacksmith Southgate) (viewed 05/07/2013)
Powell, Margaret, *Below Stairs*, reprint London 2011
Powell-Smith, Anna, *Open Domesday*; cf. http://domesdaymap.co.uk/place/SK4975/clowne/ (Clowne Domesday Book) (viewed 04/04/2013)
Preston, Chris, Clarke, Richard, Hulls, Samantha, *The Derbyshire War Memorials Project*; cf.

http://derbyshirewarmemorials.wikispaces.com/R.+DEL+MONACO (Ronald Del Monaco and family) (viewed 05/08/2013)
Pritt, Colin, *Pleasington New Hall*, 2012, cf. http://www.blackburnpast.com/2012/04/pleasington-new-hall.html (Pleasington New Hall) (viewed 16/06/2013)
Pugin, Augustus Welby, *The True Principles of Pointed of Christian Architecture and An Apology for the Revival of Christian Architecture*, London 1841
Richards, James, *Life in Britain for German Prisoners of War* (BBC History); cf. http://www.bbc.co.uk/history/british/britain_wwtwo/german_pows_01.shtml (German POWs) (viewed 05/04/2013)
Richmond, Lesley, Turton, Alison, *The Brewing Industry: A Guide to Historical Records*, Manchester 1990
Riden, Philip (with the assistance of Dudley Fowkes), *A History of the County of Derby III: Bolsover and Adjoining Parishes*, Woodbridge/Rochester 2013
Riden, Philip, *Barlborough*, in: VCH Derbyshire, On-line Texts in Progress, June 2011; cf. http://www.victoriacountyhistory.ac.uk/sites/default/files/work-in-progress/barlborough_manors_and_estates_jun_2011.pdf (Barlborough) (viewed 04/04/2013)
Riden, Philip, *Clowne*, in: VCH Derbyshire, On-line Texts in Progress, April 2011; cf. http://www.victoriacountyhistory.ac.uk/sites/default/files/work-in-progress/clowne_introduction_apr_2011.pdf (Clowne) (viewed 16/03/2013)
Riden, Philip, *Clowne, Manors and other Estates*, in: VCH Derbyshire, On-line Texts in Progress, April 2011; cf. http://www.victoriacountyhistory.ac.uk/sites/default/files/work-in-progress/clowne_manors_estates_apr_2011.pdf (Clowne manors and estates) (viewed 10/10/2012)
Riden, Philip, *Clowne, Religious Life*, in: VCH Derbyshire, On-line texts in Progress, April 2011; cf: http://www.docstoc.com/docs/144581158/Clowne-Religious-Life---Victoria-County-History (viewed 17/06/2014)
Riden, Philip, *Elmton*, in: VCH Derbyshire, On-line Texts in Progress, May 2011; cf. http://www.victoriacountyhistory.ac.uk/sites/default/files/work-in-progress/Elmton_Introduction_MAY2011.pdf (Elmton) (viewed 03/06/2013)
Roberts, Harriet, http://poundday.org.uk/tag/orphanage/ (donkey at Pleasington Old Hall) (viewed 06/09/2013)
Robinson, James, *Friends of Memorial Park Great Harwood*; cf. http://www.greatharwoodfomp.co.uk/content/indenture (Great Harwood/John (5) Erdeswick Butler-Bowdon) (viewed 16/03/2013)
Robinson, John Martin, *The English Country Estate*, London 1988
Rosevear, Alan, *Turnpike Roads in England*; cf. http://www.turnpikes.org.uk/ (turnpikes) (viewed 05/03/2014)

Ross, David, *Georgian Architecture;* cf. http://www.britainexpress.com/architecture/georgian.htm (Georgian architecture) (viewed 23/07/2013)
Ross, David, *Mediaeval Manor Houses;* cf. http://www.britainexpress.com/architecture/mediaeval-manors.htm (viewed 02/04/2013)
Ross, David, *Social Unrest in Britain 1815-1820;* cf. http://www.britainexpress.com/History/Post-Napoleonic-Britain.htm (post Napoleonic Britain) (viewed 16/07/2013)
Rotherham Metropolitan Borough, Archives and Local Studies Section, *Ref. No. 213/C/53/2;* cf. http://www.nationalarchives.gov.uk/a2a/records.aspx?cat=198-213c&cid=4-40-2#4-40-2 (Staniforth, lease in Millgate, Rotherham) (viewed 03/07/2013)
Rowlett, Russ, *How many? A Dictionary of Units of Measurement;* cf. http://www.unc.edu/~rowlett/units/dictO.html (Oxgang) (viewed 07/03/2014)
Scott Stokes, Charity, "Margery Kempe, Her Life and the Early History of her Book", in: *Mystics Quarterly 25*, Bibliography (Early printed extracts and reprint), 1999; cf. http://college.holycross.edu/projects/kempe/text/biblio.html (Margery Kempe general) (viewed 25/03/2013)
Schiano, Michael, Adams, Brian, Strafford, Dan, *SongMeanings;* cf. http://songmeanings.com/songs/view/3530822107858610588/ (Noël Coward, The Stately Homes of England) (viewed 01/08/2013)
Shakespeare Centre Library and Archive, *Ref. No. DR 422/77* (Ferrers of Baddesley Clinton, 1650; 1712-1938, 165 items); cf. http://www.nationalarchives.gov.uk/a2a/records.aspx?cat=188-dr422&cid=74#47 (grant of Mary Martha Ferrers) (viewed 12/06/2014)
Sheffield Archives, *Ref. No. MD5439;* cf. http://www.calmview.eu/SheffieldArchives/CalmView/Record.aspx?src=CalmView.Catalog&id=MD5026-5663&pos=1 (inventory of husbandry ware) (viewed 24/01/2014)
Sheffield Archives, *Ref. No. MD5444;* cf. http://www.calmview.eu/SheffieldArchives/CalmView/Record.aspx?src=CalmView.Catalog&id=MD5026-5663&pos=1 (inventory Beighton Fields 1691, Bowdon pedigree 1547-1803) (viewed 24/01/2014)
Sheffield Archives, *Ref. No. YWD 1013/4;* cf. http://www.nationalarchives.gov.uk/A2A/records.aspx?cat=199-ywd&cid=-1#-1 (leased land in Little Sheffield) (viewed 09/06/2013)
Sheffield Archives, *Ref. No. YWD 1047/1;* cf. http://www.nationalarchives.gov.uk/A2A/records.aspx?cat=199-ywd&cid=-1#-1 (closes of land) (viewed 09/06/2013)

Sheffield Archives, *Ref. No. YWD 1047/3a-b*; cf. http://www.nationalarchives.gov.uk/A2A/records.aspx?cat=199-ywd&cid=-1#-1 (conveyance) (viewed 09/06/2013)
Sheffield Archives, *Ref. No. YWD 1047/3a-b*; cf. http://www.nationalarchives.gov.uk/A2A/records.aspx?cat=199-ywd&cid=-1#-1 (land) (viewed 09/06/2013)
Sheffield Archives, *Ref. No. YWD 870 1793*; cf. http://www.nationalarchives.gov.uk/A2A/records.aspx?cat=199-ywd&cid=-1#-1 (grant) (viewed 09/06/2013)
Sheffield Archives, *Ref. No. YWD 923/14a*-b; cf. http://www.nationalarchives.gov.uk/A2A/records.aspx?cat=199-ywd&cid=-1#-1 (lease documents) (viewed 09/06/2013)
Sheffield Archives, *Ref. No. YWD 923/15a-b*; cf. http://www.nationalarchives.gov.uk/A2A/records.aspx?cat=199-ywd&cid=-1#-1 (lease documents) (viewed 09/06/2013)
Shepheard, Mathé, *The Stained Glass of John Hardman and Company under the Leadership of John Hardman Powell from 1867 to 1895*, Vol. I, Birmingham 2010
Sitwell, Osbert, *Queen Mary and Others*, London 1974
Spencer, Michael, *Yesterday's Journeys, Law and Order*, cf. http://homepages.rootsweb.ancestry.com/~spire/Yesterday/LawOrderC-D.htm (Bowdens of Hayfield) (viewed 12/07/2013)
Spencer, Michael, *Yesterday's Journeys, Settlement Examinations*, cf. http://homepages.rootsweb.ancestry.com/~spire/Yesterday/SettlementExaminationsC-D.htm (Bowden, Malkin & Co) (viewed 12/03/2014)
Spencer, Mike, *Barlborough Burials 1757*, in: Derbysgen-L Archives/RootsWeb; cf. http://archiver.rootsweb.ancestry.com/th/read/DERBYSGEN/2011-12/1324763791 (George Staniforth) (viewed 21/06/2013)
Spencer, Mike, *Clowne Burials*; cf. http://www.genuki.org.uk/big/eng/DBY/Clowne/burials.txt (Clowne burial register) (viewed 19/03/2013)
Staley, Lynn (ed.), *The Book of Margery Kempe*, Mediaeval Institute Publications, Kalamazoo, Michigan 1996; cf. http://www.lib.rochester.edu/camelot/kempint.htm (Margery Kempe) (viewed 16/03/2013)
Staley, Lynn, *The Book of Margery Kempe* (translated and edited by Lynn Staley), New York 2001
Staley, Lynn, *Margery Kempe's Dissenting Fictions*, State College/University Park Pennsylvania 1994
Staples, Teresa, *My Parish The Sacred Heart and Our Lady of Victories Clowne*, Clowne 1999
Stock, M, *Roman Rotherham*; cf. http://www.rotherhamunofficial.co.uk/history/roman (Icknield/Ryknield Street) (viewed 04/03/2014)

Stroud, Gill, *Derbyshire Extensive Urban Survey, Archaeological Assessment Report*; cf. http://ads.ahds.ac.uk/catalogue/adsdata/arch-881-1/dissemination/pdf/EUS_Texts/Eckington/Eckington.pdf, 1999 (history of Eckington) (viewed 26/03/2013)
Talen, Emily, *The Codes Project*; cf. http://codesproject.asu.edu/node/37 (English Settled Land Acts) (viewed 21/05/2013)
Tarplees, Merilyn, Boag, Dorinda, *Grimshaw's Origin and History*; cf. http://www.grimshaworigin.org/Webpages2/ErrwoodGoyt.htm#DoloresShrine (Grimshaw family, Dolores de Bergrin) (viewed 26/09/2013)
Teymur, C Ekrem, *Felicia Dorothea Hemans*; cf. http://www.poemhunter.com/felicia-dorothea-hemans/biography (Felicia Dorothea Hemans) (viewed 04/03/2014)
The Jacobite Intelligencer, *Jottings of a Jacobite Antiquary, Non-Jurors*; cf. http://jacobite.wordpress.com/non-jurors (viewed 11/07/2014)
The Library of Birmingham, *Rewriting the Book, MS 175 - John Hardman and Company and Hardman and Powell and Company, Stained Glass and Metalwork Manufacturers*; cf. http://calmview.birmingham.gov.uk/calmview/Record.aspx?src=CalmView.Catalog&id=MS+175 (records John Hardman & Company and Hardman Powell & Company in Birmingham Archives) (viewed 27/11/2013)
The National Archives, *Domesday, Britain's finest treasure*; cf. http://www.nationalarchives.gov.uk/domesday/ (Clowne Domesday Book) (viewed 04/04/2013)
The National Archives, *Ref. No. HO 334/83/3986, Naturalisation Certificate: Enrico del Monaco (known as Henry del Monaco)*; cf. http://discovery.nationalarchives.gov.uk/SearchUI/details/C11934739, (Henry Del Monaco) (viewed 05/08/2013)
The National Archives, *Ministry of Works: Historic Buildings Council for England: minutes and papers*; cf. http://discovery.nationalarchives.gov.uk/SearchUI/details?Uri=C16593 (Ministry of Works) (viewed 10/05/2013)
The National Archives, *Ref. No. PROB 11/1127/281, Will of Mary Bowdon, Widow of Barlborough, Derbyshire*; cf. http://www.nationalarchives.gov.uk/SearchUI/details/D414056?descriptiontype=Full&ref=PROB11/1127/218 (last will of Mary Bowdon) (viewed 07/06/2013)
The National Archives, *Ref. No. PROB 11/832/232, Will of George Staniforth, Gentleman of Barlborough, Derbyshire* ; cf. http://discovery.nationalarchives.gov.uk/SearchUI/details/D578229?descriptiontype=Full&ref=PROB+11/832/259 (last will of George Staniforth) (viewed 21/06/2013)
The National Archives, *Ref. No. STA* (1928-1955), Hawley Collection Trust; cf. http://www.nationalarchives.gov.uk/a2a/records.aspx?cat=2746-sta&cid=0#0 (Staniforth) (viewed 14/06/2013)

The National Archives, *Special Collections: Hundred Rolls and Eyre Veredicta*; cf. http://discovery.nationalarchives.gov.uk/SearchUI/details?uri=C13523 (Hundred Rolls) (viewed 04/03/2014)

The National Archives, *Wills 1384-1858*; cf. http://www.nationalarchives.gov.uk/records/wills.htm (Canterbury Wills) (viewed 05/10/2013)

The Original Catholic Encyclopedia, *Angela Merici, Saint*; cf. http://www.oce.catholic.com/index.php?title=Angela_Merici%2C_Saint (Saint Angela Merici) (viewed 03/06/2014)

The Original Catholic Encyclopedia, *Basil the Great, Saint*; cf. http://www.oce.catholic.com/index.php?title=Basil_the_Great%2C_Saint (Saint Basil) (viewed 03/06/2014)

The Original Catholic Encyclopedia, *Bernard of Clairvaux, Saint*; http://www.oce.catholic.com/index.php?title=Bernard_of_Clairvaux%2C_Saint (Saint Bernard) (viewed 03/06/2014)

The Original Catholic Encyclopedia, *Helena, Saint*; cf. http://www.oce.catholic.com/index.php?title=Helena%2C_Saint (Saint Helena) (viewed 03/06/2014).

The Original Catholic Encyclopedia, *Leonard of Limousin, Saint*; cf. http://www.oce.catholic.com/index.php?title=Leonard_of_Limousin%2C_Saint (Saint Leonard) (viewed 03/06/2014)

The Original Catholic Encyclopedia, *Monica, Saint*; cf. http://www.oce.catholic.com/index.php?title=Monica%2C_Saint (Saint Monica) (viewed 03/06/2014)

The Original Catholic Encyclopedia, *Teresa of Jesus (Avila), Saint*; cf. http://www.oce.catholic.com/index.php?title=Teresa_of_Jesus_%28Avila%29%2C_Saint (Saint Teresa of Ávila) (viewed 03/06/2014)

The Tablet, The International Catholic news weekly, *Births, Marriages and Deaths, 14th October 1933* (14/10/1933, p. 16); cf. http://archive.thetablet.co.uk/article/14th-october-1933/16/births-marriages-and-deaths (Alice Del Monaco) (viewed 17/10/2013)

The Tablet, The International Catholic news weekly, *Et Cietera, 26th October 1918* (26/10/1918, p. 21); cf. http://archive.thetablet.co.uk/article/26th-october-1918/21/et-cietera (Basil Butler-Bowdon) (viewed 20/05/2014)

Thomas, Roger J C, *Prisoner of War Camps (1939-1948), Twentieth Century Military Recording Project, Project Report*, English Heritage, Swindon 2003; cf. http://www.english-heritage.org.uk/publications/prisoner-of-war-camps/prisoner-of-war-camps.pdf/ (POW) (viewed 05/04/2013)

Thorndon Hall Management Company Ltd., *History of Thorndon Hall*; cf. http://www.thorndonhall.co.uk/thorndon-hall-history.htm (Thorndon Hall, Petre family) (viewed 05/03/2014)

Thorne, R G, The *History of Parliament, British Political, Social and Local History*; cf. http://www.historyofparliamentonline.org/volume/1790-1820/member/sitwell-sitwell-1769-1811 (Sitwell Sitwell) (viewed 27/03/2013)

Toler T Maunsell, D, "Provident Dispensaries or Independent Sick Clubs from a Practical Point of View", in: *British Medical Journal 1872* September 7; 2 (610): p. 265–266; cf. http://www.ncbi.nlm.nih.gov/pmc/articles/PMC2297056/?page=1 (Sick-clubs) (viewed 25/06/2013)
Torn, Alison, "Margery Kempe: Madwoman or Mystic - A Narrative Approach to the Representation of Madness and Mysticism in Mediaeval England", in: *Narrative and Fiction: an Interdisciplinary Approach*, Huddersfield 2008, p. 79-89; cf. http://eprints.hud.ac.uk/4830/2/Chapter_9_Alison_Torn.pdf (Margery Kempe) (viewed 27/03/2013)
Turner, Richard H, "A More Unobserved and Convenient Location: A Derbyshire School Reopened", in: *Recusant History: A Journal of Research in Reformation and Post-Reformation Catholic History in the British Isles*, Vol. 29 (2) (The Catholic Record Society), London 2008, p. 175-194
University of Glasgow, *John Bernard Hardman*, Mapping the Practice and Profession of Sculpture in Britain and Ireland 1851-1951, University of Glasgow History of Art and HATII, online database 2011; cf. http://sculpture.gla.ac.uk/view/person.php?id=msib4_1237375927 (John Bernard Hardman) (viewed 31/10/2013)
University of Glasgow, *John Hardman Powell*, Mapping the Practice and Profession of Sculpture in Britain and Ireland 1851-1951, University of Glasgow History of Art and HATII, online database 2011; cf. http://sculpture.gla.ac.uk/view/person.php? =ann_1263316086 (John Hardman Powell) (viewed 31/10/2013)
University of Nottingham, *Ref. No. PI E12/6/26/6/10*, cf. http://mss-cat.nottingham.ac.uk/DServe/dserve.exe?dsqIni=Dserve.ini&dsqApp=Archive&dsqCmd=Show.tcl&dsqDb=Catalog&dsqPos=0&dsqSearch=%28PersonCode%3D%3DNA66123%29 (Bowdon/land in Whitwell) (viewed 15/06/2013)
University of Nottingham, *Ref. No. Pl E12/9/6/1/31-175*; cf. http://mss-cat.nottingham.ac.uk/Dserve/dserve.exe?dsqIni=Dserve.ini&dsqApp=Archive&dsqCmd=Show.tcl&dsqDb=Catalog&dsqSearch=%28PersonCode==NA61159%29&dsqPos=213 (Bowdon/Duke of Portland) (viewed 31/03/2013)
University of Nottingham, *Ref. No. PI E12/10/1/26/1-12*; cf. http://mss-cat.nottingham.ac.uk/DServe/dserve.exe?dsqIni=Dserve.ini&dsqApp=Archive&dsqCmd=Show.tcl&dsqDb=Catalog&dsqPos=0&dsqSearch=%28AltRefNo%3D%27Pl%20E12%2F10%2F1%2F26%2F1-12%27%29 (memoranda of lands held by the Bowden family) (viewed 15/06/2013)
Victoria & Albert Museum, *Cope*; cf. http://collections.vam.ac.uk/item/O93441/cope-unknown/ (Victoria and Albert Museum, Butler-Bowdon Cope) (viewed 14/06/2013)
Victoria & Albert Museum, *The Syon Cope*; cf. http://collections.vam.ac.uk/item/O93171/the-syon-cope-syon-cope-unknown/ (Victoria and Albert Museum, Syon cope) (viewed 14/06/2013)

Victoria & Albert Museum, *Style Guide: Gothic Revival*; cf. http://www.vam.ac.uk/content/articles/s/style-guide-gothic-revival/ (Augustus Welby Northmore Pugin) (viewed 01/10/2013)
Walker, Paul D, *Church of the Immaculate Conception Spinkhill*, Sheffield 1990
Waugh, Evelyn, *Brideshead Revisited, The Sacred & Profane Memories of Captain Charles Ryder*, Harmondsworth 1983
WDR, *Heimkehr mit Verzögerung, 12. Juli 2008 - Vor 60 Jahren: Letzte deutsche Kriegsgefangene aus England*; cf. http://www1.wdr.de/themen/archiv/stichtag/stichtag3598.html (German POWs) (viewed 05/04/2013)
Wheeler, Heather, *World War Two - German Prisoners of War in Britain*; cf. http://www.historyonthenet.com/WW2/german_pow_britain.htm (German POWs) (viewed 05/04/2013)
White's *1875 Directory of Derbyshire*; cf. http://freepages.history.rootsweb.ancestry.com/~claycross/732-744.htm, 2004 (White's 1875 Directory) (viewed 29/10/2012)
Williamson, Samuel H, *MeasuringWorth*, cf. http://measuringworth.com/ukearncpi/ (currency converter) (viewed 16/09/2013)
Wilson, John Marius, *Imperial Gazetteer of England and Wales (1870-72)*; cf. http://www.genuki.org.uk/big/eng/LAN/Pleasington/ (Pleasington Old Hall) (viewed 16/06/2013)
Windeatt, Barry A (translator), **Kempe, Margery**, *The Book of Margery Kempe*, London 2004
Worpole, Ken, "Cemeteries, Churchyards and Burial Grounds", in: *Commission for Architecture and the Built Environment (CABE, 2005)*; cf. http://webarchive.nationalarchives.gov.uk/20110118095356/http:/www.cabe.org.uk/files/cemeteries-churchyards-and-burial-grounds.pdf (cemeteries in the UK, burial customs) (viewed 10/04/2013)
Young, Bonnie, "Opus Anglicanum", in: *Ecclesiastical Vestments of the Middle Ages: An Exhibition, The Metropolitan Museum of Art Bulletin, v. 29, no. 7* (March, 1971), New York 1971, p. 291-298

Other on-line sources

http://cambridgeshire.gov.uk/leisure/archives/catalogue/holdings/m_p/pettysessions.htm (Petty Sessions) (viewed 09/09/2013)
http://companycheck.co.uk/company/05119198 (John Hartman Trading Company Ltd.) (viewed 15/10/2013)
http://en.wikipedia.org/wiki/Eckington,_Derbyshire (Eckington) (viewed 27/03/2013)
http://en.wikipedia.org/wiki/Henry_Pepwell (Henry Pepwell) (viewed 16/03/2013)
http://en.wikipedia.org/wiki/Neo-Druidism (Neo-Druidism) (viewed 14/06/2014).

http://en.wikipedia.org/wiki/Toll_house (toll houses) (viewed 30/04/2013)
http://exhibitsonline.org/tombstone-art-and-symbolism.htm (tombstone symbolism) (viewed 10/04/2013)
http://planningdesignpractice.blogspot.de/2009/10/october-2009-newsletter_30.html (Southgate Old House, Eckington, outbuilding) (viewed 27/03/2013)
http://search.ancestry.co.uk/cgibin/sse.dll?gl=ukicen&rank=1&new=1&so=3&MSAV=0&msT=1&gss=ms_f-80&gsln=De%20monaco&uidh=000 (Ireneo Del Monaco) (viewed 05/08/2013)
http://search.ancestry.com/cgi-bin/sse.dll?rank=1&new=1&MSAV=1&msT=1&gss=angs-g&gsfn=George&gsln=Staniforth&msbdy=1735&msbpn__ftp=Eckington%2C+Derbyshire%2C+England&msddy=1737&msdpn__ftp=Eckington%2C+Derbyshire%2C+England&cpxt=0&catBucket=rstp&uidh=000&cp=0&gl=42&so=2 (Staniforth) (viewed 26/06/2013)
http://search.lib.cam.ac.uk/?itemid=|collpwdb|501567 (Pepwell edition Margery Kempe) (viewed 05/03/2014)
http://search.lib.cam.ac.uk/?itemid=|cambrdgedb|3584483 (de Worde edition Margery Kempe) (viewed 05/03/2014)
http://shelf3d.com/Vladimir%Osipovich%Sherwood (Vladimir Osipovich Sherwood) (viewed 05/03/2014)
http://sjweb.info (AMDG, Jesuits) (viewed 14/11/13)
http://wiki.answers.com/Q/How_much_was_a_pounds_worth_in_England_in_the_1800%27s (English Pound) (viewed 15/05/2013)
http://web.archive.org/web/20070814061819/http://www.ian.a.paterson.btinternet.co.uk/orgartillery.htm#RHA106 (Lancashire Hussars WWII) (viewed 04/03/2014)
http://www.angelfire.com/realm/gotha/Part15.htm (Butler-Bowdon birth and death dates) (viewed 15/08/2013)
http://www.avictorian.com/mourning.html (Victorian burial customs) (viewed 11/06/2014)
http://www.birminghamheritage.org.uk/pugin.html (Augustus Welby Northmore Pugin) (viewed 02/11/2013)
http://www.blackburncitizen.co.uk/touristguide/947207.Tourist_guide_to_Pleasington/ (Pleasington) (viewed 16/06/2013)
http://www.bowdenhall.co.uk (Bowden Hall) (viewed 12/07/2013)
http://www.burrows.co.uk/bolsoverguide/10TheM.htm (Clowne local history) (viewed 19/05/2013)
http://www.britishnewspaperarchive.co.uk/ (viewed 27/10/2012 and 29/10/2012)
http://www.ccel.org/g/gardner/cell/cell16.htm (Pepwell edition Margery Kempe) (viewed 16/03/2013)
http://www.chapel-en-le-frithparishcouncil.gov.uk/history.htm (John Slacke) (viewed 16/07/2013)

http://www.clownevillage.co.uk/clowne-hist/noatable%20dates2.htm (Clowne local history) (viewed 19/05/2013)
http://www.clownevillage.co.uk/feedback/feedback.htm (Southgate Camp) (viewed 19/05/2013)
http://www.clownevillage.co.uk/history/history.html (Clune, river name) (viewed 10/07/2013)
http://www.clydesite.co.uk/clydebuilt/viewship.asp?id=19107 (SS Transylvania) (viewed 05/03/2014)
http://www.colorado-cemeteries.com/symbols.html (tombstone symbolism) (viewed 10/04/2013)
http://www.communigate.co.uk/chesh/altrincham/page3.html (Bowdon History) (viewed 30/11/2013)
http://www.construction.co.uk/company_515210.htm (Pugin Hardman & Powell Ltd) (viewed 31/10/2013)
http://www.derbyshireheritage.co.uk/Menu/Townsandvillages/Barlborough.php (Barlborough village) (viewed 27/03/2013)
http://www.derbyshireheritage.co.uk/Menu/Townsandvillages/Spinkhill.php (Mount St. Mary's College, Spinkhill) (viewed 31/08/2013)
http://www.derbyshireuk.net/pickford.html (Joseph Pickford) (viewed 29/01/2014)
http://www.desertrats.org.uk/orgartillery.htm#RHA106 (RHA) (viewed 04/03/2013)
http://www.dictionary.reference.com/browse/thorp (definition "thorpe") (viewed 02/02/2014)
http://www.dd-wast.de/frame_e.htm (POW) (viewed 21/05/2013)
http://www.domesdaybook.co.uk/glossary.html (Carucate) (viewed 02/02/2014)
http://www.findmypast.co.uk (Parish Record Collection/Baptism Records for Carburton and Clowne) (viewed 23/10/2013)
http://www.findmypast.co.uk (Parish Record Collection/Marriage Records for Barlborough) (viewed 23/10/2013)
http://www.footpathmaps.com (on-line maps) (viewed 15/05/2013)
http://www.edinburgh-gazette.co.uk/issues/17817/pages/263/page.pdf (A Maxfield) (viewed 16/05/2013)
http://www.guarlford.org.uk/remember_charles_andrew.htm (Bruno Aloysius Butler-Bowdon) (viewed 02/04/2013)
http://www.historyfiles.co.uk/KingListsBritain/BritainCoritani.htm (Corieltauvi) (viewed 03/04/2014)
http://www.houseofnames.com/bowden-family-crest (Bowden name) (viewed 10/04/2013)
http://www.humphreyocean.com (Humphrey Anthony Erdeswick Butler-Bowdon) (viewed 09/09/2013)
http://www.information-britain.co.uk/famousbrits.php?id=1882 (Charles Harvard Gibbs-Smith) (viewed 05/03/2014)

http://www.inside-eckington.co.uk/abouteckington.html (Eckington) (viewed 27/03/2013)
http://www.jesuit.org.uk (AMDG, Jesuits) (viewed 14/11/2013)
http://www.jesuiten.org/home.html (AMDG, Jesuits) (viewed 12/05/2014)
http://www.legislation.gov.uk/ukpga/Vict/45-46/38/section/25 (English Settled Land Acts) (viewed 21/05/2013)
http://www.legislation.gov.uk/ukpga/1997/23/section/2 (Deputy Lieutenant) (viewed 04/03/2014)
http://www.legislation.gov.uk/ukpga/Vict/16-17/134/section/1 (Burial Act 1853) (viewed 04/06/2013)
http://www.legislation.gov.uk/ukpga/Vict/18-19/128/section/18 (Burial Act 1855) (viewed 04/06/2013)
http://www.legislation.gov.uk/ukpga/Geo4/10/7/contents (Roman Catholic Belief Act 1829) (viewed 05/03/2014)
http://www.london-gazette.co.uk/issues/18349/pages/779/page.pdf (bankruptcy note George (9) Bowdon) (viewed 08/06/2013)
http://www.london-gazette.co.uk/issues/18487/pages/1381/page.pdf (bankruptcy note George (9) Bowdon) (viewed 10/12/2013)
http://www.london-gazette.co.uk/issues/19940/pages/112/page.pdf (from Butler to Butler-Bowdon) (viewed 16/06/2013)
http://www.london-gazette.co.uk/issues/19948/pages/303 (John Bruno Bowdon High Sheriff 1841) (viewed 22/07/2013)
http://www.london-gazette.co.uk/issues/29812/supplements/10656/page.pdf (Alice, Bernard, Corona Del Monaco) (viewed 17/10/2013)
http://www.london-gazette.co.uk/issues/42901/pages/ (Cornelis Josef van Dijk) (viewed 29/10/2012)
http://www.london-gazette.co.uk/issues/43685/pages/5754/page.pdf (A Maxfield) (viewed 16/05/2013)
http://www.london-gazette.co.uk/issues/44842/pages/4807/page.pdf (A Maxfield) (viewed 16/05/2013)
http://www.london-gazette.co.uk/issues/49692/pages/4761/page.pdf (Henry Del Monaco) (viewed 04/09/2013)
http://www.losttrekkers.com/detail.asp?iType=199&iAd=2193 (POW) (viewed 18/05/2013)
http://www.marstons.co.uk/about/Heritage.aspx (Mansfield Brewery) (viewed 07/03/2014)
http://www.mortimers-property.co.uk/property/residential-sales/pleasington-lane-pleasington-blackburn-62205_1396.html (Pleasington Lodge) (viewed 07/09/2013)
http://www.msmcollege.com/msm-school/the-school (Mount St. Mary's School) (viewed 31/10/2013)
http://www.nps.gov/jofl/historyculture/stories.htm (Victorian burial customs) (viewed 04/06/2013)

http://www.pugin-society.1to1.org/JHPowell.html (John Hardman Powell) (viewed 21/10/2013)
http://www.rootschat.com/forum/index.php?topic=159766.0 (Settlement Examinations) (viewed 12/03/2014)
http://www.rootschat.com/forum/index.php?topic=641499.0 (Bowdens of Hayfield) (viewed 12/07/2013)
http://www.rotherhamweb.co.uk/genealogy/verelst.htm (Verelst family) (viewed 21/11/2013)
http://www.shiptonhallewellsolicitors-chesterfield.co.uk/ (solicitors in Chesterfield) (viewed 10/05/2013)
http://www.stjohnclowne.org/history.htm (church in Clowne) (viewed 22/05/2013)
http://www.surnamedb.com/Surname/Boden (Bowden name) (viewed 10/04/2013)
http://www.surnamedb.com/Surname/bowden#ixzz2gI0QxBJo (Bowden name) (viewed 29/09/2013)
http://www.surnamedb.com/Surname/butler#ixzz2gI0gFEKf (Butler name) (viewed 29/09/2013)
http://www.thepuginsociety.co.uk (Augustus Welby Northmore Pugin) (viewed 02/11/2013)
http://www.treetonweb.co.uk/features/org.htm (Rotherham Equalised Druids) (viewed 03/06/2013)
http://www.tribalpages.com/tribe/familytree?uid=akfraser&surname=Bowden (Bowdens of Hayfield) (viewed 12/07/2013)
http://www.uk.mundia.com/gb/Search/Results?surname=BUTLER%20BOWDON&birthPlace=United%20Kingdom (genealogy Butler-Bowdon family) (viewed 25/05/2013)
http://www.vandykhotel.co.uk/assets/vision-mag-spring-2012_web.pdf (Van Dyk Hotel) (viewed 25/10/2012)
http://www.wepsite.de/Noel_Coward,The_Stately_Homes_of_England.htm (Noël Coward, "Operette" 1938, The Stately Homes of England) (viewed 31/07/2013)
http://www.wintonforum.co.uk/fampoux.html (Fampoux) (viewed 29/05/2014)
http://www.yell.com/ucs/UcsSearchAction.do?keywords=farmers&location=clowne&scrambleSeed=61856656&searchType=&M=&bandedclarifyResults=&ssm=1 (farms in Clowne and Creswell) (viewed 16/10/2013)
http://www.zoominfo.com/p/Joseph-Badger/656577613 (Joseph Badger) (viewed 03/07/2013)
https://groups.google.com/forum/#!topic/alt.talk.royalty/rN-0VLYBiBE (origin of the Butler-Bowdons from James I) (viewed 21/05/2014)
https://maps.google.de/maps?hl=de&tab=wl (on-line maps) (viewed 06/05/2013)

https://www.gov.uk/medals-campaigns-descriptions-and-eligibility (DSO) (viewed 03/04/2014)

Genealogy and Censuses

Burke, John, Burke, John Bernard, *A Genealogical and Heraldic History of the Landed Gentry of Great Britain and Ireland, Volume I, A - L*, London 1847
Burke, Sir Bernard, *The General Armory of England, Scotland, Ireland, and Wales; Comprising a Registry of Armorial Bearings from the Earliest to the Present Time*, London 1884
Cochran, Holly, Whitehead, Tony, *Durham Records Online;* cf. http://durhamrecordsonline.com/updates/2010/09/17/added-explanation-of-1841-census-age rounding/ (Census rounding) (viewed 31/10/2012)
Office for National Statistics, *Derbyshire Area Monitor, 200 years of the census in Derbyshire;* cf. http://www.ons.gov.uk/ons/guide-method/census/1991-and-earlier-censuses/census-bicentenary/area-monitors/regions/derbyshire/index.html (Census Derbyshire) (viewed 15/04/2013)

Other on-line sources on censuses

http://en.wikipedia.org/wiki/United_Kingdom_Census_1901 (Census 1901) (viewed 31/10/2012)
http://search.ancestry.co.uk/search/db.aspx?dbid=6598 (Census 1891) (viewed 31/10/2012)
http://search.ancestry.co.uk/search/db.aspx?dbid=7572 (Census 1881) (viewed 31/10/2012)
http://search.ancestry.co.uk/search/db.aspx?dbid=7619 (Census 1871) (viewed 31/10/2012)
http://search.ancestry.co.uk/search/db.aspx?dbid=8767 (Census 1861) (viewed 31/10/2012)
http://search.ancestry.co.uk/search/db.aspx?dbid=8860 (Census 1851) (viewed 31/10/2012)
http://search.ancestry.co.uk/search/db.aspx?dbid=8978 (Census 1841) (viewed 31/10/2012)
http://www.1901censusonline.com/ (Census 1901) (viewed 31/10/2012)
http://www.1911census.co.uk/Content/default.aspx?r=24 (Census 1911) (viewed 29/10/2012)